THE
ATOMISTIC
CONGRESS

★ ★

THE
ATOMISTIC
CONGRESS

AN INTERPRETATION
OF CONGRESSIONAL
★ CHANGE ★

Allen D. Hertzke
Ronald M. Peters, Jr.

M. E. Sharpe, Inc.
Armonk, New York
London, England

Library of Congress Cataloging-in-Publication Data

The Atomistic Congress: an interpretation of congressional change /
[edited] by Allen D. Hertzke and Ronald M. Peters, Jr.
p. cm.
"Based upon an April 1990 Carl Albert Center conference,
commemorating the bicentennial of the United States Congress and
the centennial of the University of Oklahoma"—Pref.
Includes bibliographical references and index.
ISBN 0–87332–870–1 (cloth).
ISBN 0-87332-871-X (paperback).
1. United States. Congress—Congresses.
I. Hertzke, Allen D., 1950–.
II. Peters, Ronald M.
III. Carl Albert Congressional Research and Studies Center.
JK1021.A86 1992
328.73′09—dc20
91–12342
CIP

Printed in the United States of America

The paper used in this publication meets the minimum requirements of
American National Standard for Information Sciences—Permanence of Paper for Printed
Library Materials, ANSI Z39.48-1984.

MV   10 9 8 7 6 5 4 3 2 1

Dedication

The editors and contributors to this volume dedicate it to the Honorable Carl B. Albert, forty-sixth Speaker of the United States House of Representatives, in honor of his service to his country.

Contents

Part II Institutional Change in the Atomistic Congress

Figures

Tables

Preface

This volume is based upon an April 1990 Carl Albert Center conference commemorating the bicentennial of the United States Congress and the centennial of the University of Oklahoma. The conference was entitled, "Back to the Future: the United States Congress in the Twenty-first Century." Its focus was on the nature of change in Congress and on the likely direction of congressional change as the new century approaches.

From among the two dozen papers presented at the conference, we have selected eight for inclusion in this volume; in addition, we have included a very fine recent study of Senate Majority Leader George Mitchell. These essays were selected for the significance and originality of the research they report, and for the relevance of the research to an understanding of the process of congressional change over time.

In considering the evidence reported by these researchers and other research reported at the conference, we were struck by two things. On the one hand, contemporary congressional scholarship does an excellent job of charting the changes that Congress undergoes; on the other hand, contemporary congressional scholarship has failed to produce an overarching framework within which the process of congressional change can be understood. A review of other compendia of studies of Congress confirmed this impression.

We therefore decided that our editorial contribution should be to try to provide such a framework. In undertaking this task, we were increasingly led to think in terms of the larger cultural trends that seem to be shaping modern politics today. Due perhaps in part to our intellectual biases, but due most certainly in part to the reality of American political life today, we concluded that the research that congressional scholarship typically produces is best understood in terms of a historical and interpretive intellectual framework. Through it, we have sought to analyze the research reported in this book. We hope that it will spawn a dialogue about the interpretation of congressional change in which our authors and other political scientists will join.

Since this volume is the product of an event as well as of the effort of the authors and editors, we are indebted to many people. Our colleague Gary Copeland shared with us the planning and execution of the conference. Its success was due largely to the efforts of LaDonna Sullivan and Kathy Wade, which the three of us gratefully acknowledge. LaDonna Sullivan's assistance in the preparation of the book manuscript was also invaluable. We want also to thank the graduate and undergraduate Fellows of the Carl Albert Center who contributed both intellectually and logistically to the conference.

A special feature of the conference was the participation of several prominent congressional scholars as panel chairs and discussants. In addition to their contributions to the conference, these scholars offered constructive advice to us in the process of editing the papers for publication. We would like to thank Stanley Bach, Joseph Cooper, Roger Davidson, Richard Fenno, John Johannes, Charles Jones, Thomas Kazee, Thomas Mann, Samuel Patterson, Nelson Polsby, and Steven Smith.

We would like to thank our editor, Michael Weber, and Alexandra Koppen, project editor, of M.E. Sharpe, Inc.

Finally, the participants in the conference were privileged to have been joined by Speaker Carl Albert in all of the conference activities. His appreciation of congressional scholarship is the natural product of his academic inclinations. We are honored to dedicate this volume to him.

THE
ATOMISTIC
CONGRESS

★ ★

ALLEN D. HERTZKE AND
RONALD M. PETERS, JR.

Introduction: Interpreting the Atomistic Congress

This book is about the United States Congress. We have entitled it *The Atomistic Congress* to convey our impression that Congress is, in the final analysis, a group of individuals rather than a collective whole. Thus it is best understood as a product of the individual aspirations of its members, rather than a function of the collective public will. We suggest that because of its fundamentally atomistic character, change in Congress is shaped by changes in society and the political culture that have had ramifications through the American political system. We think that an emphasis on cultural foundations aids in the interpretation of congressional change, a topic of great academic interest and practical import. This volume searches for an understanding of how and why Congress changes over time. Unlike the atoms of the physical universe, whose behavior can be explained and predicted up to a point, the atomistic Congress seems often to defy prediction. We believe that a broader cultural interpretation, while perhaps not yielding a set of specific predictions, nonetheless offers the best basis for thinking about the future. The societal dynamics we catalogue are likely to be with us for a while, and even if we cannot divine the future, we may at least be able to comprehend some of the forces producing it.

Why does Congress change? An answer to this question is both easy and difficult. It is easy enough to say that Congress changes because all human things do; or because political institutions reflect the changes that take place in the political system around them; or because the political system is a product of changing cultural, economic and technological forces; in sum, that Congress changes because we do. But it is difficult to say precisely why Congress changes in the way that it does, just as it is difficult to identify with precision the factors that cause it to change. Is this an intelligible process, or must we simply chronicle the evolution of this vital American political institution like a newspaper reporting daily events? That Congress does change is not in doubt. The literature bearing upon Congress produced by American political science has, over the past two decades, been dominated by accounts of how Congress has changed. Since the enactment of the Legislative Reform Act of 1970 and the ensuing political reforms of the early 1970s, the Congress has by all accounts undergone a remarkable transformation. The stodgy, clubby, conservative, and geriatric institution that was so well captured in the work of Ralph K. Huitt, Charles O. Jones, Nelson Polsby, Charles Goodwin, Randall Ripley, Donald Matthews, and Richard Fenno was put to rest as soon as its political enemies were strong enough to kill it.[1] The attack on the entrenched, conservative power structure by younger and mostly more liberal members was obviously the proximate cause of its downfall. An explanation of the reform movement that relies upon the ostensible motives of the participants, however, leaves unexplored the underlying factors that made the revolution possible.

The Reformed Congress and Congressional Scholarship

Most accounts of the reform movement have focussed on the specific practices and arrangements that undergirded the old order, the struggle to change them, and the new protocols that emerged. The result is an anthology that is rich in description but less satisfying in explanation. In order to illustrate this let us consider several studies of the "post-reform" Congress. Among the first major books seeking to characterize Congress in the 1970s was *Congress in Change*, edited by Norman J. Ornstein.[2] Ornstein and his fellow scholars were convinced that Congress was changing in ways that would have a lasting impact on public policy. "By observing the ways in which Congress changes, we can gain a better understanding of how and why the institution responds to the society and, through its actions, shapes public policy" (p. ix). The book addressed both changes brought about by the reform movement and those occasioned by the evolution of society. "Change in Congress can, of course, come about in many ways. It can be planned or accidental; brought about through institutional reform or individual personalities; be evolutionary or instantaneous" (p. xi). Just as change can occur in a variety of ways, it can appear in a variety of contexts. "Change in institutions, change in personnel, evolutionary change, structural reforms, and informal change are among the topics covered . . . in the following pages" (p. xii).

And indeed, in eighteen chapters changes in Congress were explored in such diverse areas as turnover, the seniority system, the committee/subcommittee system, party leadership, congressional norms, and the role of the media. Each study found that Congress is a changing institution—yet the scholars who contributed to this volume did not seek to provide a broader explanation of the process of change itself. Instead, their focus was on the changes they observed and their proximate causes in the societal or institutional context of Congress. That Congress was being transformed into a new and different kind of institution, one that would be more open, participative, democratic, and responsive, was evident. These changes were not only compatible with but also contributed to the "resurgence" of Congress against the executive branch.[3] But why did this transformation take place in the 1970s instead of the 1930s or 1950s or 1990s?

The contributors to *Congress in Change* did not answer this question, but two years later Lawrence C. Dodd and Bruce I. Oppenheimer and another group of scholars again considered congressional change in the first edition of *Congress Reconsidered*.[4] Fourteen chapters traced the evolution of Congress and the effects of the reform movement. They addressed such diverse subjects as committee reform, the role of the conservative coalition, elections, the budget process, oversight, and congressional-executive relations. In a concluding essay Lawrence C. Dodd offered a cyclical theory to explain the evolution of Congress as the product of a struggle for power in which the presidency inexorably expands its influence at the expense of Congress. According to Dodd, in the typical cycle new members quest for power and seek to alter institutional arrangements to obtain it (decentralization), the system falls into chaos as a result (disintegration), the executive branch then asserts its authority, and Congress responds with a resurgence of centralized power. Each cycle, however, leaves the presidency with more influence over Congress. The reason why Congress is the consistent loser in the power game is due to its endemic constitutional weaknesses, the product of the Madisonian theory that guided the country's founders.[5]

In retrospect, the onset of the Carter administration may have been an inauspicious moment to have declared the presidency the probable winner in the power struggle. The Carter administration struggled in its relationship with Congress, leading some observers to conclude that problems endemic to the system had created paralysis while others laid the blame squarely at Carter's feet. In issuing the second edition of *Congress Reconsidered* in 1981, Dodd and Oppenheimer focussed on the results of the 1980 election and their implications for electoral realignment.[6] Impressed by the magnitude of Ronald Reagan's defeat of Jimmy Carter and by the new Republican control of the Senate, the editors considered the immediate problem of divided government and the deeper question of whether a fundamental political realignment was about to redesign the Washington landscape for the first time in a half-century.

With that time frame lending perspective, Lawrence Dodd shifted ground in a new concluding essay. The more narrowly defined cyclical theory of the first edition gave way to a broader canvas that sketched congressional eras spanning decades. The era of confrontation ran from the founding to the Civil War. An era of expansion occupied the years from 1875 until 1910. From 1920 through 1965 the political system witnessed the period of consolidation. The ten years thereafter marked the "age" of reform. In 1981 the nation was embarked on a new era of "reassessment" in which the government was experiencing a crisis of "legitimation." Still viewing the Madisonian system as inherently flawed, Dodd called for fundamental change in the Constitution to rescue the system (and hence Congress) from its own infirmities.

In another 1981 study, *The New Congress,* contributors described it as an institution on the run.[7] In this book, edited by Norman J. Ornstein and Thomas E. Mann, eleven essays described the manner in which the new Congress differed from the old, touching upon things as diverse as the culture of the Washington community, committees and subcommittees, leadership and coalition building, the role of the media and of congressional staff, and the relationship between Congress and the presidency in the policy process. Unlike *Congress in Change,* which found causes of change everywhere but failed to produce a coherent theme about them, and the first two editions of *Congress Reconsidered,* which appeared to shift emphasis as the circumstances changed, these descriptive studies had a simple theme: Congress is shaped largely by forces external to it. Thus Thomas Mann anticipated that "a new set of political ideas will emerge to give shape and substance to party competition" (p. 54). Roger Davidson held that "Congress is inevitably a reactive institution ... it mirrors the nation's political life—its values, standards, and organizing principles" (p. 131). Similarly, Barbara Sinclair concluded that "Congress is a reactive institution; it cannot anticipate. It is not, however, impervious to strong stimuli from its environment" (p. 220). In a concluding essay, Norman Ornstein blamed Congress's problems on Congress's constituents. "It is more accurate these days to criticize the whole of the citizenry for not coalescing around a set of policy ideas or a single direction in energy, economic, or foreign policy than it is to criticize Congress for failing to do so" (p. 382). The emphasis that these essays placed upon the manner in which Congress is shaped by external forces was not matched, however, by a corresponding explanation of how the shaping takes place.

As Ornstein's concluding essay in *The New Congress* suggested, the changes in the Congress that had seemed so promising to the contributors to *Congress in Change* in the mid-1970s had produced an institution that by the early 1980s seemed not to be functioning very well. Lawrence Dodd's concern about the "crisis of legitimation," was simply one among many interpretations that evoked a crisis of confidence in the American system. A main theme of congressional scholarship in the early 1980s was the diffusion of power that had been wrought by the reform movement, the attitudes of a new generation of members, and a vexing public policy agenda.

The frustration with Congress was felt earlier, of course, during the Carter administration, when the government was often inhibited in doing the nation's business due to internal turmoil in Congress and conflict between it and the administration. This paralysis of government was all the more striking since the Democrats held the White House and sizable majorities in both houses of Congress. The conventional wisdom of that day attributed the causes of this deadlock to the incompetence of President Carter and some in his administration and to the diffusion of power in Congress. Congress was too internally fragmented to be led by its own elected leadership, and Carter did not fill the vacuum with forceful presidential influence. In part due to the difficulties Democrats experienced in governing, in 1980 the Republicans won the presidency, majority control of the Senate, and came within twenty-six votes of controlling the House of Representatives. This shift in partisan control of the institutions of government did not, however, enable it to function more efficiently, except for the eight-month Reagan honeymoon in 1981. The story of the 1980s was one in which Congress and the presidency were typically at odds, public policymaking was often stalemated, and the federal government piled up a mountain of public debt.

By mid-decade frustration with Congress had reached into the forums of enlightened public opinion.[8] The litany of criticisms found members of Congress preoccupied with their own reelections and the institution bogged down in trivia, pulled apart by too many leaders and too few followers, weakened by budget paralysis, and generally incompetent to do the public's business. While public frustration with the institution increased, academic political science seemed to have given up on the task of explaining the changes that were occurring. In the third edition of *Congress Reconsidered,* published in 1985, Dodd and Oppenheimer replaced twelve of their eighteen previous contributors in favor of more timely alternatives and, more significantly, abandoned the attempt to provide editorial interpretation.[9] Implicit in the restructuring of the volume was the recognition of the difficulty that interpretation encounters in keeping pace with reality. The interpreter searches for the Archimedean point from which to explain political change, but the ground consistently shifts beneath his feet. What, after all, was the fundamental factor driving Congress in the 1980s?

In 1988 James L. Sundquist joined Lawrence Dodd in locating the problem in the Constitution. Unlike Dodd, who had emphasized the inherent weakness of Congress, Sundquist stressed the fundamental schism in the American regime caused by the constitutional separation of powers. America was in the midst of a "new era of coalition government," in which the presidency and Congress were controlled by opposing political parties most of the time.[10] From 1981 through 1986 the Republicans controlled the White House and the Senate while the Democrats controlled the House. After 1986 the Democrats controlled both houses of Congress, but the Republicans retained their grip on the White House. Sundquist concluded that this was the new norm of American politics and called for new theorizing about how the country might survive the institutional crisis into which it had unwittingly fallen.

Meanwhile, the congressional scholars were at work in the vineyards of research, and once again they found a new political topography. The ultimate response of congressional Democrats to the

Republican reign in the White House was a reassertion of centralized leadership. This tendency was particularly evident during the attenuated House speakership of Jim Wright and seemed to refute the received wisdom about the inexorable tendency toward decentralization in Congress. The second law of political thermodynamics seemed to have succumbed to a Newtonian centripetal force.

It was an abashed Lawrence Dodd and Bruce Oppenheimer who led their scholarly troops to the ramparts in the fourth edition of *Congress Reconsidered.*[11]

> One benefit we have derived from preparing four editions of *Congress Reconsidered* is an increased sensitivity to institutional change. . . . In truth, we did not foresee the fluidity of the modern House, particularly the possibility of a new House oligarchy, nor do we know of anyone who did. In 1977 the signs pointed to the spread of power among a diverse range of actors. . . . The failure to anticipate the current swing to greater centralization, a stronger speakership, and more cohesive parties in the House . . . presents us with several questions. . . . First, why was the potential for centralization so badly underestimated by numerous scholars and observers?

In searching for an explanation, the editors focussed on the underlying changes in congressional elections and their financing, the long-run effects of the Voting Rights Act of 1965, the strengthening of party leaders by the reform movements, and "the sensitivity of the reformed House to the influence of environmental context" (p. 445). Surprisingly, however, the Senate seemed impervious to the changes that transformed the House from a relatively decentralized to a relatively centralized institution. The Senate differs from the House in having less party cohesiveness, less rigid rules and procedures, and longer terms of office, hence greater independence of individual senators. The factors that caused the House to change did not, therefore, affect the Senate in the same way.

The fourth edition of *Congress Reconsidered*, like its predecessors and most other congressional scholarship in the 1980s, demonstrated the limits imposed upon political science by its own subject matter. Political science is torn between long-term trends that defy rigorous scientific explanation and short-term fluctuations that seem impossible to predict. It is caught between banality and bedlam. Perhaps, though, it might be helped, if not saved, by a reorientation in its goals. The catch–22 in which political science is caught derives from its dependence upon the explanation-prediction model. By departing from it in favor of an interpretive approach, we hope to provide a framework that will guide thinking about the problem of congressional change, even where it cannot yield precise predictions. We believe that this framework has some explanatory power, but its chief value lies less in prediction than in its capacity to foster intelligent understanding of Congress and its role in the American political system. Relying on it, we seek to interpret the research reported in this volume.

A Framework for Interpreting Change

What is needed, then, is not simply more description of institutions and of the way in which they are changing; what is required is an understanding of the process of political and institutional change itself. We want to know why Congress changes the way it does. What is required is a conceptual framework within which the process of change can be better understood, and not simply an account of changes themselves.

We here propose such a framework. The framework emphasizes the interrelationship of two forces that have shaped the American polity: the order imposed by the constitutional regime, and the permutations within that order caused by the evolution of American political culture. We share with Aristotle the conviction that a polity's fundamental law (its politia or regime) determines its character. We also share with Tocqueville, however, the belief that a political system is fundamentally shaped by its surrounding political culture, as channeled through the constitutional regime. American political institutions are formed, at any point in time, by the interaction of these two forces. The evolution of Congress illustrates this.

Figure 1 provides a schematic presentation of our view of political change. The upper and lower lines suggest the continuity of the constitutional regime. The arrows suggest the manner in which the political culture shapes the political system and how the political system in turn affects political institutions within it. The schema, as well as the framework that it illustrates, necessarily represents an oversimplification of the reality of political change. Its value lies in its tendency to force us to think about the problem of political change in a larger context than is usually undertaken in studies of Congress.

Figure 1 will remind some readers immediately of the "funnel of

Figure 1. **Political Change**

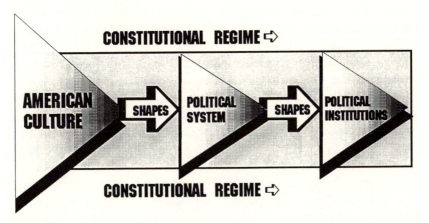

causality" familiar to the philosophy of social science. Other readers will find it reminiscent of systems theory and wonder why there is no feedback loop. Suitably unpacked, both of these observations lead to a consideration of the befuddling problem of causality. Political science, to the extent that it is a science, must search for cause and effect. To address the problem of change is to presuppose a cause-and-effect relationship. To think intelligently about political change is not possible otherwise. The problem lies in being precise. Students of change in Congress who are careful begin by searching for the most proximate causes of the changes they observe. Typically, this leads them to scour the vicinity for such things as membership turnover, new rules and norms, shifting political coalitions, leadership styles, new issues, and so forth. The search for proximate causes (what Aristotle called the "efficient cause") of change has the advantage of precision but carries with it the great liability of being insufficiently comprehensive. When Dodd and Oppenheimer, for example, say that the greater centralization of power that occurred in the House of Representatives in the late 1980s came about due to such things as the Voting Rights Act of 1965, the strengthening of the party leadership by reforms, and so forth, they are not wrong; they are merely arbitrarily narrow. A broader explanation might address the peculiar diffidence of members, who are virtually assured of reelection, that led them to be so deferential to a Speaker like Jim Wright. We believe that this phenomenon has more to do with contemporary American culture than with the campaign financing system or the rules of the House; and we believe that the same cultural forces shaping the contemporary House also serve to account for the contemporary Senate, where no trend toward centralized leadership developed.

We do not, however, believe that causal relationships can be ascertained with the kind of precision normally expected in the hard sciences. Understanding politics is a matter of *interpretation* more often than it is a matter of *explanation.* To put it another way, the explanations that contemporary political science produces themselves require interpretation in a broader context than a search for explanation (in the scientific sense) will allow. Our schema is a way of thinking about the process of political change that will permit us to provide an interpretation of the evidence reported in this volume. It is a reflection of the historical and phenomenological approaches for which we have respectively argued.[12]

We begin, then, with the constitutional regime, at all times the common denominator of American political experience. When the founders decided that the Senate would be comprised of two members from each state and that representation in the House of Representatives would be based upon population, they ensured that Congress would reflect the diversity of American culture. When the states decided to base representation in the House on geographically defined districts, they accentuated the tendency of the Constitution to incorporate "the spirit of party and faction into the necessary and ordinary operations of government."[13] When, in 1917, the Constitution was amended to provide for the direct election of senators, the arena of party and faction was shifted from the state legislatures to the people of each state. The result has been to produce a government that is moved primarily by factional force and that is in need of counterbalancing centralizing influences. Historically, the political party system provided the glue that held the system together; but in the latter part of the twentieth century the party system was undermined by a new political culture in which politicians were able to sustain their tenure in office independently of party support. Thus the constitutional fragmentation of power has, over time, been amplified by the transformation of the political culture from one dominated by party to one lacking a dominant centralizing force.

A variety of factors contributed to this transformation of American political culture, among which we mention three trends as illustrations.

The broadest tendency affecting American political culture is the power of its liberal regime. As Tocqueville saw most clearly, societies based on the principle of equality of rights have a definite tendency toward individualism, the consumptive concern with self.[14] This tendency affects all citizens of a liberal democracy, including those who choose to become involved in politics. Related is a second trend in the public policy agenda. The era of economic nationalism that produced the strong two-party system in the late nineteenth century gave way in the twentieth century to the demand for equity in the form of the welfare state. The demand for equity led to the desire for government benefits in infinite variety. This desire fed the creation of a political system anchored in distributed benefits and surrounded by the organized interests that such benefits produce. Third, and perhaps paradoxically, the postwar era's emphasis on education and training produced new generations of Americans whose attitudes toward public policy and the process that produces it are "rational" and "problem-solving" in character. Thus, a host of basically self-centered politicians seek electoral security by pandering to the demands of organized interests while presuming to solve the nation's problems by the rational intervention of "policy entrepreneurs." By the 1980s the result was a Congress in which over 90 percent of incumbents were typically reelected while the nation tripled its debt.

Isn't this just an adaptat- ion?

The decline of the party system is perhaps the most evident manifestation of the impact of the new political culture on the political system, but it is not the only one. Lawrence Dodd's thesis that the presidency must grow in power in relation to Congress is but one among several contemporary interpretations that search for a remedy in our political institutions to a problem that is endemic to our political culture. The search for institutional fixes is not new. At the height of the strong party era Mary Parker Follett called for collaborative government between the president and the Speaker of the House.[15] In the 1950s James MacGregor Burns bewailed the division of power between the presidential and congressional parties in his "four party system."[16] In the 1960s Richard Neustadt argued that a Machiavellian president could solve the dilemma of democratic governance in America, and in the 1970s James Sundquist found reassurance in a resurgent Congress.[17] It is fair to say, however, that in the 1980s the search for institutional solutions gave way to a sense of despair that any were available.

Both the search for institutional remedies and the frustration in not finding them reflect the underlying reality of American political culture. Institutions are a reflection of the political culture and hence are unlikely to be able to counteract its main tendencies. Instead, political institutions *reflect* the political culture in revealing ways. They are not like antibodies, capable of restoring health; they are like prosthetic devices, enabling the body politic to function with minimal effectiveness. It is from this perspective that the "reform" movement of the early 1970s should be viewed. Congress was not fixing itself when it sought reform in its rules and norms; it was merely adapting to a new political culture in which the old rules and norms cut against the interests of individual members and organized groups. The result was to create as many or more problems as were "solved" by the reforms. New institutional adaptations such as the emergence of informal groups, new leadership strategies and techniques, more ephemeral policy coalitions, and more frequent recourse to ad hoc decision making were merely the institutional manifestations of the new political culture.

This overview may serve to flesh out the perspective on political change that Figure 1 only captures in simplified form. But even this discussion is inadequate to a more complete understanding of the process of change. That fuller grasp requires the kind of spadework at which contemporary congressional scholars excel. We are privileged that the present volume is able to report research findings on the new frontier of congressional scholarship, findings that we believe have interpretive power when placed in the framework that we are suggesting. In Part I four chapters address the relationship between Congress and the electoral system, the relationship between members of Congress and their constituencies, and the manner in which a changing electorate is producing a different kind of Congress. The five chapters comprising Part II examine the legislative process, the role of leadership in it, and the shifting tides of policy coalition. As we discuss this research, we will explore more fully the cultural forces that illustrate the value of our framework for interpreting change.

Changing American Culture, Congressional Elections, and Representation

As a highly institutionalized body, Congress changes glacially when compared, say, to musical trends in southern California. Indeed, some scholars continue to be impressed with congressional stability[18] or with cyclical patterns of activity and stalemate.[19] But great sea changes in society and politics ultimately ramify through the national legislature, and it is that complex process that we wish to capture.

Fascinating paradoxes lie at the heart of social and political change in America. Many of the founders were wary of mass democracy, and indeed they designed a constitutional architecture to frustrate majoritarian government.[20] Yet one of the most important forces driving change in America has been democracy. From the founding era to contemporary times we see a dramatic and sustained expansion of political rights. The political system had to adapt as suffrage was extended to successive segments of the population—religious minorities, the nonpropertied, women, native and black Americans—and as rights of free expression, assembly, and union organization were assured. But as political rights became more robust, so did the popular demands on governing institutions. James MacGregor Burns sees an inherent tension here.[21] The constitutional structure frustrates strong governmental action, while expanding democracy demands it. Only in a few rare circumstances—a crisis such as the Depression, war, or a president able to lead a unified party in Congress—do we see effective and sustained mobilization of a governing majority.

But there is a deeper paradox here, one that liberal enthusiasts such as Burns often fail to see. A preoccupation with individual rights, which constitute claims prior to the state, along with an expanding language of rights in the political culture, undermines collective political action. For rights not only enable popular majorities to organize for redress of grievances, they also allow self-interested minority factions to check majoritarian action at all levels of government. Moreover, collective political action probably requires a kind of communal solidarity in which individuals are willing to sacrifice for the good for the group.[22] Otherwise only those elite, easy-to-organize sectors of society will gain effective representation.[23] Thus a political culture that stresses rights to the exclusion of obligations and sacrifice may frustrate nonelite political mobilization.

A good way to illustrate this, perhaps, is the case of African-American representation. Expansion of political rights—first in the form of an end to slavery, then in laws protecting voting rights and civil rights— was absolutely essential to effective black representation. But facilitating social and cultural structures were also required. Ironically, it was the long and unique legacy of slavery, segregation, and discrimination that created in black communities a set of social bonds that were centered in churches.[24] These communal church institutions facilitated civil rights organizing, voter registration efforts, congressional campaigns, and Jesse Jackson's presidential crusades. Effective collective political mobilization occurred through institutions that embodied racial solidarity and pride, fostered leadership, and encouraged individual sacrifice. The language of rights was thus merged with a corresponding religious and community language of obligation and sacrifice for the broader good. We believe that the role of mediating institutions such as those fostered by organized religion play a fundamental role in ameliorating the tendencies of democratic individualism, but they are less strong today than they have been during previous periods in American history.

Political culture is a slippery concept to capture with any precision, but we must grapple with it to understand how citizens develop the preferences and values that ultimately impinge on political institutions. While scholarly disagreement exists about the origins and influences of political culture, there are key convergences as well. Aaron Wildavsky, defining culture as "shared values that justify social action," has suggested that the democratic ethos in America has produced an interplay between egalitarian and individualistic political cultures. A third cultural motif that he terms hierarchical—a concern with stability, tradition, continuity, and organic community—has grown vastly weaker than the other two. Wildavsky's analysis illuminates the paradoxes described above because it explains the profound American ambiguity about effective leadership and government administration.[25] The individualistic political culture, with its emphasis on rights versus obligations or sacrifice, fosters personal autonomy and entrepreneurial achievement to the point of atomism.[26] The egalitarian culture, in contrast, reflects the American emphasis on democratization and the attempt to use collective means to achieve greater social equality. While radically different, these two cultures, Wildavsky argues, blend in ways that frustrate leadership and communal sacrifice for the collective good. Neither culture is comfortable with routine leadership, individualists because such leadership is unnecessary and egalitarians because it tends toward an acceptance of differential status and hierarchy. Charismatic leadership, the kind often found in the black community, may be the only form of leadership acceptable to egalitarians, but it remains suspect to individualists.

Other scholars of political culture have placed their emphasis on the corrosive influence of individualism alone. Bellah's celebrated study concluded that the ethos of autonomy and moral relativity undermined communities that nurture healthy citizens.[27] Merelman uses the phrase "loosely bound" to describe individuals who have loose ties to neighborhoods, churches, unions, and other community institutions.[28] To be sure, there are critics of this line of inquiry. Bellah's method and sample heavily weight the bi-coastal perspective and largely ignore the heartland. And as Fowler has suggested, elite scholars often write more of their own academic culture than the lives of ordinary Americans, who remain, in his view, still rooted in church communities that provide a modicum of relief from the demands or isolation of an individualistic society.[29] Similarly, in *Democracy in America*, Tocqueville stressed the significance of America's "point of departure" in Puritan culture.[30] But where is the point of departure for American culture today? If we are to judge by political consequences, a case can be made for the California Jacuzzis in which so many Americans sit. The tension between individualism and collective political action is directly related to the sources of congressional behavior today.

One of the enduring features of American life concerns the tension between "free persons and public good."[31] The founders, while realists about self-interest, nonetheless expected a modicum of civic virtue to leaven individual striving.[32] Moreover, throughout much of American history the "individualism" celebrated in folklore and political theory was restrained by a practical set of religious, moral, and communitarian social contexts and norms.[33] Free individuals, as Tocqueville suggested, were thus often constrained from exercising their freedom in ways destructive to their communities. By mid-twentieth century, however, broad economic, technological, and social forces radically altered the delicate balance between individual freedom and social order. Mobility, cosmopolitan education, and mass communication, especially, served to undermine the socializing power of local communities, and the triumph of the marketplace rendered values a matter of individual taste and preference. Tocqueville's fear of a rootless people driven by individual self-interest seemed a possibility. Indeed, as more individuals enjoy liberation from morally intrusive local contexts, autonomy becomes a potential reality for the mass of citizens, not just an elite.

Sprawling suburbs, obsessive television viewing, and the youth culture are the symbols of this emerging mass society of autonomous individuals unconnected by local geography.

The political implications are rich. As early as 1953 Robert Nisbet warned of the deleterious political consequences of an emerging mass society of individuals uprooted from traditional ties to family, village, and religion.[34] Daniel Bell argued that the counter-culture of the 50s and 60s was merely the mass realization of what had been advocated forty years earlier by a tiny cadre of intellectual Bohemians.[35] Thus, Bellah's recent concern that individualism is eroding civic "habits of the heart" culminates decades of musings about profound societal changes.

It is perhaps too facile to say that the problem of a culture of individual autonomy is the loss of civic virtue. Hard to measure and equally hard to compare with past eras, a dose of civic responsibility, sacrifice, or concern for the public good is probably necessary to the healthy functioning of any democratic society. But civic responsibility may be like the faith that measures a grain of mustard seed; a tiny amount goes a long way. The problems for the polity involve more than the loss, however measured, of civic virtue among politicians and voters. For four decades scholars from diverse fields have pointed to the weakness of collective political action in a societal milieu that promotes individual autonomy. Nisbet suggested that the vacuum created by the weakening ties to local communities would be filled by a quest for some national community, which he viewed as inevitably futile.[36] Echoing Nisbet, Merelman argues that Americans have become so loosely attached to social institutions, churches, and local communities that citizens are stripped of effective avenues for cohesive group action.[37] Yet the real world of political power is about collective action.[38]

The breakdown of communities has posed concrete problems for politicians, especially traditional ones. Richard Fenno, in his classic study of House members in their districts, suggested that traditional campaigning is difficult in atomistic contexts (which require cash to buy modern techniques of computer-generated voter contact, direct mail, market research, polling, and mass media appeals). Fenno noted how hard it was for some congressional members to connect with their constituents due to the decline of viable community institutions. He quotes the lament of one member of Congress about a part of his district: "It's a mystery to me. I go there and all I see are row after row of mobile homes and apartment houses. It's just a collection of shopping centers. . . . It's not a community. They have no rotary clubs or groups like that. It's just a bunch of houses. . . . I don't know how you would campaign there."[39] The period of Fenno's account—the mid-1970s—stands at the hinge of dramatic change in Congress. Perhaps his account presaged the replacement of a generation of party- and community-oriented politicians with a cadre of individual entrepreneurs epitomized by the Watergate babies.[40] Politicians who could not adapt to the new candidate-centered, technologically sophisticated milieu were ultimately replaced by those more comfortable with modern demands. Today, members of Congress are as likely to attend "town meetings" called by their staffs as they are to attend a church social or a local PTA meeting. Instead of holding forth in the back room of a local pub, as Tip O'Neill did for two decades, the members travel around the district in "representation vans," like the mobile home, a reflection of the ephemerality of modern American culture.

Not surprisingly, then, the postwar era that saw dramatic social changes in American life also witnessed key political developments. One of the most important sea changes in American politics has been the much lamented decline of party strength,[41] especially in the electorate. While parties have shown signs of institutional life and adaptability[42] and resurgence in Congress itself, the decay at the electoral level continues unabated. Split-ticket voting and increasing numbers of voters identifying themselves as independent are only a part of the story. Marty Wattenberg has documented with meticulous detail the fact that voters simply do not have the affective, emotional attachment to parties they once did.[43] Voters may state that they have an affiliation, but when probed they reveal that their attachment is weak, a fact not surprising in light of the atomizing forces described above.

This decay has momentous implications for our political system, contributing to the decline in voting rates and the rise of candidate-centered campaigns. In the past politicians rose or fell with partisan tides or presidential fortunes, and they ran party-oriented campaigns rooted in partisan voter loyalty. Now congressional candidates develop a personal following and insulate themselves from national trends. The concept of a personal vote,[44] indeed, suggests an atomistic polity. Technological advances, along with the rise of a professional campaign industry of pollsters, consultants, and media gurus, allow candidates to purchase the equivalent of a personal party structure for each election. What was once performed by ward heelers—voter research, strategic advice, voter contact—is now purchased in the free market by the highest bidder. No doubt many first-time successful congressional winners receive critical help from national and state parties. But the average member of Congress, well financed by willing contributors and well known personally by virtue of the perks available to incumbents, can tailor his or her pitch at will. Not only are candidates loosely bound to their party, but they are able to avoid the consequences of institutional weakness or governmental failure. A uniquely disturbing feature emerges in the American candidate-centered system: members run for Congress by running against it. Voters love their representative but hate Congress; individual members are not held accountable for the collective sins of the body.[45]

As Jacobson has shown, the collective accountability once provided by parties is seriously weakened with candidate-centered politics, which arise, as we have shown, from the individualistic forces at play in the broader society. Parties, with their roots in nineteenth-century community structures, must compete with modern cultural and technological entities—the mass media, PACs, and pressure groups with their narrow, laser-like focus.[46]

Party ties that do exist seem somewhat artificial, like Kurt Vonnegut's "granfalloon."[47] What a contrast this is to an era not long gone by, when American parties were creatures of tightly knit community structures. To be a Democrat in Boston, for example, involved a set of mutually reinforcing structures—ethnic clubs, union locals, Catholic parishes, along with the party ward heelers and bosses— which drew the faithful in a tight bond. Similarly, the Yankee shop owner in Vermont, Republican to the core, found his compatriots in the congregational church, in the merchants association, and so forth, reinforcing his identity and sense of civic responsibility. The stronger the collective strands of the bond are, the less likely is a temporary defection to the other party, split-ticket voting, or partisan dealignment. Today the chronic decline in voter turnout and the rise of public cynicism and apathy suggest there is a shrinking public connected to politics in meaningful ways.

Historically, parties integrated an otherwise disparate electorate and assured some measure of electoral accountability. Voters with minimum information could register an eloquent yes or no to those running the government because the "government"—meaning Congress and the presidency—was usually controlled by the same party. Divided party government, with all its attendant problems, is but another manifestation of the social forces described here. Voters who are less attached to their parties, who respond to the signals from the candidates that stress the personal over the partisan, register as an echo chamber what is fed them. Thus congressional elections seem increasingly detached from presidential elections, forcing scholars to reassess the assumptions underlying predominate theories of American government.[48]

The candidate-centered era, of course, has benefited the parties differentially, favoring the Republicans nationally and the Democrats in the states and Congress. Moreover, a kind of perverse logic governs the electorate's current habits. As James Buchanan and Gary Jacobson both show, rational voters can register their collective concerns about the state of the economy and national defense even while voting for parochial interests that may violate those sentiments. The budget deficit is a powerful metaphor for the tragedy of the commons that occurs when voters are able to simultaneously register their unrealistic wishes for lower taxes and more programs.

A related problem is the quality of representation. In the cash-rich context of modern campaigning, members of Congress increasingly spend legislative time raising funds and doing casework for out-of-state contributors and PACs.[49] Thus an "investor"-oriented system has replaced a voter-driven one.[50] All of this has left the polity at the mercy of economically focussed interests, willing and able to feed the money machine that drives modern elections. The unsavory spectacles we witnessed in the 1980s—the gothic falls of Tony Coehlo and Jim Wright, the S&L mess, and the Keating Five—suggest an atmosphere of self-serving behavior on the part of incumbents which is relatively unchecked by collective political forces.

In summary, American society is less communal in its social organization than in the past, and this fundamental change has broad ramifications for politics. One of the most important consequences of the rising individualism is the decay of party strength in the electorate. Candidate-centered campaigns, entrepreneurial representation in Congress, and other manifestations of this individualism resonate throughout our political affairs. The chapters in Part I of this volume illuminate the consequences of these social trends on congressional

politics, but they also may suggest ways in which our brush paints too
broadly. For there are cross-currents and eddies as well as prevailing
currents. So we move now from the broad to the specific, from the
global discussion of societal change to the more focussed delineation
of congressional change.

Candidate-centered Politics
and Congressional Change

The four chapters on representation and elections are remarkably complementary to one another and illustrative of themes developed here.
Campbell, Canon, and Maisel explicitly ground their work in an understanding of the candidate-centered nature of the electoral system, while
Swain's analysis suggests that black representatives are increasingly
acting like individualists and less as representatives of the national
black constituency. Thus the characteristics, decisions, and representa-
tional styles of individual candidates and members of Congress emerge
as the key units of analysis, lending support to our contention that key
social and technological trends drive change in the political system.
Those forces that led to the declining salience of party in the electorate,
consequently, magnified the importance of candidate characteristics.
Thus not only did mobility, mass communication, and cosmopolitan
education heighten individual autonomy in local communities, but because they undermined the traditional ties of citizens to parties, they
helped accentuate the emphasis on individual candidates. Individualism wins coming and going.

Nothing illustrates this maxim so well as the changing nature of
electoral politics. A generation ago the idea of a candidate-driven party
realignment would not have made sense. But as Canon shows, southern realignment was spurred in part by party-switchers (officeholders
and prominent candidates), who brought voters with them into the
GOP. Yet, as Campbell argues, the GOP failed to capitalize on presidential coattails (and favorable trends) simply because it could not
recruit quality candidates in a number of congressional districts won
by Republican presidents. Maisel's analysis corroborates Campbell's
and suggests that the problem of quality candidates is not restricted to
the South but is endemic for the Republican party nationally, a finding
consistent with a new study by Gary Jacobson.[51] Canon's ambition
theory helps to provide a plausible rationale for this dearth of good

candidates. As he shows, the ambition of aspiring politicians accounts logically for both the initial Republican gains in the South as well as their current stagnation. Aided by Maisel's account, we might extend the implications of that theory and speculate that something inherent in the Republican message or its core constituencies and investors makes recruitment problematic.

There are some interesting contrasts among these studies. While Campbell suggests that favorable opportunities will not be squandered forever (meaning there is hope for the GOP), Canon shows how the logic of courthouse politics and the solidarity of the black vote combine to send signals to aspiring individuals that the Democratic party remains a good vehicle for their political ambition. Maisel's analysis, too, suggests that the dearth of quality candidates in the GOP may continue to plague the party. Thus broad social forces that undermine strong party ties in the electorate and exaggerate the importance of individual candidates work to the detriment of Republican congressional hopes (even as they probably aid the party at the presidential level). The puzzle of Republican weakness at the state and congressional level will receive fuller analysis as we turn below to a more detailed review of the studies in this volume devoted to elections and representation. A broader concern, however, is the quality of political representation generally, especially the quality of leadership held collectively accountable for its decisions.

A good place to begin is James Campbell's analysis of the changing presidential pulse in congressional elections. Impressive in its scope, Campbell's chapter charts the pulse over the full 120 years from the post–Civil War era to the election of George Bush. His data are uniquely comprehensive and provide a fresh perspective on questions of enormous importance: Does the president have coattails? Is there a surge and decline from the presidential to the midterm election? How has the presidential effect changed over time? Critically essaying the tendency to discount the link between congressional and presidential elections, Campbell shows that something like a presidential pulse reverberates through congressional elections, beating in one election cycle, resting in the other. Our framework suggests to us that the more significant finding is the "weakening of the pulse," the eroding link between presidential and congressional contests, as we would expect in light of declining partisan ties in the electorate. Campbell notes the signs of this dealignment and concurs with our conclusion that Congress members seem better able to insulate themselves from national forces than they once were.

However, he offers an unusual explanation for the weakened presidential pulse: wasted coattails. Using the 1972 landslide election of Richard Nixon as a critical turning point, Campbell finds that "surge effects" were relatively stable until that year. But Nixon's coattails were remarkably weak in light of his impressive electoral achievement: his party gained only thirteen seats, while he carried forty-nine states and 62 percent of the vote. Nixon did particularly well in the South, but the failure of the GOP to recruit candidates there prevented the party from realizing coattail effects, thus negating a presidential surge. Remarkably, in thirty-five southern congressional districts that Nixon carried handily, the GOP fielded no candidates. Indeed, Nixon carried some districts by over 80 percent where the Democratic candidate went uncontested to Congress. Campbell shows that this pattern continued with the Republican presidential victories of 1984 and 1988. In 1984, for example, Reagan's ability to bring Republicans in on his coattails was hampered by the fact that over forty congressional districts he won went uncontested; there were just too few candidates to take advantage of the presidential surge. Campbell's evidence is convincing, but his suggestion that the presidential pulse might strengthen in the future with successful Republican party recruitment remains speculative. There are, we suggest, broader social forces that undermine the link between the presidential and congressional elections. Moreover, Campbell does not consider what might happen with a successful Democratic presidential effort. Suppose, for the sake of argument, the GOP makes a grand and successful attempt in 1992 to recruit in those districts that have been trending Republican, but then the Democrats win the White House. The Republicans might win some congressional seats, thus checking the *Democratic* presidential pulse.

David Canon's analysis of the emergence of the Republican party in the South is a nice complement to Campbell's analysis. As Canon suggests, "In an era of split-ticket voting, local politics, and independent voters, a candidate-based theory of secular realignment is more likely to explain patterns of political change." Thus focussed on the importance of individual candidates, Canon develops an ambition theory that helps to explain a gradual, long-term, realignment in the South. Based on the calculations of politically ambitious individuals, his theory of elite-driven realignment suggests that it took the dramatic external shock of the 1964 Goldwater success to upset the prior equilibrium. From that point on, the calculations of ambitious politicians could include the GOP as a viable alternative. Indeed, the increasing number of experienced Republican candidates in the South is evidence that seasoned aspirants are taking the Republican party seriously. In providing fascinating support for his theory of an elite-driven realignment, Canon shows that considerable Republican electoral success came from party-switchers (prominent Democrats who switched to the Republican party, taking candidate-loyal voters with them). Part of the reason for this is the difficulty of recruiting candidates of sufficiently high quality to defeat incumbent Democrats. Better to convert the incumbent than defeat him.

In spite of GOP gains, Canon sees the same pattern identified by Campbell: a stalled realignment. After making steady gains from the late 1960s on, GOP congressional strength stagnated at the very time it should have been growing—during the mid-to-late 1980s. Republican strength in the Senate peaked at 50 percent in 1980–1982, but then dropped precipitously to around a third in 1988. House strength rose more gradually through the 1970s but flattened out in the 1980s at around a third too. Part of the explanation for stagnating GOP gains is a surging and highly organized black vote—loyally Democratic—that has both forestalled GOP advances and altered the calculations of ambitious politicians. Black registration and voting in the South mushroomed in the 1980s, spurred by the galvanizing threat of the Reagan era and by aggressive efforts by black groups, Democratic organs, and Jesse Jackson's presidential campaigns. The potential of the black vote was enhanced at the very time that Republicans should have been making their greatest inroads. In a sense, then, a realignment did take place in the South from 1964 to 1988, but the enfranchisement of an entirely new group of African-Americans helped to make up for Democratic losses among white voters. Canon's ambition theory can account for GOP stagnation through the altered calculations of political aspirants; that still begs the question of the broader social forces that led to those altered calculations. An enlarged, energized black electorate deserves, we suspect, a richer analysis than Canon's ambition theory provides, economical though it is.

Carol Swain's chapter helps to provide some of the rich context of change that is so central to politics in the South and elsewhere. Moreover, her description of change in black representation illustrates what we have been arguing about individualistic forces at play in American society. Her analysis is the first systematic catalogue of black representation in Congress extant, and it demonstrates how forces external to Congress affect its membership. As Swain shows, blacks were represented in both the House and the Senate in the Reconstruction Era following the Civil War. All were Republicans, reflecting loyalty to the party of Lincoln and the Union. However, changing conditions in the South, particularly the Northern detachment and the assertion of white power, undermined black voting rights. By the turn of the century blacks were effectively disenfranchised in the South and Congress saw its only remaining black representative depart. For nearly three decades there was no black representative in Congress, and then, as Northern urban enclaves began to coalesce, a few black politicians, increasingly Democratic, began to make inroads. It was not until forces were unleashed by the civil rights movement, however, that black representation began to take on the contours it now enjoys in the House (the Senate remains a fortress against black representation). Swain's analysis shows how the voting rights legislation increased descriptive black representation. As important, she demonstrates how blacks strategically voted for white Democrats to increase their clout in Congress.

Intriguingly, Swain's analysis of the different forms of representation provided by national black elected officials suggests that some of the atomizing forces at play in the larger society are beginning to affect black politics. She notes how the cadre of officials elected in the 1960s created the Congressional Black Caucus to articulate collective concerns. Black House members, indeed, did not view themselves as representing their districts solely or exclusively, but rather saw themselves as representatives of black interests generally. But as some rose in seniority and influence, they found themselves departing from the "protest" agenda of the caucus to work as leaders in their party or stewards of important committees and policy arenas. Moreover, a new generation of black officials, such as Mike Espy, seem to be responding to local conditions in the same way white members do—paying attention to constituent service and district concerns even if such attention means an occasional departure from the party agenda or Black Caucus concerns. In short, black representatives appear to be increasingly conforming to our expectations about legislators generally: they pursue individual goals of reelection, policy influence, and leadership in a body that rewards such individual calculations. Swain suggests that this pattern reflects the assimilation of black leaders into the mainstream of the political culture.

Black representation, in summary, moved from an emphasis on communal solidarity—with black congressional members viewing themselves not as individual representatives of individual districts but as spokespersons of the needs and aspirations of their collective community—to a more district-oriented, individualistic representation. Ironically, then, as black opportunities for advancement and participation increased, so have the individualistic trends in the culture increasingly seeped into black communities and political action.

The final chapter in Part I, Sandy Maisel's, extends our understanding of an individualistic, candidate-driven electoral milieu and its significance for political representation. In a sense, his analysis overlaps with all four in its concern with elections and representation. Maisel confirms and expands the discussion of stalled realignment by showing convincingly that the GOP did not recruit quality candidates in many House and Senate races and thus failed to capitalize on national trends or the opportunity to ride presidential coattails. But while Campbell and Canon concentrate on the unique context of the South, Maisel shows that recruitment is a nationwide problem for the Republican party, a problem that continued through the 1990 election cycle. The GOP congressional weakness is seen in the fact that in spite of a decade of presidential control, Republican representation in the 102nd Congress will be the same as it was eight years earlier, a paltry 38 percent. The weakening of the presidential pulse is seen in the 1988 election, when Bush failed to carry anyone on his coattails (indeed, the Republicans lost a handful of seats while he was carrying 54 percent of the presidential electorate). The Republicans have seen their numbers in the House decrease in each of the last three electoral cycles. As Campbell, Canon, and Maisel all suggest, a big part of the answer to this riddle of GOP weakness congressionally during a time of Republican presidential hegemony is the issue of the quality of party candidates. As Gary Jacobson contends, Democrats attract candidates of higher quality, because the Democratic agenda of activist government makes public service more attractive.[52] Naysaying, however legitimate or needed, is just not appealing as a career focus. Add to this the fact that business elites and entrepreneurs find it inconvenient or practically impossible to run for congressional office, and the Republican party is left with few good candidates. By contrast, the Democratic party enjoys a base of potential aspirants in law, education, and elected officialdom.

This Republican weakness has spawned a number of intriguing responses. After the disastrous loss of the Senate in 1986, largely attributable to an activated black electorate, Lee Atwater established what he called "command focus" on increasing the black GOP vote. That effort apparently was submerged in presidential politics two years later as Willy Horton became a household name. More recently, Swain notes, the GOP has developed an explicit redistricting strategy aimed at creating a strange-bedfellow alliance with minorities. Concentrating minorities in certain districts may result in the election of more Hispanics and blacks to Congress but simultaneously would create more competitive districts elsewhere that Republicans can win. The Republican National Committee has devoted serious resources to this effort, so the question arises: what kind of representation should be striven for, descriptive representation on the basis of membership in the minority population or substantive representation on the basis of policy concerns? Swain warns her fellow African-Americans against falling into the GOP trap. But the dilemma is a poignant one.

Maisel's analysis, however, suggests that something more than GOP weakness is at work. His research indicates a weakness generally: both parties are having difficulty recruiting high-quality candidates, even in some open seats. The incumbent advantage, of course, looms as large as ever, in spite of supposedly testy voters and anti-incumbent sentiment in 1990. As Maisel laments, "Something's happenin' here, what it is ain't exactly clear." Perhaps what is happening is a glimpse into the consequences of a system cast adrift from traditional partisan and community moorings. As Fowler and McClure show, in a candidate-dominated system personal considerations by potential candidates largely determine political representation. Voters are presented with choices already severely delimited by the exigencies of fund raising, personal risk, family burdens, sacrifices of influential state positions, months of arduous campaigning, and the political calculations of potential aspirants. In short, voters see only candidates who choose to endure the slings and arrows of running modern, personally built campaigns. Fowler and McClure worry that there may not be enough good candidates willing to pay the costs of winning a congressional seat to provide adequate representation.[53] Brooks Jackson paints a slightly different, though related picture of inordinate influence of money on recruitment decisions and campaigns. Indeed, he suggests that an investor-driven electoral system is emerging in which "investors" receive service of a more substantial and disturbing sort than did traditional constituents,[54] a theme that is echoed by Ferguson and Rogers.[55]

Maisel is concerned about representation because genuine competition—the hallmark of our representative government—is absent in many congressional races. This lack of competition, even for open seats, leads him to question the assumptions of ambition theories that posit a ready pool of potential candidates for federal office. Perhaps the hassles of Washington representation are not worth giving up the real influence in policy available at the state level.

This brings us back to the issue of societal forms that inhibit collective action by citizens. Interest-group scholars have noted for years that organized lobbying was the province of the easy-to-organize, focussed, and self-interested, in contrast to the diffuse constituencies of the less well-to-do or otherwise hard to organize. The antidote to this elite bias in the pressure system, as Schattschneider and others argued, was a party-driven electoral politics. With the weakening of that system, our electoral politics is more driven than ever by the mobilized as against the unorganized. Thus with the decline of strong community structures, average citizens have fewer means of exercising collective influence over political decisions. True, members of Congress slavishly cater to their districts in one sense, but they increasingly raise money from out-of-state investors in order to intimidate challengers. And they seem relatively unconcerned about nonvoters and unorganized interests. Thus whatever collective accountability that exists in the system seems to bend to opposing, atomizing influences.[56]

If this depiction of the electoral milieu is correct, how, then, can we account for apparently contrary trends toward party unity or leadership in the contemporary Congress? As we will show, the individualistic cultural forces that drive the electoral system create special problems for a collective lawmaking body, problems that lead individual members to accept a certain type of structure and leadership for their own individual aims.

Institutional Change in the Atomistic Congress

Part II of this volume presents five studies of institutional change in Congress. As we have argued above, institutional change comes about as the result of changes in political culture, the political system, and the policy agenda. The particular shape of change is delimited by the constitutional possibilities and is affected by particular actors and events. Each of the five chapters in Part II offers an explanation of change, but all can be better understood when viewed from the perspective on the process of change that we are suggesting.

The atomistic Congress is the product of American culture. The tendencies in the electoral system described in Part I led to a new kind of representation in which politicians make reelection a primary goal of public service. How do such diffident persons behave when in Washington? How do their attitudes and aspirations shape the institutional environment of Congress? And how is the task of doing the nation's business—political leadership—affected by the new environment within which this business is done?

Each of the chapters in Part II offers a description of how and why Congress has changed. The scope of these studies varies from the particular to the more general, from a focus upon the past to a focus upon the present, from the House to the Senate, and from the personal to the institutional. But each seeks the same end, an understanding of the nature of change, and in them the reader will find one common thread. Each of these authors concludes that Congress is ultimately shaped by the aspirations and expectations of its members. This simple notion links these studies to each other and to those in Part I. So striking is this common thread of explanation that it may serve as a useful point of departure in discussing the evidence and implications presented by the authors.

Charles Stewart develops his analysis of the evolution of House committee assignments during the four decades from the 1870s to the 1920s within the framework of "principal-agent theory." This perspective stresses the control of the chamber by partisan majorities, the agents of which are party leaders. Members want committee assignments to further their political and legislative goals. Party leaders can cater to these appetites by increasing the number of committee assignments available to members of their party. They can do this by either allocating more seats to the members of their party than the party would be entitled to based on its proportionate share of the chamber's membership, or by increasing the size of the committees. Since some committee assignments are more valuable than others, the more important committees should grow in size and the ratio of majority to minority members should be greater than is the case with committees of lesser importance. Over time, the size of committees should increase relative to the size of the membership. Stewart's data support these expectations.

Of course, the historical pattern of committee assignments will depend upon what the members actually want. This will vary somewhat over time. Some committees (Ways and Means, Appropriations) are of such importance that they will always be sought; other committees are of such little importance that they are almost never sought (Acoustics and Ventilation, Useless Executive Papers). In between these extremes, the value of committee assignments varies according to member preferences that are shaped substantially by the public policy agenda. The Education and Labor Committee was the place to be during the Lyndon Johnson administration, but it was less valuable during the Reagan years. Also, the value of committees varies according to the rules and norms of the House, which are largely shaped by member attitudes and expectations. One would expect, for example, that an appointment to the Rules Committee is less valuable when it functions as an arm of the leadership than when it functions as an autonomous bastion of power. Thus any pattern of data such as that found by Stewart must be interpreted in historical context and from the perspective of the principals and agents who produced it.

In his essay on Speaker Thomas B. Reed and Ways and Means Chairman Dan Rostenkowski, Randall Strahan stresses the importance of the historical dimension and the role that individual actors can sometimes play. The role of the individual actor in shaping events has always vexed historians. The tendency of modern political science is to see all events as produced by causes that can be explained. The individual actor becomes an epiphenomenon, an appendage of his circumstance. Stewart's principal-agent theory is an example. While acknowledging that the role of party leaders is limited by circumstance, Strahan wishes nevertheless to suggest that in some circumstances what individual leaders do can have an effect on the evolution of the institution. Borrowing from Stephen Skowronek's concept of "political time," Strahan argues that institutions such as Congress run on "institutional time." Institutional time is the cycle of equilibrium, transformation, and new equilibrium that all institutions undergo. From this Hegelian perspective, Strahan suggests that at critical moments in institutional time, when the institution is ripe for transformation, individual leaders can and must serve as the catalyst for change. He discusses the role of Reed in changing the rules of the House in 1890 and the role of Rostenkowski in reshaping the norms of the Ways and Means Committee in the 1980s as examples.

One thing emerges more clearly than any other in Strahan's discussion. These two leaders sought to change the institution in which they served precisely because it was in their interest to do so. Reed said explicitly that he was tired of having to fight obstructionism (when he wasn't practicing it himself) and intended to reform the rules or resign his speakership. He did not say: "This is an important moral battle, and if I lose, I will regard it as my moral duty to resign." He said: "I'm tired of all this obstructing, and if I can't run the House by a Republican legislative majority, I've got better things to do with my time." Similarly, Rostenkowski had no reputation as an institutional reformer. To the contrary, his career had been built on fidelity to the sources of institutional power in Chicago and Washington. Rostenkowski did not say: "It is clear to me that the old way of doing business in the House was morally wrong, and I intend to be a new and different kind of leader." He said: "I want to be a powerful chairman, and I've got to figure out some new strategies to have the influence I want to have." Rostenkowski did not hold retreats for his committee because this was the way that Richard Daley had always done it; he did so because this was what his members expected of him. Stewart's principal-agent theory applies, but the concept of institutional time provides a framework for thinking about the self-interested choices that these leaders made. One cannot understand the choices without first understanding the context in which they were made, but one must also understand the aims and ambitions of those who made them.

David Rohde's point of departure is a pattern in the voting behavior of members of the House in the 1980s. During this period partisan voting increased. Both Republicans and Democrats were more likely to vote with their party than had been the case in previous decades, and the two parties were more often at odds (a majority of one party voting against a majority of the other). In searching for an explanation for this trend, Rohde settles upon two related factors: the changing nature of the congressional agenda and the changing makeup of its members, especially in the Democratic party. Of these, the most important factor was the increasing homogeneity among House Democrats due in large part to a transformation of the party's southern membership. Increased participation among black voters, the shifting of allegiance of many southern white voters to the Republican party, and the development of a new generation of southern Democratic politicians who supported civil rights and other issues that had in the past been the province of northern Democrats led to a greater convergence on issues within the House Democratic caucus. At the same time, the House Republican conference became increasingly influenced by new and more conservative members who chafed at their party's seemingly perpetual minority status and wanted to confront the majority Democrats on policy issues.

The growing ideological disparity between the two parties was reinforced by their respective political strategies. House Republicans sought to take advantage of the more open floor procedures that the reform movement had produced to offer politically damaging amendments. Their goal was to foster conflict, to sharpen perceptions of party difference. In response, the Democrats sought to use the power of party leadership to structure the agenda so as to limit the opportunities for Republican mischief and to enhance the prospects of Democratic unity. They looked for majorities within their party rather than across the aisle. This led to the use of rules that limited the opportunities for floor amendment and that sought to structure choices so as to enhance Democratic cohesion.

Rohde's study shows clearly the relationship between changes in the political system, the membership of the House, its institutional rules, and its agenda. Also apparent is the clear connection between all of those factors and the goals of party leaders and members. Democratic leaders want to unite their members; hence, they structure choice situations that encourage party unity. Democratic members want to be protected against politically damaging votes; hence, they accept greater structure in legislative choice than they might otherwise. Republican leaders and members want to win control of the House. If they cannot succeed, they want to inflict as much political damage on Democrats as they can. By attacking the Democrats legislatively, they push the Democrats together behind the Democratic leadership. The only ingredient missing is an assertive Democratic Speaker who wants to control policy. In the Hundredth Congress Jim Wright supplied that missing ingredient.

The pattern of voting that David Rohde detects is, then, the product of a transformation in the political system that has produced a new political order in the House. That pattern might be altered by the choice of different political strategies by either the Democrats or the Republicans, but the political strategies that each party has adopted are themselves the product of the goals of members in the particular historical context of the 1980s. Unless and until that context changes, the pattern of behavior that it has produced is unlikely to change either.

It is apparent in these studies that the theory that changes in Congress are produced by members as they seek to attain their goals must always be applied within a particular historical context that explains who the members are, what their goals might be, and the avenues available to the members to pursue their goals. Even within a particular historical context, however, variations can occur in the way that member choices affect institutional change. This is demonstrated in the contributions of Barbara Sinclair and Donald Baumer to this volume. Sinclair focuses on the House leadership and Baumer on the Senate leadership. In comparing the two accounts, it appears that the changes in the political culture and political system that led to enhanced power for House leaders had little corresponding effect in the Senate. The Constitution, as it turns out, makes a difference, and one main difference is between the House of Representatives and the Senate. The traces of modern political culture that we have discussed above were felt in both Houses, but to different effect.

Underlying Sinclair's analysis is an assumption that the character of legislative leadership will, in the end, be determined by the expectations of members. In an excellent discussion of the evolution of House leadership over the past thirty years, she demonstrates that the trend toward a more assertive and activist style of leadership, culminating in that of Speaker Jim Wright, came about because it was what most members of the Democratic caucus wanted. The new generation of entrepreneurial House Democrats wanted party leaders who would provide opportunities for their policymaking inclinations and who would at the same time seek policy consensus among them. Sinclair follows this proposition through the succession of House leaders beginning with John McCormack and shows the development of new leadership powers, strategies, and norms. Notwithstanding the diffusion of institutional power by the reform movement of a decade earlier, by the late 1980s the House Democratic leadership had become more powerful than at any time since Champ Clark and Oscar Underwood at the turn of the century. While Speaker Tom Foley did not wield the iron fist that Jim Wright had, the House leadership team as a whole nevertheless exercised control over the policy agenda.

In contrast, Donald Baumer's study of Senate Majority Leader George Mitchell reveals a man struggling to establish control over an institution that resists it. The very peculiar personal and political factors that had enabled Lyndon Johnson to run the Senate have not been replicated since. The reforms that fragmented power in the House had been paralleled by similar changes in the Senate; but unlike the House, the Senate had not sought to strengthen the power of its leadership to compensate. The demise of the old "club" combined with a weakened committee structure led to a Senate in which there were few levers of central control. Majority leaders Mike Mansfield, Robert Byrd, Howard Baker, and Robert Dole sought to persuade their colleagues where they could not command them. One main factor inhibiting the development of strong leadership in the Senate was the temperament of its members, most of whom had been elected in the 1970s and 1980s. Like their counterparts in the House (many of them having come from the House), these new senators were policy-oriented, politically independent, and ambitious. The natural object of ambition for a member of the House is the Senate; for a member of the Senate, it is the presidency. While the Senate of the 1980s was not an incubator of presidents, it was a cauldron of presidential ambition. The generally larger and more diverse constituencies served by senators, their much larger staffs, and their greater public visibility all combined to make of the typical senator less a policy entrepreneur than an entrepreneur of the self, for whom being a senator was a self-defined end, leading to only one other. Such men and women are not easily led.

Baumer describes the circumstances in which Mitchell came to power and the uses he made of it. He concludes that Mitchell was more successful than any of his predecessors since Lyndon Johnson in establishing the power and influence of the Senate majority leader. Such success as Mitchell had, however, was limited by the constraints on leadership endemic to the Senate today. The nature of these limitations may be illustrated here by a single example implicit in Baumer's account, the transformation of Senate norms. In the old days comity and deference were built into the fabric of the institution in ways that made a difference. Deference to seniority meant obedience to the committee system that it produced. Mutual respect was borne not just of norms, but of interpersonal relationships among members who came to know each other fairly well. In the Senate that George Mitchell leads, seniority is simply a convenient decision rule that sorts out the one-term from the two- or three-term member. The cottage industries that different Senate offices constitute are largely independent of each other. Senators do not know each other well, and the respect that often prevails is for position and not for person. What senators share is a common perception of their lot as senators. They are personally separated and phenomenologically connected.

In trying to lead the Senate, Mitchell has had recourse to many of the techniques that have been polished in the House over the last two decades. It is no surprise that, in this effort, he has enlisted as lieutenants former House members Tom Daschle of South Dakota, John Breaux of Louisiana, and Wyche Fowler of Georgia. These senators are a product of the group-think methods employed by the House Democratic caucus in the 1980s. They are leading the Senate into the new age of interpersonal communication that dominates American culture today.[57] That which works in the House works less well in the Senate, however. The reason is simple: in the House, the leadership has real power to put behind its therapeutic techniques. The Speaker of the House can control its agenda, but the majority leader of the Senate cannot. Furthermore, the struggle for survival in the House leads members to value a considerable degree of centralized leadership; those elections keep coming every two years. Senators can afford to play the field for four years before getting serious. It might be supposed that this would lead them to be more courageous, more willing to follow the leader in service of the public good. Sometimes they do. More often they don't and the reason is simple: their goals are better served by autonomy than by enlistment in the service of party.

The culture and system that makes the House what it is also makes the Senate what it is, and the two are significantly different. The stress that Baumer places on Mitchell's personal qualities reminds us of Strahan's argument that institutional change takes place when the man and the moment meet. Sinclair explains the evolution of stronger leadership in the House on the basis of member expectations, and the Senate differs only in the nature of those expectations. When Tom Daschle, John Breaux, and Wyche Fowler, and many others, went from the new House to the new Senate, they did not make the Senate like the House because their ambitions channeled them in a different direction.

Overstated!

The thread of continuity tying together the chapters in Part II and linking them to the chapters in Part I, then, suggests the relevance of the framework for interpretation that we have proposed. To say that institutions change when their members seek goals by making changes is to state a truism. It has no meaning until fleshed out by the particular historical and cultural circumstances shaping the members and defining their goals. With this thought in mind we turn, finally, to a brief exploration of the implications of our interpretation for the future.

The Atomistic Congress
in the Twenty-first Century

In the last decade of the twentieth century the United States Congress is at a crossroads in its evolution. It has been brought to this turning point by the cultural forces that have shaped it, and the direction that it finally takes will depend largely on what happens in and to American society. Unlike the rising chorus of voices claiming that the Constitution is the culprit (Sundquist, Burns, Young, etc.), we locate the problem in the consequences of an individualistic political culture. Americans are decent people when they are not busy being self-centered. In the 1970s and 1980s many were very busy being self-centered. One learns a great deal about a culture in considering its pathologies. In the 1980s, those included scandals in stock brokerage, federal housing, and private savings institutions. Linked to these catastrophes were symptomatic pathologies in Congress. Two leading members of Congress were subject to ethics charges related to vanity books. Several senators were accused of pressuring federal regulators on behalf of a major campaign contributor. A leading member of the House who gained power by skill in raising campaign money resigned rather than undergo inquiries into alleged sweetheart bond deals.

These well-known episodes were a reflection of American political culture at the century's end. Congressional members were encircled by a campaign financing system that forced them to grovel for contributions, ethics rules that limited their outside income, and a salary structure on which most could not afford to lead a life commensurate with their expectations. It is not without significance that by the end of the 1980s the only part of this dilemma that Congress had solved was to pay itself a 25-percent salary increase. Ninety-eight percent of the members of the House get reelected, and in 1990 over half of House incumbents had no challenger or a challenger with less than $25,000 to spend in running against them.[58] Yet the members remained constantly in fear of losing the one thing they seemed to cherish most, an underpaid job on the Hill. It is small wonder that men and women like this could cast votes tripling the national debt in just ten years.

Contemporary members of Congress are decent men and women. They are on average brighter, better motivated, harder working, and better suited for public service than any previous generation. They want to hang onto their jobs not merely for the honor and not at all for the remuneration; instead, they want to do good things. They want to "make policy" for America. And they are often pretty good at it. The problem is that collective representation requires more than aggregating individual policies. It requires decisions about priorities, realistic assessments of financial means and costs. Such decisions are excruciatingly zero-sum in the contemporary economy and are made the more difficult because notions of sacrifice or civic duty seem quaint compared to tangible government benefits. Moreover, such hard choices require the kinds of party mechanisms that enable leaders to fashion governing majorities. The difficulty that party leaders have in building majority coalitions is not due simply to the independence of members; it is also related to their growing competence. Members are less willing to simply go along with leaders because they know more and have positions on a wider range of issues than their predecessors. More educated, policy-oriented members, in a sense, make decisions about priorities harder, if not impossible.

The members of Congress must choose between the better and worse lights of their nature. They have rigged the electoral system to their own advantage, but they have not fulfilled the concomitant obligation to make hard choices. They must be willing to risk their positions in Congress by facing the necessity of difficult policy decisions and by facing the prospect of increased electoral opposition. They should do both at once. This will entail at a minimum significant campaign finance reform and sustained fiscal responsibility. In order to accomplish either, they must be able to agree. But they will never be able to agree as long as they put their electoral interest above the public interest. A good place to begin is in recognizing the difference between the two.

In what direction will American politics evolve? Some trends are favorable. Traditional pluralist theory stresses the factional cleavages in American politics. Both David Rohde's contention that Democrats are beginning to converge on policy preferences and David Canon's analysis of realignment in the South suggest that the South is at long last integrating itself into the mainstream of American political life, thus eliminating one past source of debilitating faction. Carol Swain's discussion of African-Americans also shows how they are being integrated into a more unified liberal-Democratic coalition. At the same time, party leaders are responding to the institutional dilemmas of our time. Both Barbara Sinclair and Donald Baumer find party leaders in Congress developing new techniques to deal with the atomistic Congress, and there runs throughout this volume an emphasis upon the capacity of these new American politicians for communication and compromise. But our analysis ultimately suggests that short of fundamental changes in the broader political culture, countertrends and therapeutic techniques will not be enough to alter the atomizing tendencies. We expect politicians, in the end, to pursue their interests, even if some are able to interpret those interests in enlightened ways. It is, we think, unrealistic to expect the members of Congress to rise much above average Americans in their willingness to sacrifice private to public good. The solution to the problem of the atomistic Congress may lie in transforming America into a less atomistic political culture. What might cause this to occur?

Because they are well educated, Americans share in a national culture mediated by television. Because they participate in an increasingly service-oriented economy, they are more dependent upon one another than ever before in the basic provision of the goods and services integral to a decent life. Perhaps this mutual dependence, coupled with the sobering recognition of the excesses of past decades, will produce meaningful responses. Perhaps as a more tempered nation moves through the 1990s, people will respond to the pathologies of contemporary culture and work to rejuvenate community structures. Growing concern about the schools, the drug crisis, and latchkey children suggests that people may be ready to try innovative means of addressing isolation and atomizing trends. Moreover, we suggest that a greater public awareness of this central cultural and political problem will enable more American citizens and leaders to nurture the better angels of their nature. Education for democracy should mean, above all, a sober appraisal of the debilitating tendencies in a liberal political order, so that measures can be taken to check them. People may be well-meaning, but their enlightened self-interest requires a knowledge of the sources of the problem if their response is to be effective.

We remain concerned, however, about the apparently diminishing influence of mediating cultural institutions—the local community, the church, the school, the trade union, the local service organization—in leavening the culture of American democracy. And even where such structures exist or are strengthened, it is not clear that they can be linked with the national political system in meaningful ways. As Tocqueville so well understood, even a mass culture can be undermined from within by the consumptive concern for self characteristic of liberal society. Just as there are strong forces pushing Americans together, there are also powerful forces pulling us apart. The problem lies not just in the most obvious areas of real and potential conflict— race, ethnicity, religion, region, sex, age, and class—but also in the daily habits of social life. In the end Americans will have to decide what they stand for as a people. In this, their representatives should lead rather than follow. If our authors are correct, they will only do so if motivated by ambition, interest, or fear. The recent interest in placing term limits on legislators suggests that the American public is ready to try the latter.

Leaders in Congress have a special responsibility to lead; that is why they are called leaders. It is of some solace that Sinclair, Strahan, and Baumer find highly competent congressional leaders seeking by innovative technique and personal ability to forge policy consensus in the House and Senate. It is less reassuring to note that these leaders are very reluctant to undertake reforms that will threaten or appear to threaten the fundamental interest members have in retaining office. In the end self-interest prevails, whether characterized as "ambition theory," "principal-agent theory," or "cost-benefit analysis." What the triumph of self-interest means depends wholly upon how those interests are defined. Congressional leaders must seek to define the interests of members in terms of the broader public interest. Members must come to view their interests in relationship to the public good. And the American public must demand of itself that which it expects of its leaders. Otherwise in confronting the crossroads of its future the American Congress is very likely to take the path most traveled. The moment in "institutional time" has arrived.

What will happen? Our framework leads us to think in terms of larger social and political trends, rather than in terms of the more immediate tendencies that typically claim attention inside the Washington Beltway. Into which category should the current disgust with Congress be placed? We believe that the public's disenchantment with Congress is rooted in factors that will endure. In the nineteenth century the public was disgusted with Congress because Congress was in the pocket of the titans of industry and everyone knew it. By the use of patronage, pork-barreling, and the protective tariff, the Republicans dominated Congress. The Crédit Mobilier scandal merely revealed the true character of things. The result was fundamental change, changes in the rules of the House, the adoption of the Seventeenth Amendment to the Constitution providing for the direct election of senators, and a proliferation in state constitutions of the provision for a direct primary.

The current Congress is not working any better than that one did. The members sustain their position through a system of campaign financing that permits special interests to dominate policy. The use of perquisites of office and sophisticated media and campaign strategies increasingly insulates politicians from their constituencies. The public is getting fed up with it, and the scope and degree of its disaffection is far greater than that which produced the reform movement itself. Perhaps public pressure will eventually force Congress to once again reform its ways. If so, the next reform movement will likely address campaign financing, other campaign reforms, congressional ethics, and congressional perquisites. If it succeeds, it will leave members less beholden to special interests, more vulnerable to electoral challenge, and more amenable to being led.

The result might be a Congress that can more effectively serve the public interest, but this result is not assured. A more vulnerable Congress will no doubt be even more diffident than one in which almost everyone is assured of reelection. A government insulated from special interests might also become indifferent to the public interest. Furthermore, some remedies, such as term limits on members of Congress, might create as many or more problems as they would solve. For example, both Sandy Maisel and David Canon suggest in their chapters that the quality of congressional challengers is declining. While a greater chance of winning might offer incentive to better people to run for office, term limits diminish the value of victory by placing specific caps on the length of service. Perhaps capable people will think it not worth the effort. Tocqueville believed that the inevitable tendency of democracy was to isolate people in the circle of private life, cut off from the wellsprings of public virtue. Term limits are a remedy of a culture steeped in Tocqueville's individualism.

As we await the next round of congressional reforms, those who hold office there will have to make do in present circumstances. Congress will continue to resist being led by its own leaders or by the president. Unified party control might affect that, but the experience of the Carter administration argues to the contrary. Congressional leaders will continue to use the new techniques of leadership to rally the troops (i.e., to "build coalitions"). Sometimes they will succeed. The record of the last decade is not barren of significant legislative accomplishments.

On the big issues, however, those of war and peace, the budget, and political reform, Congress will continue to struggle.[59] It will only succeed in addressing these issues when the public demands it, and the public will only demand it when it is sure that its fundamental interests are affected. The American people have demonstrated amply their attachment to government benefits and their aversion to government taxes. We are products of the culture that we have developed. There is no guarantee that we, as a people, will be willing to make the hard choices that our circumstances demand. Unless and until we are, it is probably unrealistic to expect our representatives, who are no different from us, to do it for us. "We have met the enemy," said Pogo, "and he is us."

Notes

1. For a good overview of the "golden age" of congressional research, see Glen R. Parker, ed., *Studies of Congress* (Washington: Congressional Quarterly Press, 1985).

2. Norman J. Ornstein, ed., *Congress in Change* (New York: Praeger, 1975).

3. James L. Sundquist, *The Decline and Resurgence of Congress* (Washington: The Brookings Institution, 1981).

4. Lawrence C. Dodd and Bruce I. Oppenheimer, eds., *Congress Reconsidered* (New York: Praeger, 1977).

5. Lawrence C. Dodd, "Congress and the Quest for Power." In *Congress Reconsidered*, 269–307.

6. Lawrence C. Dodd and Bruce I. Oppenheimer, eds., *Congress Reconsidered*, 4th ed. (Washington: Congressional Quarterly Press, 1981), Chap. 1.

7. Thomas E. Mann and Norman J. Ornstein, eds., *The New Congress* (Washington: The American Enterprise Institute, 1981).

8. Gregg Easterbrook, "What's Wrong with Congress," *Atlantic Monthly*, December 1984, 57–84.

9. Lawrence C. Dodd and Bruce I. Oppenheimer, eds., *Congress Reconsidered*, 3d ed. (Washington: Congressional Quarterly Press, 1985).

10. James L. Sundquist, "Needed: A Political Theory for the New Era of Coalition Government in the United States," *Political Science Quarterly* 103, no. 4 (Fall 1988):613–35.

11. Dodd and Oppenheimer, *Congress Reconsidered*, 4th ed.

12. See Allen D. Hertzke, *Representing God in Washington: The Role of Religious Lobbies in the American Polity* (Knoxville: The University of Tennessee Press, 1988); Ronald M. Peters, Jr., *The American Speakership: The Office in Historical Perspective* (Baltimore: The Johns Hopkins University Press, 1990).

13. James Madison, *Federalist*, no. 10.

14. Alexis de Tocqueville, *Democracy in America*, ed. J. P. Mayer (New York: Doubleday, 1969). See also Robert N. Bellah et al., *Habits of the Heart: Individualism and Commitment in American Life* (Berkeley and Los Angeles: University of California Press, 1985).

15. Mary Parker Follett, *The Speaker of the House of Representatives* (1902; reprint, New York: Burt Franklin, 1974).

16. James MacGregor Burns, *The Deadlock of Democracy: Four-Party Politics in America* (Englewood Cliffs, NJ: Prentice-Hall, 1963).

17. Richard E. Neustadt, *Presidential Power: The Politics of Leadership* (New York: John Wiley & Sons, Inc., 1962); Sundquist, *Decline and Resurgence of Congress.*

18. Barbara Hinckley, *Stability and Change in Congress* (New York: Harper, 1971).

19. Nelson Polsby, "Political Change and the Character of the Contemporary Congress," in *The New American Political System*, 2d ed., ed. Anthony King (Washington: American Enterprise Institute Press, 1990).

20. James Sterling Young, *The Washington Community, 1800–1828* (New York: Columbia University Press, 1966).

21. James MacGregor Burns (with L. Marvin Overby), *Cobblestone Leadership: Majority Rule, Minority Power* (Norman, OK: University of Oklahoma Press, 1990).

22. Mancur Olson, *The Logic of Collective Action* (Cambridge: Harvard University Press, 1965).

23. Jeffrey Berry, *The Interest Group Society*, 2d ed. (Glenview, IL: Scott, Foresman/Little, Brown, 1989).

24. C. Eric Lincoln and Lawrence H. Mamiya, *The Black Church in the African American Experience* (Durham, NC: Duke University Press, 1990).

25. Aaron Wildavsky, "Choosing Preferences by Constructing Institutions: A Cultural Theory of Preference Formation," *American Political Science Review* 81 (March 1987): 3–21. See also Michael Thompson, Richard Ellis, and Aaron Wildavsky, *Cultural Theory* (Boulder, CO: Westview Press, 1990); and Richard Ellis and Aaron Wildavsky, *Dilemmas of Presidential Leadership: From Washington through Lincoln* (New Brunswick, NJ: Transaction Publishers, 1989).

26. Robert Bellah et al., *Habits of the Heart.*

27. Ibid.

28. Richard Merelman, *Making Something of Ourselves* (Berkeley: University of California Press, 1984).

29. Robert Booth Fowler, *Unconventional Partners: Religion and Liberal Culture in the United States* (Grand Rapids, MI: Eerdmans, 1989).

30. Tocqueville, *Democracy in America.*

31. Michael Novak, *Free Persons and the Common Good* (Lanham, MD: Madison Books, 1989).

32. Thomas Pangle, *The Spirit of Modern Republicanism: The Moral Vision of the American Founders and the Philosophy of Locke* (Chicago: University of Chicago Press, 1988).

33. Barry Alan Shain, "A Study in 18th Century Political Theory: Liberty, Autonomy, Protestant Communalism and Slavery in Revolutionary America" (Ph.D. dissertation, Yale University, 1990).

34. Robert Nisbet, *The Quest for Community* (New York: Oxford University Press, 1953).

35. Daniel Bell, *The Cultural Contradictions of Capitalism* (New York: Basic Books, 1976).

36. Nisbet, *The Quest for Community.*

37. Merelman, *Making Something of Ourselves.*

38. See especially E.E. Schattschneider, *The Semisovereign People* (New York: Holt, Rinehart & Winston, 1960); and Mancur Olson, *The Logic of Collective Action.*

39. Richard Fenno, *Home Style* (Boston: Little, Brown, 1978), 235.

40. Burdett Loomis, *The New American Politician* (New York: Basic Books, 1988).

41. See especially David S. Broder, *The Party's Over* (New York: Harper, 1971); William Crotty, *American Parties in Decline*, 2d ed. (Boston: Little, Brown, 1984); and Martin Wattenberg, *The Decline of American Political Parties* (Cambridge: Harvard University Press, 1986).

42. See Leon Epstein, *Political Parties in the American Mold* (Madison: University of Wisconsin Press, 1986); and Paul Herrnson, *Party Campaigning in the 1980s* (Cambridge: Harvard University Press, 1988).

43. Wattenberg, *The Decline of American Political Parties.*

44. Bruce Cain, John Ferejohn, and Morris Fiorina, *The Personal Vote* (Cambridge: Harvard University Press, 1987).

45. Fenno commented on this phenomenon in *Homestyle*. For the popular assessment, see "Keep the Bums In," *Time*, 19 November 1990, 32–42.

46. Gary Jacobson, *The Electoral Origins of Divided Government* (Boulder, CO: Westview Press, 1990).

47. Kurt Vonnegut, Jr., *Cat's Cradle* (New York: Dell Publishing Co., Inc., 1963), 82.

48. Sundquist, "Needed: A Political Theory."

49. Brooks Jackson, *Honest Graft* (Washington: Farragut Publishing Company, 1990).

50. Thomas Ferguson and Joel Rogers, *Right Turn: The Decline of the Democrats and the Future of American Politics* (New York: Hill and Wang, 1986).

51. Jacobson, *Electoral Origins.*

52. Ibid.

53. Linda L. Fowler and Robert D. McClure, *Political Ambition: Who Decides To Run for Congress* (New Haven: Yale University Press, 1989).

54. Jackson, *Honest Graft.*

55. Ferguson and Rogers, *Right Turn.*

56. See Gary Jacobson and Samuel Kernell, *Strategy and Choice in Congressional Elections*, 2d ed. (New Haven: Yale University Press, 1983).

57. Peters has elsewhere described the "therapeutic" culture of the modern House, borrowing the concept from Robert N. Bellah et al., *Habits of the Heart.* See *The American Speakership*, 13–14, 245–54.

58. David S. Broder, "A Congressional Sham," *Washington Post National Weekly Edition*, 17–23 December 1990, 4.

59. Should the congressional debate over the Persian Gulf crisis in January 1991 be understood as an exercise in responsible government or as a further reflection of Congress's endemic difficulties? The answer is, both. On the one hand, the members of Congress demonstrated their capacity for sober and responsible debate leading to a vote that counted; on the other hand, it is evident that a good deal of political positioning took place between parties, between chambers, and among aspirants to legislative and executive leadership positions. In the end the closeness of the vote proved that Congress was deeply divided, and that individual members were unwilling to accept direction from the president or the leaders of their chambers. The vote was the product of the atomistic Congress.

Part I

Candidate-centered Politics and Congressional Change

JAMES E. CAMPBELL

1 | The Presidential Pulse of Congressional Elections, 1868–1988

There is a presidential pulse to congressional elections. Presidential campaigns affect congressional elections by their presence in on-year elections and by their absence in midterm elections. The first of these effects is most obvious: presidential coattails. The winning presidential party in presidential elections gains congressional votes and seats in proportion to its presidential vote. The second effect, the effect of the absence of the presidential campaign in midterm elections, is less obvious. Running without the advantage of presidential coattails, congressional candidates of the president's party suffer losses in the midterm. Like on-year gains, midterm congressional vote and seat losses associated with the absence of presidential coattails are proportionate to the previous presidential victory. This cycle of electoral change is the presidential pulse to congressional elections. The amplitude of this electoral change in the House of Representatives is set by the winning vote margin in the presidential election. Although the strength of the presidential pulse has weakened in recent years, it has been and remains a continuing feature of the American electoral system.

Presidential Theories of Congressional Elections

The idea that there is something like a presidential pulse to congressional elections is not new. Louis Bean long ago suggested that congressional candidates who live by presidential coattails die by their absence in the midterm.[1] Angus Campbell developed the theory of surge and decline to explain the linkage between individual voting behavior and inter-election change in presidential and midterm elections.[2] According to this theory, the events and personalities of each presidential campaign almost always determine the presidential election winner. The intensity of the campaign causes many people having only a slight interest in politics (peripheral voters) to turn out to vote. These voters are easily swayed by the political climate of that election year. Together with defectors from the party disadvantaged by the campaign, these peripheral voters provide the winning margin for the presidential candidate of the advantaged party, and this spills over to help many congressional candidates of the winning presidential candidate's party. These advantages cannot be counted on at the midterm and, in any event, the generally lower intensity of the midterm election itself makes any short-term advantage of less consequence. Without the hoopla of the presidential contest, peripheral voters stay home. Without a presidential race to say otherwise, the partisan defectors of the previously disadvantaged party go home to their party. The fallout is that many congressional candidates of the president's party are left stranded at the midterm.

Both Bean's simple coattails theory and Campbell's surge-and-decline theory claim a presidential pulse to congressional elections. Presidential victories carry over to congressional election outcomes. Moreover, these presidential victories have repercussions for the next midterm. The loss of the favorable presidential surge or presidential coattails results in the presidential party's consistent loss of congressional support in midterm elections. The track record of the president's party in midterms is amazingly consistent: the president's party has lost seats in thirty-one of the thirty-two midterm elections held from 1862 to 1986.

The Eclipse of the Theory

Although it was once the conventional wisdom, the theory of surge and decline has been eclipsed in recent years. The theory has been challenged on four grounds.

1. Several suspected differences between presidential and midterm electorates that were suggested by the theory simply have not emerged. Specifically, while the theory implies that there should be more "independents" (presumably, more peripheral voters) and partisan defections in presidential rather than in midterm electorates,

Arseneau and Wolfinger did not find these consistent differences.[3]

While these findings raise doubts about how individual voting behavior generates the presidential pulse, there are other ways in which the presidential surge can take place. A revised theory claims that the presidential surge is a result of the presidential campaign swaying the vote choice of independent voters and influencing the turnout rates of partisans.[4] The party losing the presidential race has more cross-pressured partisans (voters who dislike the nominee of their party), and they are more inclined to stay home to avoid voting for either presidential candidate. Congressional candidates of the winning presidential party are, then, the unintended beneficiaries of the difference in partisan turnout, but only until the midterm, when there are no longer cross-pressures from the presidential race.

2. A second charge concerns the relative variability of the vote in presidential and midterm election years. The theory of surge and decline supposes greater volatility in presidential than in midterm elections. This drives turnout higher and shakes partisans away from their normal vote to vote instead for the president's party. Jacobson and Kernell interpret this to mean that the congressional vote should vary more across on-year elections than across midterms.[5] Their investigation, however, contradicts this. They find greater variation actually in midterms than in on-year elections.

Unfortunately, too much has been read into this finding. The relative variation of the vote in the two types of elections is actually of little consequence. In fact, it is quite possible for the process of surge and decline to work perfectly with little variation in on-year elections and a great deal of variation in midterms. Take the extreme hypothetical situation in which all voters are coattail voters and one party wins 100 percent of the presidential vote election after election. Despite this consistent supersurge, there would be *zero* variance in the on-year congressional vote. True, the variability of the midterm congressional vote suggests that midterms are not merely quiet descents to the normal vote. The important variation in the vote, however, is not among midterm or among on-year elections, but in the vote between midterm and on-year elections. The point is simple: what is critical to the theory is the *systematic direction of the vote change or variation between elections.* The theory argues only that the party winning the presidency also systematically wins a greater than usual share of the on-year congressional vote.

3. The third challenge to the theory comes from an alternative theory of midterms: the idea that midterms are referenda about the performance of the incumbent administration.[6] By the referenda theory, electoral change in the midterm reflects public appraisals of how well the president is doing. While this view of midterm change is often regarded as competing with the presidential pulse theories, a head-to-head test of these theories indicates otherwise.[7] The two theories are actually complementary and, when combined, offer a more complete explanation of presidential losses in midterms than either does individually.[8]

4. The fourth challenge to the theory emphasizes the importance of local rather than national forces in congressional elections. At the outset of *Unsafe at Any Margin*, Mann states what has become the prevailing view:

> Congressional elections are local, not national, events: in deciding how to cast their ballots, voters are primarily influenced not by the president, the national parties, or the state of the economy, but by the local candidates.[9]

Ragsdale stated the localism perspective pointedly in her article: "The Fiction of Congressional Elections as Presidential Events."[10] Former Speaker Tip O'Neill put the point even more bluntly. By the Speaker's reckoning, "All politics is local."

Yet even the former Speaker might admit to a bit of hyperbole, that congressional elections are not *entirely* local in character. After all, the president (the most notable national "force") remains the best known politician to most voters; the presence of a presidential contest boosts turnout in most elections by more than a third of the midterm vote; and even though weakened a bit, parties continue to link candidates together in the deliberations of most voters. Moreover, national forces take on added importance because they are more variable from one election to the next than local factors. While local forces may be more influential in explaining congressional elections in any single election year, they are undoubtedly less influential in explaining change. Many district considerations such as incumbency, campaign spending advantages, and the partisan composition of the district often do not change much between elections. On the other hand, the impact of presidential candidates can change dramatically from one election to the next.

While the theory of surge and decline can be defended against each of the above four charges, its most important defense is the positive evidence in its behalf. A variety of studies continue to find evidence of presidential coattails in House elections as well as in Senate and state legislative contests.[11] Over at least the last three decades, there is also evidence of the expected midterm repercussions from the prior presidential surge.[12]

The Questions

This chapter examines national evidence of the presidential surge in presidential election years and its repercussions in the following midterm elections. It examines the presidential surge and its midterm decline over a long stretch of American electoral history. National changes between elections of the parties' shares of seats and votes are examined for the thirty-one presidential and the thirty midterm elections from 1868 to 1988. It also explores how the presidential pulse has changed over time. Specifically, four questions will be addressed:

1. To what extent do presidential coattails affect the national congressional vote and the partisan distribution of seats?

2. What are the repercussions of presidential coattails for electoral change in midterm congressional elections? Does the president's party lose in the midterm in proportion to its coattails in the prior presidential election?

3. How has the presidential surge in congressional elections changed in recent years? Have presidential coattails diminished significantly? If so, by how much and what might have caused it?

4. Has the midterm repercussion from the prior presidential surge, like the surge itself, weakened in recent times; if so, what may have caused this change?

Electoral Change and the Presidential Surge

The analysis examines four measures of electoral change in Congress. Two are concerned with change in presidential election years: the change in Democratic congressional *votes* and *seats* from the prior midterm to the presidential election. The other two are the corresponding electoral change variables for midterms: the change in Democratic congressional votes and seats from the presidential election to the midterm. All four of these measures are adjusted to reflect a division between only the two major parties. Also, for the sake of comparability, the number of seats has been adjusted because of the growth in the total number of seats in the House over time. The adjusted number of seats reflects a constant House size of 435 members.[13] The principal explanatory variable, reflecting the direction of the presidential surge, is the Democratic percentage of the two-party popular presidential vote. The associations between the presidential vote and the four measures of change in congressional votes and seats are examined in several ways, oriented in terms of the winning presidential party in tabular analysis and in terms of the Democratic party in both bivariate and multivariate regression analyses.[14]

Surge and Decline

The Presidential Surge

As expected, in presidential election years the winning presidential party typically gains congressional votes and wins additional seats. Since 1868 the winning presidential party has gained congressional votes and seats in more than two out of three elections. It gained votes in twenty-one of the thirty-one elections (68 percent) and picked up additional seats in twenty-two elections (71 percent).

While the winning presidential party generally registers congressional gains, the magnitude of the presidential victory clearly matters. All presidential surges are not equal. Table 1.1 divides presidential election years into two categories by the magnitude of the presidential popular vote victory. The first category consists of elections won by a presidential candidate with less than 55 percent of the two-party popular vote and the second consists of presidential landslides or near-landslides. As the table shows, presidential parties narrowly winning election are just about as likely to lose votes and seats as gain them. The story is far different when the presidential surge unambiguously favors one party. In landslide and near-landslide presidential elections, the winning presidential party made congressional gains in almost every instance and these gains were typically of an impressive magnitude.

The effects of the presidential surge are revealed more systematically by regression analyses. Several regression analyses of the effects

Table 1.1

Presidential Election Year Congressional Vote and Seat Gains for the Winning Party by Margin of Presidential Victory, 1868–1988

	Narrow to moderate size presidential victories (less than 54.9% of the pres. vote)				Presidential landslides or near-landslides (55.0% or more of the pres. vote)		
Year	Presidential vote (party) (in %)	Vote gain (in %)	Seat gain	Year	Presidential vote (party) (in %)	Vote gain (in %)	Seat gain
1908	54.5 R	−1.6	−7	1924	65.2 R	+4.3	+23
1988	53.9 R	+1.1	−2	1912	64.4 D	+6.6	+45
1944	53.8 D	+4.0	+20	1920	63.8 R	+7.4	+61
1900	53.2 R	+3.2	+14	1936	62.5 D	+2.3	+13
1868	52.7 R	−2.3	−20	1972	61.8 R	+1.5	+13
1948	52.3 D	+7.9	+75	1964	61.3 D	+4.9	+37
1896	52.2 R	−3.6	−43	1904	60.0 R	+5.0	+48
1892	51.7 D	−0.5	−36	1984	59.2 R	+3.4	+15
1916	51.6 D	−1.4	−22	1932	59.2 D	+11.0	+99
1976	51.1 D	−1.4	+1	1928	58.8 R	−1.2	+31
1968	50.4 R	+0.4	+4	1956	57.8 R	+1.5	−2
1884	50.1 D	−2.2	−26	1872	55.9 R	+3.3	+54
1960	50.1 D	−1.1	−21	1952	55.4 R	+0.1	+22
1880	50.0 R	0	+33	1980	55.3 R	+2.8	+34
1888	49.6 R	+0.8	+24	1940	55.0 D	+2.2	+6
1876	48.5 R	+1.7	+41				
Median gain:		−0.25	−0.5	Median gain:		+3.3	+31
% with gains:		44	50	% with gains:		93	93

Note: The presidential vote is the percentage of the two-party vote. The number of seats prior to 1912 is calculated as though there were a constant House size of 435. Seat gains are rounded to the nearest integer.

of the presidential vote on both a party's congressional vote and seat gains were conducted. For those interested, the full results of these regressions are presented in the first section of Table A1.1 on page 72. These regressions indicate that the presidential surge has a substantial positive effect on a party's share of both congressional votes and seats. Moreover, these effects are quite consistent across different specifications of the regression equations and the different sets of elections.

My analysis reveals that a party can expect an increase of about 2 percentage points in its congressional vote from every 5-percentage-point increase in its presidential vote. The estimated effect of the presidential vote on the party's congressional vote gains is about 0.4. Given that the median winning presidential vote has been 4.5 percentage points over the 50-percent mark, a typical presidential surge boosts that party's congressional vote by nearly 2 percentage points in the congressional vote (4.5 × 0.4=1.8). To put this in perspective, this typical surge effect is roughly half the size of the average swing in the congressional vote between elections (about 3.5 percentage points).

The presidential surge also substantially affects the partisan distribution of seats. Each additional percentage point of the presidential vote adds about three more congressmen to a president's coattails. The estimated effects of a party's presidential vote on its seat gains range from just shy of three seats per percentage point of the presidential vote to nearly three and a quarter seats. A presidential victory of average proportions (4.5 percentage points) adds about fourteen seats (4.5 × 3=13.5) to that party's column.

The Midterm Decline

The short-term nature of the prior presidential surge is clearly in evidence in midterm elections. Exactly as the several presidential theories contend, congressional candidates who ride presidential coattails into office in a presidential election year often fall when those coattails are pulled out from under them in the midterm. The decline of support for the president's party in the midterm is inversely proportional to the magnitude of the presidential victory two years earlier. Table 1.2 presents midterm losses following both narrow presidential victories and landslides. While there is no appreciable difference in the consistency of losses in the two types of midterms, the presidential party lost in

Table 1.2

Midterm Election Year Congressional Vote and Seat Losses for the President's Party by Margin of Prior Presidential Victory, 1870–1986

	Narrow to moderate size prior presidential victories (less than 54.9% of the pres. vote)				Prior presidential landslides or near-landslides (55.0% or more of the pres. vote)		
Year	Presidential vote (party) (in %)	Vote loss (%)	Seat loss	Year	Presidential vote (party) (in %)	Vote loss (in %)	Seat loss
1910	54.5 R	−2.4	−63	1926	65.2 R	+0.5	−11
1946	53.8 D	−6.4	−56	1914	64.4 D	−6.8	−63
1902	53.2 R	−1.4	−12	1922	63.8 R	−8.7	−75
1870	52.7 R	−1.9	−56	1938	62.5 D	−7.7	−76
1950	52.3 D	−3.2	−29	1974	61.8 R	−5.9	−49
1898	52.2 R	−2.4	−31	1966	61.3 D	−6.2	−48
1894	51.7 D	−9.2	−144	1906	60.0 R	−2.8	−32
1918	51.6 D	−3.8	−20	1986	59.2 R	−2.4	−5
1978	51.1 D	−3.2	−15	1934	59.2 D	−0.7	+12
1970	50.4 R	−3.3	−12	1930	58.8 R	−3.1	−51
1886	50.1 D	+0.7	−15	1958	57.8 R	−5.1	−49
1962	50.1 D	−2.4	−4	1874	55.9 R	−7.7	−140
1882	50.0 R	−2.7	−71	1954	55.4 R	−2.6	−19
1890	49.6 R	−3.8	−105	1982	55.3 R	−4.8	−25
1878	48.5 R	+2.1	−2	1942	55.0 D	−5.3	−46
Median loss:		−2.7	−29	Median loss:		−5.1	−48
% with losses:		87	100	% with losses:		93	93

Note: The presidential vote is the percentage of the two-party vote. The number of seats prior to 1912 is calculated as though there were a constant House size of 435. Seat changes are rounded to the nearest integer.

nearly every instance, there are differences in the magnitude of these losses. Midterm losses were typically greater in midterms that followed presidential landslides. Bigger declines follow bigger surges. Typically, presidential party losses have been nearly twice as large in midterms following presidential landslides. This difference emerges quite clearly despite the lack of controls. It is quite plausible that the midterm repercussions of the prior presidential surge would be hidden by changes in the volatility of the congressional vote and its translation into seats over the years or by different public evaluations of presidents at the midpoint of their terms. However, they are not.

The regression analyses (reported in full in the Appendix, page 72) confirm the tabular analysis: midterm declines are proportional to the prior presidential surge. A party loses about half a percentage point of the midterm congressional vote and about four seats in the House for every additional percentage point of the presidential vote in the prior presidential election. According to the regression results, following a presidential victory of average proportions, the president's party can expect to lose more than 2 percent of the congressional vote and about eighteen seats in the midterm election.

Surge and Decline through Time

While there is general evidence of a presidential surge and its repercussions in the midterm decline of support for the president's party, these effects may have changed over time. To address the questions of possible changes or trends in surge-and-decline effects, the election series are examined in overlapping subsets of ten presidential elections and their following midterms. This time span appears to be short enough to reflect change, yet sufficiently long to permit stable estimates of surge and decline within the subset. The first subset of elections consists of the ten pairs of elections from 1868 to 1904. Each subsequent subset drops the oldest presidential election and its midterm and adds a more recent pair. Estimates of surge-and-decline effects are obtained for a total of twenty "rolling" subsets of elections.

Two pairs of elections are omitted from this trend analysis, 1932–34 and 1924–26. Critical realignment elections, like the 1932–34 New Deal elections, are atypical. The process of surge and decline depends on the effects of short-term forces in presidential campaigns receding in the midterm. The long-term forces of a critical realignment election, unlike short-term forces of a normal presidential campaign, by definition do not recede in the midterm. In this circumstance, a basic premise of surge and decline, the link between the presidential vote and short-term forces, is absent. There is no reason to expect the 1932 presidential surge to recede in the 1934 midterm since the 1932 surge, unlike that in other presidential election years, was not a temporary phenomenon.

The problem with the 1924–26 elections is a bit different. The 1924 election is a problem because of the significant third-party presidential vote (17 percent) for Progressive party candidate Robert La Follette. Because of the size and character of the La Follette vote, the two-party division of the 1924 popular vote exaggerates Republican Coolidge's support in 1924 and would cause an underestimation of both surge and decline effects if it were included. As Table 1.1 indicates, Republicans in 1924 made quite modest gains for such an overwhelming portion of the *two-party* presidential vote and, as Table 1.2 indicates, they sustained unusually light midterm losses for such a "landslide" (actually registering a gain in votes!). Although for different reasons, the inclusion of either the 1932–34 or 1924–26 elections would only obscure real surge-and-decline effects.

The Presidential Surge through Time

The effects of the presidential surge are traced through time in Figure 1.1. This figure plots the percentage of congressional votes and seats a party could expect to gain from each additional percentage point of the presidential vote that it won. These values were obtained from regression analyses for each subset of elections in the series. As is clear from both trend lines, the presidential surge is not what it used to be. From the late nineteenth century through the mid-twentieth century each additional percentage point of the presidential vote pulled in an additional half to seven-tenths of a percentage point of the congressional vote and from five to six seats. However, presidential coattails have been far shorter in more recent elections. In the latter half of the twentieth century, each additional percentage point of the presidential vote carried with it about a quarter to three-tenths of a percentage point of the congressional vote and about two and a half to three additional seats. Although coattails certainly cannot be dismissed, a one-percentage-point gain in the presidential vote has about half the effect on congres-

Figure 1.1. **Trend in Presidential Vote Effects on Presidential Year Congressional Vote and Seat Change, 1868–1988**

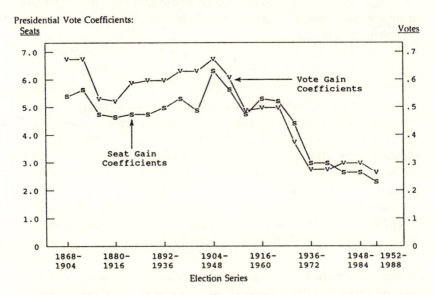

Presidential Vote Coefficients:

Note: The coefficients are unstandardized. Each series consists of ten elections. The regressions also included prior congressional votes or seats. The New Deal realignment election and the 1924 (third-party problem) election are excluded from the series.

sional elections that it once had. As a consequence of these shortened coattails, the branches of government are more commonly controlled by opposing parties following presidential elections than they had ever been. In the twenty-five presidential elections from 1868 to 1964, only three (12 percent) produced a divided government. However, in the six presidential elections from 1968 to 1988, divided government has been the result of all but one (1976).

On the basis of the above evidence it is tempting to conclude, as Ferejohn and Fiorina do in their study of coattail effects, that "House members have less to fear of national electoral tides associated with a presidential race than they have ever had before."[15] While true in one sense, it is not the full story. Although the impact of a one percentage point greater presidential victory is less than it once was, large presidential victories are more common now than they were in the late 1800s. The typical winning presidential vote in the ten presidential elections from 1868 to 1904 was only 52 percent. This compares to a typical winning presidential vote in recent years of about

55 percent. As a consequence, presidential coattails in both periods carried relatively few candidates into office, though for very different reasons. Metaphorically, the fashion of presidential coattails differed in the two periods. In the late 1800s coattails were very wide (many votes and seats per percentage of the presidential vote), but they were also very short (relatively narrow presidential victories). The point here is that while it is true that presidential landslides pack less of a punch on congressional elections than they used to, small overall effects of presidential coattails on congressional elections are not unprecedented.

The Midterm Decline through Time

The trend in the midterm decline is basically consistent with the pattern of the weakening presidential surge. Unfortunately, it is not possible, because of the lack of appropriate data prior to 1946, to control for the public's midterm approval of presidential performance throughout the entire series, so that a completely accurate view of the trend of the midterm decline can be obtained. Nevertheless, despite this methodological difficulty, the trend in the midterm decline again suggests a weakened presidential pulse in recent years.

The trend in the effects of the midterm decline is presented in Figure 1.2. The figure plots the regression coefficients for the midterm decline for the subsets of elections. The pattern in these midterm coefficients is similar to the pattern in the presidential surge coefficients observed in Figure 1.1. Like the presidential surge, their midterm repercussions were greatest in the initial few election series and are a bit smaller in the most recent series, dropping most noticeably in the last three subsets of elections.

Explaining the Weakened Presidential Pulse

The preceding analysis has found consistent evidence of a presidential pulse to congressional elections. Whether examining seat or vote change, in nineteenth-century or twentieth-century elections, there is a definite presidential election beat to electoral change in the House. Yet while these findings should give pause to claims that presidential coattails are now out of fashion, it is also clear that they have weakened. The presidential pulse is still beating but without its prior strength. For

Figure 1.2. **Trend in Presidential Vote Effects on Midterm Congressional Vote and Seat Change, 1870–1986**

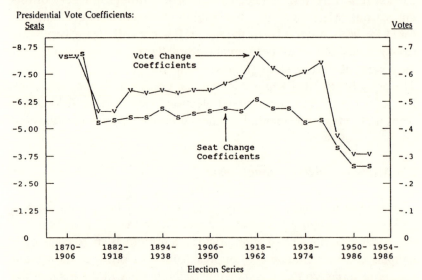

Note: The coefficients are unstandardized. Since presidential popularity at the midterm data were only available for elections since 1946, regressions for only the last three series included that variable. Each election series consists of ten elections, except the most recent, which has nine cases. The 1934 New Deal realignment and the 1926 (following the 1924 third-party problem election) midterms are excluded from the series.

one reason or another, the presidential vote is not now as closely linked to congressional vote and seat change as it has been historically.

Two interrelated explanations for the weakened link between the presidential and congressional votes are commonly mentioned: the partisan dealignment explanation and the increased incumbency advantage explanation.

Partisan Dealignment

For a variety of possible reasons—the aging of the party system, political scandals, the nomination of lackluster or extremist presidential candidates, and an increased reliance on the media—political parties seem to mean less to the public today than they once did. Although often exaggerated, the signs of dealignment are evident in many forms. There are more self-professed pure independents and apoliticals. Partisan defection rates are slightly higher. Fewer voters cast a straight party-line ticket for all offices.[16] Since the presidential surge depends upon voters associating congressional candidates with their parties' presidential candidates, dealignment may weaken the presidential pulse. If fewer voters pay attention to the partisan bonds between candidates, the impact of the presidential vote on congressional elections undoubtedly will be blunted.

Incumbency Advantages

The increased advantages of incumbency also may cause a weakened presidential pulse. Incumbents not only win by larger margins than they used to, but they also may be better able to insulate themselves from national forces. Whether by merely advertising their greater political experience and accomplishments, driving their opponents into bankruptcy with their greater financial resources, or simply scaring off quality challengers, incumbents appear better able now than ever before to divorce their contests from the national race. In a similar vein, the rise in congressional campaign spending combined with the spending limits imposed by public financing of presidential contests may have reduced the dominant attention on and thus the influence of the presidential campaign over congressional campaigns.

Wasted Coattails

While partisan dealignment and increased incumbency advantages certainly seem to be plausible explanations of the weakened presidential pulse, a third explanation may also be plausible. The weakened presidential pulse may be a consequence of wasted coattails, wasted Republican coattail opportunities in the South. Beginning with Goldwater in 1964, Republicans have employed a "southern strategy" in presidential politics. This strategy has succeeded in helping Republicans win the presidency in five of the last six presidential elections. However, while Republican presidential candidates have done exceedingly well in southern states in recent years, the traditional one-party Democratic South remains fairly well intact locally. Southern Republican parties are still in development. This has meant that many Democratic congressional candidates have gone entirely unchallenged or faced only token opposition. For most of this period, Republicans have been unable to recruit enough qualified congressional candidates to get the benefit of presidential coattails. Even ample coattails can't carry candidates who do not exist or who are not skilled enough to hold on. While dealignment and incumbency may have contributed to the weakened presidential pulse, the evidence also points to the "wasted coattail" explanation.

The 1972 Clue

The timing of the drop in the presidential surge lends some support to the "wasted coattail" interpretation of the weakened presidential pulse. Surge effects were relatively stable for election series extending as late as through the 1960s. Although they dropped a bit before this, the most pronounced drop occurred with the inclusion of the 1972 election. The magnitude of the presidential surge was cut by about a third from the 1928–68 series to the 1936–72 series. Given this sharp drop, a closer examination of the 1972 election may reveal why the presidential pulse has declined more generally in recent years.

The 1972 election was a landslide victory for Richard Nixon over Democratic candidate George McGovern. Nixon carried every state in the nation except Massachusetts (and the District of Columbia) and won nearly 62 percent of the popular vote. Despite this, Republicans gained a mere 1.5 percent of the congressional vote and only thirteen seats. By comparison, Lyndon Johnson in 1964 won by about the same magnitude as Nixon and his party gained nearly 5 percent of the congressional vote and thirty-seven seats. Based on the regressions estimates, the congressional Republicans in 1972 should have done about as well as the Democrats did in 1964. According to the regressions, Republicans should have gained 4.5 percentage points of the congressional vote and thirty-two seats. Republican gains also fell far short of the press's expectations at the time. As *Congressional Quarterly* reported, "While Nixon was overwhelming Democrat George McGovern, . . . presidential coattails materialized for his fellow Republicans in only a handful of other races."[17]

Why did Republicans fail to register larger congressional gains in the wake of Nixon's landslide? The shortfall appears to be the result of the distribution of Nixon's support. Nixon's 1972 victory was of landslide proportions because of his strength in the South. Although he won just about everywhere, he did especially well in southern states. Seven of Nixon's ten strongest states were in the South. In

Table 1.3

Southern Congressional Districts Uncontested by Republican
Congressional Candidates but Carried by Nixon in 1972

State	District	Nixon vote (in %)	State	District	Nixon vote (in %)
Alabama	7	66	Mississippi	1	80
Arkansas	1	69	Mississippi	3	79
Arkansas	2	64	N. Carolina	3	74
Arkansas	4	69	N. Carolina	6	72
Florida	1	84	Oklahoma	3	70
Florida	2	69	Texas	1	70
Georgia	1	75	Texas	10	59
Georgia	2	80	Texas	11	70
Georgia	3	78	Texas	12	62
Georgia	6	80	Texas	14	61
Georgia	9	82	Texas	15	55
Georgia	10	73	Texas	16	64
Louisiana	1	71	Texas	17	73
Louisiana	2	60	Texas	19	76
Louisiana	4	75	Texas	23	62
Louisiana	5	73	Virginia	3	72
Louisiana	6	70	Virginia	5	72
Louisiana	7	68			

Source: The uncontested seats were identified in CQ's *Guide to U.S. Elections, 2d ed.*
(Congressional Quarterly: Washington, 1985). The district vote for Nixon is from
Michael Barone, Grant Ujifusa, and Douglas Matthews (1975) *The Almanac of American
Politics, 1976* (n.p.: n.p., n.d.). The Louisiana seats did not have runoffs with Republi-
cans, though Republican candidates may have been in the initial election.

four of these states he received more than 70 percent of the vote.
Unfortunately for Republicans, many districts in these southern
states were uncontested by Republican congressional candidates.
Table 1.3 lists thirty-five southern congressional districts in 1972
that were carried by Nixon but in which congressional Democrats ran
unopposed by Republicans. Nixon not only carried each of these
districts but won all but two with more than 60 percent of the vote
and won twenty-two of the thirty-five with 70 percent or more of the
vote. This suggests that rather than Nixon's coattails being short,
there just weren't enough congressional candidates available to ride
them.

Moreover, this problem was not limited to the failure to offer a
challenge. In many long-time Democratic areas of the South, in 1972
and to this day (as Canon's and Maisel's essays in this volume attest),

many Republican challengers were not especially well-qualified candidates. Even when coattails are provided, a party needs local candidates who are serious enough to benefit from coattail help. As Nixon told political chronicler Teddy White before the election: "part of our problem is that we have a lot of lousy candidates; the good ones will go up with me, the bad ones will go down."[18] There were just not many good ones to take advantage of the available coattail help.[19] In short, *Nixon's coattails were often wasted coattails.*

The Pattern of Wasted Coattails

If Republicans wasted coattails only in 1972, we might just "write off" that election as an aberration. The question is whether 1972 was especially unusual or have Republicans continued to waste their coattails in uncontested southern Democratic districts? Figure 1.3 presents some evidence that the Republican problem of wasted coattails was not confined to 1972.

Figure 1.3 plots the number of congressional districts left uncontested by Republicans and the number of these uncontested districts that were then carried by Republican presidential candidates in presidential elections from 1952 to 1988.[20] Prior to 1964, Democratic presidential candidates carried at least two out of three of the party's uncontested congressional districts. Moreover, it was quite rare for Republican presidential candidates to carry these congressional districts by wide margins, with a vote in excess of 60 percent. In short, prior to 1964, Republicans did not waste much of any presidential coattail help they might have been able to exploit.

While the Wallace candidacy of 1968 complicates any assessment of coattails in that election and while southerner Jimmy Carter's candidacies of 1976 and 1980 interrupt the pattern, Republicans wasted substantial coattail help not only in the election of 1972 but also in 1964, 1984, and 1988. In each of these four elections, Republican presidential candidates carried more than half of districts the party left uncontested to congressional Democrats. In 1972 and 1984, Republican presidential candidates won more than 80 percent of these districts, many by wide margins. Also, most of these districts were in the South.[21] At a minimum, three out of five uncontested Democratic districts carried by a Republican presidential candidate in any election were in southern states.

Figure 1.3. **Uncontested Democratic Congressional Districts Carried by the Republican Party's Presidential Candidate, 1952–1988**

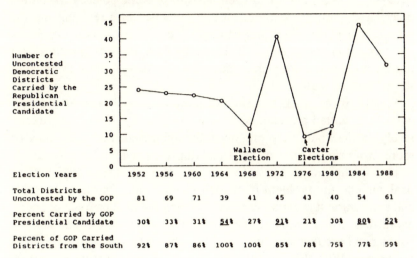

Election Years	1952	1956	1960	1964	1968	1972	1976	1980	1984	1988
Total Districts Uncontested by the GOP	81	69	71	39	41	45	43	40	54	61
Percent Carried by GOP Presidential Candidate	30%	33%	31%	54%	27%	91%	21%	30%	80%	52%
Percent of GOP Carried Districts from the South	92%	87%	86%	100%	100%	85%	78%	75%	77%	59%

Conclusion

Although the presidential pulse to congressional elections remains vital, there is no question that it has weakened in recent elections. Will this trend continue or be reversed in future elections? The future strength of surge and decline depends, in large part, on the causes of their weakening in recent elections. A weakened presidential pulse because of a growing incumbency advantage may forebode still further weakening. Some have read the 1988 congressional election to suggest that an incumbent is now only vulnerable to scandal. If so, short-term national forces are of little consequence. Surge and decline is, as Angus Campbell indicated in the title of his article, a theory of electoral change. If there is no change, if incumbents are cemented to their seats, any theory of electoral change becomes irrelevant. If this is the case, surge and decline may be rather strictly constrained to the few open-seat districts.

To the extent that the weakened presidential pulse results from partisan dealignment, we might expect a stable but weakened pulse. Ladd suggests that weakened partisan associations are a characteristic of the new party system.[22] There is no inexorable decline to nonpartisanship, just weakened partisanship compared to what we have seen in the past.

If this is true, the current presidential pulse might remain at its present strength, weaker than it had been but still of some potency. If, on the other hand, partisan dealignment is a precursor of a realignment, the presidential pulse might gain strength. Several scholars claim that a realignment is in progress.[23] If this is the case, the realignment might reinvigorate partisanship and restore the presidential pulse to much of its previous strength.

Finally, if the weakened state of the presidential pulse is a consequence of wasted presidential coattails (especially, though not exclusively, in the South), the prognosis for the presidential pulse may be more promising, if not in the short-run, then within the foreseeable future. Compared to the entrenchment of incumbents and partisan dealignment, the problem of wasted coattails may be more tractable and temporary. It is certainly more of a regional than national phenomenon. It is also a problem that one of the parties has a real stake in solving and one that may be resolved by the ambitions of aspiring local politicians. With the eventual retirements of conservative incumbent southern Democrats and the availability of coattails to prospective candidates, it seems unlikely that Republican coattails in the South will go unexploited forever. At some point, the Republican party ought to be able to recruit quality candidates in districts that their presidential candidates consistently win. However, as the data in Figure 1.3 indicate, this is a painfully slow process. More than a decade after Nixon's coattails were wasted, the situation has improved only at the margins. Republicans in the South were about as wasteful of Reagan's 1984 coattails as they were of Nixon's twelve years earlier.

Despite the continued waste of Republican coattails in the South, there are signs of change in the offing. It appears that the pool of experienced potential Republican congressional candidates in the South may be growing. One important source of viable congressional candidates is the state legislature. In running for and serving in a state legislature, candidates gain valuable experience and become better known to the electorate. According to Bullock's figures, in the 1970s the Republicans held only about 15 percent of seats in the lower houses of southern state legislatures and even a smaller share of state senate seats.[24] This was a substantial impediment to the Republicans putting forward quality challengers. In baseball terms, they just didn't have much of a minor-league system. During the 1980s, Republican ranks in southern state legislatures gradually grew. After the 1988 elections, over 27 percent of the lower houses and over 21 percent of the upper houses were Republican. Although still small in number, there are now many more Republicans positioned to contest congressional seats previously left uncontested to the Democrats. With this expanded pool of potential candidates, the prospects of Republicans seriously contesting more seats should be substantially improved.

While partisan dealignment and the advantages of incumbency may prevent the presidential pulse from being restored to full strength, it ought to regain some of its prior strength as Republicans draw more serious congressional candidates from their expanded pool of state legislators. Of course, Republican problems in the South are not purely a matter of finding quality candidates to challenge Democrats. For generations the South has been solidly Democratic and, at risk of understatement, these traditions die hard. Nevertheless, though many Republican presidential voters in these southern districts may not immediately swarm to Republican congressional candidates, undoubtedly many will opt to vote straight tickets when that option is offered to them. If so, the presidential pulse of congressional elections may beat more strongly in the future than it has for some time.

Notes

1. See Louis H. Bean, *How To Predict Elections* (New York: Knopf, 1948) and *The Mid-Term Battle* (Washington: Cantillion Books, 1950).
2. See Angus Campbell, "Surge and Decline: A Study of Electoral Change," in *Elections and the Political Order*, ed. Angus Campbell et al. (New York: Wiley, 1966). See also Angus Campbell, "Voters and Elections: Past and Present," *Journal of Politics* 26 (1964): 745-57.
3. Robert B. Arseneau and Raymond E. Wolfinger, "Voting Behavior in Congressional Elections" (Paper presented at the Annual Meeting of the American Political Science Association, New Orleans, Louisiana, 4–8 September 1973).
4. James E. Campbell, "The Revised Theory of Surge and Decline," *American Journal of Political Science* 31 (1987): 965–79.
5. Gary C. Jacobson and Samuel Kernell, *Strategy and Choice in Congressional Elections* (New Haven: Yale University Press, 1981), 63. Erikson places a great deal of weight on this charge against surge and decline. See Robert S. Erikson, "The Puzzle of Midterm Loss," *The Journal of Politics* 50 (1988): 1011–29. However, Cover takes issue with the basic finding of greater variation in the midterm vote. See Albert D. Cover, "Surge and Decline in Congressional Elections," *Western Political Quarterly* 38 (1985): 606–19.
6. There is a substantial body of research on the referenda theory of midterms. See Edward R. Tufte, "Determinants of the Outcomes of Midterm Congressional Elections," *American Political Science Review* 69 (1975): 812–26 and also his

Political Control of the Economy (Princeton, NJ: Princeton University Press, 1978); Samuel Kernell, "Presidential Popularity and Negative Voting: An Alternative Explanation of the Midterm Congressional Decline of the President's Party," *American Political Science Review* 71 (1977): 44–66; Alan I. Abramowitz, Albert D. Cover, and Helmut Norpoth, "The President's Party in Midterm Elections: Going from Bad to Worse," *American Journal of Political Science* 30 (1986): 562–76; Richard Born, "Strategic Politicians and Unresponsive Voters," *American Political Science Review* 80 (1986): 599–612; and Bruce I. Oppenheimer, James A. Stimson, and Richard W. Waterman, "Interpreting U.S. Congressional Elections: The Exposure Thesis," *Legislative Studies Quarterly* 11 (1986): 227–47.

7. James E. Campbell, "Explaining Presidential Losses in Midterm Congressional Elections," *Journal of Politics* 47 (1985): 1140–57.

8. This is precisely as Tufte originally suspected. See Tufte, "Determinants of the Outcomes of Midterm Congressional Elections," 826.

9. Thomas E. Mann, *Unsafe At Any Margin* (Washington: American Enterprise Institute, 1978), 1.

10. Lyn Ragsdale, "The Fiction of Congressional Elections as Presidential Events," *American Politics Quarterly* 8 (1980): 375–98.

11. See James E. Campbell, "Predicting Seat Gains from Presidential Coattails," *American Journal of Political Science* 30 (1986): 165–83; Richard Born, "Reassessing the Decline of Presidential Coattails: U.S. House Elections from 1952–1980," *Journal of Politics* 46 (1984): 60–79; Richard Born, "Surge and Decline, Negative Voting, and the Midterm Loss Phenomenon: A Simultaneous Choice Analysis," *American Journal of Political Science* 34 (1990): 615–45; John A. Ferejohn and Randall L. Calvert, "Presidential Coattails in Historical Perspective," *American Journal of Political Science* 28 (1984): 127–46; John A. Ferejohn and Morris P. Fiorina, "Incumbency and Realignment in Congressional Elections," in *The New Direction in American Politics*, ed. John E. Chubb and Paul E. Peterson (Washington: Brookings Institution, 1985); Randall L. Calvert and John A. Ferejohn, "Coattail Voting in Recent Presidential Elections," *American Political Science Review* 77 (1983): 407–19; James E. Campbell and Joe A. Sumners, "The Presidential Coattails in Senate Elections," *American Political Science Review* 84 (1990): 513–24; James E. Campbell, "Presidential Coattails and Midterm Losses in State Legislative Elections," *American Political Science Review* 80 (1986): 45–63; and John E. Chubb, "Institutions, the Economy, and the Dynamics of State Elections," *American Political Science Review* 82 (1988): 133–54.

12. See Barbara Hinckley, "Interpreting House Midterm Elections: Toward a Measurement of the In-party's 'Expected' Loss of Seats," *American Political Science Review* 61 (1967): 694–700, and Campbell, "Explaining Presidential Losses in Midterm Congressional Elections" and "Presidential Coattails and Midterm Losses in State Legislative Elections."

13. Third-party seats and vacancies were divided evenly between the major parties before adjusting the two-party division of seats to a constant total of 435.

14. The data for the examination of the presidential pulse come from several sources. National level partisan seat and vote data are drawn from Norman J. Ornstein, Thomas E. Mann, and Michael J. Malbin, *Vital Statistics on Congress, 1989–1990 Edition* (Washington: Congressional Quarterly, 1990), and Stokes and

Iversen's national congressional vote series found in Richard G. Niemi and Patrick Fett, "The Swing Ratio: An Explanation and an Assessment," *Legislative Studies Quarterly* 11 (1986): 75–90. The presidential vote data are drawn from *Guide to U.S. Elections*, 2d ed. (Washington: Congressional Quarterly, 1985).

15. Ferejohn and Fiorina, "Incumbency and Realignment in Congressional Elections," 142.

16. Wattenberg's figures indicate that split-ticket voting rose from the 12- to 16-percent range before 1968 to the 25- to 34-percent range in elections from 1968 to 1984. See Martin P. Wattenberg, "The Hollow Realignment," *Public Opinion Quarterly* 51 (Spring 1987): 66.

17. "An Apparent Record Landslide—With Qualifications," *Congressional Quarterly Weekly Report* (11 November 1972): 2947.

18. Theodore H. White, *The Making of the President 1972* (New York: Bantam Books, 1973), 403.

19. While much of Nixon's 1972 coattails were wasted, they were not completely wasted. Jacobson found 1972 coattails in his examination of 165 districts in twenty-five states, only two of which were in the South. See Gary C. Jacobson, "Presidential Coattails in 1972," *Public Opinion Quarterly* 40 (1976): 194–200.

20. The 1968 election is complicated by the third-party candidacy of George Wallace. Because of this complication, the figure indicates the number of uncontested districts carried by the Republican presidential candidate in 1968 in which Nixon ran ahead of Humphrey, regardless of the Wallace vote in the district.

21. The reader may question the exclusive focus on uncontested Democratic districts. However, while the number of uncontested Republican districts has grown since 1952, they still remain relatively few in number (eighteen in 1988) and Democratic presidential candidates have never carried more than two of these districts in any election since 1952.

22. Everett Carll Ladd, "As the Realignment Turns: A Drama in Many Acts," *Public Opinion* 7, no. 6 (1985): 2–7.

23. See John R. Petrocik, "Realignment: New Party Coalitions and the Nationalization of the South," *Journal of Politics* 49 (1987): 347–75; and Charles S. Bullock III, "Regional Realignment from an Officeholding Perspective," *Journal of Politics* 50 (1988): 553–74.

24. Bullock, "Regional Realignment," 566, 568. The states classified as southern are the same as those used by Bullock: AL, AR, FL, GA, LA, MS, NC, SC, TN, TX, and VA.

Appendix—Table A1.1

Effect of the Democratic Presidential Vote on Change in the Democratic Congressional Vote and Seats in Presidential and Midterm Elections, 1868–1988

	Presidential elections (1868–1988)				Midterm elections (1870–1986)			
	Democratic vote change		Democratic seat change		Democratic vote change		Democratic seat change	
Independent variables	(1)	(2)	(3)	(4)	(5)	(6)	(7)	(8)
Democratic pres. vote	+.39 (5.66)	+.39 (9.14)	+2.95 (3.94)	+3.20 (6.41)	−.48 (6.06)	−.50 (5.69)	−4.52 (3.80)	−3.62 (2.93)
New Deal	—	+2.88 (1.57)	—	+45.60 (2.33)	—	+4.47 (1.21)	—	+36.08 (.75)
Prior Dem. congressional vote or seats	—	−.53 (6.22)	—	−.46 (5.58)	—	−.05 (.28)	—	−.45 (2.22)
Early GOP era (1868–1928)	—	−2.73 (4.05)	—	−34.44 (4.73)	—	+.25 (.18)	—	+5.12 (.28)
Constant	−18.68	+9.28	−148.00	−36.96	+23.43	+26.54	+230.01	+286.95
N of cases	31	31	31	31	30	30	30	30
R^2	.53	.86	.35	.80	.57	.60	.34	.50
Adjusted R^2	.51	.84	.33	.76	.55	.54	.32	.42
Std. error	2.74	1.59	29.87	17.72	3.15	3.20	47.42	43.59

Note: The Democratic presidential and congressional votes are shares of the two-party vote. The New Deal variable is a dummy variable (1932,1934=1, otherwise=0). The Republican electoral era variable is a dummy variable (before 1932=1, otherwise=0). Prior Democratic votes and seats are from the prior midterm election. In all cases, the number of seats have been adjusted to a constant House size of 435 seats. The coefficients in parentheses are *t*-ratios.

DAVID T. CANON

2 | The Emergence of the Republican Party in the South, from 1964 to 1988

In explaining episodes of dramatic change in Congress, scholars point to three types of change in the composition of its membership: realigning, partisan surge, and secular. Congressional change during realigning periods suggests a linkage between political upheaval, institutions, politicians, and policy.[1] The second type of change, partisan surge, produces a large freshman class that reshapes the institution. A large Democratic class in 1958 brought about changes in norms and in the distribution of power; the 1964 class played a crucial role in the success of "Great Society" legislation; and effects of the "power earthquake" registered by the 1974 Watergate class are still being analyzed. Secular change in membership—a gradual shift over a period of many elections—also produces change in Congress. New members elected during the Progressive era in the late nineteenth and early twentieth centuries undermined the homogeneity of the Republican party and helped hasten the demise of its leadership. The gradual rise of the Republican party in the South over the past three decades has had the opposite impact on the Democrats by increasing Democratic party unity.[2]

While it is important to understand the linkages between membership change and institutional change, the purpose of this chapter is to provide a more complete understanding of the *process* of secular change. The instance of secular change examined here is the growth of the Republican party in the South in the 1964–88 period. Across the region Republican candidates in state legislative and gubernatorial races, and in U.S. House and Senate contests, have become increas-

Figure 2.1. **Republican Strength in the South**

% Republican (1962-1988)

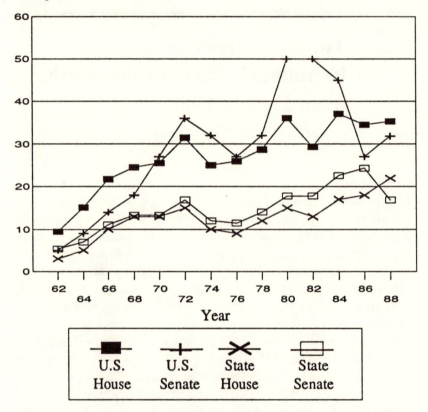

Year

■	+	✕	☐
U.S.	U.S.	State	State
House	Senate	House	Senate

Sources: Compiled by the author from *Congressional Quarterly Weekly Report* (House and Senate data) and from *Statistical Abstract of the United States* (state legislative data).

Note: Trend lines indicate the proportion of each office held by Republicans in the South. For all figures, the South is defined as Alabama, Arkansas, Florida, Georgia, Louisiana, Mississippi, North Carolina, South Carolina, Tennessee, Texas, and Virginia.

ingly competitive (see Figure 2.1). Though Democrats still have an edge in partisan identification, Republicans have closed the gap and the proportion of independents has more than doubled since the 1960s. Previous accounts of the emergence of the southern Republican party focused on the importance of racial politics, presidential candidates, shifts in the mass electorate, and demographic changes.[3]

These variables are obviously important in explaining political change in the South, but I develop a different dimension of change. I argue that decisions made by individual politicians about how to best further their political careers play a crucial role in the process of secular political change. From this basic assumption I develop an elite-based model of partisan change that may be applied to other periods of secular change, such as the 1860s. Before presenting this model I will review previous work on this topic and demonstrate the need for a new perspective. The model is then supported with anecdotal evidence, a survey of southern state party chairs, and an analysis of competition in southern House districts from 1964 to 1988. The chapter concludes with speculation on the limits of Republican growth and a discussion of the implications of secular change in the South for congressional politics.

Realignment Theory, Ambition Theory, and Political Careers

For thirty-five years, realignment theory has been a useful tool for identifying the causes and consequences of party system change. The theory predicts periodic establishment of a new majority party as new issue cleavages stimulate massive shifts in the electorate.[4] However, there is a growing frustration with realignment theory, especially with its predictive power. Professor Ladd likens waiting for the next realignment (which has been predicted by various pundits in each of the last six presidential elections) to the futile experience in Samuel Beckett's play *Waiting for Godot*.[5]

Scholars are frustrated because they are waiting for the wrong kind of realignment. Fundamental changes in the nature of politics—dealignment, split-ticket voting, candidate-centered campaigns, and the power of incumbency—reduce the likelihood of another 1930s-style realignment. A new theory is needed that reflects the reality of secular rather than sudden political change, a theory based on the calculations of strategic politicians. A decade of research on congressional elections has demonstrated the centrality of candidates in the electoral process. Explanations of candidate recruitment, the incumbency advantage, the impact of economic variables on electoral outcomes, and individual-level voting all have focused on the behavior of politicians. Tip O'Neill's famous adage that "all politics is local" is the rallying cry for students of congressional elections.

Realignment theory is at odds with this observation because it is based on national issues rather than the behavior of individual politicians.[6] Critical elections are presumed to overwhelm political careers as their cross-cutting issues hack a swathe through the political landscape. The actions of individual politicians are seen as irrelevant in the face of changing policy cleavages and dramatic shifts in voting behavior. James Sundquist supports this view:

> The attributes and qualities of individual candidates may be crucial in some elections also but, like the valence issues, they lead to deviation rather than to realignment. . . . Leadership is seen as a transitory and accidental thing, subject to change at the next election, and is not reason for permanently shifting party attachments.[7]

Ambition theory provides a better starting point for an elite-based theory of secular realignment. Ambition theory suggests that politicians respond to existing opportunity structures in a manner consistent with winning office. Though the seminal work on ambition theory assumed a relatively stable set of opportunity structures, subsequent work by Joseph Schlesinger notes that career structures can shift due to changes in rules in the "party system," or in "the relative chances that each party has of winning the various elective offices."[8] The dynamic aspect of career patterns is suggested in candidate-centered explanations of electoral outcomes.[9] This research suggests that in normal political periods politicians respond to new opportunities as the probability of winning higher office increases (ambitious Democrats jumped at the chance to run in 1974, while Republicans did so in 1980). But the broader consequences of changes in opportunity structures have received little attention, particularly the possibility that politicians might actually *switch parties* if the conditions were ripe. On the basis of evidence presented below, I suggest that conventional ambition theory must be modified to encompass the emergence of the Republican party in the South.

Secular Realignment and Political Careers: A New Perspective

Revisions of both realignment theory and ambition theory are needed to account for the behavior of politicians during periods of secular change. Classic ambition theory has ignored the dynamic aspect of political careers, and realignment theory has neglected them altogether.

The new theory of secular change offered here reflects a growing perception in the realignment literature that it is misleading to focus on the 1930s as the paradigmatic case of realignment.[10] The emergence of two-party competition in the South does not look much like the realignment of the 1930s. A better model for recent change in the South is V.O. Key's analysis of secular realignment, even though his frame of reference is the rise of the Democratic party in New England from 1892 to 1952. He said:

> [T]he rise and fall of parties may to some degree be the consequences of trends that perhaps persist over decades and elections may mark only steps in a more or less continuous creation of new loyalties and decay of old. . . . Only events with widespread and power impact or issues touching deep emotions produce abrupt changes. On the other hand, other processes operate inexorably, and almost imperceptibly, election after election, to form new party alignments and to build new party groupings.[11]

Key notes the importance of candidates in this evolution, "Attractive candidates or a fortunate sequence of events may operate to retard or accelerate the long-term trend to the advantage of one or the other of the parties."[12] However, he focuses on the changing nature of voting and party identification rather than on candidate behavior.

My new theory, then, is a dynamic version of ambition theory that borrows insights of gradual but "inexorable" change from Key and a focus on political careers from Schlesinger. The crux of this theory is on the decisions and actions of individual politicians confronted by substantial change in their electoral environment. Their interpretations of developing events and their decisions about how to react to them are integral parts of the realignment process. The key assumption here is that the strategic calculus employed by politicians encompasses, among other things, the competitive relationship of the parties and the relative success of others who have followed the same career path. The implications of this assumption can be traced through stable and changing times.

In periods of electoral stability, normal career paths develop as ambitious politicians operate within a set of constraints that vary only marginally from election to election. In these times, careers are "orderly enough to direct and guide the expectations of the politically ambitious."[13] Politicians have a clear idea of which offices they can win and what they must do to win them. For obvious reasons, in the first half of the twentieth century, individuals contemplating political careers in the South were channeled into the Democratic party. There was no other vehicle for the politically ambitious.

Electoral change disrupts normal political careers by disturbing settled patterns of party competition and by affecting the relative success of candidates at various levels of the career structure. Opportunities suddenly emerge for politicians where none previously existed. Frustrated careers may be revived, and sudden access to higher office may accelerate movement up the career structure. In the southern case, as the Republican party-in-the-electorate grew and as nominally Democratic voters began to vote for Republican presidential and congressional candidates, the calculations of politically ambitious officeholders and amateurs were profoundly affected. The Republican party suddenly became a viable vehicle for political success, but the party faced a serious discrepancy between the supply of and demand for political talent. In the early stages of secular realignment, the emerging party was forced to rely on political amateurs who had never held public office.[14] In the next stage, Republicans were able to recruit ambitious Democratic politicians seeking to advance their careers under a new party label. Finally, as Republicans began to nurture a homegrown pool of political talent in many areas, the party's prospects slowly brightened.

The following diagram elaborates the dynamics of this process. The central variable is the individual career decision, which includes the decision to enter politics for the first time (and in which party), to seek higher office and to switch parties after winning office. Many scholars use ambition theory to explain these various decisions,[15] but no model addresses the complete set of career moves. The same constellation of forces—the nature of two-party competition, party recruitment, policy or ideological motivations, and district and national conditions—operate for each decision. The importance of most of these variables is self-evident and well developed in the literature, at least for the decision to seek higher office. For example, a southern Democrat would be more likely to switch to the Republican party in 1964 or 1984 than in 1974, for the same reasons that an experienced Republican would be more likely to seek higher office in those years. However, each variable does not work equally for each type of decision. While party efforts are generally not that important in the decision to run for Con-

Figure 2.2. **A Model of Elite-Driven Secular Realignment**

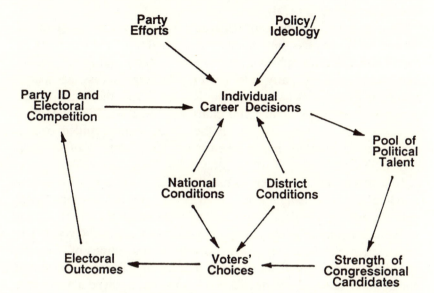

gress,[16] the Republican party *has* played an important role in recruiting switchers. Similarly, policy motivations play a larger role in the initial decision to run for office and to switch parties than in the decision to seek higher office.[17]

The central relationships in the model are between party competition, individual career decisions, the strength of a party's congressional candidates, and electoral outcomes. In this dynamic model, an external shock or trigger mechanism is needed to upset the equilibrium. In the case examined here, that event was Barry Goldwater's success in the South in the 1964 presidential campaign. The external shock changed the relative electoral prospects of the parties, which in turn affected individual career decisions: the Republican party was suddenly a viable alternative. This reinforced the effects of the initial electoral shock by providing the emerging party with new political talent in future elections. Furthermore, as these candidates won office and advanced under the new party's banner, their experiences were factored into the calculations of others seeking to win political offices and of voters who were given a viable alternative. Relatively small initial changes in the behavior in the electorate can trigger a set of elite decisions that dramatically alter the context in which voters' choices will be made in the future. In this manner, the whole cycle repeats as the secular realignment proceeds.

This model is a significant departure from previous treatments of the realigning process, but it cannot be applied to all realignments. In the 1930s, electoral upheaval shattered one party and swept a new, innovative majority party into power. Massive "across-the-board" change in electoral behavior brought Roosevelt into the White House and generated huge Democratic gains in Congress. The magnitude and speed of electoral change in the 1930s simply spilled over a stable career structure and washed out a large number of political careers.[18]

It is misleading, however, to use the 1930s as a model for understanding all other realignments. In an era of split-ticket voting, local politics, and independent voters, a candidate-based theory of secular realignment is more likely to explain patterns of political change. The next section elaborates on how the decisions and actions of elites responding to changes in the major variables in this model (electoral competition, national and district conditions) have played a major role in shaping the new competitive party system in the South.

Evidence for the Elite Model of Secular Change

A complete test of this model will be part of a larger project on partisan realignments and political careers, but preliminary evidence is strongly suggestive. By examining the strength of Republican candidates in U.S. House races and the incidence of party-switching, insights can be gained into the nature of elite responses to electoral change. At this point, the impact of elite behavior on voting and predictions about the future remain more speculative.

Amateurs and Experienced Politicians

Republicans in the South have been forced to rely heavily on political amateurs because there were virtually no experienced Republican state and local politicians in some districts. Those who were serious about careers in politics found their way to the Democratic party. While amateurs may occasionally run successful campaigns for House seats,[19] in the initial stages of Republican resurgence amateur candidates were mostly prominent local businessmen who ran to promote their nonpolitical careers or party leaders simply willing to provide a Republican line on the ballot. V.O. Key was skeptical that these candidates would ever build a competitive party; he described southern Republicans at mid-century in the following manner:

> They are not politicians and are not desirous of office. They are sound, reputable people—and undoubtedly they are. They are honest, and, again, undoubtedly they are. The people, however, who build political parties are politicians. They are keenly desirous of public office, an honorable ambition, perhaps the most honorable of all ambitions. Only through the clash of such ambitions can the ideals of democracy be approached.[20]

Occasionally, "amateurism" was used as a campaign issue. For example, in Georgia Phil M. Landrum (D), was challenged by Jack Price (R), a poultry farmer, who argued that the state needed a two-party system. Landrum replied, "I am glad to see a two-party system, but I don't want to make the government a stooge. I am not ready to turn the government over to a bunch of irresponsible people just so we can have a two-party system."[21]

The Goldwater revolt began to change the southern equation, but the process was slow. In 1964, Republican congressional candidates had broad success in the Deep South for the first time since Reconstruction. The southern Republican party benefited from the salience of national issues which alienated voters from their traditional Democratic attachments, but its supply of political talent was woefully limited. Of the nine newly elected Republican House members from the South in 1964, seven were amateurs. Through time, the lack of attractive candidates constrained the party's capacities to exploit electoral opportunities. This is true even in states such as North Carolina, where the Republican party has been more competitive than in most Deep South states. In the 1974 senatorial race Republicans nominated a furniture company executive, William E. Stevens, Jr., a complete political amateur, to face State Attorney General Robert B. Morgan. Stevens lost, receiving only 37.9 percent of the vote. Alexander Lamis noted, "Several North Carolina observers pointed to the weakness the GOP has in fielding candidates with the credentials to give them credibility with voters, one noting that the Republican party, 'simply has no stable of talent' to draw on."[22]

As opportunities improved and as the party built a base of experienced politicians, the Republicans' reliance on amateurs diminished.

Table 2.1

Number of Previous Elective Offices for House Members from the South and Non-South, 1930–1988

		Democrats	Republicans
	1930–1961	.77 (249)	.11 (9)
South	1962–1975	.84 (69)	.55 (49)
	1976–1988	.87 (77)	.85 (52)
	1930–1961	.74 (712)	.79 (649)
Non-South	1962–1975	.77 (236)	1.01 (183)
	1976–1988	.99 (167)	.87 (163)

Source: Compiled from the *Biographical Directory of the American Congress* (n.p.: n.p., n.d.) and various editions of *Congressional Quarterly Weekly Reports.*

Note: Numbers in the cells indicate the average number of previous elective offices held. The number of newly elected House members each period are in parentheses.

From 1930 to 1961, 66.7 percent of the Republicans elected from the South were amateurs (six of nine).[23] From 1962 to 1974, this proportion fell to 38.8 percent (of forty-nine elected), and from 1976 to 1988, only 34.6 percent were amateurs—still significantly above the national average for Republicans of 24.5 percent for this period, but the South is closing the gap. The average number of previous offices held reveals the same pattern. Republicans elected in the South in the 1930–61 period had held an average of 0.11 elective offices; those elected in the 1962–75 period had held an average of 0.55; and those elected in the 1976–88 period had held an average of 0.85, nearly the same level of elective experience as their nonsouthern counterparts. In 1986 and 1988 they had even more experience (1.2 elective offices and 7.5 years' elective experience, compared to 0.9 offices and 6.4 years for nonsouthern Republicans).

Two important implications can be drawn from this trend. First, one key dimension of change in southern politics has been the Republican party's capacities to run politicians with previous political experience

Figure 2.3. **Southern House Races (No GOP Candidates)**

Percentage of Races

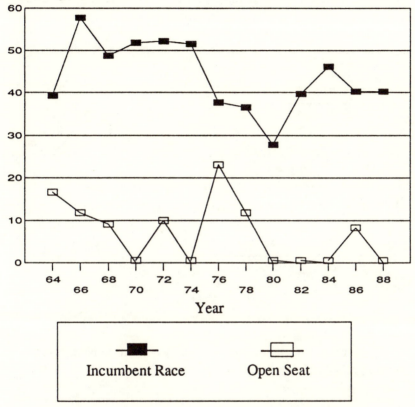

Year

Incumbent Race   Open Seat

Source: Compiled by the author from *Congressional Quarterly Weekly Reports.*

Note: Trend lines indicate the proportion of uncontested races in districts held by Democratic incumbents (incumbent races) and in open-seat races.

in races for Congress. "Challenger quality" is an important determinant of success in congressional elections, and this development has subtly increased the strength of the southern GOP. While this process has been halting because of the limited success the party has enjoyed at the state and local levels, the party's diminishing reliance on political amateurs is noteworthy.

Second, this observation forces an amendment to the strategic politicians hypothesis that in periods of high opportunity the advantaged party is able to offer attractive, experienced candidates to the elector-

Figure 2.4. **GOP Challengers in Districts with Democratic Incumbents**

Percentage of Races

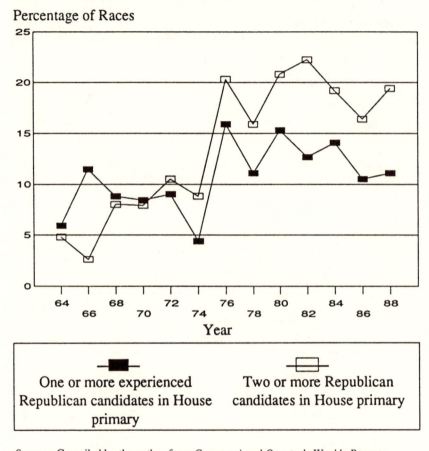

Year

One or more experienced
Republican candidates in House
primary

Two or more Republican
candidates in House primary

Source: Compiled by the author from *Congressional Quarterly Weekly Reports.*

ate.[24] In at least two periods of party system change (in the 1930s and in the South in the early 1960s), parties enjoying auspicious electoral circumstances were forced to rely on political amateurs because they lacked a large pool of experienced candidates. In these realigning periods, then, there was an inverse relationship between challengers' previous political experience and opportunity.

It would be inappropriate to move on without addressing Key's argument about the types of amateurs whom the Republicans ran in the 1940s. Clearly, the amateurs Key studied did not expect to win elective office or to have the opportunity to have significant impacts on public policy.[25] As

Figure 2.5. **GOP Challengers in Open-Seat Races**

Percentage of Races

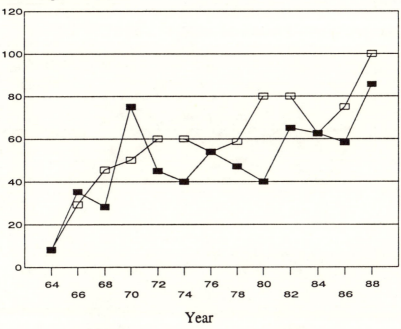

Year

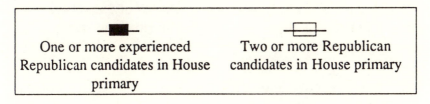

One or more experienced Republican candidates in House primary

Two or more Republican candidates in House primary

Source: Compiled by the author from *Congressional Quarterly Weekly Reports.*

the emerging party builds a more ˜competitive position, however, the amateurs do not fit Key's description. Those in the new generation of Republican amateurs are both "keenly desirous of office" and highly motivated ideologically (for example, Connie Mack of Florida, Jack Fields and Joe L. Barton of Texas, and Newt Gingrich of Georgia). Discriminating measures of the "quality" of Republican amateurs, if available, would reveal a marked increase in quality over time.

The question of how changes in party competition shape the calcu-

Figure 2.6. **Size and Quality of GOP Pool in Districts with Democratic Incumbents**

Mean Score

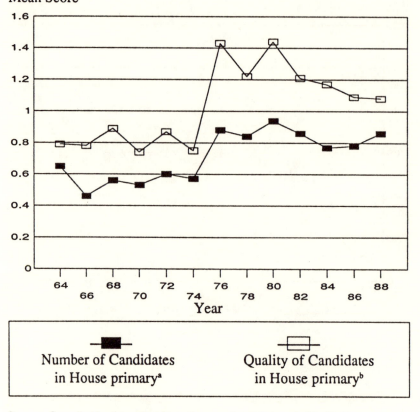

Year

| Number of Candidates in House primary[a] | Quality of Candidates in House primary[b] |

Source: Compiled by the author from *Congressional Quarterly Weekly Reports.*

Notes: [a]Mean number of candidates in Republican primary in districts with a Democratic incumbent.
[b]Mean quality of the pool in Republican primary in districts with a Democratic incumbent, where the quality of the pool is determined by summing quality score assigned to each Republican candidate. Complete amateurs were coded as 1, ambitious amateurs 2, those with some political experience 3, and those with extensive experience 4. See the text for a more extended discussion.

lations of generations of prospective politicians is an interesting one, but there are no data available on the topic. Such career calculations can be inferred from simple assumptions about individuals' motivations and an understanding of the context of congressional elections in the South, but direct evidence of candidates' decisions based on relative career opportunities within the two parties would have to be based on survey data. Such a survey is beyond the scope of this project, but some anecdotal evidence from a different context is suggestive. Bernard Asbell recounts this story about two of Maine's prominent politicians, William Cohen and Edmund Muskie:

> Cohen once told Clyde [MacDonald] that when he decided as a young Bangor lawyer to go into politics he made a calculated decision to do so as a Republican. The Democratic party was so full of talent and the Republican party so devoid of it that clearly the GOP presented the more attractive possibility of a quick rise to the top. Muskie nods, acknowledging Cohen's perfectly reasonable and craftsmanlike decision. The irony is exquisite. It is an exact reversal of what Ed Muskie perceived twenty-one years ago—a poverty among Maine Democrats and an unchallenged concentration of power among Republicans. Muskie's capture of the state capital began the tidal flow of talent to the Democrats, which Cohen now seeks to reverse.[26]

Competition in Primaries

As candidates begin to view the emerging party as a viable outlet for a political career, nominations in that party should become more highly desired and, therefore, more contested. Furthermore, the quality of the primary challengers should also increase as the pool of experienced Republicans grows. Figures 2.3, 2.4, and 2.5 support these assertions. Figure 2.3 shows the proportion of southern districts that did not have a Republican challenger from 1964 to 1988. The pattern of greater Republican activity is clearly evident from 1966 to 1980 in districts held by Democratic incumbents, but the number of uncontested seats has risen once again in the past four elections. In open seats, however, only one district did not have a Republican candidate in the 1980s. If the time period were extended back to the 1950s, the pattern would be clearer. As recently as 1958, eighty-five southern Democratic incumbents were uncontested![27]

The intensity of competition in Republican primaries has also increased in the past three decades. The proportion of open-seat primaries contested by two or more Republicans increased from 27.5 percent in the years 1964–68, to 57.1 percent in the 1970s, and to 78.8 percent in the 1980s. Republican competition to face a Democratic incumbent has increased to the point where roughly a fifth of

Figure 2.7. **Size and Quality of GOP Pool in Open-Seat Districts**

Mean Score

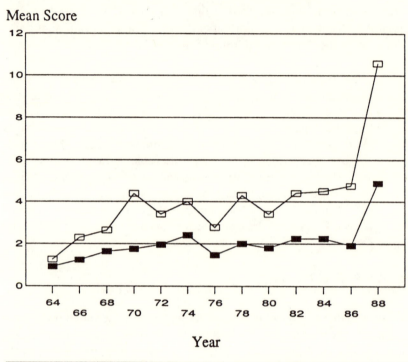

Year

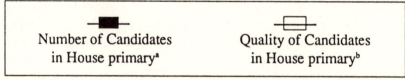

| Number of Candidates in House primary[a] | Quality of Candidates in House primary[b] |

Source: Compiled by the author from *Congressional Quarterly Weekly Reports.*

Notes: [a]Mean number of candidates in Republican primary in open-seat districts.
[b]Mean quality of the pool in Republican primary in open-seat districts, where the quality of the pool is determined by summing quality score assigned to each Republican candidate. Complete amateurs were coded as 1, ambitious amateurs 2, those with some political experience 3, and those with extensive experience 4. See the text for a more extended discussion.

such primaries are contested by two candidates. (It was 19.6 percent in the 1980s, compared to 12.3 percent in the 1970s and 5 percent in the period 1964–68.) The quality of these challenges has also increased, with nearly two-thirds of all open seat and one-fifth of Democratic incumbent districts in the 1980s having at least one Republican challenger with some previous political experience. These proportions are also up dramatically since 1964.

Figures 2.6 and 2.7 show the same pattern, using aggregate measures of the size and quality of the Republican candidate pools. These figures show that the average size of the candidate pool in a Republican primary increased from about 0.8 in the 1980s in incumbent districts. The quality of the pool[28] increased from about 0.8 to 1.4 and then fell to 1.1 by 1988. The pattern is similar for open-seat races, but rather than falling off in the most recent period, open seats are attracting very strong Republican candidates.

Party-Switchers

Of course, amateurs and homegrown experienced politicians have not been the only sources of Republican candidates in the South. Party-switchers, Democratic officeholders who move to the Republican party, have also been an important source of growth for the GOP. Why is switching an attractive alternative to some Democrats? First, the value of the party label increases with the growth of the potential Republican vote; the success of Republican presidential candidates, as well as of other southern Republicans, indicates to strategic politicians that new opportunities have emerged. Second, in one-party systems, political conflict is channeled into the dominant party, and because the nominations of the stronger party are so important they become difficult to obtain. Ambitious politicians confronting crowded paths to power within the Democratic party may be attracted to the Republican party by the ease with which its nomination can be obtained. For example, Ed Knox, a state legislator and mayor of Charlotte, North Carolina, switched to the Republican party after losing the 1984 Democratic gubernatorial primary; Knox said, "I think there is an openness in the Republican party, so that you get out there and you earn the right to run, then at least you won't be sidetracked by a power structure. I think that's the wholesome part of the Republican party. They have enough need for new faces that they use them."[29] Third, the short ideological distance between the southern Democratic and Republican parties eases the transition. Fourth, both national and state Republican party organizations have seen the value of recruiting Democratic officeholders, and they offer substantial electoral and financial support as enticements to potential switchers through their "Operation Open Door" program.[30]

This mixture of ambition, opportunity, and resources creates powerful incentives to move to the rising party. As experienced politicians move to the GOP, its electoral prospects in affected districts improve, more Republicans gain office, and the emergence of the party is reinforced. In this way, the calculations of the politically ambitious can help to drive party system change. The state chairman of the Louisiana Republican party said of his organization's efforts to convert Democratic officeholders:

> The key to building a party system of competition is to be prepared at any moment to take advantage of the next opportunity—whatever it may be at any electoral level. The trouble is, up to now we haven't had the right candidates available. . . . Now we do have the candidates, we are getting ones who have already won, winners.[31]

Wolfinger and Hagen indicate the specific contributions switchers make to party organizations:

> Each important switcher brings along some dozens or hundreds of local supporters: district coordinators and county chairmen and fundraisers and miscellaneous lieutenants and sergeants in his organization. These eminent defectors and their entourages will help meet the Republican party's most pressing need in the South: appealing candidates and strong campaigns for national and state legislative seats.[32]

Another southern Republican party leader explained the electoral benefits of recruiting Democrats and the strong-arm tactics that can be used to encourage switching:

> After years of Democratic control of elected office, and faced with a relatively sparse "bench" of potential Republican candidates, it is much cheaper to get a person with an established backing to switch parties than to try and knock them off. In those districts with basically Republican sentiments and a Democrat in office, we were not afraid to threaten them that unless they switched we could no longer allow them to go unchallenged. After the switch, our ability to sell our position along with the personal support of the converted official often turned a once safe Democratic seat in to a toss-up or even a Republican seat. This had the further effect of allowing more voters to conceive of themselves as Republicans.[33]

Of particular importance here is the suggestion that successfully enticing someone to switch has implications for the growth of the

Republican party-in-the-electorate. The presence of a Republican officeholder and the voters' satisfaction with that politician's performance may lead voters to alter their partisan attachments, thus improving the climate for other Republican candidates.

How prevalent is party-switching? Biographies in *Politics in America* indicate that twenty of the forty-eight southern Republican members of the House and Senate in the 101st Congress had once been Democrats.[34] The two most recent switchers are Bill Grant of Florida and Tommy Robinson of Arkansas. While it is more difficult to gather information on switchers who run and lose, there is some evidence from a survey of state party chairs. Between 1972 and 1986, South Carolina Republicans ran eleven candidates for House seats who had previous political experience; *six* of these candidates had held elective office as Democrats earlier in their careers. In addition, of course, Senator Strom Thurmond is an ex-Democrat, as is Republican Floyd Spence. The state chairman of the South Carolina Republicans reported that switchers at the state and local level "have been a major source of growth for our party," especially since 1980, and that the party has pressed its efforts to attract converts at the state legislative level. Virginia officials reported that three of thirteen experienced Republican House candidates had been Democrats (and one other not mentioned by them, John F. Herrity, was a switcher), while the Democratic chair in Florida notes that Republicans have encouraged switching and that "they are continuing with a full court press." Half of the Republican state legislators in Mississippi in the past fifteen years were Democrats, as were Republican Webb Franklin and Senator Trent Lott. A sample of fifty-six Republican state House candidates in Louisiana from 1972 to 1983 revealed that *all* of the winners and 65 percent overall had formerly been Democrats.[35] In an April 1988 special election in Louisiana, former-Democrat Jim McCrery became the first Republican elected in the Fourth Congressional District in 114 years.

Given the evidence that 41.7 percent of current Republican members of Congress and substantial numbers of Republicans in lower office are party-switchers, it is clear that individual career decisions have been important in the emergence of the southern Republican party. The success of the Republicans in attracting experienced challengers, and the impact of their success on the calculations of other politicians, have played a major role in driving party system change in the region.

Because ambition theory has not yet adequately incorporated policy goals, however, it would predict far more switching at high levels of the career structure than actually has occurred. When confronted with a choice between a stagnated career or a new opportunity, a purely ambitious politician would have no trouble—he or she would do what would be necessary to advance the career. As Aldrich points out, an ambitious politician will switch parties if the net probability of winning as a Republican is greater than the net costs of running as a Republican; this is shown in the left-hand side of the inequality:[36]

$$(P_R - P_D) > (C_R - C_D)$$ Where P is the probability of winning
R is the Republican party
D is the Democratic party
and   C is the cost of running

However, it is clear that politicians do not always display purely ambitious behavior. Why? The simple answer to this question can be brought within the ambit of ambition theory by expanding the concept of the political career. More is involved in a career than a simple progression from office to office in an opportunity structure. During the 1984 presidential campaign Walter Mondale asserted that "I am what I am" in response to urgings that he alter some political positions and his style. This means that over the course of a career in politics, candidates develop an "identity" which introduces constraints on the positions they can plausibly take and binds them to the old party.[37]

Former Representative Kent Hance learned of the constraints that a political identity can place on one's political career choices when he left the Democratic party to run in the Republican gubernatorial primary in Texas in 1986. Republican Representative Jack Fields responded, "Kent has to recognize he's new to the party; he did some work for (Lloyd) Doggett (Phil Gramm's opponent in his 1984 Senate election), he did some work for Mondale, and this might not be the best time for him to run for governor." Republican Mack Sweeney simply said, "It would have to take a lot of persuasion for me to turn around and support a born-again Republican."[38] Apparently, Texas Republicans agreed because Hance received only 20 percent of the vote in a three-way primary.

This example illustrates the importance of the terms on the right-hand side of the inequality shown above: the *costs* of running will not be the same for those who are just beginning a political career as for those who are politically experienced. The latter have developed political ties and a political identity that may be hard for them to shake when they attempt to switch parties. This simple argument suggests a hypothesis: electoral change is far more likely to have effects on the calculations of ambitious candidates at the lower levels of the career structure, where identities are still ill-formed and malleable, than at the higher levels of the structure, where candidates clearly "are what they are"—their political identities are firmly established, and the costs of abandoning them for simple advancement of the career may be unacceptably high. At present there is little data available to test this hypothesis or to reveal the extent of switching that has occurred below the level of winners in congressional contests.

Of course, some switching has occurred at very high levels of the career structure. Strom Thurmond and Andrew Ireland are prominent examples, and they are interesting because it cannot be said that either moved to the Republican party to advance his career. Both were electorally safe at home, and their decision to change labels was clearly motivated by policy considerations. On the other hand, it was widely perceived that Bill Grant switched parties for political reasons. As Lawrence Smith (D-FL), for example, observed, "I think it was strictly for political gain for Bill Grant. I think he made a deal with the Republicans and they are going to support him in a state-wide Cabinet race. I think it was very cavalier of him. I think he ought to resign."[39]

In most cases, though, it is impossible to discern the extent to which policy or career goals have governed decisions to switch parties. One reasonable, if imperfect, way to determine which motivations governed switching behavior is to see how long switchers who actually hold office stay in their current office before trying to make a move up the career structure. Castle and Fett found that 65 percent of switchers who actually held offices when they changed parties attempted to move to higher offices within two years of joining the new party. From this they infer that the switch was, at least in part, electorally motivated.[40] The intensive method used by Rothenberg in his study of party-switchers could be combined with a careful examination of individuals' careers to shed additional light on this question.

District-level Effects

Conventional wisdom holds that the southern Republican party has grown because of changes in the electorate and changes in issue cleavages, namely race.[41] I argue that the interaction between electoral success and changes in the issue cleavages in the electorate is more fluid and interactive. Elites anticipate the direction of change in voter preferences and then help *lead* the change. In the modern South, Republicans who win office draw voters closer to the Republican party and create safe Republican or highly competitive seats through their effective policymaking and careful exploitation of the resources of their offices. Therefore, the actions of candidates and politicians are, in part, driving the realigning process. As voters increasingly base their votes on incumbency and less on party and crosscutting issues, candidates will be at the forefront of secular partisan change.

If this argument is correct, several patterns should be evident. First, voter identification, which has gradually shifted from Democratic to Republican and independent loyalties, should occur in stepwise rather than continuous fashion. When a prominent Democrat changes parties, thousands of Democratic voters are more likely to think of themselves as Republicans. Similarly, if a Democratic seat is captured by a popular Republican politician and transformed into a safe seat, voters may quickly shift their allegiances. This hypothesis, while not tested here, follows logically from the theory of elite-driven alignment. Second, if incumbency is a growing component of the vote in the South today at the expense of party, more candidates of the insurgent party should be elected to open seats than when a Democratic incumbent is running. Furthermore, once the Republicans win those seats, they should manage to win reelection on the basis of incumbency voting. Third, the seats of successful Republican challengers should become increasingly safe as voters become accustomed to voting for the new party.

Republican candidates have taken control of formerly Democratic districts in three types of situations: winning open seats, defeating an incumbent, and switching parties. As expected, open seats have been the most important vehicle for southern Republican gains in the House. Open-seat wins for Republicans may be the result of fortuitous circumstances, favorable redistricting, or more normal circumstances. In each case, it is crucial that the party nominate a strong candidate who can exploit the opportunity.[42] From the 1960s through the 1972 redistricting, Republicans took advantage of the newly created districts, winning nine of the seventeen new districts. However, Republicans managed to win only two of the eight new southern seats in the 1982 reapportionment. With retiring Democratic incumbents, Republicans have won twenty-six seats from 1964 to 1990 (compared to Democrats winning only eleven seats that were formerly held by Republican incumbents). Between 1972 and 1978 Republicans won a *net* of ten open seats. Since then they experienced a net loss of three, however, so open seats have not been uniformly profitable, especially of late.

Republican challengers have also defeated incumbents twenty-six times in the years 1964–88, but in many of these instances the districts reverted back to the Democrats in the following election. Overall, Republicans have gained only a net of four seats through incumbent defeats in this period. Incumbent defeats tend to be bunched in elections with strong national tides: twenty-one of the twenty-six Democratic defeats in this period came in 1964, 1966, 1980, and 1984; fourteen of the twenty-two Republican defeats came in 1974 and 1982.

Party-switches seem to be the most effective way to gain a seat and hold it. Andy Ireland, Phil Gramm, and Albert Watson all managed to win reelection after switching parties as an incumbent House member. Others, such as Trent Lott, Sonny Callahan, and William Dickinson won election as Republicans in strongly Democratic districts after leaving the Democratic party. In several of these districts, the switchers have been able to pass along the district to another Republican. Floyd Spence (another switcher) followed Watson, Joe Barton followed Phil Gramm, and Harrison County Sheriff Larkin Smith succeeded Trent Lott, who was elected to the Senate in 1988 (however, Democrats regained this seat in a special election in 1989 after Smith died in a plane crash).

The argument for incumbency-based voting in the South is further supported by the number of formerly safe Democratic districts that are now firmly in the Republican column. Since 1978, about one-fourth of all southern Republican incumbents have been uncontested. This compares to only 5.8 percent of northern Republicans in the same period. Another measure of the success Republicans have had in establishing safe districts in the South is the pre-election survey conducted by Congressional Quarterly. In 1964 only two Republican districts were classified as "safe." Through the 1970s and 1980s, the number increased from fifteen to thirty, to the point that 83.3 percent of southern Republican incumbents were seen as safe in 1988.

The Limits of Republican Growth

Despite impressive Republican gains in the South, realignment is stagnating and long-term structural forces may prevent the Republicans from becoming the new majority party there. David S. Broder says, "[T]here is no Republican bulldozer moving inexorably across the South, flattening every Democrat who stands in the way."[43] One immediate indicator was the surprising loss by southern Republicans of four Senate seats and five House seats in the 1986 midterm elections. Also, Republicans lost two special elections in 1989, the Alabama Third and Mississippi Fifth Districts; the latter had been held by Republicans since 1973 (however, Republicans did win Claude Pepper's old seat in Florida and narrowly missed picking up Jim Wright's district in two other special elections).

The data presented in Figures 2.3, 2.4, and 2.6 show that the frequency and strength of challenges to Democratic incumbents in the South peaked in the early 1980s (though the upward trend continues in open-seat races). The ability of Republicans to make continued gains will depend on the recruitment of experienced politicians from the Democratic party and electoral success at lower levels of the career structure. The latter may prove to be the most resistant to change.

Some Republican strategists look to the 1992 elections with great anticipation because of the addition of seven to eleven House districts in the South (mostly in Texas and Florida, where Republicans have done especially well) and an above-average number of retirements. However, if the trend established in the 1980s continues, Republicans will make only marginal gains (recall, they gained only one new seat through reapportionment in 1982 and they actually lost some ground in open-seat races).

Four fundamental reasons may explain the limits of Republican growth in the South: the solid Democratic base in lower political office, the response of Democratic national and state party organizations, which has helped increase the costs of party-switching, and the growing importance of race in southern politics.

The State and Local Base

Democratic strength increases dramatically the deeper one goes in the political career structure. This reservoir of strength provides a pool of political talent for higher office, but it also serves as an anchor for partisan attachments. "The courthouse has been our rock against the tide of Republicans statewide," said state legislator Clifton (Chip) Woodrum (D-VA). "Without it, we would have been washed away." Voters remain registered Democrats in many states because the action in primary elections is predominantly within their party.[44]

Although Republican primaries at the congressional level are slowly becoming more contested, most local offices are still uncontested by Republicans in the South. Democrats also dominate state-level offices, holding approximately three-fourths of the state legislative seats and nearly all of the constitutionally established state offices below governor; between 1982 and 1987, Democrats won 98 of 100 such races, losing only the lieutenant governorships of Florida and Louisiana.[45] This lack of Republican success undermines GOP efforts to recruit strong challengers in House races. In the recent special election in Alabama's Third District, Democrats fielded nine candidates, including six officeholders. The Republicans had only three amateurs and one party-switcher, John Rice, who was trounced in the general election, 68 to 32 percent. Rhodes Cook notes that in "the heart of Dixie, the GOP has run into a fire wall, in large part because it has no farm team of candidates seasoned and ready to run."[46] The absence of a "farm team" prevented southern Republicans from taking full advantage of presidential coattails in 1972 and in the 1980s, thus weakening the strength of the "presidential pulse."[47]

Democratic Response

The Republican challenge has awakened moribund Democratic organizations in many southern districts in which the Republicans have been especially aggressive. Fred Slabach, director of the Mississippi Democratic party (and a former Republican) observed,

> Many local Democrats felt as if they were under siege, and when that happens, sometimes it just brings people together and gets them working for a common goal. They really went out and tried to find the best

people they could. They urged them to run and told them they'd do everything they could to help them win.[48]

The Republicans' effectiveness in recruiting and funding candidates and in attracting party-switchers was bound to stimulate responses by Democratic politicians and organizational leaders. The stakes are high, the Democrats still control important offices, and they still have a strong grip on voters, especially in races for local offices. It is highly unlikely that the party would simply roll over for the Republicans.

Slabach argued that the Democrats were able to beat back the Republican advance by targeting switchers to woo them back to the party and running aggressive campaigns against politicians who had switched.

> Once we got these folks elected and once the people that switched were defeated, other people who had been thinking about switching decided not to. A specific case happened in Lincoln county. It had been rumored that several members of the Board of Supervisors were thinking about switching parties. They had, in fact, told a member of our executive committee that if the people on the municipal level were successful in getting elected as Republicans, that they were all going to switch and run for reelection in 1987 as Republicans. Well, now that we defeated the switchers there, they said it doesn't make political sense to switch, and they're not going to do it now.[49]

The recent failure of John Rice in Alabama shows that the Republican party can often provide an easy path to the general election, but it cannot guarantee success. Kent Hance's experience in Texas shows that ambitious switchers may not even jump that first hurdle. If Democrats actively work to increase the costs of party-switching, the effectiveness of this tactic may also be undermined.

Race

The overwhelming commitment of black voters to the Democratic party and their increased participation in the past twenty-five years are a powerful constraint on Republican resurgence in the South. Blacks have long played a role in electoral politics in "rim-South" states such as Tennessee and North Carolina, but where their numbers are the greatest in the Deep South, blacks were largely disenfranchised for one hundred years. After the Voting Rights Act of 1965, black voters changed the face of southern politics. When the black population exceeds 20 percent (which it does in virtually all southern and border states), the Republicans are at a major disadvantage, needing to carry 65 percent of the nonblack vote in order to win. In 1986, Jeremiah Denton of Alabama carried 61 percent of the nonblack vote, Mack Mattingly of Georgia 59 percent, and W. Henson Moore of Louisiana 60 percent, but these sizable majorities were not enough to overcome the strength of the black vote for their Democratic opponents.[50]

At the congressional district level, Republicans have also been more successful when the black population is less than 20 percent than in more heavily black districts. Twenty-four of the thirty-seven southern House Republicans in the Hundredth Congress, or 65 percent, were elected from districts where less than 20 percent of the voters are black. The comparable figure for the Democrats was thirty-nine out of eighty-one, or 48 percent. This difference is reasonably large, and it is deflated by the lingering strength of older southern Democrats in some heavily white districts, as well as by the strength of Democrats in many rural, nonblack constituencies.[51] Large black populations are not an absolute bar to Republican success—Mississippi's Second District, with the third largest black population of any southern district (54 percent) was represented by a Republican from 1983 to 1987—but the continuing strength of the Democrats among black voters is an important barrier to expanding Republican success in southern elections.[52]

Implications for Congressional Politics

It may seem obvious that the changing partisan composition of the southern congressional delegation has an impact on congressional politics. But the changes have been more far-reaching than would be predicted by the shift of several dozens seats from Democratic to Republican control. Not only has the nature of representation changed in those districts, but the very basis of congressional politics in the South has been transformed: southern Democrats in Congress are almost as liberal as their nonsouthern counterparts. The "conservative coalition" is nearly dead.

The roots of this change are far too complex to summarize here.[53] Clearly, race has played an important role. On crucial issues such as the appointment of Robert Bork to the Supreme Court and the Martin Luther King, Jr., holiday, southern Democrats led the national party.

Wayne Dowdy (D-MS) says, "The Voting Rights Act gives me the luxury of being independent of the typical Southern conservative position. You couldn't be on the right half of the spectrum and win a primary in my district." Martin Frost (D-TX) agrees, "There's no room left for conservative Democrats."[54]

The dynamics of secular change outlined here have also played a role in this transformation. When southern Democrats voted with Republicans in Congress in the 1950s to 1970s, there was an expectation that the national Republican party would discourage challenges to the loyal defectors. Now there are no such guarantees. The example that most southern Democrats point to is the defeat of Jack Hightower of Texas. He had voted with the conservative coalition 88 percent of the time, but he was beaten by a Republican who distorted his record on school prayer. "People from the South talk about Hightower all the time," reported one Texas House member:

> He came back up here after the election and talked about what a mean, scurrilous campaign the Republicans had run against him. He told everybody that no matter how conservative they voted, Republicans would lie, cheat and steal to beat them. What's the percentages for some of these people to do business with the Republicans when they see the treatment Hightower got?[55]

A systematic study of inter-party competition and roll-call voting would test the validity of this claim.

Conclusion

In this chapter I have argued that party system change in the South has had important consequences for political careers and that the decisions and actions of politicians in the face of electoral instability have, in turn, affected the realigning process. Previous discussions of the emergence of the southern Republican party have focused largely on voters; I have turned empirical and theoretical attention to the *elite side of the realigning process*. The modern South is a virtual laboratory for the study of party system change and political ambition; it is crucial for political scientists to recognize the analytical opportunities afforded by a generation of politicians forced to deal with a dramatically altered set of political conditions.

More specifically, I have shown that the Republican party's reliance on political amateurs, very heavy in the early years of the party's resurgence, declined as the GOP nurtured a base of experienced politicians and persuaded numbers of Democratic officeholders to abandon their old party for new opportunities in the rising party. The lack of quality challengers, however, has slowed the party's political advance.

What does the future hold? Because incumbents are increasingly insulated from national forces, it is not likely that the nation will soon experience a 1930s-style realignment. Instead, a party looking to fashion a new majority, such as the GOP in the South, must rely on strong and attractive candidates to do its work. Obviously, the argument does not work in an ideological or party vacuum, but certainly the candidate side of realignments requires more attention.

Notes

An earlier version of this paper was presented at the 1988 Annual Meeting of the Southern Political Science Association, with David J. Sousa. I would especially like to thank David Sousa for his contribution to the development of this paper.

1. See especially David Brady, *Critical Elections and Congressional Policy Making* (Stanford, CA: Stanford University Press, 1988).

2. On the "governing side" of realignments, see David W. Brady, *Critical Elections and Congressional Policy Making*; Jerome M. Clubb, William H. Flanigan, and Nancy H. Zingale, *Partisan Realignment: Voters, Parties, and Government in American History* (Beverly Hills, CA: Sage Publications, 1980). On the 1958 class, see David W. Rohde, Norman H. Ornstein, and Robert L. Peabody, "Political Change and Legislative Norms in the U.S. Senate, 1957–1974," in *Studies of Congress*, ed. Glenn R. Parker (Washington: Congressional Quarterly Press, 1985). On the 1964 class, see Christopher Deering and Charles E. King, "The Class of '64: An Examination of a Watershed House Cohort" (Paper presented at the Annual Meeting of the Midwest Political Science Association, Chicago, Illinois, 5–7 April 1990). On the 1974 class, see Burdett Loomis, *The New American Politician* (New York: Basic Books, 1988). On the Progressive era, see David W. Brady, Richard Brody, and David Epstein, "Heterogeneous Parties and Political Organization: The U.S. Senate, 1880–1920," *Legislative Studies Quarterly* 14, no. 2 (May 1988): 205–23 and Peter Swenson, "The Influence of Recruitment on the Structure of Power in the U.S. House, 1870–1940," *Legislative Studies Quarterly* 7, no. 1 (February 1982): 7–36. On the recent South, see David W. Rohde, "Variations in Partisanship in the House of Representatives, 1953–1988: Southern Democrats, Realignment and Agenda Change" (Paper presented at the Eighty-fourth Annual Meeting of the American Political Science Association, Washington, D.C., 1–4 September 1988).

3. See Earl Black and Merle Black, *Politics and Society in the South* (Cambridge: Harvard University Press, 1987) for a review of the literature.

4. See V.O. Key, "A Theory of Critical Elections," *Journal of Politics* 17, no.

1 (February 1955): 3–18; Walter Dean Burnham, *Critical Elections and the Mainsprings of American Politics* (New York: Norton, 1970); James L. Sundquist, *Dynamics of the Party System*, rev. ed. (Washington: Brookings Institution, 1983). See Edward G. Carmines and James A. Stimson, *Issue Evolution: Race and the Transformation of American Politics* (Princeton, NJ: Princeton University Press, 1989), for a challenge to this conventional view.

5. Everett Carll Ladd, "Like Waiting for Godot: The Uselessness of Realignment for Understanding Change in Contemporary American Politics" (Paper presented at the Eighty-fifth Annual Meeting of the American Political Science Association, Atlanta, Georgia, 31 August–3 September 1989).

6. The literature on the "governing side" of realignments focuses on the importance of individual politicians. Effective leadership has been necessary, historically, to translate the opportunity for policy innovation offered by an electoral shock into a lasting realignment of the electorate (see Clubb, Flanigan, and Zingale, *Partisan Realignment)*. This "governing side" perspective shifts focus to the policy actions of politicians but says little about their office-seeking behavior and examines only critical, rather than secular, change.

7. James L. Sundquist, *Dynamics of the Party System*, 304.

8. Joseph A. Schlesinger, "The New American Political Party," *American Political Science Review* 79, no. 4 (December 1985): 1154. For the seminal work, see his *Ambition and Politics: Political Careers in the United States* (Chicago: Rand McNally and Co., 1966).

9. David W. Rohde, "Risk Bearing and Progressive Ambition: The Case of Members of the United States House of Representatives," *American Journal of Political Science* 23, no. 1 (February 1979): 1–26; Gary C. Jacobson and Samuel Kernell, *Strategy and Choice in Congressional Elections* (New Haven: Yale University Press, 1983); David T. Canon, *Actors, Athletes, and Astronauts: Political Amateurs in the United States Congress* (Chicago: University of Chicago Press, 1990).

10. Gerald H. Gamm, *The Making of New Deal Democrats* (Chicago: University of Chicago Press, 1989); Ladd, "Waiting for Godot"; John R. Petrocik, "Realignment: New Party Coalitions and the Nationalization of the South," *Journal of Politics* 49, no. 2 (May 1987): 347–75; Clubb, Flanigan, and Zingale, *Partisan Realignment*.

11. V.O. Key, "Secular Realignment and the Party System," *Journal of Politics* 21, no. 2 (May 1959): 198–99.

12. Ibid., 208.

13. Schlesinger, *Ambition and Politics*, 89.

14. The term "amateur" simply refers to the absence of prior political experience and is not to be confused with James Q. Wilson's reform-minded activist. See Wilson's *The Amateur Democrat* (Chicago: University of Chicago Press, 1962).

15. Canon, *Actors, Athletes, and Astronauts*; Jacobson and Kernell, *Strategy and Choice*; Rohde, "Risk Bearing and Progressive Ambition"; John H. Aldrich, "The Rise of the Republican Party, 1854–1860" (Paper presented at the Annual Meeting of the Midwest Political Science Association, Chicago, Illinois, 8–11 April 1987).

16. Jacobson, *Politics of Congressional Elections*, 18–21. See Paul S. Hernn-

son, *Party Campaigning in the 1980s* (Cambridge: Harvard University Press, 1988), for an opposing view.

17. The place of policy and ideology in this model requires elaboration. I have included policy goals as well as ambition because it is obvious that ambition alone cannot explain the behavior of politicians; the potential for influence over public policy that comes with a political career leads some to go into politics rather than another pursuit. This concern will be discussed in the section on party-switching.

18. David T. Canon and David J. Sousa, "Realigning Elections and Political Career Structures in the U.S. Congress" (Paper presented at the Eighty-third Annual Meeting of the American Political Science Association, Chicago, Illinois, 3–6 September 1987).

19. Canon, *Actors, Athletes, and Astronauts*, Chap. 4.

20. V.O. Key, *Southern Politics in State and Nation* (New York: Alfred A. Knopf, 1949), 296–97.

21. *Congressional Quarterly Weekly Report* (9 October 1964): 2354.

22. Alexander P. Lamis, *The Two-Party South* (New York: Oxford University Press, 1984), 137.

23. These figures and subsequent data on careers in the South will exclude the First and Second Congressional Districts in Tennessee. These districts have been Republican since the Civil War, so it would be theoretically inconsistent to include them with the southern districts that have been dominated by the Democratic party or increasingly competitive for most of the twentieth century. See V.O. Key, *Southern Politics*, 75–81, for a discussion of Tennessee Republicanism.

24. Jacobson and Kernell, *Strategy and Choice*.

25. Key argues that the Republican party leaders in the South hung on to skeleton organizations to have power over presidential nominations and a claim to federal patronage from Republican administrations (*Southern Politics*, 292–97).

26. Bernard Asbell, *The Senate Nobody Knows* (Baltimore: Johns Hopkins University Press, 1978), 284.

27. Peverill Squire, "Competition and Uncontested Seats in U.S. House Elections," *Legislative Studies Quarterly* 14, no. 2 (May 1989): 281–95.

28. The quality is computed from a four-level variable that is scored 1 for a complete amateur, 2 for ambitious amateurs, 3 for candidates with appointive experience or lower elective office, and 4 for state legislators, large-city mayors, and statewide officeholders. (See Canon, *Actors, Athletes, and Astronauts*, for a more complete discussion.)

29. Stuart Rothenberg, *Party Switches: Interviews about Realignment and the Political Parties* (Washington: The Free Congress Research and Education Foundation, 1985), 17. For a general discussion of this issue see Key, *Southern Politics*, Chap. 19.

30. Rothenberg, *Party Switches*, 58–59. A survey sent to state party chairs of the Democratic and Republican parties in the South revealed that money was a clear Republican advantage. (All nine who responded indicated that money was key. One chairman described Republican national funds as a "bottomless pit".) This survey is the basis for the discussion of party-switching that follows.

31. Quoted in Stella Z. Theodoulou, *The Louisiana Republican Party: The*

Building of a State Political Party (New Orleans: Tulane University Press, 1985), 117–18.

32. Raymond Wolfinger and Michael Hagen, "Southern Comfort: Prospects for a Republican Realignment in the South," *Public Opinion*, October/November 1985, 13.

33. Stephen E. Frantzich, *Political Parties in the Technological Age* (New York: Longman, 1989), 164.

34. Five were serving in Congress when they switched; thirteen had served in public office as Democrats, the other two had not held office.

35. Theodoulou, *Louisiana Republican Party*, 116.

36. Aldrich, "Rise of the Republican Party," 9–12.

37. David Sousa contributed this concept of the "political identity."

38. Quoted in David S. Castle and Patrick J. Fett, "When Politicians Switch Parties: Conscience or Calculation?" (Paper presented at the Eighty-first Annual Meeting of the American Political Science Association, New Orleans, Louisiana, 29 August–1 September 1985), 5.

39. Peter Bragdon, "Florida Democrats Rattled by Grant Jump to GOP," *Congressional Quarterly Weekly Report* (25 February 1989): 410.

40. Castle and Fett, "When Politicians Switch Parties," 7.

41. Harold W. Stanley, "Southern Partisan Change: Dealignment, Realignment, or Both?" *Journal of Politics* 50, no. 1 (February 1988): 64–88; Petrocik, "Realignment."

42. In some cases a relatively weak candidate may benefit from district-level circumstances. For example, in the Louisiana Eighth District, Republican Clyde Holloway was elected to the seat vacated by the death of Gillis Long. Long's widow, Cathy, decided not to run for reelection after her victory in a 1985 special election. Holloway had no political experience (he ran a wholesale nursery business for seventeen years), but he managed to squeak by with 23 percent of the primary vote and 51 percent in the general election. The primary was a tight five-way race among three white Democratic men, a black Democratic woman, Faye Williams, who won the primary with 25 percent, and Holloway. The district, which is liberal by southern standards (it gave 49 percent of its votes to Walter Mondale in 1984), went Republican for the first time since the district was created in 1912 when Williams did not capture enough of the white vote (the district is 35 percent black). The district may remain in Republican hands for some time, as Holloway seems ready to use his "fluke" election to establish a hold in a Democratic district.

43. David S. Broder, "Republicans Gain Strength in Region's Political Cauldron," *Washington Post*, 18 May 1986, A12.

44. Quoted in Broder, "Republicans Gain Strength," A12. Democratic dominance in primary elections is breaking down in some areas. In the 1978 gubernatorial primary in Texas, only 158,000 people voted in the Republican primary compared to 1.8 million in the Democratic primary. By 1982 the figures were 544,000 and 1.1 million, respectively.

45. Richard K. Scher and Warren W. Heyman, "Growing Pains of the Southern Republican Party" (Paper presented at the Eighty-fourth Annual Meeting of the American Political Science Association, Washington, D.C., 1–4 September 1988).

46. Rhodes Cook, "Alabama 3rd Provides Test for GOP in South," *Congressional Quarterly Weekly Report* (28 January 1989): 182.

47. See the chapter by James Campbell in this book.

48. Quoted in Rothenberg, *Party Switches*, 30.

49. Ibid., 29–30.

50. Petrocik, "Realignment," 371–72.

51. Of the forty-five Democrats from districts with fewer than 20 percent black voters, fifteen are from mostly rural districts in Texas.

52. An unusual alliance between blacks and Republicans aimed at creating several additional black-majority districts may weaken this advantage for Democrats in 1992. Democrats obviously prefer to spread the influence of their black partisan loyalists. Whether this attempt will be successful and to what extent it will alter the partisan balance in the South remains to be seen.

53. See Rohde, "Variations in Partisanship," and his forthcoming book on the Democratic party in the South. See also Carmines and Stimson, *Issue Evolution*.

54. *Congressional Quarterly Weekly Report* (1 August 1987): 1704.

55. Ibid.

CAROL M. SWAIN

3 | Changing Patterns of African-American Representation in Congress

> Twenty years ago, black members couldn't even eat in the House dining room. It was an unwritten rule. . . . Now I'm chairman of the committee that has jurisdiction over that dining room.
> (Representative Augustus Hawkins, March 11, 1983)[1]

In 1870 the first African-Americans, beaten down by slavery but rejuvenated by Lincoln, took their seats in Congress.[2] In the intervening century and a quarter, vast changes have taken place in the political status of African-Americans on and beyond Capitol Hill, especially in the House of Representatives. By 1989 the House majority whip was an African-American, five blacks chaired full House committees, and seventeen chaired subcommittees. The penetration of blacks into the House power structure represents a dramatic change for a group whose numbers have fluctuated over time. Their progress from the Reconstruction Era through the twentieth century was not linear; it was slow and unsteady, punctuated by regressions and resurgences.

By the 1990s the number of African-American representatives continued to increase, as did the diversity of the districts from which they were elected and their views on policy and ways of fulfilling their responsibilities as representatives. In particular, more and more blacks were elected from districts that were not predominately black, and they were falling into the traditional congressional pattern of giving the interests of their districts first priority and other matters second priority.

In order to examine the changing pattern of black representation in

Congress, from the Reconstruction Era to the present, it is necessary first to consider what the notion of representation entails. Representation, W.B. Gallie observes, is an "essentially contested concept"—that is, one that is used with discrepant meanings and assumptions which can lead scholars into empty debates.[3]

Of the many analyses of the concept, that of Hannah Pitkin is most useful for present purposes. Pitkin distinguishes between *descriptive representation* and *substantive representation*. The first is the statistical correspondence of the characteristics of the representatives and those of their constituents, the second is the substantive correspondence of the representatives' goals and those of the majority of their constituents.[4]

Descriptive representation can be examined by comparing the incidents of particular characteristics—for example, race, gender, religion, occupation, or age—in the population and in the representation. Black Americans are descriptively represented to the extent that they are represented by black officeholders. Shared race or ethnicity, however, is not necessary for substantive representation, and it says little about a member's actual performance. "Being typical may be roughly synonymous with being representative," Bernard Grofman points out, "but it is neither a sufficient nor necessary condition for effective representation."[5]

Students of African-American politics such as Robert Smith, Diane Pinderhughes, and Mack Jones recognize that more black faces in political offices may not lead to tangible gains for African-Americans.[6] They refer to a third form of representation, namely *symbolic*, to refer to the failure of black (and, by extension, any) elected officials to advance the policy interests of their group.[7] In effect, these scholars are referring to descriptive representation that is not accompanied by substantive representation.

In what follows I first trace the descriptive representation of blacks in Congress in the Reconstruction Era and then ask whether descriptive representation was accompanied by substantive representation in that period of American history. I then consider black representation in Congress in the twentieth century, also examining descriptive representation and its substantive implications, in effect comparing the extent to which blacks were substantively represented in Congress in the two periods. In a brief concluding section I explore the outlook for the future of black representation in Congress.

Black Representation in the Reconstruction Era

The Reconstruction Era began in 1870 and is traditionally viewed as having ended with the Compromise of 1876. In that year disputed electoral votes in the presidential contest resulted in a constitutional crisis that ended when Samuel Tilden, the Democratic candidate with an undisputed 184 of the 185 electoral votes needed to win, conceded to Rutherford Hayes, the Republican candidate who was then declared president. In exchange for the needed electoral votes, the Republican party abandoned its attempts to advance the interests of African-Americans and in effect left the South to deal with its black population as it saw fit.[8] For purposes of this chapter, I extend the discussion of the Reconstruction Era through 1901, when the last African-American representative from the first wave of black electoral activity left Congress.

Twenty-two African-Americans served in Congress between 1869 and 1901—twenty in the House of Representatives and two in the Senate. They are enumerated by Congress and years of service in Table 3.1 and listed by name, party, and state in Table 3.2. The influence of Lincoln and emancipation was overwhelmingly evident in their party affiliations—all were Republicans.

African-Americans served in Congress for three decades in the post–Civil War period. The initial breakthrough was in the Forty-first Congress (1869–71), which had three black members. Between the Forty-first and Forty-fourth Congresses, the number of black legislators grew rapidly but peaked early in the Forty-fourth Congress (1875) with eight members. After 1875 Congress was characterized by the sporadic and dwindling presence of African-Americans. No blacks served during the Fiftieth Congress, three served during the Fifty-first, and between the Fifty-second and Fifty-sixth Congresses the institution averaged one black member per session.

Table 3.3 shows the distribution of black members of Congress by state and percentage black. As might be expected, the first African-American representatives came from states with high black populations—the former slave states of the South. No state outside the South elected African-American representatives until well into the twentieth century. South Carolina (59 percent black) elected eight blacks to the House. Mississippi (54 percent black) and Louisiana (50 percent black) each elected one black, and the former sent two blacks to the Senate.

Table 3.1

African-American Representatives by Year and Congress: Reconstruction Era

Year	Congress	Number
1869–71	41st	3
1871–73	42nd	5
1873–75	43rd	7
1875–77	44th	8
1877–79	45th	4
1879–81	46th	1
1881–83	47th	2
1883–85	48th	2
1885–87	49th	2
1887–89	50th	0
1889–91	51st	3
1891–93	52nd	1
1893–95	53rd	1
1895–97	54th	1
1897–99	55th	1
1899–1901	56th	1

Source: Compiled from data found in the Congressional Research Service, Library of Congress.

Five other states with sizable black populations—Alabama, Florida, Georgia, North Carolina, and Virginia—elected the remaining twenty black representatives. Although blacks were elected to Congress only in states with high percentages of blacks, the exact percentage was uncorrelated ($r = -.0006$) with the number of blacks elected. Far more important was the percentage of blacks within each district. Over 90 percent of the Reconstruction Era black representatives were elected from districts with black majorities.[9]

Despite the large black populations of the South, African-Americans elected fewer black politicians than some historians imply. Allan Nevins, for example, asserts that the North granted ''the Negro a full participation in the rights and duties of free society'' and that it took ''the millions of former slaves . . . [and] placed them in charge of the delicate and complicated mechanism of modern democracy.''[10]

Nevins's statement is an exaggeration. Several former slave states—Arkansas, Tennessee, Texas, and West Virginia (part of a former slave state)—never elected black representatives. In fact, far fewer African-Americans served in Congress than might be expected by the size of the black population. The same can be said for state governments.

Table 3.2

African-American Representatives by Party, State, and Congress: 1869–1901

Senate

Hiram R. Revels	(R-MS)	41st
Blanche K. Bruce	(R-MS)	44th, 46th

House

Joseph H. Rainey	(R-SC)	41st, 42nd, 43rd, 44th, 45th
Jefferson F. Long	(R-GA)	41st
Robert C. Delarge[a]	(R-SC)	42nd
Robert B. Elliot[b]	(R-SC)	42nd, 43rd
Benjamin S. Turner	(R-AL)	42nd
Josiah T. Walls	(R-FL)	42nd, 43rd, 44th
Richard H. Cain	(R-SC)	43rd, 45th
John R. Lynch	(R-MS)	43rd, 44th, 47th
James T. Rapier	(R-AL)	43rd
Alonzo J. Ransier	(R-SC)	43rd
Jeremiah Haralson	(R-AL)	44th
John A. Hyman	(R-NC)	44th
Charles E. Nash	(R-LA)	44th
Robert Smalls	(R-SC)	44th, 45th, 47th, 48th, 49th
James E. O'Hara	(R-NC)	48th, 49th
Henry P. Cheatham	(R-NC)	51st, 52nd
John M. Langston	(R-VA)	51st
Thomas E. Miller	(R-SC)	51st
George W. Murray	(R-SC)	53rd, 54th
George White	(R-NC)	55th, 56th

Source: Congressional Research Service, Library of Congress.
Notes:
[a] Unseated by contested election.
[b] Resigned.

Despite the black majorities in several southern states, only 794 African-American state legislators served between 1870 and 1901.[11]

The high visibility of black politicians during this period nevertheless led many white southerners to view them as part of an "unholy triumvirate" with "scalawags" and "carpetbaggers," the white southerners and relocated northerners who took part in the Reconstruction Era governments.[12] The electoral success of blacks during the first three decades after the Civil War was partially traceable to structural changes and the efforts of the federal government to empower the newly freed slaves and partially to black mobilization and coalition building with sympathetic whites. But these successes were remarkably limited, even with respect to descriptive representation.

Eric Foner writes that during the Reconstruction Era of 1865–77,

Table 3.3

Correlation between Reconstruction Era African-American Representatives and the States' 1870 Percentage Black

State	% black	Congress		Total
		Senate	House	
South Carolina	59	0	8	8
Mississippi	54	2	1	3
Louisiana	50	0	1	1
Florida	49	0	1	1
Alabama	48	0	3	3
Georgia	46	0	1	1
Virginia	42	0	1	1
North Carolina	37	0	4	4

N = 22

r = .0006

Source: Compiled from data found in U.S. Department of Commerce, Bureau of the Census, Current Population Reports, series p–23, no. 67, 17.

African-Americans embraced ''an affirmation of Americanism that insisted that blacks formed an integral part of the nation and were entitled to the same rights and opportunities that white citizens enjoyed.''[13] Although the majority of African-Americans who emerged from slavery were illiterate, with few qualifying as voters,[14] by 1867 many had joined with whites in political organizations such as the Friends for Universal Suffrage, National Equal Rights League, and Union Free State party.[15] They studied the Declaration of Independence, eagerly embracing its tenets that ''all men are created equal . . . [and] are endowed by their creator with certain inalienable rights.''[16] Through the Freedmen's Aid organizations the federal government provided the newly freed slaves with access to voting registrars, who instructed them in American history and government.[17]

The earliest biracial coalitions resulted in the election of sympathetic white politicians from the ranks of the scalawags and carpetbaggers, but a growing frustration with the tendency of these coalition strategies to cast blacks as ''junior partners'' led African-Americans to demand more representation in the descriptive sense. In 1870 blacks in South Carolina demanded a fairer share of political offices. They gained concessions which resulted in African-Americans being elected to four of the eight state executive offices, three of the five congressional seats, and the placement of one on the state supreme court.[18] An observer at the 1873 South Carolina state legislative session noted: "The Speaker is black, the clerk is black, the doorkeepers are black, the little pages are black, the chairman of the Ways and Means Committee is black, and the chaplain is coal-black."[19]

In Mississippi, blacks were partially responsible for the election of the two black senators of the Reconstruction Era. The first breakthrough occurred when delegates to that state's Republican convention demanded that the legislature select a black to fill the unexpired term of Jefferson Davis, the former president of the Confederacy. Hiram Revels, who thus became the first African-American senator, explained the circumstances surrounding his nomination:

> An opportunity of electing a Republican to the United States Senate to fill an unexpired term occurred, and the colored members after consulting together on the subject, agreed to give their influence and votes for one of their own race for that position, as it would be in their judgment a weakening blow against color line prejudice, and they unanimously elected me for their nominee. Some of the [Democrats] . . . favored it because they thought it would seriously damage the Republican Party. When the election was held everything connected with it was quiet and peaceable and I [was] elected by a large majority.[20]

Galvanized by their success, African-American delegates at Mississippi's 1873 Republican State Convention moved that three of seven state-level vacancies be filled by African-Americans. In introducing this motion, the delegates argued that they were entitled to a proper share of state offices and were tired of voting for white men.[21] Black voter strength in the state eventually led the first governor of the reconstructed Mississippi, a white, to declare his intent to "vote with the Negro, discuss politics with him, sit if need be, in council with him, and form a platform acceptable to both."[22]

In summary, the newly emancipated African-Americans appeared to believe that they were entitled to the same rights enjoyed by white men, including the right to elect members of their own race. Blacks made it evident that they believed that democratic principles guaranteed them a right to share in governance. After their coalitions with whites yielded few black officeholders, they demanded descriptive representation, i.e., more black faces in political office.

A majority of the African-Americans who served in Congress between 1870 and 1901 were former slaves, but they were not illiterate. Half had attended college and five were graduates. Their colleges and universities included Oberlin (Ohio), Howard (District of Columbia), Knox (Illinois), Shaw (North Carolina), University of South Carolina, and Wilberforce (Iowa). Only of Benjamin S. Turner (R-AL) was it said that "he could write his name and nothing more."[23] The historian Terry Seip, who has closely examined their performance, concludes that "most demonstrated a command of the language equal to that of their white peers."[24] As a group, they had a remarkable amount of political experience for blacks in the period following Emancipation: seventeen of the twenty-two had held prior elective office.

Nor were black representatives poor. Seip reports only one with an estate less than $1,000.00, while five had estates ranging from $5,000 to $20,000, which were respectable fortunes in that era.[25] Among the wealthiest were Josiah Walls, who was able to use his salary to buy a huge estate from a former Confederate general, and Blanche K. Bruce, who was said to have acquired a fortune in real estate.[26] Thus African-American representatives had economic interests more like whites than blacks.[27] Perhaps as a consequence, they did not seek economic revolution. Indeed, many worked to return lost economic power to white southerners.[28]

Apart from being black in terms of the legal definition (one-eighth black ancestry), many of the blacks in Congress were not even representative of African-Americans in appearance. Photographs published in *Black Americans in Congress* show twelve with marked Caucasian features, which suggests that many of them may have identified more with whites than blacks.[29] Some of them may have shared the ambivalence sometimes associated with mixed racial ancestry. This was expressed by a black candidate for a South Carolina office, who declared in 1868, "I never ought to have been a slave, for my father was a gentleman. . . . If there ever is a nigger government—an unmixed nigger government . . . I shall move."[30]

The *Congressional Globe* of the era shows petition after petition introduced by black representatives seeking the return of the lost political rights of the former rebels. In general, the freed slaves who took part in Reconstruction Era politics evinced little vindictiveness. Even in states such as South Carolina, where blacks had substantial political power, they made no concerted efforts to subjugate whites. In an 1871 speech before the U.S. House of Representatives, Representative Joseph Rainey brought this to the attention of his colleagues when he asked rhetorically whether blacks had presumed to take improper advantage of the majority they hold in the state [South Carolina] by disregarding the interests of the minority? "They have not," he replied. "Our convention which met in 1868, and in which the Negroes were in a large majority, did not pass any prescriptive or disfranchising acts, but adopted a liberal constitution, securing equal rights to all citizens, white and black, male and female. . . . Mark you we did not discriminate, although we had a majority. Our constitution towers up in its majesty with provisions for the equal protection of all citizens."[31]

Most of the twenty-two blacks in Congress served on at least one committee. Six served on the Education and Labor Committee, four on Agriculture, and four on Public Expenditures. Blacks were also represented on the District of Columbia, Library of Congress, Manufactures, Mining, Militia, Pensions, and War Claims committees. There was only one black chairman, however, and he served on a minor committee—Levees and Dikes of the Mississippi River. Black representatives sought to advance both national issues affecting their states and districts—for example, public education and protective tariffs for local products—as well as more specifically black issues, such as relief for depositors of the failed Freedman's Savings and Trust Company. They also worked for more equitable treatment of Indians.[32] Their successes, however, did not go beyond easily obtained political patronage appointments such as postmaster, customs inspector, and internal revenue agent for their constituents. They had few legislative accomplishments; most of their bills languished in committee.[33] Not all blacks pursued the interests of their African-American constituents. Manning Marble notes that although the black Republicans were in favor of suffrage for black males, many "openly flirted with denying voting rights to the poor."[34] For example, John Langston (R-VA) who served on the House Committee on Education, introduced a measure which would have disenfranchised a significant proportion of the former slaves by requiring all voters to be able to read and write before voting in federal elections.[35]

Alert to their minority status, the African-American representatives presented their legislative goals as measures affecting both races so as to garner white support. South Carolina Congressman Joseph Rainey, for example, in a speech in support of civil rights legislation, acknowledged "a certain degree of truth" to the claim that the legislation was "for the protection of colored people" but declared that it would also protect "those loyal whites, some to the manor born . . . who, in the exercise of their rights as American citizens, have seen fit to move thither from other sections of the states, and who are now undergoing persecution simply on account of their activity in carrying out Union principle and loyal sentiments in the South."[36]

The constraints on what black Reconstruction Era representatives could accomplish are suggested by their own poignant references to personal experiences with discrimination. Each of the seven blacks in the Forty-third Congress gave speeches in support of the Civil Rights Bill of 1875, many of them citing a litany of public humiliations. One spoke of being ousted from a Virginia streetcar, another of being forced to sit in a railroad smoking car with undesirables, still others of being denied service in inns and restaurants.[37]

A number of events and forces spelled an end to Reconstruction and black representation in Congress: the Hayes-Tilden compromise of 1877, Supreme Court decisions that negated the effect of the Fourteenth Amendment and the Civil Rights Act of 1875, intimidation of black voters by the Ku Klux Klan, and all of the other concomitants of the return to power of the former confederates and their allies. By the turn of the century black representation seemed about to end, even at the descriptive level. Only one black member remained, George White of North Carolina.

In an 1899 speech White observed that he and his compatriots had been modest in their demands:

> Our representation is poor. . . . We have kept quiet while numerically and justly we are entitled to fifty-one members of this House; and I am the only one left. We kept quiet when numerically we are entitled to a member of the Supreme Court. We never had a member, and probably never will; but we have kept quiet. . . . We should have the recognition of a place in the President's Cabinet. . . . We are entitled to thirteen United States Senators, according to justice and our numerical strength, but we have not one and possibly will never get another; and yet we keep quiet.[38]

White was to be the last African-American to serve in Congress for twenty-eight years. In his 1901 farewell address, White expressed a view that must have been shared by other black politicians: "This, Mr.

Chairman, is perhaps the Negro's temporary farewell to the American Congress; but let me say Phoenix-like he will rise up someday and come again. These parting words are in behalf of an outraged, heart-broken, bruised and bleeding, but God-fearing people. . . ."[39]

White's departure occurred during the Jim Crow era of white primaries, literacy tests, and grandfather clauses.[40] It represented his voluntary decision in an increasingly hostile environment. The racist climate that led blacks to conclude that staying in Congress was futile was captured in a 1900 cartoon published in the *Raleigh News and Observer* which depicted White "as a creature with a human head, dragon's spine, and an elephant's trunk dipping into a container," representing the public till. The caption read, "He doesn't let go, but most people think our Negro Congressman has had it [his salary] long enough."[41]

The first African-American congressmen were clearly trail blazers, but there is disagreement about their actual impact. W.E.B. DuBois quotes two commentators with differing interpretations of the group and its impact. One concluded that, "They left no mark on the legislation of their time; none of them, in comparison with their white associates attained the least distinction." The other made an observation carrying more positive implications: "The colored men who took seats in both Senate and House did not appear ignorant or helpless. They were as a rule studious, earnest, ambitious men, whose public conduct . . . would be honorable to any race."[42]

The second observation seems to have been more accurate, but as responsible as these pioneers were, the times, the precariousness of their situations, and the attitudes of their white colleagues kept them from accomplishing much in the way of substantive representation.[43] Even their descriptive representation was inadequate in that their numbers never approximated the ratio of blacks to whites in the population, their educational and financial achievements exceeded that of almost all blacks, and indeed many of them were not black in appearance.

Black representatives may have made a nonlegislative contribution. Some white colleagues must have been struck by the many petitions that they introduced on behalf of their former masters. The eloquence of speakers like Elliot and Rainey and their sophistication and reasoning undoubtedly helped, however modestly, to break down their white colleagues' notions of black inferiority. However, the twentieth century brought eloquence *and* effectiveness in the second wave of blacks in Congress.

Black Representation in the Twentieth Century

After the resignation of George White in 1901, no blacks served in Congress for twenty-eight years (the Fifty-seventh–Seventieth Congresses). A number of forces resulted in gradual but significant increases in the number of blacks in Congress. These included urban migration, which made possible the concentration of large numbers of blacks in cities like Chicago, Philadelphia, Detroit, and New York, court decisions affecting reapportionment and redistricting, and the passage and implementation of the Voting Rights Act of 1965. Safe electoral seats made it possible for African-American representatives to gain the seniority necessary to rise in power in a way that was not possible during the Reconstruction Era. Increasingly, congressional blacks have come to be as favorably situated in the opportunity structure as are whites.

Tables 3.4 and 3.5 list twentieth-century blacks by Congress, year, name, party, and state. Virtually all of the twentieth-century black representatives have been college educated. During the 101st Congress, for example, only two of the twenty-four black members lacked college degrees. Five held law degrees and cited attorney as their prior occupation. Another five held masters degrees. One had a Ph.D. and another was in a Ph.D. program. This educational level contrasts strikingly with that of the African-American population, where in 1980 only about eight percent had attended college.[44] Thus the twentieth-century blacks in Congress are like those in the Reconstruction Era in being uncharacteristic of the African-American population.

As in the Reconstruction Era, many of twentieth-century congressional blacks held prior political office—most often in state legislatures and city councils. Others are clergymen, teachers, professors, and former business executives.[45] In terms of education, income, and occupation, these black representatives resemble their white counterparts more than they do their African-American constituents.

The turnover rate of twentieth-century African-American representatives has been low. Only a handful of those who left Congress were defeated (all in primaries)—Adam Clayton Powell, Jr. (1945–67, 1969–71), Robert Nix (1958–78), Katie Hall (1982–84), Bennett Stewart (1979–81), and Alton Waldon (1986). The one black Republican senator, Edward Brooke, was defeated in a general election after serving in the Senate for twelve years.

Table 3.4

African-American Representatives by Year and Congress: Twentieth Century

Year	Congress	Number
1901–1929	57th–70th	0
1929–1935	71st–73rd	1
1935–1943	74th–77th	1
1943–1945	78th	1
1945–1955	79th–83rd	2
1955–1957	84th	3
1957–1963	85th–87th	4
1963–1965	85th–95th	5
1965–1967	89th	6
1967–1969	90th	6
1969–1971	91st	11
1971–1973	92nd	14
1973–1975	93rd	17
1975–1977	94th	18
1977–1979	95th	18
1979–1981	96th	17
1981–1983	97th	19
1983–1985	98th	21
1986–1988	99th	21
1988–1990	100th	23
1990–1991	101st	24
1991–1993	102nd	26

Source: Compiled from data found in the Congressional Research Service, Library of Congress.

The second wave of black electoral activity began in 1928 with the election of Oscar DePriest (R-IL) from an inner-city Chicago district. Like the Reconstruction Era blacks before him, DePriest was elected from a majority black district. He won office after black constituents, tired of voting for white politicians, agitated for a black representative. DePriest's election made him a celebrity. He came to be viewed as the national representative of the then eleven million African-Americans. In fact, the modest descriptive representation he provided conveyed little substance: he introduced no legislation during his first congressional term. During his second term his performance improved only slightly. He sponsored an unsuccessful bill calling for the integration of the House Restaurant.[46] (Real desegregation of the restaurant was not destined to occur until three decades later.) After serving in the Seventy-third and Seventy-fourth Congresses, DePriest was defeated

Table 3.5

African-American Representatives by Party, State, and Congress

Senate	Edward W. Brooke III	(R-MA)	90th–95th
House	Oscar DePriest	(R-IL)	71st–73rd
	Arthur W. Mitchell	(D-IL)	74th–77th
	William L. Dawson	(D-IL)	78th–91st
	Adam C. Powell, Jr.[b]	(D-NY)	79th–90th, 91st–92nd
	Charles C. Diggs, Jr.	(D-MI)	84th–96th
	Robert C. Nix, Sr.	(D-PA)	85th–95th
	Augustus F. Hawkins	(D-CA)	88th–101st
	John Conyers, Jr.	(D-MI)	89th-
	Shirley Chisholm	(D-NY)	91st–97th
	William L. Clay	(D-MO)	91st-
	George W. Collins	(D-IL)	91st–93rd
	Louis Stokes	(D-OH)	91st-
	Ronald V. Dellums	(D-CA)	92nd-
	Ralph H. Metcalfe	(D-IL)	92nd–95th
	Parren J. Mitchell	(D-MD)	92nd–99th
	Charles B. Rangel	(D-NY)	92nd-
	Walter B. Fauntroy[c]	(D-DC)	92nd–101st
	Yvonne B. Burke	(D-CA)	93rd–95th
	Cardiss Collins	(D-IL)	93rd-
	Barbara Jordan	(D-TX)	93rd–95th
	Andrew Young, Jr.	(D-GA)	93rd–95th
	Harold E. Ford	(D-TN)	94th-
	Julian C. Dixon	(D-CA)	96th-
	William H. Gray III	(D-PA)	96th-
	Melvin Evans[c]	(D-VI)	96th–97th
	Mickey Leland[a]	(D-TX)	96th-
	Bennett M. Stewart	(D-IL)	96th–97th
	George W. Crockett, Jr.	(D-MI)	96th–101st
	Mervyn Dymally	(D-CA)	97th-
	Gus Savage	(D-IL)	97th-
	Harold Washington	(D-IL)	97th–98th
	Katie Hall	(D-IN)	97th–98th
	Alan Wheat	(D-MO)	98th-
	Major Owens	(D-NY)	98th-
	Edolphus Towns	(D-NY)	98th-
	Charles Hayes	(D-IL)	98th-
	Alton R. Waldon, Jr.	(D-NY)	98th–99th
	Mike Espy	(D-MS)	100th-
	Floyd Flake	(D-NY)	100th-
	Kweisi Mfume	(D-MD)	100th-
	John Lewis	(D-GA)	100th-
	Donald Payne	(D-NJ)	101st-
	Craig Washington	(D-TX)	101st-
	Maxine Waters	(D-CA)	102nd-
	Gary Franks	(R-CN)	102nd-
	William Jefferson	(D-LA)	102nd-
	Barbara Rose-Collins	(D-MI)	102nd-
	Eleanor Holmes Norton[c]	(D-DC)	102nd-

Source: Mildred Amer, ''Black Members of the United States Congress 1789–1989,'' Congressional Research Services, August 10, 1989.
Notes: [a] Died in office. [b] The 90th Congress refused to seat him. [c] Nonvoting delegate.

in 1934 by Arthur Mitchell, the first black Democrat elected to Congress. DePriest's defeat was traceable to his failure to represent his district's interests, as evidenced by his failure to support Roosevelt's emergency legislation even though it would have helped his district.[47] More than five decades were to pass before another black Republican was elected to the House.

Arthur Mitchell's 1934 election was followed two years later by the 1936 Democratic landslide and was part of the New Dealers electoral realignment in which African-Americans transferred their loyalties en masse from the Democratic to the Republican party. Mitchell was considerably more active in Congress than was DePriest. He supported New Deal legislation and sponsored several bills of his own covering civil service reform, anti-lynching, desegregated interstate travel, and the creation of a Negro exposition. Still, he may have struck some of his black constituents as being overly conciliatory when he declared that 19,000 whites voted for him and he intended to represent them too, and when he supported the Supreme Court nomination of Hugo Black, a former Ku Klux Klansman, declaring that Black should be judged on his merits. "It is no more fair . . . to say that because a white man is from the South he is an enemy to the Negro than it is to say because you are a Negro you are worthless as an American citizen," Mitchell stated. "Other Congressmen may draw the color line, but I have not done it."[48]

In 1942, after eight years of service, Mitchell resigned and William Dawson succeeded him. Two years later, Adam Clayton Powell, Jr., was elected from Harlem. For the first time since 1891 there was more than one black representative in the House. In 1950 there was another breakthrough for black representation when Dawson gained enough seniority to become the first African-American to chair a standing committee, Government Operations. In 1960 he was followed by Powell, who became chairman of the Education and Labor Committee.[49]

Still another breakthrough came in 1966, when Senator Edward W. Brooke (R-MA), the third black senator in American history, was elected from a state less than 3 percent black. Brooke served until his defeat in 1978. Just as race had not earned him his office, it was not a factor in his defeat. Insiders had considered him vulnerable long before then. He rarely returned home and authored no major legislation. As if this was not enough, he underwent a highly publicized divorce.

Brooke's election was a harbinger for the elections of other blacks from majority white constituencies. Four years after his victory, Ronald Dellums (1970) was elected from a 75-percent white district. Thereafter, Andrew Young (1972), Harold Ford (1974), Alan Wheat (1982), Katie Hall (1982), and Gary Franks (1990) were elected from majority white districts, and not from the traditionally liberal constituencies in Massachusetts and Berkeley, California, which sent Brooke and Dellums to Washington. Since the early 1970s a much larger group of black representatives—Barbara Jordan (1972), Julian Dixon (1978), Mervyn Dymally (1980), Mickey Leland (1978), Floyd Flake (1986), and Craig Washington (1990)—have been elected in districts where no racial group constitutes a majority. Others, like William Clay (1968) and Charles Rangel (1970), held their seats as their majority black constituencies become majority white or Hispanic.

By 1990, 40 percent of the blacks in Congress represented districts that were less than 50 percent black. Black majorities are not the black politician's only route to Congress, thus refuting the conventional wisdom that majority black districts, preferably 65 percent or greater, are needed to elect black politicians.[50]

The election of black representatives from minority black districts is of the utmost importance for African-American representation. There are severe limitations on what can be achieved by relying on black majorities to elect black politicians, given the present distribution of the black population and the paucity of areas capable of sustaining new majority black districts. Indeed, the upper limit of possible black representation from majority black congressional districts has already been reached, and politically ambitious African-American politicians who hope to win national office are frustrated and blocked in their aspirations.

The contrast between the two eras of black representation could not be sharper. In the nineteenth century black representation decreased; in the twentieth century it increased. In the nineteenth century, blacks served short terms; in the twentieth century they have had continuous service and have risen in seniority. In the nineteenth century all black representatives were Republican; in the twentieth century, with few exceptions, all were Democrats. In the Reconstruction Era 92 percent of the blacks came from majority black congressional districts; in the twentieth century African-American representatives were no longer dependent on black majorities as their sole means to Congress. In the next section I consider what the above changes mean for the substantive representation of African-Americans.

The substantive representation of African-Americans had an unpromising start under Oscar DePriest but gained in vigor with the passage of time. Arthur Mitchell, William Dawson, and Adam Clayton Powell, Jr., were pioneers in attempting to bring a more substantive form of representation to African-Americans. While DePriest, Mitchell, and Dawson worked within the system to accomplish their goals through coalition-building, Powell was an outsider[51] who was perceived by his colleagues as an irritant. Because of their historical significance and because they represent polar types, Dawson and Powell are of particular interest. I shall discuss them in great detail, drawing on James Q. Wilson's classical analysis.[52]

Largely because of his confrontational manner, Powell was viewed as too militant by many whites, while some blacks viewed Dawson as too conciliatory. They won recognition for very different accomplishments, Dawson for gaining power in the House and the respect of his white colleagues, Powell for giving African-Americans a source of pride in the spectacle of a fearless black man who was ready to stand up to whites.

Politicians are strategic calculators of advantage.[53] Dawson and Powell, Wilson argues, were influenced by the nature of their respective political organizations and resources.[54] Dawson was a master politician, using the traditional patron resources of the Chicago machine and serving the black community within the confines of the Democratic party. Dawson once admonished his black constituents: "We must play the game according to the rules. I always play that way and I play with my team. If you are on a baseball team you stick with your team or you might not be able to play much longer."[55]

Powell, in contrast, relied on his personal charisma and his constituents' admiration of him. "I've always got my mouth open, sometimes my foot is in it, but it is always open," he once declared. "It serves a purpose; it digs at the white man's conscience."[56] Powell had a devoted following. He saw himself as a representative of the masses with a mandate to fight racism throughout the nation. His strength in the district allowed him to be militant, but his confrontational style eventually led to a multitude of troubles. He was sued by one of his constituents, who charged him with slander. At one time he was expelled from Congress on charges that he padded his payroll. When the Supreme Court ruled that Congress used illegal procedures in ousting him, he was reseated but stripped of his seniority. Finally, he was defeated in 1970 by Charles Rangel, Harlem's current representative.

If any one action of Powell typified his confrontational style it was the so-called Powell Amendment—his "killer amendment" to an education bill. In 1956, when Democratic party leaders sponsored a bill providing for federal funds for the construction of new schools, Powell used the occasion to strike a blow at segregation. He proposed an amendment that funds could go only to schools that desegregated in compliance with *Brown v. Board of Education of Topeka*.[57] The Powell Amendment, in effect, put civil rights ahead of education. The amendment passed when conservative Republicans opposed to federal aid to education strategically joined forces with liberal Democrats and voted in favor of the substitute language. In the end, however, the amended bill was defeated when the conservative Republicans, aligned this time with southerners opposed to integration, voted against its final passage.

The Powell Amendment posed a serious problem for white representatives of northern urban districts who favored school aid and represented large numbers of black constituents. Essentially, they were placed in a prisoner's dilemma situation.[58] If they voted against the amended bill, it could look to their constituents as if they favored segregation and would give a challenger an issue to place before black constituents. If they voted in favor of the amended bill, they were killing school aid because the amendment made the bill less attractive to southerners and they were defying their party's leadership. The Democratic leadership could issue sanctions, but only if defections were low. Members, caught up in the dilemma, were safe only if most Democrats voted the same way.[59] Representative Dawson voted with the Democratic leadership and voted against the Powell Amendment despite his black majority district. Most white northern representatives with black constituents supported the Powell Amendment, however, knowing full well that it would kill the school aid bill by making it less attractive to the southerners. In the above instance, Dawson was clearly supporting the substantive representation of African-Americans, since the passage of the unamended legislation would have resulted in new schools for blacks as well as whites. On the other hand, Powell's actions, while drawing attention to school segregation, had the short-term implications of denying better schools to both races, which occurred when his amendment passed and the final bill was defeated. As chairman of the Education and Labor Committee, Powell was capable of acting within the congressional system, presiding over much of the civil rights legislation that emerged from that committee during the 1960s.

The Institutional Aspects of Black Representation

Dawson and Powell operated without the formal organization that African-American representatives were to establish in later years, the Congressional Black Caucus (CBC). The caucus was formed in 1971, when the nine black members of the House organized to coordinate their individual efforts at representing African-Americans. According to Marguerite Barnett, "the CBC saw itself as Congressmen at large for 20 million Black people," with its creation being partially a response to renewed interest among blacks in electoral politics and partially a response to the Nixon administration's unofficial policy of "benign neglect" toward African-American interests.[60] The organization gathered information and articulated black interests, and it coordinated such activities as casework or scholarships.

The caucus was initially chaired by Charles Diggs, but members switched the chairmanship to Louis Stokes when it became clear that Diggs was not sufficiently aggressive. It took until 1990 for Ronald Dellums with almost twenty years of seniority to advance to the chairmanship; prior to that, CBC members considered him too assertive for the job.[61]

Early studies of the Black Caucus were critical of its performance. The more serious indictments implied that the caucus was not a dominant voting cue for its members and that it served more as a social organization than as an effective political entity.[62] Bruce Robeck concluded that the caucus and the blacks on the Hill made little difference in policy outcomes. He claims that it would not matter much if all black representatives were replaced by white northern Democrats.[63]

Marguerite Barnett's indictment was as severe.[64] She charged that the caucus was failing in its mission to deliver the types of legislation most needed by African-Americans. Barnett saw the organization as transforming itself through a series of stages characterized by different views of representation. In stage one, caucus members emphasized collective action to advance the interests of a national black constituency. In stage two, caucus members attempted to become "just legislators." According to Congressman Louis Stokes, "Our conclusion was this: if we were to be effective, if we were to make a meaningful contribution to minority citizens in this country, then it must be as legislators. This is the area in which we possess expertise—and it is within the halls of Congress that we must make this expertise felt."[65] The caucus's third stage blends the strategies of the first and second stages. It both mobilizes behind legislation and serves as a national forum for black interests. At present, the organization appears to be firmly entrenched in the third stage.

In spite of early legislative failures, the Black Caucus received much national attention for such activities as its 1971 boycott of Nixon's State of the Union address and for issuing its own message to the nation after Nixon refused to meet with the caucus. In 1972 the caucus sponsored a series of hearings on "Racism in the Media" and began a concerted effort to identify and respond to the needs of a "national black constituency." In 1974 it made a major substantive advance by wrestling an agreement from the House leadership to place at least one black member on each of the major committees.

In 1975 the caucus established the Action-Alert Network aimed at targeting white representatives in districts greater than fifteen percent black and threatening to mobilize their black constituents if they voted against legislation favored by the caucus. This "stick" approach was especially controversial given congressional norms of collegiality. From the start some African-American representatives disagreed with the tactic.[66] To the extent Mayhew is correct in describing congressmen as "single-minded seekers of reelection," then the activities of the caucus members were bound to be threatening to the white representatives they targeted.[67]

In 1988 the Black Caucus supplemented the controversial Action-Alert Network with a "carrot." At the urging of Alan Wheat (D-MO), a black representative from a 75-percent white district, the caucus opened its membership ranks to whites.[68] Forty-one white congressmen immediately joined as nonvoting associate members who pay $1,000 annual dues but are not allowed to attend its closed-door meetings (black members pay $4,000). White membership in the caucus makes the organization seem more mainstream and gives the white representatives an easy forum for position-taking. As recently as 1975 the caucus denied membership to Fortney Stark (D-CA), a white representative from a racially diverse constituency.

By 1989 the history of the Black Caucus appeared to be a complete success. At least one African-American sits on all major committees. Indeed, in 1989 one-quarter of all standing committees in the House were chaired by African-Americans. The caucus had established its own foundation, research group, and political action committee. Still, there are signs that the organization may be imperiled by its own successes. The sense of relative deprivation which led to its creation is gone and it may be difficult for individual caucus members to criticize the institutional arrangements of Congress when they are so much a part of the system. It is instructive that senior black members such as Ronald Dellums and John Conyers, once viewed as militants, now rarely criticize the system.[69] As one observer put it, "There's been a recognition . . . that you can't stand outside the castle and throw rocks anymore."[70]

Of course, the behavior of African-American representatives is affected by the characteristics of their districts.[71] Most blacks in Congress represent majority black districts, but increasing numbers are now from racially diverse constituencies. Some represent majority white districts. Although Black Caucus members come together for issues such as South African sanctions, civil rights, and busing, they are not cohesive in their voting behavior. Like white representatives, most appear to respond first to the electoral considerations imposed by their districts and second to their own values.[72] If the two are not in conflict, however, they are likely to go along with the preferences of the Black Caucus.

Accordingly, in recent years members of the Black Caucus have become more diverse in the issues they have supported and in their voting behavior. Representative Mike Espy (D-MS), for example, supports the death penalty and belongs to the National Rifle Association (NRA). In the past, African-American representatives have unanimously opposed the death penalty and are traditional supporters of tough gun control laws.

Many of the changes have occurred because the type of behavior that was consistent with the rise of blacks to power is not necessarily consistent with the requirements of being in power. To the extent that Congress is an organization where one must "go along to get along," then there are important trade-offs for black representatives. Some will be accommodating to the white majority. Others, like Chicago's Gus Savage, will remain militant and angry. Given such possibilities, it is not surprising that the Black Caucus has weakened in recent years. It has not been able to get unanimous support from its members for its annual alternative to the national budget since 1986. It is difficult to anticipate the future of the caucus, but as more and more African-Americans climb the leadership structure, it seems likely that it will cease being an organization geared primarily toward advancing a black agenda.

Important changes have occurred for blacks with regard to the committee structure. During the early 1970s, African-American representatives joined with other Democrats to pass a series of rules changes permanently altering the relationships between committee chairs and subcommittees. Changes predicted by Raymond Wolfinger and Joan Hollinger, who foresaw the rise of northern Democrats with the seniority to challenge aging southern Democrats in congressional longevity, have come to pass.[73] Blacks especially have benefited from these changes.

Moreover, the caucus arrangement for blacks to be assigned highly prized positions on the exclusive committees represented an important institutional change.[74] Prior to 1974, African-American representatives sat on nonexclusive and minor constituency committees. Table 3.6, listing committee assignments and ranks of black members of the 101st Congress, shows them well represented across committees. High seniority has led to five chairmanships. Also during the 101st Congress, two African-Americans chaired Select Committees, while seventeen chaired subcommittees. Presently over 75 percent of the African-Americans in Congress chair some committee or subcommittee.

In 1988 Walter Fauntroy commented on how in the early 1970s African-American representatives complained about the seniority system, but, he stated, "the longer we stay, the more we like it."[75] Representative Dellums (D-CA) explained that the chairmanship gave him "the opportunity to set the agenda, explore issues, bring in witnesses that have never been presented."[76] With more and more blacks chairing committees, there is an opportunity to effect a wide range of outcomes. This extends the influence of African-American representatives. Congressional norms of universalism, where committees try to include benefits in their legislation for as many members as possible, and reciprocity ensures that the system will operate to benefit majorities of all types.

The first real effort of African-Americans to rise to leadership positions occurred in 1971, when Representative John Conyers (D-MI) challenged Carl Albert (D-OK) for the speakership of the House. He was defeated 220 to 20 and dismissed by his colleagues as a prankster.[77] Representative Shirley Chisholm also made inroads, but the real penetration of African-Americans into the House power structure did not begin until after the 1978 election of Pennsylvania's William Gray III. Gray quickly moved from the co-chairmanship of the Democratic Leadership Council to Budget Committee chairman, to Democratic Caucus chairman, to majority whip.

Other African-Americans are also in crucial positions. After losing by a wide margin just three years earlier, Charles Rangel (D-NY) was elected deputy whip in 1989. During the 101st Congress, Rangel was joined by Mike Espy, John Lewis (D-GA), and Kweisi Mfume (D-MD), who were at-large whips. In addition to the whip posts, Harold Ford was a member of the Democratic Steering and Policy Committees, while William Clay (D-MO), Mervyn Dymally (D-CA), and Mike Espy sat on the Democratic Congressional Campaign Committee. Never in history have African-Americans been so close to the Speaker's chair.

With insider positions comes a special conflict between individual and collective goals. African-American representatives' quest for re-election and advancement may not coincide with caucus goals. For example, in recent years Representatives Gray and Espy have voted "present" rather than support the Black Caucus's alternative to the national budget. The passage below describes the circumstances leading to such stances:

> This new breed of black legislators bears striking similarities to the relatively independent lawmakers in both parties who have been elected to the House during the last decade. First, they worked painstakingly to build their own organizations to win election. Once in the House they have become issue activists and coalition builders eager for influence, not necessarily inclined to await the delayed rewards of the seniority system.[78]

Gray explained his position by stating, "It's not an issue of [being] black. The issue is: I'm chairman of the Budget Committee, a Demo-

Table 3.6

African-American Democratic Members of the House: Committee Assignments and Rank-standing Committees of the House, 101st Congress

Committee	Democratic members	African-American members and rank	
Exclusive			
Appropriations	35	Stokes	— 7
		Dixon	—19
		Gray	—25
Ways and Means	23	Rangel	— 4
		Ford	— 7
Rules	9	Wheat	— 7
Semi-Exclusive			
Agriculture	27	Espy	—22
Armed Services	31	Dellums	— 4
Banking, Finance and Urban Affairs	31	Fauntroy	— 3
		Flake	—25
		Mfume	—26
Education and Labor	22	Hawkins	— 1
		Clay	— 4
		Owens	—10
		Hayes	—11
		Payne	—14
		Mfume	—22
Budget	21	Espy	—12
Foreign Affairs	28	Crockett	— 7
		Dymally	— 9
		Payne	—28
Judiciary	21	Conyers	— 4
		Crockett	—11
Energy and Commerce	26	*Leland	—10
		Collins	—11
Public Works and Transportation	31	Savage	— 9
		Towns	—14
		Lewis	—18
Science, Space and Technology	29	None	

Nonexclusive

House Administration	13	Clay	— 8
District of Columbia	8	Dellums	— 1
		Fauntroy	— 2
		Gray	— 4
		Dymally	— 5
		Wheat	— 6
Interior and Insular Affairs	26	Lewis	— 2
Post Office and Civil Service	15	Clay	— 2
		*Leland	— 5
		Dymally	—11
Government Operations	24	Conyers	— 1
		Collins	— 2
		Owens	—13
		Towns	—14
		Payne	—22
Standards of Official Conduct	6	Dixon	— 1
Veterans Affairs	21	None	
Merchant Marine and Fisheries	26	None	
Small Business	27	Savage	—10
		Hayes	—16
		Conyers	—17
		Mfume	—19
		Flake	—20

Select Committees

Narcotics Abuse and Control	18	Rangel	— 1
		Collins	— 5
		Towns	—14
		Mfume	—16
Aging	39	Ford	— 1
		Crockett	—17
Hunger	18	*Leland	— 1
		Espy	—10
		Flake	—11
Children, Youth and Families	18	Wheat	—13

Sources: Congressional Black Caucus Publications; *Politics in America, 1990: The 101st Congress* (Washington: Congressional Quarterly, 1989); Barone, M. and Ujifusa, G. *The Almanac of American Politics 1990* (Washington: National Journal, 1989).

Note: *Died in office (August 1989).

crat. I build a consensus. I walk out with a budget. Now do I vote against my own budget? . . . that doesn't make a lot of sense.''[79]

His position has evoked criticism from other members of the Black Caucus. According to John Conyers, members "take exception" to Gray's refusal to show solidarity, especially when Gray has actively campaigned against caucus initiatives.[80] The tensions are apparent. In a recent interview a Black Caucus member quipped "Study Bill Gray. Which constituency does he represent? Is it the one who elects him, or is it the one that keeps him in power?"[81]

It is no less accurate for having been said so often that Congress is a club, where certain norms must be observed to advance in rank. Most leadership positions are either elective or appointed. Writing before the reforms of the 1970s, Herbert Asher summarized congressional norms as: (1) maintaining friendly relationships; (2) realizing the importance of committee work; (3) knowing procedural rules; (4) avoiding personal attacks during floor debates; (5) being willing to specialize; (6) being willing to trade votes; and (7) being willing to serve apprenticeships.[82] African-American representatives have not always observed these norms, but the newest African-American representatives appear to have no difficulty adhering to them.

In short, African-American representatives are assimilating just as other ethnic representatives have. One does not have to be a seer to see the direction and magnitude of the changes. They are becoming more like white liberal Democrats. They no longer automatically seek the traditional constituency committees, such as Education and Labor, Public Works, and Post Office. As Table 3.6 shows, they are represented throughout the committee structure, including the Rules, Ways and Means, and Appropriations committees. In these new positions, most seek to advance the legislative agenda advocated by black groups such as the National Association for the Advancement of Colored People and the National Urban League. But depending on their constituencies, they may depart from the positions taken by such groups. Mike Espy's positions on the death penalty and gun control, for example, are perfectly consistent with the preferences of his conservative, rural Mississippi constituency.

Increases in the number of blacks in Congress have been influenced by changes in the structure of political opportunities in the United States, particularly changes in the electoral system. During the Reconstruction Era federally facilitated black voter registration and educational programs led to the election of black politicians at all levels of government. Twentieth-century blacks were also aided by urban migration and the machine politics that facilitated competition for the black vote. In some areas, loyal blacks were rewarded with congressional seats once the black population reached a certain percentage and the white incumbent either died, retired, or became enmeshed in some type of scandal.

African-Americans were also greatly assisted by the decision of the Supreme Court to enter the "political thicket" of redistricting and reapportionment.[83] The Court's decision in *Reynolds v. Sims*[84] resulted in more representation for urban areas and increased the number of African-American state legislators, a traditional stepping stone to Congress. Similarly, the 1965 Voting Rights Act gave African-American politicians another big boost when it removed many of the barriers reducing the influence of southern blacks.

Finally, progress in race relations and the willingness of whites to support black candidates have meant an increase in the number of blacks who represent white constituencies. These blacks are more district-oriented than others, and they seek to bring substantive representation to all their constituents. Blacks are no longer representing just blacks. Still, the race of the voters is a dominant consideration in many official decisions regarding black representation.[85] This has led policymakers to emphasize descriptive representation—more black faces—over substantive representation.

More black faces in the halls of Congress have not transformed the circumstances of African-Americans. Black communities are beset with massive problems. It becomes clearer and clearer that the needs of these communities cannot be adequately addressed by the handful of blacks in Congress, or even the larger numbers that can come from districts that do not have large black populations. The blacks in Congress will need to coalesce with alliances with similar-minded white and Hispanic representatives to pass legislation beneficial to blacks and other disadvantaged Americans. Although twentieth-century black representation has been more substantive than ever before, further progress requires coalition-building that in turn calls for recognizing black representation when it comes from white members.

Conclusion

What is on the horizon for black representation in America? The picture is complex and not wholly consistent. First, the incumbency advantage in reelection will allow more black members to gain seniority; this will make for additional strength in committees and on the Hill. But the blacks in power may become less prone to advocate controversial issues that are in the interests of the disadvantaged majority of American blacks. More blacks may become traditional legislative brokers. These changes may further weaken the Black Caucus as more blacks pursue their individual goals. Similarly, a loss of influence will come with retirements, such as that of Augustus Hawkins, chairman of the Education and Labor Committee, who left in 1990 after twenty-eight years of service.

Second, the substantive representation of African-Americans is likely to be reduced by the Republican party's 1990s strategy of providing voting rights activists with the technology to draw black and Latino majority districts in the next round of redistricting.[86] This strategy, while ingenious on the part of the Republicans, has the potential to reduce black representation by increasing the number of Republicans in Congress. This occurs because once minorities are removed from the districts of white Democrats, they often lose to conservative Republicans. Thus the gain of one black representative may come at the expense of several white Democrats who might have provided additional votes for overriding a presidential veto or promoting a black-preferred legislative agenda.[87]

Third, because black representation is so heavily tied to the fortunes of the Democratic party, it is subject to change if and when the Democrats lose control of the House. If this happens, the majority of African-Americans quickly and automatically become minority members of the minority party. Gone will be the committee chairmanships, the leadership posts, and other key assignments. Black influence on the Hill is heavily dependent on the ability of the Democrats to organize Congress, at least the House of Representatives.

The rise of black Republicans may reduce the problem of being dependent on Democratic control. Since the early 1980s, several black Republicans have run and received their party's nomination. All lost in the general election until 1990, when Gary Franks of Connecticut, a conservative black, became the first black Republican House member since 1935.[88]

Prior to Franks's election, black Republicans ran almost exclusively in no-win situations with limited financial support from their party. In fact, they were routinely promoted in races where they stood a "snowball's chance in Hell of winning." Examples of the latter include Virginia's 1988 senatorial race, in which Maurice Dawkins, a black, ran against former Governor Chuck Robb, an extremely popular opponent; and Alan Keyes (R-MD), who took on incumbent Paul Sarbanes in a state where Democrats outnumber Republicans three to one. Both senatorial candidates complained of financial problems and a lack of party support.

The 1990 election of a black Republican changes the racial and partisan composition of the House, bringing descriptive representation to all blacks, with the ironic result of doing relatively little to ameliorate the condition of poor inner-city blacks. Still, one cannot say dogmatically that the election of black Republicans will diminish the representation of African-Americans; not all blacks are poor or ideologically liberal. The existence of a growing black middle and professional class, often geographically and socially separate from poorer blacks, makes it extremely difficult to say what (if anything) is in the black interest.

Other changes can be envisioned. In addition to the election of black Republicans, we can expect black representation to be enhanced by the presence of black Democrats in the Senate. This has never occurred in the history of the institution (all three black senators were Republicans), but all signs point in that direction. In North Carolina's 1990 senatorial race, for example, Harvey Gantt, a black Democrat, beat several white primary opponents, won the runoff election against a single white opponent, and came within seven points of defeating Jesse Helms, the arch conservative incumbent in a state that is 20 percent black. Despite speculation that racism was a major factor in the final outcome, Gantt's vote percentage (47 percent) was consistent with that of Helms's previous white opponents. He was able to hold Helms to his usual marginal victory.[89] Gantt's gains, along with the increasing number of blacks elected to statewide offices elsewhere in the nation, illustrate the potential for electing blacks to the Senate. Indeed, the signs point toward a time when the U.S. Congress will be composed of a racially diverse and partisan body.

It is clear that African-Americans have moved unevenly from the point at the nation's founding, when they were not counted as full human beings in the constitutional formula for reapportionment, through two waves of black representation in Congress. Now, 6 percent of the House of Representatives (to 12 percent of the nation) is black, and black descriptive representation in the Senate seems likely in the not-too-distant future. But how the increase in black descriptive representation will affect the increasingly varied substantive representation of blacks—and especially those on the bottom of the heap—remains to be seen.

Notes

I would like to thank Douglas Arnold, Richard Fenno, Fred Greenstein, and William Keech for their comments on earlier drafts of this chapter. I am also indebted to the National Science Foundation (SES-8723080) and the American Association of University Women for their generous financial support.

1. "For Blacks Racism and Progress Mix," *New York Times*, 11 March 1983.

2. I use the terms African-American and black interchangeably to refer to individuals of African descent.

3. W. B. Gallie, "Essentially Contested Concepts," *Proceedings of the Aristotelian Society* 56 (London, 1955–56), reprinted in *The Importance of Language*, ed. Max Black (Englewood Cliffs, NJ: Prentice-Hall, 1962): 121–46.

4. Hannah F. Pitkin, *The Concept of Representation* (Berkeley, CA: University of California Press, 1967); J. Roland Pennock and John W. Chapman, eds., *NOMOS X: Representation* (New York: Atherton Press, 1968); Ronald Rogowski, "Representation in Political Theory and in Law," *Ethics* 91 (April 1981): 395–430; Robert Weissberg, "Collective vs. Dyadic Representation in Congress," *American Political Science Review* 72 (1978): 535–48.

5. Bernard Grofman, "Should Representatives Be Typical of their Constituents?" In *Representation and Redistricting Issues*, ed. Bernard Grofman, Arend Lijphart, Robert McKay, and Howard Scarrow (Lexington, MA: Lexington Books, 1982), 99.

6. Robert C. Smith, "The Death of Black Politics," 1990 speech; Diane Pinderhughes, *Race and Ethnicity in Chicago Politics* (Chicago: University of Illinois Press, 1987), xix; Mack H. Jones, "Black Office-Holding and Political Development in the Rural South," *The Review of Black Political Economy* (Summer 1976).

7. Their usage differs from Pitkin's use of *symbolic representation* as a phenomenon, which occurs when constituents believe in the legitimacy of the representative because of what he or she is perceived to be, rather than what one actually achieves in office. Unlike descriptive representation, which can be discerned by the presence of shared demographic characteristics, or substantive representation, which can be identified through activities, symbolic representation is more ambiguous and less useful for characterizing black members of Congress.

8. W.E.B. DuBois, *Black Reconstruction in America* (New York: Harper and Row, 1935); Eric Foner, *Reconstruction 1863–1877* (New York: Harper and Row, 1988); John Hope Franklin, *Reconstruction: After the Civil War* (Chicago: University of Chicago Press, 1961).

9. Terry Seip, *The South Returns to Congress* (Baton Rouge: Louisiana State Press, 1983), 103–4.

10. Allan Nevins, *A History of American Life*. In *The Emergence of Modern America, 1865–1878*, ed. Arthur M. Schlesinger, Sr., and Dixon Ryan Fox, vol. 7 (New York: Macmillan, 1927), 27–28.

11. *National Roster of Black Elected Officials*, vol. 6 (Washington: Joint Center for Political Studies, 1976). Individuals are counted once regardless of the number of terms served.

12. Seip, *South Returns to Congress*, 2–3.

13. Foner, *Reconstruction 1863–1877*, 26.

14. Franklin, *Reconstruction*, 86.

15. Charles Vincent, *Black Legislators in Louisiana during Reconstruction* (Baton Rouge: Louisiana State Press, 1976).

16. Foner, *Reconstruction 1863–1877*, 283.

17. Ibid., 282.

18. Ibid., 352.

19. Francis Butler Simpkins, *South Carolina during Reconstruction* (Chapel Hill: University of North Carolina Press, 1932), 123–24.

20. Senator Hiram Revels, as quoted in Maurine Christopher's *Black Americans in Congress* (New York: Crowell, 1976), 3.

21. James W. Garner, *Reconstruction in Mississippi* (New York: Macmillan, 1901), 263.

22. Governor James Alcorn, as quoted in *Reconstruction in Mississippi*, 174–80.

23. Maurine Christopher, *America's Black Congressmen* (New York: Crowell, 1971); Edward Clayton, *The Negro Politician* (Chicago: Johnson, 1964), 32.

24. Seip, *The South Returns*, 20.

25. Ibid., 27–29.

26. Foner, *Reconstruction 1863–1877*, 360–61.

27. Marble, *Black American Politics* (London: Verso, 1988), 157.

28. Franklin, *Reconstruction*, 91–92.

29. Bruce Ragsdale and Joel Treese, *Black Americans in Congress* (Washington: Office of the Historian, U.S. House of Representatives, 1990).

30. Cited in Marble, *Black American Politics*, 149.

31. DuBois, *Black Reconstruction*, 630.

32. Ragsdale and Treese, *Black Americans in Congress*.

33. Foner, *Reconstruction 1863–1877*, 450.

34. Marble, *Black American Politics*, 151.

35. Christopher, *America's Black Congressmen*, 147.

36. Representative Joseph Rainey, as cited in the *Congressional Globe*, Part 1, First Session, Forty-second Congress 169:393–94. Similarly, Representative Robert Elliot asserted:

> I do not wish to be understood as speaking for the colored man alone when I demand instant protection for the loyal men of the South. No, sir, my demand is not so restricted. In South Carolina alone, at the last election, twelve thousand of the working white men in good faith voted the Republican ticket, openly arraying themselves on the side of free government. . . . The white Republican of the South is also hunted down and murdered or scourged for his opinions. (Ibid.)

37. Foner, *Reconstruction 1863–1877*, 533–34.

38. George White, as quoted in Christopher's *Black Americans in Congress*, 164–65.

39. George White, as cited in Clayton, *Negro Politician*, 37.

40. C. Vann Woodward, *The Strange Career of Jim Crow* (New York: Oxford University Press, 1974).

41. Christopher, *America's Black Congressmen*, 166.

42. DuBois, *Black Reconstruction*, 627.

43. See Foner, *Reconstruction 1863–1877*, 112.

44. Robert C. Smith, "The Black Congressional Delegation," *Western Political Quarterly* (June 1981): 209–10.

45. Charles Hayes (D-IL), with a high school education and a prior occupation of trade unionist president, is the exception to the norm. Still, he is clearly a member of the black middle class.

46. Matthew Holden, "Tabulation of Bills and Proposed Resolutions Relative to Afro-Americans, the 57th–80th Congresses (1901–1948)" (3 March 1987), unpub. archival data, University of Virginia.

47. Christopher, *America's Black Congressmen*, 174–75.

48. Arthur Mitchell, as cited in Maurine Christopher, *America's Black Congressmen*, 179–80.

49. Seven years later Powell was stripped of both his seniority and chairmanship after having been charged with an ethics violation.

50. Kimball Brace, Bernard N. Grofman, Lisa Handley, and Richard Niemi, "Minority Voting Equality: The 65 Percent Rule in Theory and Practice," *Law & Policy* 10, no. 1 (January 1988): 42–62; Bernard Grofman and Lisa Handley, "Minority Population Proportion and Black and Hispanic Congressional Success in the 1970s and 1980s," *American Politics Quarterly* 17, no. 4 (October 1989): 436–45.

51. Ralph K. Huitt, *Working within the System* (Berkeley, CA: Institute of Governmental Studies Press, 1990), Chap. 3.

52. James Q. Wilson, "Two Negro Politicians: An Interpretation," *Midwest Journal of Political Science* 5 (1960): 349–69.

53. Gary Jacobson and Samuel Kernell, *Strategy and Choice in Congressional Elections* (New Haven: Yale University Press, 1981); Roger Davidson and Walter Oleszek, *Congress and its Members* (Washington: Congressional Quarterly, 1985).

54. Ibid.

55. Clayton, *Negro Politician*, 73.

56. Ibid.

57. *Brown v. Board of Education of Topeka*, 349 U.S. 294, 1954.

58. A Prisoner's Dilemma Game refers to a two-player situation with players confronted by a choice of cooperating or defecting. Each player must make his/her choice in ignorance of the other player's move. Defection always yields a higher payoff than cooperation. The dilemma occurs because mutual defection leaves both players worse off than if they had cooperated. See Robert Axelrod, *The Evolution of Cooperation* (New York: Basic Books, 1984).

59. Arthur Denzau, William Riker, and Kenneth Shepsle, "Farquharson and Fenno: Sophisticated Voting and Home Style," *American Political Science Review* 79 (December 1985): 1117–35.

60. Marguerite Ross Barnett, "The Congressional Black Caucus," *Congress against the President*, reprinted in *Proceedings of the Academy of Political Science* 32, no. 1 (1975): 35–36.

61. Personal communications with CBC members (January 1989).

62. Arthur Levy and Susan Stoudinger, "Sources of Voting Cues for the Congressional Black Caucus," *Journal of Black Politics* 7: 29, 46.

63. Bruce Robeck, "The Congressional Black Caucus" (Paper delivered at the Annual Meeting of the American Political Science Association, Chicago, Illinois, 29 August–2 September 1974), 73.

64. Barnett, "The Congressional Black Caucus," *Proceedings of the Academy of Political Science*; "The Congressional Black Caucus," in *The New Black Politics: The Search for Political Power*, ed. Michael Preston, Lenneal Henderson, Jr., and Paul Puryer (New York: Longman, 1981).

65. Excerpt from Louis Stoke's July 1973 speech, as quoted in Barnett, "Congressional Black Caucus," 39.

66. Charles Jones, "Testing a Legislative Strategy: The Congressional Black Caucus's Action-Alert Communications Network," *Legislative Studies Quarterly* 12, 4 (November 1987): 521–37.

67. David R. Mayhew, *Congress: The Electoral Connection* (New Haven: Yale University Press, 1974).

68. Personal communications with Alan Wheat, October 1988.

69. Beth Donavan, "The Wilder-Dinkins 'Formula' Familiar to Blacks in the House," *Congressional Quarterly* (11 November 1989): 3099.

70. Ibid., 3100.

71. Richard Fenno, *Home Style* (Boston: Little, Brown, 1978).

72. Leo Rennie, "The Congressional Black Caucus: Confronting Individual and Collective Goals," unpub. seminar paper, Princeton University, 25 May 1989.

73. David Vogler, *The Politics of Congress*, 5th ed. (Needham Heights, MA: Allyn and Bacon, 1988), 152–57; Raymond Wolfinger and Joan Hollinger, "Safe Seats, Seniority, and Power in Congress," in *Readings on Congress*, ed. Raymond Wolfinger (Englewood Cliffs, NJ: Prentice-Hall, 1971), 54–55.

74. Barnett, "The Congressional Black Caucus."

75. Walter Fauntroy, speech made during the Congressional Black Caucus party, Atlanta, Georgia, July 1988.

76. "For Blacks Racism and Progress Mix," *New York Times*, 11 March 1983.

77. *Human Events Weekly*, 29 January 1971, 2.

78. Richard Cohen, "New Breed for Black Caucus," *National Journal* (26 September 1987): 2432.

79. William Gray, as quoted in "The Congressional Black Caucus May Be a Victim of Success," *The Washington Post National Weekly Edition*, 12 October 1987, 14.

80. Ibid.

81. Personal communications with Black Caucus member, August 1990.

82. Herbert B. Asher, "The Learning of Legislative Norms," *American Political Science Review* 67 (June 1973): 499–513.

83. Reapportionment concerns the redistribution of the nation's 435 congressional seats based on decennial census data of population shifts. Redistricting

involves the politics of how district lines are to be drawn within the individual states. Although there are certain criteria such as compactness, contiguity, and equal population, the process is highly political and the outcomes are often based on which party controls the state legislature. For a list of some of the relevant theoretical studies, see Q. Whitfield Ayres and David Whiteman, "Congressional Reapportionments in the 1980s," *Political Science Quarterly* 99, no. 2 (Summer 1984): 303–14.

84. *Reynolds v. Sims,* 377 U.S. 533 (1964).

85. Ayres and Whiteman, "Congressional Reapportionment"; Abigail Thernstrom, *Whose Votes Count?: Affirmative Action and Minority Voting Rights* (Cambridge: Harvard University Press, 1987); Frank R. Parker, *Black Votes Count* (Chapel Hill: University of North Carolina Press, 1990).

86. Peter Bragdon, "Democrats' Ties to Minorities May be Tested by New Lines," *Congressional Quarterly* (2 June 1990): 1739–42; James Barnes, "Minority Mapmaking," *National Journal* (7 April 1990): 837–39.

87. Charles Bullock, "Racial Representation Issues: The Role of the Experts in Determining Dilution of Minority Influence," *PS* 4 (Fall 1985): 759–68; Kimball Brace, Bernard Grofman, and Lisa Handley, "Does Redistricting Aimed To Help Blacks Necessarily Help Republicans," *Journal of Politics* 49 (1987): 169–85.

88. "Bleak Outlook for an Ohio Candidate Underlines Difficulties of GOP Blacks Running for Congress," *Wall Street Journal,* 28 August 1986; "GOP Conservatives after Eight Years in Ascendancy Brood Over Lost Opportunities," *Wall Street Journal,* 17 August 1988; "GOP Candidate Seeks To Open Eyes to Tokenism," *Wall Street Journal,* 2 September 1988; "A Black Congressional Hope in Connecticut," *New York Times,* 9 August 1990; "In Cincinnati House Contest, GOP Takes Aim at Elusive Goal: Victory for a Black Republican," *Wall Street Journal,* 17 August 1990.

89. "Helms Kindled Anger in Campaign, and May Have Set Tone for Others," *New York Times,* 8 November 1990.

L. SANDY MAISEL

4 Quality Candidates in House and Senate Elections, from 1982 to 1990

> Something's happenin' here,
> What it is ain't exactly clear.
>
> (Buffalo Springfield)

As both parties prepared for the 1990 congressional elections, windows of opportunity opened. Three United States senators were retiring and another was seeking his state's governorship. At least eleven representatives were retiring; another sixteen had announced they would leave the House to run for other offices. But interestingly, one of the common themes in the stories discussing these open seats was the reluctance of prominent potential candidates to throw their hats into the ring. In Idaho, the Republicans had two well-known candidates for the Senate seat being vacated by James McClure, but Congressman Richard Stallings and former Governor John V. Evans both declined to seek the Democratic nomination, leaving that slot on the ballot open for a less experienced candidate. Similarly in Colorado, Republican Congressman Hank Brown was seeking the seat vacated by William Armstrong, but all of the prominent Democrats mentioned as strong contenders decided not to run.[1] If this was the case in open seats, it was even more the case where challengers were sought to oppose incumbents. *Congressional Quarterly*'s Special Report, "Early Readings on '90 Elections," featured seat after seat in the House and Senate in which prominently mentioned challengers had decided not to take on potentially vulnerable incumbents.

Congressional elections justly receive a great deal of attention in both scholarly research and in the work of political journalists.[2] The electoral process is central to the functioning of a representative democracy. Only through elections can the citizens hold the government accountable; and only through competition can elections be effective agents of democracy. Thus the concern in recent research is that competition in House elections is approaching such a critically low level as to threaten the responsiveness of our political system. While a majority of the research has dealt with elections to the House, recent attention has turned to the Senate as well.

My research deals with the quality of candidates for Congress. More specifically, I am concerned with decisions by potential candidates *not* to seek seats in the House and Senate. Candidate quality is important because abundant evidence exists to show that better candidates—defined in a variety of ways—run more competitive campaigns and therefore present the electorate with a more meaningful choice.

In this chapter I examine the candidate pools for the 1982, 1984, 1986, and 1988 House and Senate elections; I also include preliminary analysis of those who sought congressional seats in 1990. By developing practical definitions of "candidate quality," I analyze the appearance of quality candidates in congressional races in the last decade. By looking at the entire pool of congressional candidates—in the House and Senate, in primaries and general elections, in open seats as well as those in which incumbents seek reelection—I hope to move toward a rethinking of recruitment patterns and of political ambition. In addition, I give attention to changing temporal contexts, noting the evolving nature of congressional campaigns.

Electoral Competition

The starting point for this examination is a concern for a lack of electoral competition in congressional elections. Every undergraduate student who has taken a course in American government knows that over 90 percent of those incumbents who have sought reelection to the House of Representatives in recent years have been successful. In fact, as Table 4.1 reveals, only once in the last two decades have fewer than 90 percent been reelected, and that was in the 1974 election, in which the Republicans suffered the backlash of Watergate. Many have already commented on the extraordinary success rates for House incumbents in the 1986 (98.0 percent), 1988 (98.5 percent), and 1990 (96.1 percent) elections, noting that electoral defeat now seems reserved for

Table 4.1

House and Senate Incumbents' Electoral Success, 1968–1990

Year	Total seeking reelection	Defeated in primary	Defeated in general	Reelected	Percentage successful
House elections					
1968	409	4	9	396	96.8
1970	401	10	12	379	94.5
1972	390	12	13	365	93.6
1974	391	8	40	393	87.7
1976	384	3	13	368	95.8
1978	382	5	19	358	93.7
1980	398	6	31	361	90.7
1982	393	10	29	354	90.1
1984	409	3	16	390	95.4
1986	393	2	6	385	98.0
1988	408	1	6	402	98.5
1990	407	1	15	391	96.3
Senate elections					
1968	28	4	4	20	71.4
1970	31	1	6	24	77.4
1972	27	2	5	20	74.1
1974	27	2	2	23	85.2
1976	25	0	9	16	64.0
1978	25	3	7	15	60.0
1980	29	4	9	16	55.3
1982	30	0	2	28	93.3
1984	29	0	3	26	89.6
1986	28	0	7	21	75.0
1988	27	0	4	23	85.2
1990	32	0	1	31	96.9

Sources: Data gathered from election issues of the *Congressional Quarterly Weekly Report*, and reported in various forms in many sources, including Norman J. Ornstein, Thomas E. Mann, and Michael J. Malbin, *Vital Statistics on Congress, 1989–1990* (Washington: Congressional Quarterly Press, 1990).

those who are involved in personal or political scandals. Studies of elections in the 1970s differentiated the difficulty which Senate incumbents had from the relative easy reelections faced by their House counterparts.[3] In the last six elections, however, at least three out of every four senators seeking reelection have also been successful, and the 1990 return rate of 96.9 percent is the highest since senators have been directly elected. Thus the Senate pattern in the last decade seems to be closer to that in the House than it ever was before.

Table 4.2

House and Senate Incumbents' Victory Margins, 1982–1990

Year	Incumbents in general election	Uncontested by other major party (a)	Hopeless challengers (<30%) (b)	Total (a+b)	Percentage of incumbents with little or no competition
House elections					
1982	383	56	104	160	41.8
1984	406	68	131	199	49.0
1986	391	74	157	231	59.1
1988	407	81	159	240	59.0
1990	406	83	89	172	42.3
Senate elections					
1982	30	0	3	3	10
1984	29	1	9	10	34.5
1986	28	0	4	4	14.3
1988	27	0	2	2	7.4
1990	32	4	5	9	28.1

Sources: Data gathered from annual editions of the *Congressional Quarterly Almanac*, Appendices on election returns.

Electoral victory is only one measure—albeit the most important one—of electoral competition. A slightly different picture emerges if one looks at victory margins. Electoral competition requires some opposition. The least competitive elections are those in which an incumbent faces no major party challenger. But elections in which incumbents score overwhelming victories over challengers also demonstrate that no real competition existed. When Gary Jacobson correlates vote margin in one election with the frequency of incumbent defeats in the next, his data suggest that unless a challenger polls more than 30 percent of the vote in the initial House election, the likelihood that the incumbent will be defeated the next time approaches zero.[4] Table 4.2 presents data on uncontested elections and elections contested by "hopeless" challengers in the decade of the 1980s; the 30-percent cutoff figure has been substituted for the more common 40-percent figure, which has traditionally been used to connote "marginality." House-Senate differences are apparent.

Table 4.2 reveals not only that incumbent members of the House of Representatives win an overwhelming percentage of the races they run, but also that they are facing no competition or hopeless competition more frequently. In 1988 nearly one-fifth of the House members seeking reelection faced no major party competition; another two-fifths faced competitors unable to mount serious campaigns. The fact that 98.5 percent of the incumbents seeking reelection did so successfully becomes even more meaningful when one realizes that very few of them faced any serious challenge. The level of competition in 1988 was not very different from that in 1986, but in these two elections 10 percent more of the incumbents seeking to return to Congress did so with little or no competition than had been the case in the first two elections under study. The 1990 election revealed a different pattern. In many districts no challenger emerged, but the victory margin for those incumbents who were challenged decreased significantly. Only 22 percent of the challengers ran "hopeless" campaigns, by far the lowest percentage in the decade. Political commentators felt that incumbents would be in trouble in 1990. In fact they won, but fewer of them in landslides. A logical explanation of this is that voters were dissatisfied but were thwarted in expressing this dissatisfaction because of the low quality of challengers.[5]

The more meaningful contrast is with the Senate. The data in Table 4.1 show that senators in the 1980s seem to be safer in reelection bids than they and their counterparts had been a decade earlier. However, Table 4.2 shows that those senators who were reelected faced more serious competition than did members of the House. During the first four elections studied, only one incumbent senator seeking reelection (Bennett Johnston of Louisiana in 1984) did not face major party competition.[6] Moreover, a vast majority of those running for reelection faced competitors who were able to poll at least 30 percent of the vote (though the amount of competition using this index also declined in 1990). Even if one uses the more restrictive 40-percent definition of a competitive race, approximately half of the incumbents who won during this period (and obviously all of those who lost) faced serious competitors.

Thus as our starting point we note that few House or Senate incumbents were defeated in the four elections studied. Further, we note that few of the representatives who won faced serious competition, but more senators did so. We also can see (from Table 4.1) that the number of incumbents who lost primary elections in either house has been on the decline. Primary competition against incumbents rarely stands as more than a slight annoyance on the road to reelection. Our next step then is to examine those who have challenged incumbents to determine if changes in the quality of challengers can be observed.

Quality of Congressional Challengers

No consensus exists on how to determine, before a race has actually been held, if a candidate is going to present a formidable challenge to an incumbent. The "quality" of a challenger is in essence either a subjective characterization or one that can only be definitively determined after an election has been held. Nevertheless, a number of scholars have attempted to arrive at surrogate measures in order to characterize challenger quality in advance of an actual election.

What characteristics are likely predictors of a competitive challenger? The answer, simply, is those traits needed to run a good campaign: the ability to gather a campaign staff and set up an effective organization; the ability to raise a sufficient amount of money; the ability to gain name recognition (or to have it in advance); the ability to relate to voters, one-to-one, in public forums and through the media; the ability to convince the voters that one is competent to hold the job sought, that one is trustworthy, in essence, that one has the personal traits that voters seek in officeholders; and ability or desire to pursue the goal of elective office with sufficient commitment. The list of characteristics could be expanded, but the qualities mentioned serve as a good starting point.

A decade ago, Gary Jacobson and Samuel Kernell suggested that previous electoral experience was a good surrogate measure for candidate quality.[7] Scholars have attempted to refine that definition in a number of ways since that time. Elsewhere Linda Fowler and I have reviewed the various definitions which have been attempted.[8] Our conclusion is that previous experience, if modified to eliminate that experience so old as to be irrelevant, is still the best objective measure for candidates for the House of Representatives. We believe that measures which have added more "sophistication" to the definition have frequently sacrificed accuracy—which often can only come with knowledge of the local context—for seeming precision. Further, Jacobson has demonstrated that there is a high correlation among the results obtained using the various measures.

On the other hand, it does seem possible to add more precision to the discussion of quality candidates in Senate races. This is possible largely because the number of candidates and seats involved is smaller and knowledge of the "local" context is more widespread. Thus, for example, governors, who by definition have run and won elections in the same electorate as they face as Senate candidates, stand out as extremely high-quality candidates. Those leaving House seats to run for the Senate have real advantages in terms of relevant legislative experience; but the extent to which their electoral experience is relevant depends, in part at least, on the number of seats their state has in Congress and on the media markets involved.[9] Other officeholders who have run and won statewide may have the appropriate electoral experience—though this depends in part on the prominence of their positions and the types of campaigns necessary to win them—but their "on-the-job" experience may not seem comparable to the electorate. The "ambitious amateur" category which David Canon has perceptively isolated is more easily operationalized for Senate races than for House races.[10]

For all of these reasons I have used different definitions of quality challengers in the analysis of House and Senate races below. For House races the definition of experienced candidates is those who are currently holding elective office, those who held office in the previous term (and might arguably have given up that office in order to seek election to the House), and those who have run credible campaigns for Congress in the district (defined as receiving 40 percent of the vote or more) in the past. As noted, this definition is not very different from Jacobson's, nor from Canon's, except that it includes those whose past performance would seem to make them competitive while excluding those whose previous officeholding may no longer be relevant because of the amount of time that has passed.

For the Senate races I have listed the different relevant experiences separately in order to examine whether the more prominent officeholders (1) have in fact been more successful, and (2) are seeking seats in the Senate more or less frequently. I have looked at governors and ex-governors, those who previously served in the United States Senate, members of Congress and former members, and other statewide elected officeholders or former holders of those offices. I added a final category labelled "celebrity," which attempts to capture the "ambitious amateurs" identified by Canon, i.e., those without previous electoral experience but who, because of their prominence in other fields, are

Table 4.3

Primary Challengers to Incumbents, 1982–1988

Year	Total seeking reelection	Unopposed in primary	Number of experienced challengers	Incumbents defeated	Defeated by experienced challengers
House elections					
1982	393	242	32	10	4
1984	409	254	24	3	0
1986	393	264	20	2	1
1988	408	318	14	1	0
Senate elections					
1982	30	15	1	0	0
1984	29	17	1	0	0
1986	28	16	1	0	0
1988	27	17	1	0	0

thought likely to be strong candidates.[11] This analysis thus allows for comparison across relevant experiences and over time. To compare House and Senate races in the decade, I have summarized the Senate races for the various kinds of "quality" candidates.

Primary Challengers to Incumbents

Table 4.3 deals with primary challengers to House and Senate incumbents seeking reelection. It can be summarized very briefly. Most incumbents face no primary opposition whatsoever. Those who do rarely face experienced challengers. And even those who face serious challengers rarely lose.

The exceptions tend to prove the rule. In 1988 the only incumbent senator facing an experienced challenger was David Karnes (R), of Nebraska who had been appointed to his seat upon the sudden death of Edward Zorinsky (D) in March 1987. Many thought that Republican Governor Kay Orr would appoint Harold J. Daub, a popular Republican congressman from Omaha, to succeed Zorinsky. When she appointed Karnes instead, she created a primary opponent for her choice. Though Karnes defeated Daub in the primary, former Governor Robert Kerrey won the general election.

In 1986 South Dakota's Republican Governor William Janklow was constitutionally ineligible to succeed himself and decided to challenge his party's incumbent junior senator, James Abdnor, who seemed vulnerable. Again, the incumbent won the primary but lost the general election. In 1982 and 1984 the experienced challengers were members of the House who were ideologically at odds with senators of their party seeking reelection (Tom Corcoran, who challenged Charles Percy in the Illinois Republican primary, and Jim Santini, a party-switcher who challenged Howard Cannon for the GOP nod). In both of these cases, as in the previous two, the incumbents won the primary but lost the general election.

The House examples are not so clear-cut, in part at least because of the less precise way in which experienced challengers are identified. However, it is clear that more and more incumbents are unopposed for renomination, that fewer and fewer experienced challengers are contesting nominations of incumbents, and (consequently) incumbents are virtually assured of their party's nod for reelection. Only two of the incumbents beaten in the last three elections were beaten by experienced challengers, and even those examples are really exceptions. In 1990 Ohio Republican Donald E. "Buz" Lukens finished third in a primary, losing to State Representative John Boehner and also finishing behind former Congressman Thomas Kindness. However, Lukens's defeat was not unexpected. A year before the primary he had been convicted of a misdemeanor as a result of a sexual liaison with a sixteen-year-old girl. His party had deserted him, and he did not even declare for renomination until a week before his defeat.

In a Democratic primary in 1986 Floyd Flake beat incumbent Alton Waldon, who had won the seat in a special election to fulfill the unexpired term of Democrat Joseph Addabbo, who had died suddenly in April. Waldon beat Flake by 276 votes in the special election, a margin won on contested absentee ballots. Flake, categorized as an experienced candidate because he had done well in that special election, reversed the decision in the Democratic primary held only two months later, before Waldon could garner many of the benefits of incumbency.

The only other two cases of incumbent defeats involve Republicans who had little seniority and were thought of as far out of touch with their constituents. Mark Siljander lost in Michigan's Fourth District in 1986 and Ernest Konnyu in California's Twelfth District in 1988; both were defeated by more mainstream Republicans who, nonetheless, were inexperienced candidates. Fred Upton, who defeated Siljander, was a former congressional staffer; Tom Campbell, Konnyu's successor, had been a Stanford professor before going to Congress. In each case the incumbent's record more than the challenger's ability led to the upsets.[12] The conclusion seems to be that experienced potential challengers act like strategic politicians. Those who do not run have something of value to lose and see little chance of succeeding in their quest for a higher office. Those who do run decide to do so only when circumstances indicate that the incumbent is vulnerable and could well be defeated.

Primary Challengers to Opposition Incumbents

Table 4.4 presents the background information on those who have sought the nomination to challenge an incumbent of the other party, that is, Democrats seeking to challenge incumbent Republicans and Republicans seeking to challenge incumbent Democrats. The number of districts (for House elections) and seats (for Senate elections) represents the number of incumbents of the other party seeking reelection. Thus in 1982 168 Republicans and 219 Democrats were seeking reelection to the House of Representatives; eleven Republicans and nineteen Democrats were seeking to return to the Senate. The number of experienced challengers represent those who sought the nomination, whether they were successful or not in so doing.

Examining data for the House of Representatives we see that after 1982, the number of experienced Democrats seeking to challenge Republicans, either in raw numbers or as a ratio to the number of seats to be contested, has remained approximately constant. For the Republicans, on the other hand, a downward trend is evident. While many more Democrats ran in the first election following the redistricting after the 1980 census, the same was not true for the Republicans. Moreover, in each election under study the proportion of experienced Republicans to contested seats has been lower than for the Democrats. And in each election that Republican ratio has declined from the election before, to the point that in 1988 only one experienced Republican sought nomination for approximately every nine seats held by Democrats, a proportion half of that for Democrats challenging Republicans. If experienced challengers do make better candidates, neither party has been very successful in recruiting these challengers, but the Republicans have been noticeably less so. These data do not speak to causality,

Table 4.4

Experienced Candidates Seeking Nominations to Challenge Incumbents in General Elections

	1982		1984		1986		1988	
	Dems	GOP	Dems	GOP	Dems	GOP	Dems	GOP
House elections								
Experienced challengers (a)	86	50	42	51	43	39	39	31
Number of districts[a] (b)	168	219	164	258	160	235	175	260
Ratio (a/b)	.51	.23	.26	.20	.27	.17	.22	.12
Senate elections								
Experienced challengers								
Governors	1	0	2	0	3	0	2	0
Ex-governors	1	0	1	0	2	2	3	0
Ex-senators	0	0	0	0	0	0	0	1
Congressmen	3	10	6	6	11	6	5	5
Ex-congress-men	2	1	1	0	2	1	1	2
State elected officials	3	0	4	0	3	0	5	1
Ex-state elected officials	0	0	0	0	1	0	0	0
Celebrities	1	1	0	2	2	3	2	1
Total (a)	11	12	13	8	24	12	18	10
Number of seats[a] (b)	11	19	17	12	19	9	12	14
Ratio (a/b)	1.00	.63	.76	.67	1.26	1.33	1.5	.71
Others								
State legislators	5	7	7	3	7	3	4	7
Ex-state legislators	2	0	2	6	1	0	0	1
No experience	14	31	25	15	23	12	3	17

Note:
[a]The number reported in each column is the number of seats held by the other party for which these experienced challengers were contesting.

but they do speak volumes about competition faced by congressional incumbents and about the Republicans' inability to challenge the Democrats' hold on the House.

If, on the other hand, one looks at Senate data, a different and more complex picture emerges. First, recall that experienced challengers have been defined in a way that is more clearly relevant for every seat than was the case for the House. But, as mentioned above, even though the definition used is more relevant to the Senate and perhaps more precise, the electoral qualifications of all candidates categorized as "experienced" in these races are far from equal. For instance, House members from less populous states, who therefore each represent a larger segment of the whole state, are likely to be better candidates than House members whose districts encompass much smaller portions of their states.[13] This caveat becomes even more important when one realizes that at least half of the experienced candidates for the Senate in every election studied in each party, with the exception of the Democratic candidate pool in 1988, were members of Congress or former members.

Even with that caveat noted, it is apparent that more candidates enter primaries to run against incumbent senators than is the case for the House. In many cases, more than one qualified candidate was running; thus it would seem that the primary electorate also had a meaningful choice in these races. Further, one can see that the trend toward fewer experienced candidates seeking nomination, which was seen in House races, is not evident in the Senate. No clear pattern emerges, though again more Democrats tend to run than do Republicans.

Differences between the major parties are again apparent. Many more Democratic governors and other statewide officeholders run for the Senate than is true of Republicans. This finding seems to be particularly relevant because we know that every statewide elected official has run and won a race in the exact same electorate that decides the Senate race. That is, the experience in office may not be as directly relevant to service in the Senate as is congressional or state legislative experience, but the campaigning experience may well be more relevant.

A temporal pattern also emerges from an examination of Senate primary candidates. Fewer and fewer state legislators are running for the United States Senate; further, fewer and fewer "nonqualified" candidates (especially if celebrities are removed from that list) are seeking Senate nominations. These declines may well reflect a recognition of the fact that running for the Senate is a serious business, expensive in terms of money and time required, and that few without relevant experience—such as that held by those in the offices identified in Table 4.4—are successful in seeking nominations.

Nominees against Opposition Incumbents

Table 4.5 presents background information and general election success rates for those who won primary nominations. A comparison of Tables 4.4 and 4.5 reveals that a high percentage of those experienced candidates who sought nominations did so successfully. As is not surprising, given what we know about strategic politicians, many of the experienced candidates who lost nominations did so to other experienced candidates, as more than one candidate saw a possibility to go to Congress. However, Table 4.5 reveals clearly for House candidates that even experienced nominees are not often successful in general elections. That is, politicians might have seen these elections as their best chance to win a seat in Congress, but it was often not good enough.[14] Experienced challengers do fare better than inexperienced challengers in House elections, but even seemingly qualified candidates do not present serious obstacles to incumbents' relatively easy reelections to the House.[15]

In Senate races Democrats and Republicans also seem to be following different courses. First, over half of the Senate Democratic nominees in the 1986 and 1988 (though not in the 1990) elections were experienced, well-qualified challengers to incumbent Republicans. Democratic nominees in these two elections appear to have been much better qualified than were their predecessors in 1982 and 1984. The 1986 candidate pool is a reflection, in part at least, of an intense effort on the part of George Mitchell (D-ME), then chair of the Democratic Senatorial Campaign Committee and currently the Majority Leader, to recruit strong Democratic candidates. The 1988 candidate pool reflects continued strong interest on the part of Democratic officeholders to move to the Senate, perhaps because the party had regained control of that body. One can only speculate on why this trend was not followed in 1990; perhaps Democratic activists were more concerned with protecting seemingly vulnerable seats they currently held than with encouraging challengers in seats which looked difficult to capture.

Table 4.5 also reveals that all the Democratic winners who helped their party regain control of the Senate by defeating incumbent Re-

Table 4.5

Experienced Nominees Challenging Incumbents in General Elections

	1982		1984		1986		1988	
	Dems	GOP	Dems	GOP	Dems	GOP	Dems	GOP
House elections								
Incumbents[a]	168	219	164	258	160	235	175	260
Experienced nominees	56	38	27	39	32	31	24	25
Experienced successful nominees	16	1	1	1	4	1	1	0
Inexperienced successful nominees	6	0	2	12	1	0	3	2
Senate elections								
Incumbents[a]	11	19	17	12	19	9	12	14
Experienced nominees	4	5	7	3	11	3	7	3
Experienced successful nominees	1	0	2	0	6	0	3	0
Inexperienced successful nominees	0	1	0	1	0	0	0	0

Note:
[a]The number reported in each column is the number of seats held by the other party for which these experienced challengers were contesting.

publicans in 1986 were experienced challengers. The three Democrats who took seats previously held by Republicans in 1988 were also experienced, qualified candidates, though the only challenger to defeat an incumbent in 1990 (Paul Wellstone in Minnesota) was not. A closer look at these winners is important. Whereas most of the experienced candidates seeking to challenge incumbent senators have been members of Congress, six of the nine winners had previously won statewide elections—two as governor, three as other statewide officeholders, and one (Tom Daschle of South Dakota) as his state's only representative in Congress. Two of the other winners (Richard Shelby of Alabama and Wyche Fowler of Georgia in 1986) were members of Congress; the final successful Democratic challenger (Brock Adams of Washington) had represented his state in

Congress before leaving that position to serve as secretary of transportation in the Carter cabinet. The two experienced Democratic winners in 1984 (Tom Harkin of Iowa and Paul Simon of Illinois) left seats in the House to go to the Senate, though Simon had also previously run and won statewide. The sole Democratic winner in 1982, Jeff Bingaman of New Mexico, had been his state's elected attorney general before running for the Senate. However, this case proves the importance of looking carefully at each instance. Though Bingaman was elected statewide, he gained few of the advantages one normally associates with running and winning, because his race was uncontested. He was not widely known.

Republican experience running against incumbent Democrats contrasts markedly with that presented above. While Table 4.4 did not reveal a noticeable drop-off in experienced Republicans seeking nominations to run for the Senate, the figures in Table 4.5 show that very few of the supposedly qualified candidates won nominations and none beat the incumbent Democrat he or she opposed. The only two Republicans unseating incumbent Democratic senators since 1980 have been Chic Hecht, a former state senator who defeated Howard Cannon in Nevada in 1982, and Mitch McConnell, a county judge who defeated Dee Huddleston in Kentucky in 1984. In both cases the quality of their campaigns, probably not predictable from their previous experience, contributed significantly to their victories. Interestingly, these were two of the closest races examined, with each decided by fewer than 6,000 votes. All other experienced Republican candidates—many of them members of Congress, governors, or in one case a renowned and highly recruited Rhodes scholar and ex–All American football player, Pete Dawkins in New Jersey—lost.

The conclusion which one draws must be tentative. However, it is clear that party differences exist. One would have thought that the Republicans, who had taken over the Senate in 1980, would have been successful in convincing quality challengers to take on the nineteen Democrats seeking reelection in 1982 and the twelve who had to run against the Reagan reelection tide in 1984. But the quality of the Republican candidates was not equal to that of the Democrats, who seemingly were running against a national tide. A total of only five incumbents lost in these two elections, leading observers to wonder if the Senate was becoming as safe for incumbents as the House. However, the Democrats demonstrated that incumbents could be beaten in

1986 and 1988, running more qualified candidates, particularly those who had been successful in statewide elections, and winning more seats. Whether Republican candidate recruiters will counter this trend has yet to be seen.

Open Seats

Studying open-seat races is important because a disproportional number of seats switching from one party to the other come from those districts or states in which no incumbent is running. Between 1980 and 1990, 38 of the 104 House seats (36.5 percent) and 9 of the 26 Senate seats (35.6 percent) that changed party hands were in open races, despite the fact that fewer than 10 percent of the House races and 15 percent of the Senate races did not involve incumbents. The professional literature is full of references to strategic politicians who wait until a seat is open in order to run. Thus one would imagine that more qualified candidates seek party nominations in open seats, that more do so successfully, that the races are more hotly contested, and that more experienced candidates win. These expectations, however, are only partially fulfilled.

While many seat changes are indeed in open races, inter-party competition is not so strong in open seats as one would expect. In fact, in this study only in 1984 were as many as two-thirds of the seats decided by a margin of less than 20 percent of the votes cast. In the 1982, 1986, 1988, and 1990 elections, the percentage of open seats in which the winner polled more than 60 percent of the votes were 43.1, 43.2, 44.4, and 44.8 respectively.[16]

Second, while on the average more experienced candidates run for open-seat nominations and more are in fact nominated than is the case for incumbents' challengers, only slightly more than half of the open seats in 1982 and 1984 were won by experienced candidates. Moreover, differences between the parties have become apparent in the last two elections. Democrats have more experienced candidates seeking their nomination in open seats for the House, but fewer and fewer experienced Republicans are running—and fewer and fewer of those are winning nominations and elections, to the point that only five experienced Republican candidates won in open-seat races in 1988.[17] Republicans seem to be finding their candidates, including their successful candidates, elsewhere. Our data do not permit us to reach definitive conclusions about why fewer experienced Republicans run for office; that would require a serious study of candidate decision making which focuses on potential candidates who decide not to run. However, we were able to demonstrate that the Republicans' inability to recruit quality candidates in open-seat races hinders further their efforts to reclaim majority status in the House.

Because of the small number of open Senate seats in any one election, analysis is more liable to idiosyncratic variations. Still, some aspects of Table 4.6 stand out. First, not since 1982 has a candidate without those political experiences deemed relevant for Senate races won in an open seat. In that election, multimillionaire Frank Lautenberg (D) in New Jersey defeated a sitting representative to capture an open seat. San Diego Mayor Pete Wilson (R) defeated three members of the California congressional delegation (and President Reagan's daughter Maureen) to capture the Republican nomination in order to run against—and eventually defeat—Democrat Edmund G. (Jerry) Brown, Jr., the state's governor who was constitutionally ineligible to succeed himself and who had run an unsuccessful campaign for his party's presidential nomination two years earlier.[18] In the last three elections the vast majority of the nominees and all of the winners in open seats have been qualified, experienced candidates. As was the case with House seats, the Democrats have been more successful than the Republicans at fielding qualified candidates, though one is hesitant to conclude much from these data because of the small numbers involved. Furthermore, as was observed for challengers to incumbents, the Democrats, more than the Republicans, have been putting forward candidates with previous experience running statewide. Democratic winners in open seats have included two governors (Rockefeller of West Virginia and Robb of Virginia), a former governor (Sanford of North Carolina), a lieutenant governor (Kerry of Massachusetts), and a sitting representative who had served as lieutenant governor and had run unsuccessfully in a previous Senate race (Reid of Nevada). Former Governor Christopher (Kit) Bond of Missouri was the only Republican candidate who had served in a statewide elective office before running for an open Senate seat during this period. One is led to question if the Democrats have hit upon a (certainly obvious) source of successful candidates which the Republicans have been slow to identify. In any case, it is abundantly clear that the races in open Senate seats are not

Table 4.6

Number of Experienced Candidates in Open-Seat Elections

	1982		1984		1986		1988	
	Dems	GOP	Dems	GOP	Dems	GOP	Dems	GOP
House elections								
Open districts[a]	58	56	27	26	43	44	27	26
Experienced candidates	73	61	34	27	59	39	41	25
Experienced nominees	29	31	11	12	27	22	19	12
Experienced winners	16	15	4	10	18	14	12	5
Senate elections								
Open seats	3	3	4	4	7[b]	7[b]	5	5
Experienced candidates	5	6	7	3	10	6	10	3
Experienced nominees	2	2	3	2	6	6	4	3
Experienced winners	0	1	3	1	5	2	2	3

Notes:
[a]Excludes uncontested races.
[b]John B. Breaux (D) won the Louisiana election by gaining more than 50 percent of the vote in the nonpartisan primary, thus avoiding a general election contest.

for amateurs, not even for those amateurs who have been able to convert fame in other fields to success in politics.

Interpretation

This analysis has been unself-consciously what some have described, often unflatteringly, as "thick description." No attempt has been made to assert causality. Yet the data do not speak for themselves, and some interpretation is warranted. It is important to recall why this topic is important. We have just celebrated the bicentennial of Congress as a representative institution. Our system of representative democracy depends on the citizens having the ability to express their views at the polls, whether those views be evaluations of the individuals holding office, of the parties they represent, or of the policies they favor. But citizens cannot express any views in the absence of competition. And it is abundantly clear that true competition occurs only when candidates with certain qualities contest elections. This chapter started and ends with a concern that that is not happening— though it is not entirely clear why. Before speculating on the causes of the patterns observed during the 1980s, it is appropriate to review briefly the most recent electoral experience.

The 1990 Election

For the most part, this analysis has presented data on the elections of 1982, 1984, 1986, and 1988. The data in Tables 4.1 and 4.2 demonstrate that the pattern of decreased competition noted for some time continued in 1990. Incumbents are almost always renominated, frequently without competition, for seats in the House and the Senate. They are most often reelected, again often without competition or with limited competition. But it should be noted that an anti-incumbent mood of the electorate did lead to decreased victory margins in 1990, even though it did not lead to incumbent defeats.

In the House in 1990 familiar patterns recurred. Of the 407 members who sought renomination, 406 were renominated. Of these, 391 were reelected, 83 without major party opposition; however, the percentage of incumbents with over 70 percent of the general election vote declined significantly, leading to speculation that incumbents might have fared worse had they faced more experienced, better-funded challengers. All 32 of the incumbent senators seeking renomination were chosen by their party. Of these, 4—Republicans Cochran of Mississippi and Warner of Virginia and Democrats Nunn of Georgia and Pryor of Arkansas—faced no opposition. Such token opposition confronted 12 others that four months before the general election they each had raised more than fifty times the amount of money raised by their opponents.[19] Of the 32 renominated, 31 won reelection, the 4 mentioned facing no opposition and 22 others polling more than 70 percent of the vote. Furthermore, while all data have not yet been analyzed, it seems clear that qualified challengers were even more rare in 1990 than they had been in the past. Thus while in some ways the 1990 election continued the trend observed earlier, in other respects it seems to have exaggerated the trend.

House-Senate Differences

It has been clear for some time that quality candidates are not challenging incumbents in the House of Representatives. Others have hypothesized on why this is so, examining the impact of a variety of variables on the presence of qualified candidates for Congress and on the ability of candidates for Congress to raise enough money to run credible campaigns. Their research and their findings are important, but when I examine that body of literature, I am reminded of Aristotle's warning:

> Our discussion will be adequate if it has as much precision as the subject matter permits for. Precision is not to be sought for alike in all discussions. . . . It is the mark of an educated man to look for precision in each class of things just so far as the nature of the subject permits.[20]

After all, it is politics that we are seeking to explain, the decisions made by individuals who are pursuing political careers. It is not only the contextual circumstances leading to quality challengers which interest us, but it is also the individual decisions made by those who decide not to run for Congress. Years ago Lasswell told us about the political personality.[21] We should not forget some of the lessons he taught and how they can be applied to current situations.

Fewer and fewer qualified candidates are running for the House than is the case for the Senate. Despite exceptions in Idaho and Colorado noted earlier, for virtually all open seats in the Senate see experienced candidates run for both major parties' nominations. Many of the Senate races are hotly contested. In twelve of the open-seat races in the five elections studied, the winner polled less than 55 percent of the vote and in only five did he or she poll more than 60 percent. On the other hand, many open-seat races in the House are not competitive, and in many cases experienced candidates do not win either parties' nomination.

If this is the case for open seats, it is even more the case for nominations to oppose incumbents. Senate nominations are still deemed valuable by experienced contenders, though again the 1990 experience gives some pause. In the most recent election, Republicans were unsuccessful in convincing Tom Kean of New Jersey, Pete DuPont of Delaware, and Lamar Alexander of Tennessee to take on tough races against incumbents Bradley, Biden, and Gore. Similarly, the Democrats could not convince former Vice President Mondale to reenter the political fray against Rudy Boschwitz; nor could they persuade former governors Jerry Baliles of Virginia or Jim Hunt of North Carolina to challenge John Warner or Jesse Helms. Because of the small number of cases in any one election year, it is difficult to separate patterns from idiosyncrasies in Senate elections. Even with the 1990 experience, however, it seems fair to conclude that qualified candidates seek and receive the nominations and can provide real competition in a majority of Senate races.

This does not seem to be the case for nominations to oppose incumbent members of the House. And in this case the 1990 experience reinforces what has been seen in recent years. Qualified candidates do not come forth on their own and are not successfully recruited to challenge incumbent members of House. Thus member after member faces either no competition or only token competition in seeking to return for another two years in Washington. This finding is a source of concern for democratic theorists; lack of competition raises serious questions about representative democracy, at least in the House of Representatives. The voting public's inability to convert dissatisfaction with incumbents into a changing of the congressional guard in 1990 is evidence of this problem. Presumably, concern over the character of the two houses of our bicameral legislature should follow.

Ambition Theory

My research suggests that ambition theorists need to reexamine some of their assumptions. John Hibbing has raised important questions about whether "progressive ambition"[22] merits redefinition. He mentions members of the House who define for themselves progressive careers within that body.[23] But just as easily one could focus on state legislators who define their careers as progressing within those legislatures rather than moving on to Washington.[24] These reevaluations of career paths undoubtedly have a number of causes, some relating to personal matters, some to political, and some to policy.

For instance, state legislators have an incentive to seek advancement within those bodies because of the increasing role which states have come to play in establishing policy as a result of changes instituted during the Reagan administration. Whereas once most domestic and social policymaking took place in Washington, today more and more of it occurs in state capitals. State legislatures are becoming more professional—in terms of salary, staff resources, and the like—and more influential. Legislators can gain the psychological rewards of important public service without enduring the personal costs which a move to Washington would entail.

Members of Congress are more satisfied with their positions because of the accelerated paths to power in the House which have followed from the reforms of the 1970s. Whereas once power in the House only followed long apprenticeships, now subcommittee leadership and increased staff can be anticipated and then enjoyed relatively early in one's career. More and more representatives have a significant say in the formulation of public policy on important matters. They see this increased influence as a significant progression in power and thus look forward to moving "up" within the House rather than "up" to the Senate.

The relative ease of reelection to the House—which dissuades state legislators from challenging incumbents, on the one hand, and encourages members of Congress to stay in the House rather than face the more difficult prospect of election and reelection to the Senate, on the other—provides an additional incentive to "progress" within an institution rather than seek advancement by moving to another house or a higher legislative body. Whereas once the constant treadmill of election campaigns was considered onerous by House members, particularly in comparison to the six-year cycle enjoyed by their Senate counterparts, now House reelections are relatively routine and senators are the ones who frequently complain of the "treadmill life-style" once bemoaned by their colleagues in the House. Unless they want to be accused of remoteness, senators are expected back in their states almost as often as representatives are in their districts, and they still face more difficult reelection contests.

If ambition theory requires rethinking in terms of "progression" within state legislatures rather than from them to Washington, if state legislators and others are also defining career "progression" in terms different from those with which we are familiar, then a closer examination of the pool of candidates for the House, successful as well as unsuccessful, is called for. If ambition theory requires rethinking in terms of "progression" within the House rather than from the House to the Senate, this has obvious implications for the likely pool of Senate candidates. And in those lights, indicators of the qualifications for success will also require modification.

Democratic-Republican Differences

Perhaps the most dramatic finding of this chapter is that Democratic candidates have differed from Republican candidates in ways which would not have seemed obvious. If anything, the differences are in the opposite direction from those which would have been anticipated.

Conventional wisdom about recent changes in party organization holds that the Republicans have progressed much more quickly than have the Democrats.[25] The Republicans raise more money; they have built up a party infrastructure to aid candidates; they have reached out into the country with political directors in charge of geographic regions; they have worked on building state and local organizations. They have a plan aimed at regaining control of the House after the post-1990 census redistricting.

However, the data presented here reveal a different picture. In election after election the Republicans have not done as well as the Democrats in finding qualified candidates. For House elections, fewer qualified candidates are seeking nominations and fewer are winning in races against incumbents; even more dramatic is that fewer Republican candidates in open seats are experienced campaigners who can be strong contenders. Two results have followed from this recruitment pattern. First, successful Republican candidates have come from untraditional backgrounds, or at least from backgrounds which would have made prediction of their success unlikely. Second, the Republicans have not made partisan gains—either in open-seat races or in those few races in which incumbents are defeated—despite their supposed organizational and financial advantages. In fact, more open seats previously held by Republicans have gone to Democrats than vice versa in the last five elections.[26] In terms of congressional elections the resurgence of the Republican party organization seems more fiction than fact.

Much the same conclusion about party differences is in order if one looks at Senate races. The Republican candidates—in open seats and as challengers to incumbents—did not match their Democratic counterparts as experienced campaigners. The Democrats were more successful in finding candidates who had run successfully in statewide elections to contest for—and to win—Senate seats. They realized a net gain of one in the open seats during this period; they defeated eleven more incumbents than have the Republicans.

Thus during the 1980s—a period of a popular Republican president who won reelection by a landslide, a period of a reputed resurgence in the Republican party organization that the Democrats have struggled to emulate, a period of economic growth and prosperity, and a period in which more Democratic than Republican seats had to be defended—Democrats fielded more qualified candidates and fared better in the elections. Perhaps the standards used to measure organizational development by political parties have missed the mark.

Why should this be so? A number of possibilities suggest themselves. One set of possibilities revolve around Republican politicians. If Republicans philosophically believe that government should be kept closer to the people, then they are more comfortable working at the state or local level, especially with the recent trend toward more meaningful decision making in those arenas. That is, Republican politicians in state and local government are not anxious to move "up" to the national level because they do not believe important decisions should be made in Washington and they are convinced that fewer of them are in fact now made there. The Republican National Committee has made a major effort to improve their position in state legislatures. In anticipation of redistricting after the 1990 census, they have invested time and money in winning state legislative races and in convincing conservative Democrats, particularly in southern legislatures, to change party affiliation. One unintended by-product of this may well be a corps of Republican state legislators who are not anxious to move. The 1992 candidate pool will provide the first measure of the success of this strategy.

Of course, added to those incentives is the disincentive for Republicans to move to Congress because of their seemingly permanent minority status in the House. Thus not only do they not believe decisions should be made in Washington, but they do not play as influential a part in those decisions which are made. This reasoning leads to something of a self-fulfilling prophecy which does not augur well for Republican chances in the House in the future. Some of this same reasoning may apply to potential Senate candidates, especially after the Democrats regained control in 1986.

Another set of possible explanations revolves around "breeding grounds" for successful politicians. Democratic politicians have traditionally come up through the ranks—and they continue to do so. They are politicians who see political progression as their chosen career path. Can one say the same of Republicans? I am less certain. Is it overstereotyping to say that Republicans define success more in terms of business success than political success? If it is not, then does it not follow that successful Republican politicians come out of the business community—or elsewhere in the private sector—rather than up through the political ranks? And in this age of candidate-centered campaigns, in which a candidate can win a party nomination by running his or her own campaign through the media, does that path not make just as much sense for a Republican aspiring to high elective office? If this line of reasoning has merit, further redefinition of predictors of quality candidacies is called for.

Other explanations can be offered. Democrats are better campaigners. Republicans are waiting for new House districts in 1992. Republican Senate candidates are also waiting for 1992, to challenge the Democrats who beat incumbent Republicans in 1986. The best potential Republican candidates took positions in the Reagan and Bush administrations and are seeking influence through appointive, executive office not through elective, legislative office. Whatever the explanation, the party difference is significant and merits attention in the future.

Temporal Trends

The 1980s were supposed to be the years of the Republican resurgence. They were not—and they were not, in part at least, because Republicans failed to field competitive candidates in the races they needed to capture if they were going to retain control of the Senate and make inroads on Democratic control of the House. Republican enthusiasm was dashed by the 1982 election. The GOP mounted a major effort to recruit and support candidates in 1982. Despite the fact that the Democrats had to defend more seats than the Republicans, the partisan balance in the Senate was virtually unchanged. And in the House, the Republicans suffered a net loss of twenty-six seats, not unusual for a president's party in a midterm election, but reversing all but eight seats of the gain made in 1980 and effectively deflating what some saw as a rising Republican balloon.

The 1984 election stands out from the others in the series under study. Each party had the lowest ratio of experienced candidates to seats available of any of the Senate elections examined. Both parties also saw a decline in experienced challengers and in experienced nominees for House and for Senate races. For the Democrats the decreased numbers seem logical; a popular Republican president was running for reelection in a time of peace and prosperity. No one thought 1984 would be a good Democratic year; strategic Democratic politicians stayed on the sidelines. But for Republicans, the rationale was less clear. It did look like a good Republican year. That the Republicans did not do as well as anticipated—gaining fourteen seats in the House, but losing two in the Senate—was attributable in part at least to a lack of qualified candidates.

A new pattern emerged in the last two elections of the decade, with fewer strong Republicans and more strong Democrats running. In 1986 the Democrats regained control of the Senate, though they picked up only five seats in the House, low for a midterm election but not surprising because of the size of their majority. In 1988 despite another Republican presidential landslide, the Democrats gained two seats in the House and broke even in the Senate. And the Republicans who contested the 1990 elections, a midterm election which did not seem likely to favor their party, certainly did not constitute a strong corps of challengers. One could argue that qualified Republicans were awaiting the 1992 election, when another popular Republican president presumably will run for reelection, when the Senate Democrats whose first elections helped their party regain majority status in 1986 face their first reelection campaigns, and when House district lines will have been redrawn following the census. But a reemergence of qualified, experienced Republican candidates in that election would have to reverse a trend that by then will have progressed unabated for a decade. Clearly, a new kind of party commitment will be necessary if this reversal is to eventuate.

Conclusion

Two final comments seem in order. First, the evidence presented in this paper supports the hypothesis that the American polity has indeed entered an era of divided government.[27] Incumbent advantages are only partially responsible for this division. Institutional changes are partially responsible. Decisions made by potential candidates for office are also partially responsible. And the consequences for governing require further study.

In addition, more of a time series needs to be developed, particularly for the Senate. As a discipline we have not developed historical data on primary contestants for either branch of our national legislature.[28] Because of the work of Gary Jacobson and others, we do have a good deal of data on and analysis of House elections.[29] We have much less on Senate elections. Yet Senate elections have changed dramatically over time. The most evident change was the move to direct election of senators, and the impact of that change for recruitment patterns cannot be overstated. But campaigning for the Senate has also changed significantly in recent decades.

No accurate financial records exist for the period before 1974, when the reporting requirements of the Federal Election Campaign Act became operative. However, in that year the average Senate campaign cost under $500,000. In 1988 Democratic incumbents spent an average of over $2.5 million to be reelected, defeating Republican challengers who averaged more than $1.5 million in spending. Republican incumbents outspent their Democratic challengers by almost two to one, averaging expenditures of over $4 million in their campaigns. The average spent per candidate in open seat races was almost $3 million. Television advertising was a major component of virtually every race; in the 1950s television was rarely used. We have demonstrated that the candidate pool was transformed somewhat during the 1980s. One can speculate on changes before that time—and on the implications of those changes for certain types of candidacies, for elections, and for the Senate—but more data must be gathered and analyzed. No one doubts that some Senate campaigns, even in the era before television, cost a great deal of money. But others—the renowned penny-pinching campaigns of senators such as Margaret Chase Smith (R-ME) and William Proxmire (D-WI)—were profoundly different, with expenditures measured in the hundreds of dollars. Those types of campaigns for the Senate have vanished, and the kind of candidates who won them are no longer around.

Thus this chapter does indeed end as it began. We have documented changes in the quality of candidates running for the House and for the Senate, changes which have been different for the Democrats than for the Republicans, changes which have been different in the House than in the Senate, changes which have implications for our understanding of political ambition, changes which have obvious implications for the Congress of the future. We have looked at these changes in the recent past and raised speculation about the more distant past. We have speculated further about the causes for these changes. But we are still left with questions about what it means for the future. Something is happenin' here, but what it means ain't exactly clear—at least not to this observer at this time.

Notes

This chapter is part of an ongoing project on candidate recruitment. In this endeavor I have benefited from the wisdom and advice of my collaborators, Linda Fowler, Ruth Jones, and Walter Stone. I would also like to thank my colleagues Tony Corrado and Cal Mackenzie, the participants at the "Back to the Future" conference at the Carl Albert Center of the University of Oklahoma, particularly Tom Kazee and Tom Mann, and the panelists at the Northeast Political Science Association Annual Meeting for comments on earlier drafts of this work. This chapter was made possible in great part by the work of my research assistant, Gretchen Anglund, who I hope knows the debt I owe to her. Of course, none of these friends and colleagues bear any responsibility for errors of fact or interpretation.

1. Phil Duncan, "Large Turnover Seems Unlikely, but Campaign Won't Be Dull," *Congressional Quarterly Weekly Report* (17 February 1990): 447–48, 456.

2. The literature is familiar and extensive. As examples on congressional elections generally, see Gary C. Jacobson, *The Politics of Congressional Elections*, 2d ed. (Boston: Little, Brown, 1987) and his "Strategic Politicians and the Dynamics of House Elections, 1946–1986," *American Political Science Review* 83 (1989): 773–93; Jacobson and Samuel Kernell, "National Forces in the 1986 U.S. House Elections," *Legislative Studies Quarterly* 15 (1990): 65–88; Linda L. Fowler and L. Sandy Maisel, "The Changing Supply of Competitive Candidates in House Elections, 1982–1988" (Paper presented at the Eighty-fifth Annual Meeting of the American Political Science Association, Atlanta, Georgia, 31 August–3 September 1989). On incumbency return rates, see Jeffrey S. Banks and D. Roderick Kiewiet, "Explaining Patterns of Candidate Competition in Congressional Elections," *American Journal of Political Science* 33 (1989): 997–1015; Fowler and Maisel, "Changing Supply" and the references they cite. On House-Senate differences, see Peverill Squire, "Challengers in U.S. Senate Elections," *Legislative Studies Quarterly* 14 (1989): 531–48; Alan I. Abramowitz, "Explaining Senate Election Outcomes," *American Political Science Review* 82 (1988): 385–404; Barbara Hinckley, "House Re-elections and Senate Defeats: The Role of the Challenger," *British Journal of Political Science* 10 (1980): 441–60. On the ability of the electorate to express policy preferences through elections, see Gerald C. Wright and Michael B. Berkman, "Candidates and Policy in United States Senate Elections," *American Political Science Review* 80 (1986): 567–88; David Austen-Smith and Jeffrey Banks, "Elections Coalitions, and Legislative Outcomes," *American Political Science Review* 82 (1988): 405–22; Gerald C. Wright, "Policy Voting in the U.S. Senate: Who Is Represented?" *Legislative Studies Quarterly* 14 (1989): 465–86; Robert S. Erikson and Gerald C. Wright, "Voters, Candidates, and Issues in Congressional Elections," in *Congress Reconsidered*, 4th ed., ed.

Lawrence C. Dodd and Bruce I. Oppenheimer (Washington: Congressional Quarterly Press, 1989); Robert A. Bernstein, *Elections, Representation, and Congressional Voting Behavior* (Englewood Cliffs, NJ: Prentice-Hall, 1989). On factors leading to significant challenges to incumbents, see Gary W. Copeland, "Choosing To Run: Why House Members Seek Election to the Senate," *Legislative Studies Quarterly* 14 (1989): 549–66; L. Sandy Maisel, *From Obscurity to Oblivion*, rev. ed. (Knoxville: University of Tennessee Press, 1986). On the impact of political action committee money, see Peverill Squire and John R. Wright, "Fundraising by Nonincumbent Candidates for the U.S. House of Representatives," *Legislative Studies Quarterly* 15 (1990): 89–98; Frank J. Sorauf, *Money in American Elections* (Glenview, IL: Scott, Foresman, 1988).

3. Hinckley, "House Re-elections and Senate Defeats"; Alan I. Abromowitz, "A Camparison of Voting for U.S. Senator and Representative," *American Political Science Review* 74 (1980): 633–40.

4. Gary C. Jacobson, "The Marginals Never Vanished: Incumbency and Competition in Elections to the U.S. House of Representatives," *American Journal of Political Science* 31 (1987): 137.

5. Supporting this conclusion is the finding that eight incumbents who did not face any major party opposition still managed less than 80 percent of the vote and another five less than 85 percent. Voters cast their ballots for minor party or independent candidates—those with little or no chance of winning—to show unhappiness with incumbents.

6. Louisiana has a unique "nonpartisan" primary system in which all candidates appear on the primary ballot together. If any candidate receives a majority of the primary vote, he or she is declared to have been elected. If no candidate receives a majority, there is a runoff between the top two candidates, regardless of party affiliation, on the date of the general election. Johnston faced two Republican challengers in his "nonpartisan" primary. As he received over 85 percent of the vote, he was declared the winner with no general election competition.

7. Gary C. Jacobson and Samuel Kernell, *Strategy and Choice in Congressional Elections* (New Haven: Yale University Press, 1981).

8. Fowler and Maisel, "Changing Supply"; also see Jon R. Bond, Cary Covington, and Richard Fleisher, "Explaining Challenger Quality in Congressional Elections," *Journal of Politics* 41 (1985): 510–20; Jonathan S. Krasno and Donald Philip Green, "Preempting Quality Challengers in House Elections," *Journal of Politics* 50 (1988): 920–36; David T. Canon, "Political Amateurism in the United States Congress," *Congress Reconsidered*, 4th ed.; Banks and Kiewiet, "Explaining Patterns."

9. See Squire, "Challengers in U.S. Senate Elections," and Copeland, "Choosing to Run."

10. See Canon, "Political Amateurism," and his *Actors, Athletes, and Astonauts: Political Amateurs in the United States Congress* (Chicago: University of Chicago Press, 1990).

11. See Canon, *Actors, Amateurs and Astronauts*. Inclusion in this category involves subjective judgment as to who is a true celebrity. When in doubt, I have erred on the side of inclusion rather than exclusion, including, e.g., President Reagan's daughter Maureen, who ran for the Senate from California. On the other hand, I have not used the celebrity category for House races, a decision with

which some of my colleagues disagree. However, Fowler and I have concluded that the "celebrity" category for House races is too tied to local knowledge to be useful for scholars researching all congressional districts. Thus we would all identify television personalities Fred Grandy (R-IA) and Ben Jones (D-GA) and basketball star Tom MacMillan (D-MD), but many scholars would misclassify Amory Houghton (R-NY), the CEO of the leading employer in his district, and Claudine Schneider (R-RI), who had been a local television personality before running for the House in 1980. See Fowler and Maisel, "Changing Supply."

12. Michael Barone and Grant Ujifusa, *The Almanac of American Politics 1988* (Washington: National Journal, 1988), 589–90, 805–7; Michael Barone and Grant Ujifusa, *The Almanac of American Politics 1990* (Washington: National Journal, 1989), 110–12.

13. See Squire, "Challengers in U.S. Senate Elections"; Copeland, "Choosing To Run"; and John Hibbing, "The Career Paths of Members of Congress" (Paper prepared for the "Conference on Career Paths of Elected Politicians," Institute of Politics, John F. Kennedy School of Government, Harvard University, December 1989).

14. Compare L. Sandy Maisel, *From Obscurity to Oblivion*, and Banks and Kiewiet, "Explaining Patterns."

15. Fowler and Maisel, "Changing Supply."

16. Ibid.

17. Preliminary analysis of 1990 data reveals that the gap between the parties closed somewhat in this instance; furthermore, two-thirds of the open seats were won by experienced candidates—though two-thirds of the losers were not experienced.

18. It is worth noting that neither New Jersey, with fourteen congressional districts and no dominant media market within the state, nor California, with forty-five congressional districts and a large number of media markets within the state, is a state in which a representative in Congress would have a large electoral advantage. In fact, as mayor of San Diego, Wilson had been elected by a constituency more than twice as large as that of any of the members of Congress he defeated.

19. Paul Taylor, "Be All That You Can Be," *Washington Post National Weekly Edition*, 13–19 August 1990, 13–14.

20. Richard McKeon, ed., *The Basic Works of Aristotle, Ethics*, trans. W.D. Ross (New York: Random House, 1941), Book 1, Chap. 2, 936. I am indebted to Robert McArthur for locating this precise reference for me.

21. See, for example, "The Political Personality," Chap. 3, in Harold D. Lasswell, *Power and Personality* (New York: The Viking Press, 1948) and the work of Lasswell's students, such as James David Barber, *The Lawmakers: Recruitment and Adaption to Legislative Life* (New Haven: Yale University Press, 1965).

22. Joseph A. Schlesinger, *Ambition and Politics* (Chicago: Rand McNally, 1966).

23. Hibbing, "Career Paths of Members of Congress."

24. Linda L. Fowler and Robert D. McClure, *Political Ambition: Who Decides to Run for Congress* (New Haven: Yale University Press, 1989).

25. See, for example, Xandra Kayden and Eddie Mahe, Jr., *The Party Goes*

On (New York: Basic Books, 1986); Larry J. Sabato, *The Party's Just Begun: Shaping Political Parties for America's Future* (Glenview, IL: Scott, Foresman, 1988); and Paul S. Herrnson, "Reemergent National Party Organizations," in *The Parties Respond: Changes in the American Party System*, ed. L. Sandy Maisel (Boulder, CO: Westview Press, 1990).

26. The Democrats have made a net gain of 17 seats during the period; 17 Democratic incumbents lost to Republicans, while 34 Republican incumbents lost to Democrats and the open-seat switches split evenly.

27. See Morris P. Fiorina, "An Era of Divided Government" (Center for American Political Studies, Harvard University, Occasional Paper 89–96), rev. and reprinted in *Developments in American Politics*, ed. Bruce Cain and Gillian Peele (London: Macmillan, 1990).

28. I am indebted to David Canon for sharing data with me on Senate primary contestants in the 1970s. These data reveal no clear pattern, raising the added flag of caution about the need to view Senate data skeptically because of the small number of elections in any one year.

29. Jacobson, "Strategic Politicians."

Part II

Institutional Change in the Atomistic Congress

CHARLES STEWART III

5 | The Growth of the Committee System, from Randall to Gillett

A fundamental problem that faces legislators is how to organize the legislature so the will of the majority, if it exists, will be implemented. This problem is much like that posed by Madison in *Federalist* 51 when he discussed the more general problem of organizing a government that was simultaneously effective and accountable:

> In framing a government which is to be administered by men over men, the great difficulty lies in this: you must first enable the government to control the governed; and in the next place oblige it to control itself. A dependence on the people is, no doubt, the primary control on the government; but experience has taught mankind the necessity of auxiliary precautions.

Thus Madison thought it important to distinguish *authority* from *autonomy* when thinking about the organization of government. In his view, it was vital that government be given the authority to provide effective governance. The trick was in ensuring that effective governments would not become autonomous from the desires of citizens.

In much the same way that the framing of the Constitution was an act of citizens balancing authority and autonomy to create the institutions that would govern them, the creation and reform of legislative institutions reflects legislators balancing these same goals. Thus in thinking about how Congress has been organized as an institution over the decades, it is useful to imagine that each chamber is a miniature society trying to find the right configuration of institutions that will not only be effective in legislating, but will also be responsive to the desires of the legislative majority.

Therefore, in framing a legislature, legislators create subunits such as committees to do the legislature's work, and then they create oversight mechanisms to control these subunits. Some of this oversight is done directly by the legislators themselves, as when they vote on whether to pass, reject, or amend committee proposals. Other mechanisms are less direct. For instance, party leaders are deputized to appoint members to legislative committees so that these committees will recommend measures a majority of the legislature wants to pass. Committees have wide latitude in influencing legislation, but legislators also have ways to ensure that committees remain the agents of policy majorities. What is interesting to political scientists is understanding precisely how these mechanisms of control work in general and discovering how successful they are in producing optimal legislative outputs.

The fifty-year period beginning around 1875 provides a very interesting case for studying how Congress has addressed its organizational problems, especially how chamber majorities used the structure of the House to pursue partisan policy ends. Prompting the transformation in congressional organization during these years were a series of major changes in Congress's external environment. The final product was the modern, institutionalized House (to use Nelson Polsby's term) that is usually the subject of academic and journalistic attention today.[1]

The House of the 1910s was quite different from the House of the 1870s:

1. *It was larger.* Between 1877 and 1919 the House grew by 48 percent, from 293 to 435 members.

2. *Its membership was more stable.* Fifty percent of the members of the Forty-fifth Congress (1877–79) were in their first term, compared to 28 percent in the Sixty-sixth (1919–21).[2]

3. *It had more committees and opportunities for committee service.* The Forty-fifth Congress had forty-eight standing committees and 431 committee slots. The Sixty-sixth Congress had fifty-nine committees and 716 slots.

4. *Committee membership was more stable.* Eighteen percent of all committee members in the Forty-fourth Congress returned to their appointments in the Forty-fifth. In contrast, 41 percent of committee assignees in the Sixty-fifth Congress returned to service on the same committees in the Sixty-sixth. If we restrict our attention only to members who were actually reelected to the next Congress, this increase in

continuity is also evident: 56 percent of all members who were re-elected to the Sixty-sixth Congress were reappointed to the committees on which they had served in the Sixty-fifth, compared to 36 percent at the beginning of the Forty-fifth Congress.

5. *Committee leadership was more stable.* Thirty percent of the committee chairs in the Forty-fifth Congress had chaired the same committee in the Forty-fourth. In comparison, 43 percent of the members who chaired committees in the Sixty-sixth Congress had been the ranking minority member in the Sixty-fifth Congress. (Republicans regained control of the House in the intervening election.)

Other differences are also well documented, if less amenable to quantitative description. For instance, Speakers alone appointed committees in 1877, while the floor held formal authority to elect committees in 1921. A system of property rights in committee seats, part of what we call the "seniority system," became increasingly entrenched. Speakers in the 1870s controlled the floor partially through their domination over the Rules Committee. By 1921 not only did Speakers not control the Rules Committee, they were prohibited by the rules from even serving on it. The list could go on.

Between the 1870s and 1920s, then, House organization grew more sprawling, lines of authority became less well defined, and the locus of power shifted from party leaders to committees. Congressional service became a career in itself, rather than a way station en route to other political pursuits.

The purpose of this chapter is to present some new evidence about the transformation of the House committee system between 1875 and 1921 and to make an argument about how one should interpret this evidence. The evidence centers on the pattern of committee appointments during this period, particularly the size of the various committees that were appointed over the course of several decades. This evidence about the size of committees is embedded in data on approximately sixteen thousand House committee assignments that were made between the Forty-fourth and Sixty-sixth Congresses.

The general argument reflects the discussion of the balancing of authority and autonomy with which I began this chapter: while the *authority structure* of the House was different during most of this period compared to the present, the fundamental degree of *autonomy* exercised by those in authority remained essentially unchanged. In the particular case of committee assignments this means the following: although Speakers exercised seemingly unilateral control over committee rosters up until 1911, the latitude they exercised by having the authority to make committee assignments was seriously constrained by the preferences of legislative majorities.

This argument runs counter to traditional views of Congress about this period of its history. Scholars of congressional history have traditionally been ambivalent about the central period covered by this chapter, the era of "czar rule" in the 1890s and 1900s. Most commonly, this period is portrayed as one of unbridled control of the House floor by strong party bosses, especially Speakers, and reflects in large part the scholarship and rhetoric of the turn of the century, which were both infused with Progressive ideals.[3]

By calling into question this traditional view of the speakership, I am aligning myself with recent research that has questioned the degree to which any subdivision of Congress, such as the committee or leadership system, could long operate autonomously from chamber majorities. This new research to which I refer frequently operates under the rubric of "principal-agent theory."[4] It is not necessary to explore this literature in any depth here but only to note the central claim that principal-agent theorists have made in the application of this theory to legislatures: so long as the rules of procedure can be changed by a majority vote of the legislature, the subdivisions of the legislature that are given authority to act on the legislature's behalf (such as committees and leaders) must always gauge their actions with the aim of maintaining majority support in mind.

If committees regularly report out bizarre legislative proposals and party leaders ignore pivotal blocs in the party, they are likely to be sanctioned. This does not mean that committees and party leaders always "do what the legislature wants," since it is meaningless to talk of *a* legislative will.[5] It does mean that committees and leaders must somehow correlate their actions with the preferences of legislative majorities, or else they run the risk of being overthrown. It also means that the costs that leaders and committees impose upon the rank and file must also be accompanied by palpable political benefits.

Interestingly enough, an expression of this view of the historical House of Representatives is provided by Mary Parker Follett in her classic study of the speakership:

The construction of the committees is a duty requiring the utmost caution and deliberation. In it is involved a multitude of considerations. . . . What this officer [i.e., the Speaker] does attempt to do is so to balance the various considerations as to accomplish his own aims, please his party, satisfy individuals, meet the reasonable expectations of the minority, and appear respectable to the country—a laborious task greatly increased by the large number of new men and the importunity of members for particular places. First among influential considerations are the numerous claims which have grown out of [the Speaker's] election: he must remember the men who have voted for him in the party caucus, he must recognize the preferences of his party as expressed in the other nominations for the Speakership, and he must redeem the promises by which he has secured his choice.[6]

Engaging in a comprehensive study of how Speakers attempted to be responsive to legislative majorities would be a major undertaking, much beyond the scope of this chapter. What I *can* do, however, is focus on one simple way in which Speakers and party leaders were responsive to the needs and desires of the rank and file when they made committee assignments from 1875 to 1921, particularly when they decided how many members to appoint to each committee. A full articulation of this argument must await another forum.[7]

On the Value of Committee Assignments

Any understanding of how Speakers and the rank and file interacted over the assignment of members to committees must begin with an understanding of why committees exist in the first place and what members desire to achieve through committee membership. Because entire books have been written on this subject, the treatment here must necessarily be cursory and brief, but certain points bear emphasis.[8]

Committees provide both *individual* and *collective* benefits to legislators. Both benefit types are well-known and derive from the organizing principle of the committee system: *division of labor*. Under division of labor we can think of the committee system as (1) dividing up the policy world into compartments, called jurisdictions; (2) dividing up legislators, creating the committees themselves; and finally (3) assigning jurisdictions (i.e., policies) to committees (i.e., legislators). The most important collective benefits this provides come through specialization—members of the legislature come to know certain policy areas very well, potentially providing the legislature with the information necessary to write and enact effective legislation.

In addition to the general benefit of expertise, the committee system also provides particular, individual benefits to members of the legislature. These particular benefits *may or may not* benefit the legislature considered as a whole. For instance, when a member of the Ways and Means Committee is able to slip an unnoticed special provision benefiting a constituent into a large tax bill, this is a benefit that accrues to the legislator involved (and his or her constituent), not to the legislature (or the nation) as a whole.[9] And because there is no *guarantee* that the subject-matter expertise a member gains by serving on a committee will be shared with the legislature as a whole, it is possible for committees to lead the whole chamber down the primrose path, producing gains for the committee's members at the expense of the rest of the legislature.

Members of Congress, being professional politicians, understand quite well how the committee system can cut both ways—how it can provide the benefits of a division of labor while running the risk that expert committee members will take advantage of the rest of the chamber. To guard against the perversities that might attend a committee system, members of the House have over the years created a sometimes Byzantine system of accountability and control. For most of the period under consideration here, this control system extended from the caucus of the majority party to the committee system via the Speaker. The Speaker was entrusted with direct oversight of the committee system from top to bottom. This oversight began with the determination of the details of the system itself. Until 1910 the Speaker chaired the House Rules Committee, which was primarily responsible for recommending the standing rules of the chamber at the beginning of each Congress.[10] Almost every account of the Rules Committee during this period casts it as a partisan tool of the majority party leadership, so we can safely assume that the creation of committees, the establishment of their jurisdictions, and the fixing of their sizes—three important components of the House rules—had to pass partisan muster as reflected in the preferences of the incumbent Speaker.

In addition to the details of the system that were overseen by the Rules Committee, the Speaker had direct control over the composition of committees. Speakers set the "partisan ratio" of each committee, thus determining how large a majority the majority party would hold on each committee. They also had the authority to name members to committees (including members of the minority), in addition to determining who would chair each committee.

Students of Congress know that this system came to an end with the "revolt" against Speaker Joseph Cannon in 1910 (Sixty-first Congress). These changes removed the Speaker from the membership of the Rules Committee and formally transferred authority to appoint committees to the floor itself; the appointment authority quickly evolved in practice into a "committee on committees" in each party, still subject to majority vote of the entire floor. Thus in the last ten years covered by this chapter, 1911 to 1921, the most direct oversight of the committee system ran through the separate party caucuses and then through party committees. This system of authority has obtained to this day, with the exception of the added role of the Speaker in making committee assignments beginning in the 1970s. (Still, the power of the Speaker in 1991 pales in comparison to the Speaker's power in 1891.)

The drumbeat of criticism by Democrats, Populists, and Progressives against "czar rule" following Reed's ascent to the speakership in 1889 and the pyrotechnics associated with the "revolt against Cannon" often lead neophyte students of congressional history to believe that Speakers behaved arbitrarily when they used their unilateral power to make committee assignments around the turn of the century. The rise of seniority and party committees after 1910 is thus seen as the triumph of order against tyranny, although this new system, too, would come under constant attack in the 1960s.

Certainly, Speakers of the era of czar rule acted against the interests of opposition parties, but that was precisely the role prescribed to them by their own party caucuses. Such ruthlessness was necessary for the Republicans to overcome obstruction by the minority Democrats. Later, Cannon believed that the tactics he had used to fight against the obstructionist Democrats would be effective in fighting against the Progressive minority within the Republican party that was challenging his authority.

Of course, Cannon proved to be wrong in making this strategic calculation, but two comments deserve to be made. First, Cannon and his followers believed his actions were fully justifiable against the backdrop of past Speakers' actions. Second, and in a related vein, Cannon's actions were strategic miscalculations, but not by much. He *almost won* the vote that constituted the revolt, and even after losing that vote he won the ensuing vote on declaring the speakership vacant. Cannon failed to hold onto political support within the House, but it was unclear how much the House would change as a result.[11]

Thus in ultimately failing to hold the support of a majority of the House for his organization of the chamber, Cannon's experience allows us to focus again on what the rank and file expect out of the committee system, how they expect party leaders to implement their desires, and how they hold ultimate sanctions when leaders push their initiatives too persistently. And, as Cooper and Brady have argued, Cannon's experience allows us to witness what happens when many of these expectations change due to changes in the political environment.

On the Size of Committees

A detailed examination of all the ways in which Speakers maintained support via their committee assignment practices up until Cannon would involve several chapters of a book on organizational strategy. Short of that, I will narrow the focus in the following sections. The focus is narrowed by highlighting a single dimension of the committee assignment problem: that of committee size. The issue of committee size provides a simple target to focus on in understanding how Speakers and other party leaders balanced the collective and individual benefits that derived from the committee system. The matter of committee size is a little-considered, yet instructive, characteristic of committees. It is little-considered because it seems so mundane; it is instructive because when the size of committees is determined, the distribution of powerful resources is also determined.

We can begin this discussion by recognizing that some committees are more useful than others in helping members of the House achieve their goals. For instance, a member of Congress who represents the fishing community of New Bedford, Massachusetts, will probably find membership on the Merchant Marine and Fisheries Committee more useful in achieving his electoral and policy goals than service on the Banking, Finance, and Urban Affairs Committee. At the same time, representatives from both New Bedford and Manhattan are likely to find membership on the Ways and Means Committee very useful for most goals they might have, given this committee's oversight of such weighty topics as income taxation and social security.

We can easily imagine what would happen if members of the House were allowed simply to choose their own committee assignments absent any constraints upon their choice. One plausible scenario is this: first, most members would probably choose to serve on the committees that deal directly with important national issues, such as Appropriations and Ways and Means. Second, "lesser committees" would be heavily populated with members whose constituents had a special interest in that committee's jurisdiction. Third, committees that deal with the most mundane matters of legislative life, such as judging disputed elections, adjudicating charges of ethical violations among its members, and overseeing the printing of congressional reports, might get no members.

Thus if the House adopted such a radical version of self-selection, we might expect great disparities in the sizes of committees, with the most broadly based (e.g., Ways and Means and Appropriations) being the largest, the most narrowly defined policy committees (e.g., Agriculture) being smaller, and the housekeeping committees (e.g., House Administration) being smaller still. The housekeeping committees would have too few members to discharge legislative duties effectively, the narrowly defined policy committees would be too obviously biased to be relied on by the rest of the House for legislative advice, and the most important committees would be so large that the reason for having something like the Ways and Means Committee rather than simply a committee of the whole would be questioned altogether. In other words, the committee system would not offer the benefits a division of labor promises.

For these reasons, real-world legislatures such as the House of Representatives rarely rely on self-selection to allocate members to committees. Instead, they ration valuable committee seats and coerce membership onto less valued committees. Doing so enhances the benefits that accrue from a division of labor.

For the period covered by this chapter, the first practical institutional result of this rationing/coercion was that Speakers kept some committees, such as Ways and Means, "too small" and others, such as Ventilation and Acoustics, "too large," judged by the criteria of pure self-selection. This practice produced policy results that were beneficial to the legislative majorities that controlled the House during this time: coercion and rationing together provided the legislative personnel necessary to handle the House's mundane affairs, helped balance the policy committees against total capture by narrow interests, and ultimately channeled the most able members into the most important committees.

This control of opportunities for committee service set up an interesting dynamic between the rank and file and Speakers. On the one hand, by being the guardian of this plan, the Speaker came to exert influence over members of the rank and file. By appointing "too many" members to the least desirable committees, a class of legislators was created that was always on the lookout for opportunities to transfer onto a more desirable committee; these "institutional climbers" were thus susceptible to influence from the Speaker, who provided the route to advancement within the House. By denying anyone an inviolable right to be continuously reappointed to his current committees—there was no meaningful "seniority system" as we understand it today—Speakers could also induce House members, even the most highly elevated members, to support the party program. To the extent that party loyalty was valued by party leaders and followers alike, the implementation of a committee-seat rationing plan overseen by a single party leader helped to provide the collective benefit of consistent party legislation.

Yet members bridled at this system. While a member might agree in principle with the need to keep valuable committee assignments scarce and to reward hard work and party loyalty with increasingly attractive committee appointments, he might wonder about the justice of his own particular lot in legislative life. And if enough members became dissatisfied with their treatment under the existing regime, revolt against the leader was always a possibility.

Thus while a Speaker might hold the reins tightly, he could not hold them too tightly and still achieve his own and his party's policy goals. This need to accommodate the special needs (or demands) of the rank and file led inexorably to the loosening of the system of rationing top committee positions, and thus to the growth of many committees.

In addition, there were incentives for Speakers, just like governments in general, to pay off their "debts" by debasing the currency. In this case the debts were political, while the currency was institutional standing. Consider the following scenario: a party leader might induce policy compliance or hard work from a member of the rank and file by promising to consider that member favorably in making future committee assignments. What would happen in the next Congress if too few committee seats opened up to pay off this debt? One solution would be simply to "coin more money," which in this context would mean creating another committee assignment to reward the faithful backbencher.

Thus if Speakers had to be responsive to the demands of the rank and file in making committee assignments during this era, we can make two predictions about the size of committees over time: first, there would be a constrained inflationary tendency in the size of committees that is independent of the growth of the institution; second, if we divide committees into *types*, we would notice that the most valuable committees, such as Ways and Means, would grow faster than the least valuable, such as Ventilation and Acoustics. I will consider these predictions in order.

General Growth in the Committee System

The data in Table 5.1 show that the number of committees, the number of total committee assignments, and the average size of committees grew throughout the years covered by this chapter. (The data used here and in the rest of this chapter are discussed briefly in appendix A.) It is tempting to attribute the growth in the size of the committee system to the growth of the House itself. A combination of population growth and new-state admissions caused the House to grow from 293 to 435 members between 1875 and 1921, thus we might assume that the committee system grew largely as a consequence of accommodating these 142 new members within the committee system.

Yet two observations cast doubt on this explanation. First, the committee system grew faster than the House itself did. By the Sixty-sixth Congress there were 48 percent more House members than there had been in the Forty-fourth Congress, but there were 82 percent more committee assignments. Second, committee appointments did not grow faster when the House added seats due to the decennial post-census reapportionments. In the Forty-third, Forty-eighth, Fifty-third, and Fifty-eighth Congresses the House grew by an average of thirty-two seats due to the effects of reapportionment. In those same Congresses, an average of only fifteen new committee assignments were added. On the other hand, in the fifteen Houses between 1875 and 1921 that experienced *no* growth, either because of the lack of reapportionment

Table 5.1

Number of Standing Committees and Standing Committee Appointments in the 44th–66th Congresses, 1875–1921

Congress	Years	Entire Congress[a]		Beginning of Congress[b]	
		Committees	Seats	Committees	Seats
44	1875–77	46	457	46	397
45		48	479	48	431
46		50	537	49	475
47	1881–83	49	529	49	474
48		50	562	50	495
49		50	578	50	540
50		52	593	52	577
51		56	653	56	587
52	1891–93	55	653	55	594
53		54	699	53	576
54		56	691	56	641
55		56	677	56	624
56		58	729	58	674
57	1901–3	59	749	59	666
58		59	744	59	686
59		60	782	60	708
60		60	798	60	735
61		60	811	60	741
62	1911–13	55	799	55	683
63		57	822	57	718
64		58	810	58	757
65		59	854	59	716
66	1921–23	59	858	59	721
			15,864		14,216

Source: Committee membership data described in appendix A.

Notes:
[a]Includes all committee appointments made during a Congress, including appointments to new committees and the filling of vacancies.
[b]Includes only committees that were appointed at the beginning of a Congress.

or the admission of new states to the union, the number of committee assignments increased on average by nineteen seats.

There are more sophisticated methods for dealing with this empirical issue. One such technique is multiple regression analysis, which allows us to disentangle the contribution of increased workload, growth in the House's membership, and other partisan factors in explaining the growth of the committee system during this period. Appendix B contains a simple example of this sort of quantitative analysis. For the less technically inclined, let me summarize that analysis here. First, growth in the House size had no substantive role in explaining the growth in either the number of committees in the House or the number of committee assignments. Second, whenever partisan control of the House changed because of an intervening congressional election, the new controlling party actually *reduced* the number of assignments by about sixteen seats. This pattern is consistent with the "leadership responsiveness" argument because when the House changed partisan hands, members of the new majority party could be accommodated in committee assignments by taking over the old seats of the former majority party; the remaining members of the minority party (the erstwhile majority) were simply forced by the majority to make do with less.

Finally, even after accounting for the growth in House size, the number of committees in the committee system, and changing partisan control of the House, there is still a significant upward trend in the number of assignments made each Congress. The size of this upward drift averaged about eight committee seats per Congress. This may not seem like much, but given the small size of House committees during this period, eight committee slots essentially amounted to the leadership's adding another committee every Congress or two.

The Distribution of Committee Growth

In addition to this general inflation of committee assignments, if we look at *where* this inflation occurred, we see that it is consistent with the "leadership accountability" argument that I made in the previous section. For this argument to hold we should witness Speakers opening up the more desirable committees faster than the least desirable, in order to maintain support among the rank and file. To see this pattern, we first need to develop a method of classifying committees in order of their desirability. There are numerous ways to classify congressional committees in the political science literature.[12] For the purposes of this chapter I have chosen to classify all House committees between 1875 and 1921, placing them into categories that roughly reflect how much a member of the rank and file would give up (in terms of other committee or leadership assignments) in order to serve on a type of committee. These five categories, and their definitions, are as follows. (Although there are exceptions, I have ordered these categories roughly in the order of their hypothesized value to the average member.)

1. *Partisan/power committees.* These were the most important committees for the prosecution of party programs and for wielding the widest range of policy influence in the House. Included in this category are Ways and Means, Appropriations, and Rules. I also included Judiciary and Banking and Currency here because they were the committees that oversaw the most controversial substantive legislation of the era.

2. *Other appropriations committees.* Between 1865 and 1877 the House Appropriations Committee held undisputed jurisdiction over all spending measures in the House. Beginning with the Forty-fifth Congress, however, numerous authorizing committees and their supporters succeeded in transferring spending jurisdiction to various legislative committees, such as the Commerce Committee in 1878, Agriculture in 1880, and five other legislative committees in 1885.[13] By virtue of its oversight over most of the budget during this period, Appropriations was always a valued assignment; as these other legislative committees acquired appropriations oversight they, too, gained in power and prestige, and thus appointment to them became more valuable than appointment to other substantive committees.

3. *Substantive committees* were legislative committees that did not consider appropriations but which fell outside the "power committee" category described above and the "constituency claims" category described below. These committees considered a wide range of topics, running from Alcoholic Liquor traffic to Woman [sic] Suffrage.

4. *Private/claims committees* were committees that spent most of their time determining benefits that would flow to constituents from the federal government, such as military pensions and war claims. Consequently, private bills dominated the workloads of these committees.

5. *Housekeeping/audit committees* were those that either dealt exclusively with matters internal to the House (e.g., ventilation and acoustics) or oversaw the financial practices of particular agencies

(e.g., expenditures in the State Department). Because these committees provided so few benefits to constituents and their work was so anonymous, they were likely to be the least prized of all assignments.

Given the policy, electoral, and power goals of most members of the House, members during this period least wanted to serve on the housekeeping/audit and private/claims committees; they most wanted to serve on the power, appropriations, and substantive committees, and they would relinquish other assignments or be more willing to accede to leadership directives in order to be assigned to them.[14]

Table 5.2 reports the number of committees in each category and the number of members appointed to each type of committee in each Congress. Using the Forty-ninth Congress as the baseline,[15] we can see there is a rough correspondence between hypothesized committee value and the rates at which the committee categories grew. Between the Forty-ninth and Sixty-sixth Congresses the number of appointments to power, appropriations, and substantive committees grew by 68 percent, 38 percent, and 55 percent, respectively, while the number of seats on housekeeping committees grew by only 7 percent and the number of seats on claims committees actually shrank by 19 percent. (The House as a whole grew by 34 percent over these years, from 325 to 435 members.)

Growth in committee seats was also related to the number of committee vacancies produced in each election, as detailed analysis reported in appendix B shows. To summarize that multiple regression analysis here, except within the housekeeping category, the number of committee seats tended to grow more whenever there were relatively few committee vacancies created by defeats or retirements in the previous election. This finding is consistent with the "seat inflation" scenario I outlined in the previous section. Often, when the Speaker had a hard time moving people into committees because other veteran members already could claim committee seats, Speakers responded by simply adding more seats to committees.[16] In addition, the number of committee seats in each category, except housekeeping, grew a bit each year, even after accounting for growth that occurred because of the lack of vacancies that followed particular elections.

Therefore, although party leaders held a firm grip on the allocation of committee positions during this period, they had to periodically

Table 5.2

Number of Committees and Committee Assignments by Committee Category, 44th–66th Congresses (statistics as of beginning of the Congress)

Congress	Power		Appropriations		Substantive		Private/Claims		Housekeeping	
	Committees	Seats	Committees	Seats	Committees	Seats	Committees	Seats	Committees	Seats
44	6	53	1	10	19	205	5	52	16	87
45	6	59	2	22	20	210	5	52	17	110
46	6	69	3	45	20	208	5	55	17	128
47	6	73	3	44	19	198	5	60	18	129
48	6	69	3	41	20	214	5	64	17	121
49	6	69	8	111	15	184	5	67	17	124
50	6	75	8	110	17	210	5	67	17	129
51	6	67	8	108	19	223	5	68	19	135
52	6	74	8	105	19	232	5	65	18	133
53	6	80	8	115	18	214	5	64	17	119
54	6	87	8	130	18	227	5	68	20	146
55	6	81	8	122	18	223	5	66	20	145
56	6	87	8	133	20	266	5	66	20	139
57	6	84	8	131	21	266	5	64	20	137
58	6	86	8	133	21	270	5	66	20	147
59	6	90	8	134	21	293	5	69	21	139
60	6	87	8	140	21	305	5	70	21	149
61	6	88	8	145	21	302	5	70	21	152
62	6	107	8	152	17	244	4	55	21	142
63	6	103	8	160	18	274	4	54	22	147
64	6	113	8	160	19	296	4	59	22	150
65	6	107	8	154	20	279	4	56	22	136
66	6	116	8	153	20	286	4	54	22	133

Note: The number of committees in each category and the number of assignments are based on the actual appointment of committees at the beginning of each Congress. Thus it is likely that the number of appointments for each Congress does not equal the number of seats allocated to all committees through the House Rules, due to the failure to fill all committee slots. Similarly, the failure to appoint a committee at all at the beginning of a Congress, although it was still listed in the House Rules, would result in that committee not being accounted for in this table.

accommodate the wishes of the rank and file, who constantly desired an increase in the number of opportunities for important committee service. As the years progressed and the number of vacancies caused by electoral turnover declined, Speakers increasingly accommodated the wishes of their followers by expanding the size of the committee system.[17]

Conclusion

The data and argument I presented in the previous sections could be extended to other measures and other characteristics of the committee system. For instance, others have studied the degree to which Speakers chose committee chairs based on the norm of seniority.[18] An examination of the choice of committee chairs before the onset of the relatively strict seniority norm would generally bolster the "leadership accountability" argument that I have been making. Even when Speakers had complete authority to ignore past committee service in appointing members to chair committees, they did so infrequently. "Violations" of seniority are usually easily explained in terms of partisan goals, not the personal whims of Speakers.

Other characteristics of the committee system that could be studied for evidence of leadership responsiveness to rank and file demands include whether members tended to be promoted to increasingly attractive committees over their careers and whether such promotions were based on adherence to the party's platform. Such analysis remains to be done in the future. When it is completed, it will provide us with a more comprehensive view of the relationship between congressional leaders and followers.

An historic tendency among many students of Congress is to mistake authority for autonomy. As the House entered its second century, Speakers had tremendous authority. Whether they had autonomy, is another matter. Progressive slogans decrying "bossism" have tended to obscure the degree to which party leaders were effective agents of their caucuses around the turn of the century. Examining how Speakers executed this agency will not only help us understand an important era of congressional history, it will help us understand the web of relationships that have entangled members of Congress from the beginning and that continue to entangle them as Congress enters yet another century.

Appendix A:

Data Sources

The data set analyzed in this chapter consists of information on standing committee assignments in the House between the Forty-fourth and Sixty-sixth Congresses (1875–1921). The data about committee assignments were gathered and made available by Professor Garrison Nelson of the University of Vermont. The primary source for the assignment data was the House *Journal*, which is more authoritative and accurate than listings that appear in the *Congressional Directory*.[19] Some other data were added to this basic information about committee assignments, drawing from standard historical sources.

The Nelson data set contains information about assignments to House *standing* committees. Fortunately, Nelson included assignment data for select committees if they later became standing. The most important committee to which this pertains is the Rules Committee, which became a standing committee only in 1880 (Forty-sixth Congress), although it had been continually appointed as a select committee since the first Congress. In fact, most select committees that were appointed at the beginning of a Congress during the era covered by this chapter eventually became standing. Therefore, while the data set omits assignments to select committees that never became standing committees, Nelson's liberal definition of standing committees makes this a minor problem.[20] In all, the Nelson data set chronicles almost 16,000 separate committee assignments to seventy-one different standing committees between the Forty-fourth and Sixty-sixth Congresses. The total number of assignments at the beginning of a Congress varied from 397 seats on forty-six committees in the Forty-fourth Congress to 757 seats on fifty-eight committees in the Sixty-sixth (see Table 5.1 in the text above).

Appendix B:

Data Analysis Details

Twice in this chapter I resort to some multiple regression analysis to make points about the fluctuation of committee sizes from 1875 to 1921. For readers without a background in quantitative social science,

Table A5.1

Growth in the Number of Committees and Committee Assignments, 44th–66th Congresses

Dependent variables:	Committee assignments	Number of committees
Independent variables		
House size	0.02	0.025
	(0.38)	(0.030)
Number of committees	11.74	—
	(3.13)	
Change in party control	−15.71	−0.07
	(7.69)	(0.58)
Democratic control	8.42	−1.94
	(11.80)	(0.63)
Trend	8.03	0.26
	(4.19)	(0.41)
r^2	.62	.37
adj. r^2	.53	.25
rho	−.58	
d.w.	1.89	2.41
Method	AR1	OLS

Variables: Committee assignments: number of committee assignments made at the beginning of a Congress. *House size:* total number of apportioned House members at the beginning of a Congress. *Number of committees:* number of committees appointed at the beginning of a Congress. *Change in party control:* dummy variable equal to 1 if the party that organized the House in Congress t did not organize the House in Congress t–1, 0 otherwise. *Democratic control:* dummy variable equal to 1 if the Democrats organized the House, 0 otherwise. *Trend:* Congress –44.

Note: All variables were transformed using first differences.

I report in the text a summary of this analysis. For readers who do have such training, I provide here the tables that are the sources of those summaries.

Table A5.1 shows the result of analysis in which I modeled the total number of committee assignments in the House and the number of committees as a function of congressional workload, House size, and changes in partisanship. In addition, I used the total number of committees as a partial explanation for the growth in the number of assignments. To test for the existence of an upward trend independent of

Table A5.2

Growth in the Number of Seats in Each Committee Category as a Function of Vacancies Created through Resignation or Electoral Defeat, plus Partisan Variables, 45th–66th Congresses (N = 22)

Independent variables:	Committee type				
	Power	Appro-priations	Sub-stantive	Private	House-keeping
Trend	11.92	9.04	18.83	25.27	−2.15
	(4.69)	(2.97)	(9.39)	(10.46)	(2.99)
Vacancies	−105.56	−54.46	−61.37	−143.38	58.29
	(48.94)	(26.77)	(37.10)	(46.57)	(37.45)
Change in party control	9.09 (3.48)	7.45 (3.01)	−0.08 (5.43)	−2.58 (3.44)	−6.17 (2.32)
Democratic control	3.22 (2.79)	5.46 (3.00)	−2.94 (4.16)	−3.99 (2.48)	−3.33 (2.23)
House size	−0.08	−0.07	0.15	0.12	0.03
	(0.12)	(0.13)	(0.17)	(0.09)	(0.07)
Number of committees in category	—	9.53 (1.27)	10.11 (1.28)	−19.06 (7.05)	−2.29 (1.41)
r^2	.37	.83	.85	.69	.49
adj. r^2	.21	.78	.80	.59	.32
rho	−.42	−.61	—	.84	—
d.w.	1.92	2.61	2.35	1.94	2.19
Method	AR1	AR1	OLS	AR1	OLS

Variables: Trend, change in party control, Democratic control, and *number of committees in category* as defined in Table A5.1. *Vacancies:* the number of members of a committee in Congress *t*–1 who did not return to the House in Congress *t*.

Note: All variables are first differences, therefore the trend is measured by the constant. The number of committees in the partisan/power category is constant for the entire period and thus is not included in the analysis.

other systematic factors, I finally included a linear trend term in each analysis. The data sources for these variables were the Nelson data set and *Historical Statistics of the United States.* The dependent variables in the analyses were taken from the last two columns of Table 5.1. Congressional workload was defined as the number of bills and resolutions introduced during each Congress. Partisanship was measured in two ways. First, a dummy variable was created describing

Congresses in which Democrats controlled the House. Second, a dummy variable was created describing Congresses in which majority control of the chamber passed from one party to the other.

Because I was interested in explaining *expansion* of the committee system, not the overall size per se, I transformed all the variables to "first differences." Briefly, a regression on first differences involves transforming *all* variables in the regression by subtracting the value of each variable at time t from the value of the same variable at time t-1. So, for instance, a simple two-variable regression would be written as:

$$Y_t = a + bX_t + e_t$$

The first difference version of this equation would be:

$$(Y_t - Y_{t-1}) = b(X_t - X_{t-1}) + (e_t - e_{t-1})$$

Note that a constant subtracted from itself is equal to zero, so that the first difference regression is properly conducted without an intercept term. Also to be noted is that the parameters estimated in each equation are identical, the only difference is the method of estimation.

In the second multiple regression I was interested in seeing whether the dynamics of committee growth—measured by the number of assignments to the five different committee categories I identified in the text—were similar across the different committee types. I was also interested in seeing whether the number of more sought-after committee assignments grew whenever the number of vacancies on those committees fell. Table A5.2 reports the results of this analysis.

Notes

Some data used in this paper were generously made available to me by Professor Garrison Nelson of the University of Vermont and the Inter-University Consortium for Political and Social Research. The original draft of this chapter was prepared for presentation to a conference at the Carl Albert Center. Comments on that original paper by Joseph Cooper, Stanley Bach, Tom Gilligan, and Ron Peters were greatly appreciated. The Dirksen Center provided much-appreciated financial support for the collection and analysis of the data. The Hoover Institution at Stanford University provided computing resources and time off so that I could write the original draft.

1. On institutionalization, see Michael Abram and Joseph Cooper, "The Rise of Seniority in the House of Representatives," *Polity* 1 (1968): 52–85; Nelson Polsby, "The Institutionalization of the U.S. House of Representatives," *American Political Science Review* 62 (1968): 144–68; Nelson Polsby, Miriam Gallaher,

and Barry Rundquist, "The Growth of the Seniority System in the U.S. House of Representatives," *American Political Science Review* 63 (1969): 787–807; Allan Bogue, Jerome H. Blubb, Carroll R. McKibbin, and Santa Traugott, "Members of the House of Representatives and the Process of Modernization," *Journal of American History* 63 (1976): 275–302; Samuel Kernell, "Toward Understanding 19th Century Congressional Careers: Ambition, Competition, and Rotation," *American Journal of Political Science* 21 (1977): 669–93; H. Douglas Price, "The Congressional Career Then and Now," in *Congressional Behavior*, ed. Nelson Polsby (New York: Random House, 1971); Price, "Congress and the Evolution of Legislative 'Professionalism,' " in *Congress in Change*, ed. Norman Ornstein (New York: Praeger, 1975); Price, "Careers and Committees in the American Congress: The Problem of Structural Change," in *The History of Parliamentary Behavior*, ed. William O. Aydelotte (Princeton, NJ: Princeton University Press, 1977).

On the House more generally during this period, see Woodrow Wilson, *Congressional Government* (Boston: Houghton Mifflin, 1885); Mary Parker Follett, *The Speaker of the House of Representatives* (New York: Longmans, 1896); Lauros G. McConachie, *Congressional Committees* (New York: Crowell, 1898); O.O. Stealey, *Twenty Years in the Press Gallery* (New York: Self-published, 1906); De Alva Stanwood Alexander, *History and Procedure of the House of Representatives* (Boston: Houghton Mifflin, 1916); Chang-Wei Chiu, *The Speaker of the House of Representatives since 1896* (New York: Columbia University Press, 1928); George B. Galloway, *History of the House of Representatives* (New York: Crowell, 1961); James Holt, *Congressional Insurgents and the Party System, 1909–1916* (Cambridge: Harvard University Press, 1967); David W. Brady, *Congressional Voting in the Partisan Era* (Lawrence, KS: University of Kansas Press, 1973); Joseph Cooper and David W. Brady, "Institutional Context and Leadership Style: The House from Cannon to Rayburn," *American Political Science Review* 75 (1981): 411–25; Charles Stewart III, *Budget Reform Politics: The Design of the Appropriations Process in the House of Representatives, 1865–1921* (New York: Cambridge University Press, 1989).

2. Morris P. Fiorina, David W. Rohde, and Peter Wissel, "Historical Change in House Turnover," in *Congress in Change*, 30.

3. An important recent exception to this tendency is Cooper and Brady, "Institutional Context."

4. For representative treatments of Congress in this vein, see Mathew D. McCubbins and Thomas Schwartz, "Congressional Oversight Overlooked: Police Patrols versus Fire Alarms," *American Journal of Political Science* 28 (1984): 167–79; D. Roderick Kiewiet and Mathew D. McCubbins, *The Spending Power* (Chicago: University of Chicago Press, forthcoming); Gary W. Cox and Mathew D. McCubbins, *Parties and Committees in the U.S. House of Representatives* (Berkeley and Los Angeles: University of California Press, forthcoming); Keith Krehbiel, *Information and Legislative Organization* (Ann Arbor: University of Michigan Press, 1991).

5. William H. Riker, *Liberalism against Populism* (San Francisco: Freeman, 1982).

6. Follett, *Speaker of the House*, 222–23. It is interesting to note that in the paragraph that precedes this one, Follett provides a description of the committee

appointment process that might lead one to believe that Speakers were able to ignore the preferences of the majority altogether in making up committee lists. Such ambivalence is common to "progressive" scholarship about Congress, an even more classic example of which is Woodrow Wilson's *Congressional Government*.

7. Much of the argument and data in this paper is extracted from Charles Stewart III, "Committees from Randall to Clark: Some Preliminary Evidence about Committee Assignments in the House of Representatives, 1875–1921" (Paper presented at the conference "Back to the Future: The United States Congress in the Twenty-First Century," Carl Albert Center, University of Oklahoma, 11–13 April 1990).

8. See especially Richard Fenno, *Congressmen on Committees* (Boston: Little, Brown, 1973); Steven S. Smith and Christopher Deering, *Congressional Committees* (Washington: Congressional Quarterly, 1984); Kenneth Shepsle, *The Giant Jigsaw Puzzle* (Chicago: University of Chicago Press, 1978); Krehbiel, *Information and Legislative Organization*.

9. It is often argued that such special provisions "grease the skids" so that significant legislation that does benefit the nation as a whole can be passed. I am not disputing that point here. What I am highlighting is how members of Ways and Means are advantaged in garnering these sorts of special tax benefits for their constituents, and thus the distribution of these sorts of legislative gains tends to be unequal.

10. It was not until 1883 that the practice of writing and reporting special orders—what we now colloquially refer to as "rules"—was developed. See James A. Robinson, *The House Rules Committee* (Indianapolis: Bobbs-Merrill, 1963); Stanley Bach, "From Special Orders to Special Rules: Pictures of House Procedure in Transition" (Paper presented at the Eighty-sixth Annual Meeting of the American Political Science Association, San Francisco, California, 30 August–2 September 1990).

11. Cooper and Brady, "Institutional Context."

12. Examples of committee classification schemes according to notions of value inherent in committee service can be found in Abram and Cooper, "The Rise of Seniority," and Cox and McCubbins, *Parties and Committees*. For an example of a classification scheme based on the importance of the type of legislation considered, see McConachie, *Congressional Committees*.

13. Stewart, *Budget Reform Politics*. These five other committees were Military Affairs, Foreign Affairs, Indian Affairs, Naval Affairs, and Post Office.

14. Some evidence about the validity of this assertion is provided in the conference paper that was the basis of this chapter, "Committees from Randall to Clark." The evidence consists of committee "dominance" or "value" rankings that are derived from the observed pattern of transfers among committees during specific eras. For instance, among the thirty-five committees that were in existence for the entire period between 1875 and 1921, the following is the average value ranking of each category, along with the number of committees:

(There are more than thirty-five committees reflected in this table because of overlaps among the power, appropriations, and substantive committees.) Other than the virtual tie between claims and housekeeping committees, these average rankings reflect the hypothesized category ranking used in this chapter.

Table N5.1

Committee type	Arithmetic mean	Geometric mean	N
Power/prestige	4.0	3.0	(5)
Appropriations	7.9	6.7	(7)
Substantive	15.6	13.4	(14)
Excluding appropriating committees	20.8	19.4	(8)
Private/claims	25.0	24.7	(3)
Housekeeping/audit	24.3	22.9	(13)

15. I have taken the Forty-ninth Congress as the baseline here because that was the Congress in which five committees shifted from the substantive to the appropriations category. Otherwise, the growth rates are dominated by the effects of the "devolution of 1885," which I describe in *Budget Reform Politics.*

16. I admit to coming close to creating an anachronism here, by assuming that returning, veteran committee members could put claims on committee seats solely based on prior committee service. Even if prior service entitled veteran members to *no* claims to continued service on that committee, Speakers were still unlikely to upset prior decisions (i.e., committee assignments made in prior Congresses) wholesale in order to accommodate the current committee demands of a few members.

17. One interesting question that this assertion raises, but which we yet do not have enough data to answer, is which type of committee assignment process was more responsive to membership demands to expand the size of the committee system—the Speaker-centered system which lasted until 1911 or the party committee system which has held sway since 1911. I hazard a guess that the current system, which has party committees rather than individual Speakers making assignments, is less accommodating to demands for committee seat inflation, since responsibility for committee assignments is more diffuse.

18. Abram and Cooper, "The Rise of Seniority"; Polsby et al., "The Growth of the Seniority System"; Price, "Careers and Committees."

19. For a complete description of the data, see Garrison Nelson, "Congressional Committee Assignments, 1789–1989," photocopy, University of Vermont. Further discussion of committee assignment data can be found in Price, "Careers and Committees." For discussions about error checking of the Nelson data, see Gary W. Cox and Mathew D. McCubbins, *Parties and Committees in the U.S. House of Representatives* (Berkeley and Los Angeles: University of California Press, forthcoming); and Stewart, "Committees from Randall to Clark."

20. For instance, Stubbs reports that seventy-three standing and ninety-eight select committees existed some time between the Forty-fourth and Sixty-sixth Congresses. Almost all of these select committees were one-time affairs appointed in the course of a Congress. It is assignments to committees such as the Select Committee on Georgia Post Roads that are omitted from consideration in this paper. See Walter Stubbs, comp., *Congressional Committees, 1789–1982* (Westport, CT: Greenwood Press, 1985).

RANDALL STRAHAN

6 Reed and Rostenkowski: Congressional Leadership in Institutional Time

Thomas Brackett Reed and Dan Rostenkowski might seem at first an odd pair to focus on in an essay on leadership and change in Congress. Reed, Speaker of the House during the late 1880s and 1890s, was a Maine Yankee known for his parliamentary skill, devastating wit, and unwillingness to bend on matters of principle. Rostenkowski, chairman of the House Ways and Means Committee since 1981, is the grandson of Polish immigrants and a master practitioner of the Chicago school of machine politics, in which tangible rewards for personal and group loyalty, and sometimes not too subtle forms of intimidation rather than principled rhetoric or fine points of procedure, are the stock-in-trade of political leadership. How might a comparison of Reed and Rostenkowski as leaders help in understanding why Congress changes?

The role of leaders in bringing about institutional change in Congress has received less attention from political scientists than one might expect. Political scientists today usually view congressional leaders as being more *influenced by*, than influencing, institutional forms or other features of a political "context." When seeking to explain what congressional leaders do and how influential or successful they are, most recent work on leadership has emphasized contextual or situational factors rather than personal qualities of individual leaders. Congressional leaders are usually characterized as more or less skillful practitioners of a "leadership style," which is defined by the institutional/political context within which the leader must work. In this contextually driven framework, limited opportunities are present for a leader to act independently to define an effective leadership style or to direct the course of institutional change.

Yet both Reed and Rostenkowski stand out as innovative leaders. Reed recast the role of the majority party leadership by asserting the Speaker's control over the conduct of business on the House floor during the 1890s, while Rostenkowski reestablished a more centralized leadership style on the Ways and Means Committee after a period of democratizing reforms and permissive leadership during the 1970s. A review of the conditions under which these two leaders served finds that each encountered a similar political situation. Both served in periods during which an existing leadership regime had fallen into disfavor and dissatisfaction with institutional performance was high. Both also, for very different reasons, believed in the legitimacy of stronger legislative leadership, and each possessed skills needed to assert a new type of leadership in the particular political situation he faced. The goals of this chapter are, first, through a comparison of the cases of Reed and Rostenkowski, to explore the idea that some periods in the history of the House may in fact present opportunities for individual leaders to influence the course of institutional development and change, and second, to propose a theoretical framework for thinking about the situations that may present these kinds of opportunities and why leaders do or do not exploit them.

Leaders, Leadership, and Institutional Change in the House

A prominent example of the contextual emphasis in recent work on congressional leadership is Joseph Cooper and David Brady's analysis of the transition from the centralized, hierarchical pattern of majority leadership that was in place in the House at the turn of the century to the decentralized, bargaining-oriented leadership regime of the Rayburn years. Cooper and Brady find that

> . . . institutional context rather than personal traits primarily determines leadership style in the House. To be sure, style is affected by personal traits. Nonetheless, style is and must be responsive to and congruent with both the inducements available to leaders and member expectations regarding proper behavior.[1]

Studies of House leadership by Charles O. Jones, Richard F. Fenno,

Jr., Barbara Sinclair, Steven S. Smith and Christopher J. Deering, David W. Rohde and Kenneth A. Shepsle, Ronald M. Peters, Jr., and others have also found a contextually driven theoretical framework most useful for understanding the leadership styles and influence of leaders in the House.[2]

This emphasis on context over personal characteristics of leaders has been a needed corrective to earlier commentaries that attributed differences in leaders' styles and effectiveness primarily to personality or political skill. Congressional leaders must work within constitutional forms and a political culture that limit opportunities for establishing and maintaining hierarchical forms of authority.[3] House leaders who attempt to exercise influence beyond limits defined by the preferences of a procedural majority in the chamber risk losing their positions or being stripped of their authority—a point ably demonstrated by Charles O. Jones in an earlier leadership study comparing a Speaker (Joseph G. Cannon) and a committee chairman (Howard W. Smith).[4] The House is not an institution that invites leaders to make it over in their own images; few attempts to do so are likely to be successful. As Jones concludes in a more recent essay on House leadership, "seldom will leaders be successful in capitalizing on personal characteristics to rise above the constraints of organizational conditions."[5]

Three types of contextual factors are most important in defining the constraints or limits on leadership in the House. The first are institutional factors. These include constitutional forms and internal organization and procedures, as well as informal, but well-established, norms or practices that structure the expectations and behavior of members. Second are factors associated with electoral politics and conditions in the party system. Probably the most important factor influencing House leadership styles over the long term is the degree of unity or factionalism in the congressional party system.[6] The role of party organizations in candidate recruitment is another important factor of this type. The configuration of partisan control of Congress and the White House is important as well in defining opportunities and constraints for congressional leaders. A third set of factors that are important for understanding leadership in the House involve agenda or issue-related factors. The opportunities and constraints encountered by both party and committee leaders are defined in part by the number and types of issues on the congressional agenda, as well as institutional arrangements and partisan conditions.

The basic premise of most recent leadership studies is that leaders must work within the constraints defined by these contextual factors and can only influence leadership styles and institutional arrangements—as Steven S. Smith put it in a recent analysis of House leadership under Speaker Thomas P. "Tip" O'Neill—"at the margins."[7] Cooper and Brady offer a similar view:

> If O'Neill's leadership style is far closer to that of Rayburn, McCormack, and Albert than to Cannon or Reed, this is not attributable to basic personality similarities and differences. It is rather attributable to the fact that the House he leads is more like theirs than the House during the days of Czar rule. Similarly, though leaders remain distinct personalities (note, for example, O'Neill and Albert), the range of tolerance for personal traits that conflict with prevailing norms is restricted.[8]

That some House leaders have been involved in engineering institutional change has not gone unnoticed. David Rohde and Kenneth Shepsle have noted that ambitious leaders may turn to institutional tinkering as a strategy for maintaining office when legislative parties are factionalized.[9] Roger H. Davidson has pointed out that congressional leaders may act as resistors, managers, or sponsors of institutional innovation, though he found in a study of institutional change in the 1960s and 1970s that leaders most often acted as brokers between pro- and anti-change factions.[10] The framework proposed by Ronald M. Peters, Jr., in his recent historical study of the speakership seeks to explain the office in relation to broader patterns in American political development yet also maintains that "individual actors and events that are not historically or contextually determined will influence the House."[11]

The fact that leaders may on occasion initiate structural changes or develop new leadership styles does not mean that the emphasis on contextual factors in leadership studies is misplaced. For much of the history of the House—probably most of it—it seems reasonable to assume that leaders are best understood as constrained within fairly narrow limits defined by institutional arrangements and political conditions. And if changes in leadership styles and institutional arrangements in the House follow more or less inevitably from changes in the political context, the case for attributing an independent causal influence even to an innovative leader remains a weak one. The theoretical framework proposed by Rohde and Shepsle for understanding House leadership suggests something like this view of the limited significance of leaders:

. . . institutional arrangements, leadership style and ambition, and follower diversity all hang together. The last of these is, clearly, partly exogenous. But once this characteristic of the governing party is determined, the other two aspects *are brought into adjustment* so that follower coherence, institutional practices, and leadership strategies together loosely characterize an equilibrium.[12]

A second possibility that should be considered in thinking about why Congress changes is that the timing and scope of stylistic or structural innovations may in some cases depend on the motivations, judgment, or skills of leaders who encounter uncertain political situations. From this perspective, institutional changes or new forms of leadership that might appear inevitable in retrospect may in reality have involved uncertainty or even political risk at the time they occurred. During periods when changes in the party system or the governmental agenda have undermined established leadership styles or created unmanageable conflicts within existing institutional forms, a considerable degree of uncertainty or ambiguity may be present in the contextual limits on leadership. A high degree of contextual ambiguity may in turn present both unusual opportunities and unusual risks for those who find themselves in leadership positions. If congressional change frequently takes the form of ongoing, incremental adjustments to new contextual forces, at times, both leadership styles and structural arrangements in the House have been brought into adjustment with new contextual conditions through decisive actions initiated by a leader. In these cases the personal goals and skills of leaders may be important for explaining when institutional adjustments take place as well as the form and extent of change that occurs. To be sure, even in these cases contextual factors remain important in defining the outside parameters for stylistic or institutional innovation. As Shepsle and Rohde point out, for new leadership styles or organizational innovations to persist and become institutionalized, they must be in a kind of loose equilibrium with other features of the political/institutional context. But this process of adjustment to contextual change may be less determinate than contextualist theories of leadership suggest. It may oversimplify matters to conclude that contextual factors *always* place narrow limits on opportunities for House leaders to redefine effective leadership styles or initiate institutional changes; even if congressional leadership is correctly understood as determined primarily by contextual factors, during some periods broader opportunities for innovative leadership may be present. $_{\text{Say, Divided Gvt,}}$

Leaders and Leadership in Institutional Time

The idea that individuals are more likely to influence the course of political events in ambiguous situations or those involving conflict or instability has a long history in political analysis. Among contemporary political scientists, this idea has been developed in Fred I. Greenstein's writings on personality and politics, and it has also informed the work of Richard F. Fenno, Jr., on congressional committee leadership and House members' "home styles." These studies, together with some recent work on presidential leadership by Steven Skowronek, provide the point of departure for outlining a framework for exploring the question of leadership and change in the House of Representatives from the perspective of *institutional time.*

In *Personality and Politics*, Fred I. Greenstein offered the following propositions: "The likelihood of personal impact [on political events] varies with (1) the degree to which the actions take place in an environment which admits of restructuring, (2) the location of the actor in the environment, and (3) the actor's peculiar strengths or weaknesses."[13] The situations where individual actions matter most, Greenstein proposes, are those "in a precarious equilibrium." Physical analogies Greenstein cites to illustrate these types of situations are "massive rock formations at the side of a mountain which can be dislodged by the motion of a keystone, tinder-dry forest land, highly explosive compounds with properties like that of nitro-glycerin," and "the weakened dikes of our little-Dutch-boy."[14]

If a state of "precarious equilibrium" makes it more likely that the *actions* of a strategically placed individual will make a difference in political outcomes, the importance of the individual *actor*, according to Greenstein, will vary with the skill required to act decisively in the situation and the degree of ambiguity that is present. Skill may be important, Greenstein observes, "since the greater the actor's skill, the less his initial need for a favorable position or a manipulable environment, and the greater the likelihood that *he himself* will contribute to making his subsequent position favorable and his environment manipulable. By the same token, a singularly inept politician may reduce the manipulability of his environment."[15] Ambiguous situations, on the other hand, "leave room for personal variability to manifest itself."[16] Of the types of ambiguous situations Greenstein discusses, two seem relevant to the case at hand: (1) new situations or organizational settings where structures have yet to be clearly established and hence relatively few cues for behavior are present; and (2) situations in which various elements contradict one another or suggest different structures for action.[17]

In his analysis of committee leadership in *Congressmen in Committees*, Fenno focused on contextual factors, but he also noted that personal qualities of leaders might assume greater significance in defining an effective leadership style and in determining how a committee operated in cases where tensions or conflicts were present among committee members' goals or among the forces in the committee's political environment. "In subtle matters of balance among potentially conflicting decision rules," he observed, "personal factors are probably critical."[18] Fenno has likewise noted the greater importance of personal factors in the development of House members' "home styles" in cases where constituencies are complex or heterogeneous.[19]

Different contextual situations that create or limit opportunities for innovative leadership by House leaders may be viewed as different moments in *institutional time*. The concept of institutional time is a variation on a framework Steven Skowronek has proposed for the study of presidential leadership. Skowronek argues that opportunities for presidential leadership are defined in part by a cycle of creation and decay of national governing coalitions and regime commitments, a sequence he characterizes as political time. Noting similar opportunities and problems for exercising leadership faced by presidents who assumed office during different historical periods but at similar points in this cyclical pattern in American political development, Skowronek concludes: "The clock at work in presidential leadership keeps political rather than historical time."[20] The greatest opportunities for exercising leadership, according to Skowronek, have existed for presidents "who are able to define their leadership projects against the backdrop of the manifest failures of a recently displaced governing coalition."[21]

Opportunities for innovation by House leaders have been defined by the interplay between a sequence of institutional developments in the House and major shifts in the governmental agenda and the party system. The most important institutional developments include the establishment of the standing committee system in the early nineteenth century, the development of party organizations, the centralization of power in the speakership, the revolt against the Speaker in 1910–11, the establishment of the seniority norm for assigning committee leadership positions, and the thoroughgoing institutional reforms of the 1970s. In contrast to the view that leaders are always narrowly constrained by the institutional/political context, the institutional time approach proposes that opportunities for House leaders to redefine leadership styles or influence institutional change may vary over time, depending on the political situation and the point in the sequence of institutional development of the House at which a leader serves. Though I have borrowed from Skowronek's framework, I do not mean to suggest that opportunities for innovation by House leaders occur in anything like the neat, recurring political cycles Skowronek finds for presidents.

Instead, from the perspective of institutional time, the history of the House may be viewed as consisting of periods of *equilibrium*, which are characterized by stability or adaptive change, and *critical moments* during which contextual constraints on leadership are ambiguous, or conflicts have developed that cannot be managed within existing institutional forms. During periods of institutional equilibrium, the party system, the governmental agenda, institutional arrangements inside the House, and leadership styles are mutually reinforcing, and individual leaders have limited opportunities for innovation.[22] Critical moments in institutional time, during which contextual factors are more ambiguous or conflictual, allow greater leeway for individual leaders to initiate stylistic or structural changes. Examples of these critical periods would include the early nineteenth century, when the institutionalization of the House was in its early stages, and later periods when changes in the party system or governmental agenda have created new political forces that undermined the effectiveness of existing leadership styles and spawned conflicts that could not be managed through institutional tinkering or adjustments at the margins (1860s, 1890s, 1906–10, 1970s–80s).

Critical moments in institutional time may allow unusual opportunities for leaders to influence institutional changes and redefine leadership styles, but for innovative leadership to occur there must be an individual present who is willing and able to break with existing practices and initiate changes in response to a new political situation. There is no guarantee that those in leadership positions will have the desire or

Figure 6.1. **Leadership in Institutional Time**

Leader Type

		Traditionalist	Innovator
Contextual Conditions	Equilibrium	Maintaining leader	Frustrated "visionary"
	Critical Moment	Rejected leader	Innovative leader

the ability to do so. Speaker Joseph Cannon, who failed to accommodate reformist elements in the House Republican party in the early years of this century, and Rules Committee Chairman Howard W. Smith, who continued to block programs sought by the more liberal Democratic majorities elected to the House in the late 1950s, are two examples of leaders who failed to change their leadership styles when conditions changed. Leaders like Cannon and Smith, who attempt to maintain or work within existing forms, may be termed traditionalists. Leaders who are willing to initiate change may be termed innovators.

Figure 6.1 outlines a provisional framework for viewing leadership in institutional time. The central proposition derived from this framework is that leaders may play a significant role in influencing the course of institutional development in the House in cases where innovators occupy leadership positions at critical moments in institutional time. Whether a leader in fact plays a significant role in the process of institutional change during one of these critical periods depends on the particular configuration of contextual factors and the personal qualities and skills of the leader. Traditionalists like Cannon and Smith, who seek to maintain the status quo in the face of new political forces, will find their influence undermined (rejected leaders). An innovator who attempts to initiate major changes during an equilibrium period is unlikely to succeed (frustrated "visionary"). The final possibility within this framework is the traditionalist who occupies a leadership position during a period of equilibrium and acts to maintain existing institutional arrangements or seeks to initiate only marginal or incremental stylistic or structural changes (maintaining leader).

Though their cases differ in some significant ways, Thomas B. Reed and Dan Rostenkowski may both be viewed as innovators who assumed positions of leadership at critical moments in institutional time.

Both broke with an existing pattern of leadership and initiated institutional changes consistent with a new leadership style. To explore further this perspective on leadership and change in the House, I turn first to the case of Thomas B. Reed and the procedural reforms adopted by the House of Representatives during the Fifty-first Congress.

Leadership and Innovation: Reed and the Fifty-first Congress

Thomas B. Reed of Maine served as Speaker of the House during three Congresses, the Fifty-first (1889–91), the Fifty-fourth (1895–97), and the Fifty-fifth (1897–99). Reed's legacy as a House leader is twofold. First, upon becoming Speaker he confronted head-on the problem of minority obstructionism and won approval of a series of procedural reforms (Reed's Rules) that consolidated the Speaker's control over floor activity. Second, Reed used this and other authority vested in the Speaker to establish a highly centralized leadership style ("czar rule") in which the Speaker (with the support of a disciplined majority party) closely controlled the legislative process through his committee assignment power, chairmanship of the Rules Committee, and authority as presiding officer. Because Reed's success in establishing this new leadership style began with, and was dependent upon, the procedural reforms that occurred during his first term as Speaker, the discussion will focus on Reed and the Fifty-first Congress.

Reed was first elected to the House in 1876, after serving in both houses of the Maine legislature and as the youngest attorney general in the history of the state. A member of the Republican minority during his first two terms, he quickly developed a reputation as an aggressive partisan and became known for his biting, sarcastic humor. When Republicans regained control of the House in the Forty-seventh Congress (1881–83), Reed was appointed to a position on the Rules Committee. He remained on the Rules Committee during the following three Democratically controlled Congresses and had become the de facto leader of his party by the Forty-eighth (1883–85). At the beginning of the Forty-ninth Congress (1885–87), Reed received his party's nomination for Speaker and thus became floor leader for the Republican minority. When the Republicans regained control of the House after the 1888 elections, Reed was elected Speaker.

When the record of Reed's political career is reviewed, a number of personal qualities stand out. First, if his biographers and contemporaries are accurate in their portrayals, Reed took little interest in the patronage politics or opportunities for personal gain that preoccupied many politicians of his time.[23] Though he was ambitious for political prominence, pursuing first the speakership of the House and later the Republican presidential nomination (in 1896), Reed reportedly refused to promise either favors or appointments in exchange for support for either office.[24] Though personally ambitious, Reed appears to have been equally committed to at least two other types of objectives. First, he held strong views on a number of public policy issues. He was for a system of protectionist tariffs and a gold-backed currency, and he was opposed to new territorial acquisitions in the Caribbean and the Pacific. In the latter case, Reed chose in 1899 to relinquish the Speaker's chair and resign from the House rather than accommodate the overwhelming Republican sentiment in support of annexation of the Philippines.[25] Second, though Reed's views on party governance evolved over the course of his House career, by the time of his election to the speakership in 1889, he was firmly committed to the goal of establishing a system of responsible party governance in the House. To this end he had conceived a specific program of institutional reform, and (by his own account) was willing to risk his newly won leadership position in the attempt to bring it about.

In a floor debate during his second term in the House, Reed had commented: "The best system is to have one party govern and the other party watch, and on general principles I think it would be better for us to govern and the Democrats to watch."[26] But he did not in the early stages of his House career view strict control by the majority over the conduct of business as essential to effective governance in the House. When the procedural reform on which Reed would later stake his speakership—elimination of the "disappearing quorum"—was proposed in the course of a debate on House rules in January 1880, Reed actively defended the right of the minority to refuse to vote even if the result was to delay action for lack of a quorum. "It is a valuable privilege for the country," Reed contended, "that the minority shall have the right by this extraordinary mode of proceeding to call the attention of the country to measures which a party in a moment of madness and of party feeling is endeavoring to enforce upon the citizens of this land. And it works equally well with regard to all parties, for all parties have their times when they need to be checked."[27] From his third term on, however, Reed began an ongoing effort to establish a system of rules and procedures through which the Speaker and the majority party could both control and be held responsible for the actions of the House.

Reed first began to act on this view of party governance during the Forty-seventh Congress. In May 1882, after members of the Democratic minority had blocked action on a contested election case for seven days, Reed brought forth a special report from the Rules Committee establishing strict limitations on dilatory motions during consideration of election cases. When Democrat Samuel J. Randall of Pennsylvania continued to offer delaying motions, Reed raised a point of order against dilatory motions during consideration of rules changes. The point of order was sustained on appeal of Speaker J. Warren Keifer's favorable ruling, enhancing both Reed's reputation as a parliamentary strategist and opportunities for using special orders from the Rules Committee to expedite floor action. In a wide ranging defense of his position, Reed made clear his view of the Speaker's responsibilities: "Whenever it is imposed upon Congress to accomplish a certain work, it is the duty of the Speaker, who represents the House, and who in his official capacity is the embodiment of the House, to carry out that rule of law or of the Constitution. It then becomes his duty to see that no factious opposition prevents the House from doing its duty. He must brush away all unlawful combinations to misuse the rules and must hold the House strictly to its work."[28]

In the second session of the Forty-seventh Congress, Reed again used his position on the Rules Committee to introduce a special report which would allow the majority to work its will in the face of resistance from the minority. When tariff legislation appeared unlikely to be enacted as the session was drawing to a close, Reed introduced a report making it in order to suspend the rules and send the bill to conference with a simple majority rather than a two-thirds vote. This action was heatedly denounced by Democratic leaders as yet another partisan attack on the time-honored rights of the minority, but according to De Alva S. Alexander's account, Reed had also come very close to the limits of what his own party members would accept in the way of procedural innovations. As Alexander describes the situation:

[Reed] was too shrewd to stake his growing prestige on this latest adventure without due warrant, and so he spent several days in overcoming scruples and obtaining pledges. His precaution, however, scarcely justified his final action, for the disappearance of thirty-two members of his own party left him without a quorum. Even the next morning when he appeared with a file of recruits, failure stared him in the face until several Nationalists, suddenly seized with a desire to go on record in opposition, swelled the vote to a quorum.[29]

Reed continued to propose procedural changes to allow the majority to conduct business more efficiently in the three Congresses that followed (Forty-eighth–Fiftieth, 1883–89), but Democratic majorities under the leadership of Speaker John G. Carlisle of Kentucky allowed few opportunities for advancing the cause of procedural reform. A large Democratic majority in the Forty-eighth Congress had repudiated rules changes restricting dilatory motions, and most of the Democratic leadership continued to support the principle of protecting minority rights. By the Fiftieth Congress (1887–89), minority obstructionism had reached a new peak in the House.

In 1889, before the Fifty-first House was to convene with a newly elected Republican majority, Reed published two essays on the House of Representatives. In both he criticized the existing state of affairs in the House and advocated rules changes to allow the majority to govern. There is only one way to deal with the problem of obstruction by a minority, Reed declared in March 1889,

... and that is to return to the first principles of democracy and republicanism alike. ... It is the old doctrine that the majority must govern. Indeed, you have no choice. If the majority do not govern, the minority will; and if tyranny of the majority is hard, the tyranny of the minority is simply unendurable. The rules, then, ought to be arranged to facilitate the action of the majority.[30]

"When a legislative body makes rules," Reed wrote in a second essay appearing in the October 1889 *North American Review*, "it does not make them, as the people make constitutions, to limit power and provide for rights. They are made to facilitate the orderly and safe transaction of business."[31] Reed made it clear that when the House reconvened, an effort would be made "to establish rules which will facilitate the public business—rules unlike those of the present House, which only delay and frustrate action."[32]

The Fifty-first Congress in Institutional Time

As Reed began his service as Speaker in December 1889, the chronic legislative congestion in the House had attracted widespread criticism in the press, and a newly elected Republican majority stood ready to act on an agenda of tariff revision and other measures. No one doubted that House rules would be revised to facilitate action by the majority. Still, the narrowness of the Republican majority and the determination of Democratic leaders to protect the traditional prerogatives of the minority made the situation a precarious one for Reed. A brief account of the contextual forces at work at the beginning of the Fifty-first Congress will show why this period in the history of the House may be considered a critical moment in institutional time. Uncertainty regarding the limits of leadership in this situation was resolved only by Reed's act of counting a quorum, after which he was able to complete his program of restructuring House procedures and lay the foundation for a new leadership regime.

Institutional Factors

The distinctive institutional feature of the post–Civil War House had been the maintenance of procedures under which a minority could delay or block legislative action. The most commonly used tactics for obstructing legislation were to deprive the House of a quorum by refusing to vote (the so-called disappearing quorum) and to make and demand votes on various motions (such as motions to recess or adjourn) simply for purposes of delay. The problems of conducting business under these procedures had been offset to some degree by the increasing authority of the Speaker's office and use of the Rules Committee, but by the late 1880s the flow of legislation had slowed to a trickle as only uncontroversial measures or privileged legislation were assured of reaching the House floor for consideration. Democrats generally supported a system of rules that protected minority rights, but the resulting dominance of the legislative process by the tight-fisted Appropriations Committee (due to the privileged status of its legislation and the "Holman Rule" allowing legislative riders to appropriations bills if the riders reduced expenditures) produced a bipartisan revolt against the committee and a major restructuring of its jurisdiction in 1885.[33] For proponents of a more activist legislative program, the condition of the House had reached crisis proportions by the Fiftieth Congress. As Alexander observes: "By the time Carlisle had reached his third term as Speaker it became so easy to muster a sufficient number of disgruntled members to delay or prevent legislation that the House in the Fiftieth Congress, although in continuous session longer than any of its predecessors, passed only one [major] measure except such as received unanimous consent."[34]

Partisan Factors

Levels of partisan voting had been relatively low during the 1880s, but a number of factors converged at the outset of the Fifty-first Congress to encourage greater party unity, especially among Republicans. Over the three Congresses preceding the Fifty-first, the percentage of votes pitting 90 percent of one party against 90 percent of the other ranged from 7.0 to 16.6. During the Fiftieth Congress only 8.7 percent of roll calls produced this level of polarization in voting.[35] According to David Brady's analysis of House politics during this period, both parties experienced major factional splits on economic policy issues, though Democrats were the more deeply divided.[36]

In comparison with the preceding Congresses of the 1880s, two factors encouraged greater partisan unity among the Republican majority elected to the House for the Fifty-first Congress. For the first time in fourteen years, Republicans controlled both houses of Congress and the presidency and were anxious to enact new tariff legislation and other measures. Second, Cooper and Brady have shown that the constituency bases of the Democratic and Republican parties in the Fifty-first House were polarized along agricultural/industrial lines to a degree that would not reappear until the realigning elections of 1894–96.[37]

Finally, among the partisan factors that helped define opportunities for leadership in the Fifty-first Congress, it is important to note that this was a period in which many members of both parties were products of party machines. As Peter Swenson has argued: "The gradual fusion of partisan leadership with hierarchical authority was granted the Speaker and Rules Committee by machine-style congressmen willing to delegate the task of managing legislative business, and above all, in the case of the 1890 rules change, of taming the minority party, and excluding it from the fruits of congressional office."[38] Machine congressmen, Swenson points out, were interested primarily in matters of patronage and distribution of material benefits. Their attitudes toward authority "were those of men trained and selected to seek advancement within a multi-layered system of suzerainty, and to suppress demands for [individual] power."[39] Thus, Reed assumed the speakership at a point at which institutional arrangements in the House still allowed individual members or small groups from the opposition party to determine the fate of legislation, even though many members had come up through party organizations where hierarchy and party control were taken for granted.

Agenda Factors

In addition to the desire of members of the Republican party to act on the tariff issue and other matters on the agenda of the Fifty-first Congress, the continued pressure of a growing workload also contributed to a favorable climate for procedural reform. As Mary Parker Follett observed in her study of the speakership published in 1896: "As the territory extends and the population grows, as railroads and corporations, commerce and manufactures increase, the business of the country is greatly multiplied and legislation must keep pace. To legislate for seventy millions of people even with the way made smooth is no easy task; but the systematic filibustering which has hitherto been allowed causes the business of the country to accumulate to an alarming extent."[40]

As it turned out, the specific issue on which Reed challenged the existing system of minority prerogatives was a contested election case. Whatever the ebb and flow of partisanship on other issues on the legislative agenda, decisions in contested elections had consistently been highly partisan affairs for decades.[41]

Reed as an Innovative Leader

The critical point for Speaker Reed's attempt to assert the control of the majority over business in the House occurred early in the Fifty-first Congress, when on January 29, 1890, two Democratic members withdrew their votes on the question of taking up a contested election case from West Virginia, Smith v. Jackson. The vote stood at 162 yeas, 3 nays, 163 not voting. Because a quorum consisted of 165 members and only 161 Republican members could be assembled on the floor, a change of two members to nonvoting status would bring business to a halt for lack of a quorum. Amid cries from Democrats of "No quorum!" Reed broke with precedents traceable as far back as the 1830s by directing the clerk to record the names of members who were present and refusing to vote. Reed's ruling provoked a vigorous protest from Democrats on the House floor, during which the Speaker's ruling was appealed by Charles F. Crisp of Georgia. The issue was then debated before the House for two days. On the second day (January 31), Reed refused to entertain an appeal when he again counted a quorum on a vote to approve the Journal and, in response to a motion to adjourn offered by Democrat William M. Springer of Illinois, ruled that the Speaker would no longer entertain motions made only for purposes of delay. Each of Reed's rulings was sustained by the Republican majority, clearing the way for the House to take up and approve a thoroughgoing revision of House rules in February 1890.[42]

In a speech to his own constituents in September 1890, Reed played down his role in bringing about the changes enacted by the Fifty-first Congress. "Great events do not turn upon one man," he explained. "The House of Representatives was ready and ripe for change, and the people stood ready to approve. What all the world wanted was easy to do."[43] However, Reed's actions at the time and his later recollections suggest that he was in fact less certain his initiative would succeed. According to one of Reed's biographers, Samuel W. McCall, Reed had discussed his plan to count a quorum beforehand with Elihu Root, and he had made plans to resign the House and join Root's New York law firm if the House failed to sustain his ruling.[44]

In a later interview, Reed recalled:

> I knew just what I was going to do if the House did not sustain me. . . . I should simply have left the chair, resigning the Speakership and my seat in Congress. There were other things that could be done, you know, outside of political life, and for my own part I had made up my mind that if political life consisted in sitting helplessly in the Speaker's chair and seeing the majority powerless to pass legislation, I had had enough of it and I was ready to step down and out.[45]

Reed's determination to establish the conditions for party government in the House and his political skill should not be discounted in the attempt to explain the important institutional changes that occurred in the House during the Fifty-first Congress. By forcing the issue of the Speaker's authority to count a quorum and refuse dilatory motions in the highly partisan atmosphere of a contested election case, Reed acted strategically to mobilize Republican support for procedural innovations under the most favorable possible conditions. As William A. Robinson's biography of Reed observes:

> The case of Smith vs. Jackson . . . had given an excellent opportunity to demonstrate the evils of obstruction. Democratic tactics on this occasion had furnished ample excuse for heroic treatment. The case was settled before it could be confused by a protracted discussion of new rules, and the Speaker's ruling on the quorum assured the passage of the new code when it should be submitted.[46]

Though most of the Reed Rules were repudiated by the large Democratic majority elected to the House for the Fifty-second Congress (1891–93), Reed continued to press the issue of procedural reform as leader of the Republican minority. The Democrats controlled a narrower majority in the Fifty-third Congress (1893–95), and Reed and the Republicans repeatedly brought the business of the House to a halt by refusing to vote or by employing other delaying tactics. Reed's actions forced Speaker Charles F. Crisp and the Democratic majority to choose between losing control of the floor or reintroducing procedures to check minority obstructionism. In April 1894 the Democratic leadership grudgingly gave in, proposing that the House reenact a rule allowing a quorum to be established by counting members who were present but not voting. The adoption of this rule by the Democratically controlled House signaled the final success of Reed's project of establishing a system of party government under the control of the Speaker.

Reed did not create the conditions that allowed the assertion of a stronger speakership and a major revision of House rules during the 1890s. But due to his strong commitment to party governance and his parliamentary expertise, Reed was willing and able to act decisively at a critical moment in institutional time when existing institutional arrangements were no longer adequate to manage the agenda of the House and the partisan and factional conflicts it evoked. A more conventional leader might have been hesitant to initiate sweeping procedural reforms in the Fifty-first Congress with such a slim majority; a less skilled leader might have botched the task of maintaining a unified majority in support of expanding the Speaker's prerogatives. Though it is unlikely that House rules allowing minority obstructionism would have survived the large Republican majorities elected after 1894, the new leadership regime established by Reed allowed the Republican majority of the Fifty-first Congress to pass an extensive body of new legislation and permitted the Speaker to be the dominant figure in the governance of the House until the revolt against Speaker Joseph G. Cannon occurred in 1910.

Leadership and Innovation: Rostenkowski and the Postreform Ways and Means Committee

Dan Rostenkowski's chairmanship of the House Ways and Means Committee during the 1980s offers a second case in which a House leader encountered a situation that allowed opportunities for asserting a new leadership style and initiating institutional change.[47] Rostenkowski reasserted an active leadership style on the Ways and Means Committee in the aftermath of a period of structural reform and highly permissive leadership on the committee. Consistent with this more assertive leadership style, he has restructured the committee staff and attempted to rein in subcommittee chairmen. Rostenkowski is not an innovator of the same type or on the same scale that Thomas Reed was. The institutional changes he has initiated as committee chairman are limited in scope, and in some respects it would be accurate to say that he has restored elements of an *old* leadership style to the Ways and Means Committee rather than defining an entirely new one. Yet like Reed, he fits the pattern of leader who initiated structural and stylistic changes at a critical moment in institutional time.

Dan Rostenkowski was first elected to the House from the Eighth District of Illinois in 1958. His father was the Democratic committeeman for the Thirty-second Ward in Chicago. Rostenkowski worked his way up through the Chicago Democratic organization, serving two terms in the state legislature and as treasurer of the Cook County Young Democrats before winning the approval of Mayor Richard J. Daley to run for the House in 1958. Rostenkowski won a seat on the Ways and Means Committee in 1964, attracted primarily by the political clout associated with the committee due to the committee assignment function then exercised by Ways and Means Democrats.[48] After Al Ullman of Oregon was defeated for reelection in 1980, Rostenkowski became Ways and Means chairman in 1981.

Rostenkowski's political style bears an unmistakable imprint from his political apprenticeship in the Chicago Democratic organization. As Leo Snowiss observed in an article written in the 1960s, members recruited by the Chicago machine tended to be nonideological types who were "well schooled in . . . quiet bargaining, negotiation and compromise," who "value[d] party cohesion as a positive good in need of little or no justification," and who viewed politics "as a cooperative, organizational enterprise."[49] They were also politicians who were accustomed to working within "a relatively hierarchic structure of authority throughout the city and county."[50] Consistent with this view of the political world, Rostenkowski has pursued two basic objectives as chairman of Ways and Means: he has sought to enhance the power and reputation of both the chairmanship and the committee, and he has attempted to support partisan objectives of House Democrats. "Rostenkowski," a senior Republican stated, "is the ultimate expression of the Chicago view that the function of politics is control." "If anything characterizes him," a Democrat commented, "it's that he wants to win." Said another Democrat: "He wants his committee to look good, to pass legislation." A committee Republican likewise observed:

> His main objective is to have a committee that is respected. He is very interested in having the respect of the committee's marketplace—the House floor and people who deal with the committee. He wants respect for the committee and the product. . . . I think he is more interested in respect than the substance.

Rostenkowski has shown limited interest in substantive policy issues that fall within the jurisdiction of Ways and Means.[51] But committee members emphasized that the chairman does want to be seen as a leader of a committee that is responsible and willing to make difficult decisions when necessary. As a senior Republican described the chairman's attitude toward the committee's economic policy jurisdiction: "My sense is that he feels a tremendous sense of responsibility." Or as a senior committee staffer put it: "Rostenkowski has the sense of being a manager . . . and we are responsible for managing Social Security, Medicare, AFDC, the tax system."

When asked to describe Rostenkowski, committee members and staffers also emphasized the chairman's loyalty to the Democratic party as an institution. Though a number of members commented that

Rostenkowski is very much a legislative pragmatist who prefers to assemble bipartisan coalitions to enhance the prospects of passing committee bills on the House floor, others noted a deeply ingrained sense of loyalty to party. One senior Republican observed, with what appeared to be a sort of grudging respect: "Danny is a good Democratic chairman." On Rostenkowski's approach inside the committee, a junior Republican commented:

> In the preliminary steps of almost every issue he makes an extra effort to be bipartisan and let everybody be a player. However, when push comes to shove ... he has a natural reaction to become extraordinarily partisan.

As was the case with Reed, Rostenkowski assumed a position of leadership in the House during an unsettled period. Extensive reforms, a new agenda, and dissatisfaction with the leadership of his predecessor had created an ambiguous situation in which opportunities were present for innovation.

Ways and Means Committee in Institutional Time

Comparisons of Reed and Rostenkowski are complicated by the fact that party and committee leaders work within very different institutional contexts in the House. Selective recruitment patterns for committees, the smaller size of the group, and the responsibility for only a specific legislative jurisdiction are among the important differences that must be taken into account in comparing these types of leaders. For the purpose of exploring how different contextual situations may allow opportunities for innovation by leaders a similar framework is nonetheless useful. As was the case with party leadership in the late nineteenth century, opportunities for innovation on the postreform Ways and Means Committee may be considered in relation to institutional, partisan, and agenda factors.

Institutional Factors

Rostenkowski became chairman in the aftermath of the extensive reforms enacted in the House during the 1970s. Between 1970 and 1974, major structural reforms had been enacted in the House, including changes to reduce the autonomy of standing committee chairmen by requiring caucus election and limiting their control over committee organization and procedures. Under the new procedures committee leaders were no longer assured their positions simply on the basis of seniority, and they had to be attentive to concerns of rank-and-file Democrats or risk removal by the majority caucus (as occurred with three senior chairmen in 1975). The Budget and Impoundment Control Act of 1974 had established a new set of organizational units and procedures and evolved an effective mechanism (reconciliation) for coordinating tax and spending decisions.

The Ways and Means Committee and its influential chairman, Wilbur D. Mills of Arkansas, had been principal targets of House reformers during the 1970s. The reforms targeted at the Ways and Means Committee—including changes in the closed-rule procedure to allow amendments to Ways and Means bills to be proposed by vote of the Democratic caucus, a requirement that subcommittees be established, and expansion of the committee's size from twenty-five to thirty-seven members—were intended specifically to bring an end to the centralized, consensus-oriented leadership regime that had been nurtured by Mills since the late 1950s.[52] Thus by the time Dan Rostenkowski became chairman, the committee had been restructured to decentralize power and increase the committee's responsiveness to the majority caucus.

But the House reform movement had run its course by the late 1970s, and members found themselves faced with the day-to-day problems of making the new organizational arrangements work. Based on interviews conducted between 1981 and 1983, Steven S. Smith and Christopher J. Deering found that "the most common complaint . . . heard about committee leadership from committee members and staff was that chairs are no longer responsible for their committee's actions."[53] Some Ways and Means members who had served on the committee during the late 1970s voiced very similar complaints. During the years Al Ullman served as chairman (1975–80), one Democrat explained, "you had true democracy at work. The committee doesn't work well in that way unfortunately." Said another Democrat: "It was chaos under Ullman." A committee Republican described the late 1970s as "this time of wandering in the desert," adding: "Service on the committee during that time was frustrating. There was no unity of purpose, no common direction." As further evidence of the emergence of a "postreform" institutional climate in which concerns with restoring decision-making capabilities had begun to compete with demands for openness, participation, and decentralization, the return by the Ways and Means Committee to the traditional practice of closing bill-writing sessions to the public in 1983 excited little interest or criticism.[54]

Reform era changes in the House also resulted in new patterns in committee recruitment. Fewer prestige-oriented legislators have been attracted to the Ways and Means Committee than in earlier years, while more members have sought seats because of interest in the policy issues in the committee's jurisdiction.[55] This more diverse, more policy-oriented membership has made reaching agreement on how the committee should operate more difficult than in the Mills era, when most members accepted the view that partisan and ideological conflicts should be muted in order to maintain committee prestige. After 1974, the chairman of the Ways and Means Committee faced an institutional environment in which the committee had been expanded and restructured, and a broader range of views was present among committee members about how the committee should function. But by the 1980s, reform era demands for openness, decentralization, and participation had begun to wane perceptibly, creating an institutional context somewhat more amenable to the exercise of influence over committee politics by the chairman.

Partisan Factors

Because Ways and Means Committee politics have long reflected the politics of the parent chamber, the contextual situation faced by the committee chairman is defined also by the size of partisan majorities in the House and by the degree of unity or factionalism in the majority party. Some fairly striking increases in party unity have been visible among House Democrats during the 1980s. Increased Democratic unity may in part reflect changes in electoral politics in the South.[56] But increased Democratic unity on issues in the jurisdiction of Ways and Means also has occurred due to more short-term agenda factors. Hence, this development is treated in the section that follows.

The distinctive features of the partisan context during the 1980s were the election of Republican presidents and the presence of a Republican majority in the Senate from 1981–86. Though Democrats maintained majorities in the House throughout the decade, the majority was relatively small in the Ninety-seventh Congress (1981–82), when Democrats held only a 55.9 percent majority in the chamber. As a Republican Ways and Means member pointed out, on tax and budget issues "a conservative majority controlled the House floor." After the 1982 elections, House Democrats held more comfortable majorities— 61.6 percent in the Ninety-eighth Congress (1983–84) and 58.2 percent in the Ninety-ninth (1985–86), 59.3 percent in the Hundredth (1987– 88), and 59.8 percent in the 101st (1989–90).

Agenda Factors

Issue- or agenda-related factors are important for understanding leadership on the Ways and Means Committee due to a series of major shifts in the issues within the committee's jurisdiction during the 1980s. By the late 1970s, the poor performance of the economy and a growing "tax revolt" had produced a shift in the economic policy debate away from a liberal agenda focusing on distributional equity toward a more conservative agenda focused on reducing tax burdens across the board and stimulating economic growth. This new agenda created serious strains on Democratic unity in the Ways and Means Committee and in the House as liberals continued to stress distributional issues, while other elements in the party sought to respond to the new agenda.

The committee agenda of the 1980s was dominated initially by the tax- and budget-cutting initiatives of the new Reagan administration, then by the deficits that followed enactment of the president's program. The tax and budget initiatives submitted by the administration in 1981 divided the Democratic majority in the House. But after 1981, an agenda dominated by large budget deficits and attempts by a Republican White House to reduce deficits through additional domestic budget cuts helped to produce increased partisanship in House voting and greater party unity among House Democrats on economic and fiscal policy issues.[57] Thus after the initial successes of the Reagan administration in winning Democratic support to enact its economic program, a deficit-driven agenda has resulted in a more unified Democratic coalition in the House, offering opportunities for a committee leader to assemble partisan coalitions in committee and on the House floor.

Along with encouraging partisan polarization in the House, deficit politics have also created pressures for greater centralization as a means of setting priorities and reestablishing some autonomy from clientele demands. As Roger H. Davidson has pointed out: "The painful fiscal choices of the 1980s would seem to dictate a reversal of . . . [decentralizing] structural tendencies, as party leaders and the budget-making apparatus tug at the decentralization that was the legacy of the 1970s reforms."[58]

During the Ullman chairmanship extensive structural reforms, the breakdown of a consensus on how the committee should operate, and the divisive issues that dominated the Ways and Means Committee's agenda had combined to create an unsettled and difficult context for exercising leadership from the chair of the Ways and Means Committee. The configuration of partisan control and the committee agenda were perhaps even less favorable for a Democratic committee leader at the outset of Dan Rostenkowski's chairmanship, but concerns with restoring decision-making capabilities after the reform era, the presence of a highly contractive agenda, and increased unity among House Democrats in the context of deficit politics all created opportunities for more active leadership and greater organizational centralization.

Restoration as Innovation: Rostenkowski as an Innovative Leader

With his background in a strong party organization, Rostenkowski is a politician who values hierarchical authority more than do most contemporary House members, and thus he did not hesitate to centralize authority and assert a more active leadership style when he became chairman in 1981. His machine background also inculcated a political style and a set of skills that have worked surprisingly well for exercising leadership on the postreform committee. As one Democrat commented on Rostenkowski's approach to leadership:

> He has a very interesting set of values that is very un-eighties, if you will. He talks about [Ways and Means as] the Cadillac of committees and I say that you should refer to it as the Mercedes-Benz of committees. But he believes in these values of loyalty and stability, that there's a boss and the wise and compassionate boss checks it out with his minions before he leads them into battle. And he rewards and punishes. You know, these are all very Old Testament-type values. And they've worked very well.

Al Ullman had exercised a very permissive style of leadership on Ways and Means between 1975 and 1980, allowing other committee members to take the lead in assembling coalitions in the full committee and allowing subcommittee chairmen a great deal of autonomy in hiring committee staff and setting their own legislative agendas. "Rostenkowski," a senior Ways and Means member observed, "is much more interested in controlling the authority, the flow of legislation, than Mr. Ullman seemed to be." As another senior member put it: "Rostenkowski is not as strong on the substance as Ullman was, but he is significantly stronger on the politics. [With Rostenkowski] . . . the power is concentrated in the chairman and he plays hardball politics."

Rostenkowski has restructured the committee staff so that it is controlled by and responsible to the full committee chairman rather than subcommittee chairmen, and he has established a much more centralized style of leadership than had been present during the Ullman years. This leadership style incorporates five basic elements: direct involvement in committee recruitment; encouragement of group solidarity; early consultation, then negotiation to win firm commitments; threatening dissidents and freezing out defectors; and centralized control over organizational resources.

In a situation where reform era institutional changes encouraged decentralization and participatory decision making while partisan and agenda factors provided opportunities for asserting stronger direction over committee politics, Rostenkowski reestablished a stronger leadership role on the postreform Ways and Means Committee. Rather than defining a new leadership style, the current chairman has attempted to restore an older style of leadership that is oriented toward group loyalty and maintaining committee prestige. Like Wilbur Mills, Rostenkowski has sought when possible to build bipartisan coalitions to enhance the chances for winning passage of committee bills on the House floor. Unlike Mills, though, Rostenkowski's style includes a strong, if pragmatic, element of partisanship. He also presides over a larger, more diverse committee and must work within a more complex institutional setting in which the committee must be responsive to influences from the party leadership, the budget process, and the House floor. Rostenkowski has enjoyed mixed success as a legislative leader. He successfully built coalitions to enact deficit reduction legislation in 1984 and tax reform legislation in 1986, yet he also lost control of major tax bills in 1981, 1982, and 1989. Only time will tell if the organizational changes and the more centralized leadership style of the Rostenkowski chairmanship represent a new equilibrium on the Ways and Means Committee.

Conclusion

In his recently published historical study, *The American Speakership*, Ronald M. Peters, Jr., offers the following observation: "While the speakership is an important position of leadership in our constitutional system, it is an important position of *institutional* leadership. The office's roots are in the legislative body, and it is affected by the forces that shape the House of Representatives."[59] The same might be said of all leaders in the House. They are institutional leaders whose actions reflect, or must be attentive to, constitutional forms, partisan dynamics, issues on the governmental agenda and organizational arrangements and institutionalized patterns within the legislative body itself. Though most recent studies of congressional leadership conclude that House leaders can play only a marginal role in defining an effective leadership style or influencing the course of institutional change, the cases of Reed and Rostenkowski suggest that *institutional leadership* may be better understood if viewed in *institutional time*. Though leaders do have limited leeway for initiating change during equilibrium periods, opportunities for more innovative leadership may be present at critical moments in institutional time, and at these critical moments individual leaders' goals and skills may affect the timing and scope of institutional change in the House.

The comparison of a nineteenth-century Republican Speaker from Maine and a twentieth-century Democratic committee chairman from Chicago suggests that in some important cases, Congress changes because leaders have the motivation and the political skill to change it. Of the two leaders considered here, Reed clearly presents the stronger case of the leader whose personal goals and political skills left an imprint on the institutional development of the House; Rostenkowski initiated change on a smaller scale and in effect took advantage of an opportunity during the 1980s to restore an older type of leadership rather than establish a new one. If the influence on institutional change that can be attributed to these two leaders varies, there remains the important similarity that both encountered political situations where the limits on leadership were uncertain and both were willing to act decisively to initiate change. That Reed and Rostenkowski are both unusual types for their respective historical periods is also an interesting finding. Reed served in a House well stocked with machine politicians, yet he enjoyed reading Balzac in French, was a prolific essayist, cared about political ethics, and disliked backslapping; Rostenkowski, one of the last of the machine politicians, values camaraderie and respects hierarchy but serves in a House full of independent "new breed" political entrepreneurs. It is possible that a distinctive view of the political world rather than mere ambition to maintain office has been an important motivating factor for innovative leaders in the House. More attention to the leaders who have initiated change at critical moments in institutional time is needed to determine if this is so.

More precise definitions of the types of situations that constitute critical moments and periods of equilibrium in the history of the House need to be developed, and more intensive study of the historical situations surrounding cases of innovative leadership is needed before this approach can contribute more than these tentative conclusions. For the time being, I would simply propose that our conclusions about why Congress changes not rule out the possibility that sometimes Congress changes because a leader has a view of how it ought to work and attempts to put that view into practice.

Notes

The author would like to thank Ronald M. Peters, Jr., Charles O. Jones, and Roger H. Davidson for their helpful comments and suggestions on an earlier version of this chapter. Research support from the Everett McKinley Dirksen Congressional Leadership Research Center and the Emory University Research Committee is also gratefully acknowledged.

1. Joseph Cooper and David W. Brady, "Institutional Context and Leadership Style: The House from Cannon to Rayburn," *American Political Science Review* 75 (1981): 423.

2. Charles O. Jones, "House Leadership in an Age of Reform," in *Understanding Congressional Leadership*, ed. Frank H. Mackaman (Washington: Congressional Quarterly Press, 1981); Jones, "Joseph G. Cannon and Howard W. Smith: An Essay on the Limits of Leadership in the House of Representatives," *Journal of Politics* 30 (1968): 6–25; Richard F. Fenno, Jr., *Congressmen in Committees* (Boston: Little, Brown, 1973); Barbara Sinclair, *Majority Leadership in the U.S. House* (Baltimore: Johns Hopkins University Press, 1983); Steven S. Smith and Christopher J. Deering, *Committees in Congress* (Washington: Congressional Quarterly Press, 1984); David W. Rohde and Kenneth A. Shepsle,

"Leaders and Followers in the House of Representatives: Reflections on Woodrow Wilson's *Congressional Government*," *Congress and the Presidency* 14 (1987): 111–33; Ronald M. Peters, Jr., *The American Speakership* (Baltimore: Johns Hopkins University Press, 1990).

3. See Joseph Cooper, "Organization and Innovation in the House of Representatives," in *The House at Work*, ed. Joseph Cooper and G. Calvin Mackenzie (Austin: University of Texas Press, 1981).

4. Jones, "Limits of Leadership."

5. Jones, "House Leadership in an Age of Reform," 129.

6. Cooper and Brady, "Institutional Context and Leadership Style;" Rohde and Shepsle, "Leaders and Followers."

7. Steven S. Smith, "O'Neill's Legacy for the House," *Brookings Review* (Winter 1987): 35.

8. Cooper and Brady, "Institutional Context and Leadership Style," 423–24.

9. Rohde and Shepsle, "Leaders and Followers," 112–14.

10. Roger H. Davidson, "Congressional Leaders as Agents of Change," in *Understanding Congressional Leadership*, ed. Frank H. Mackaman (Washington: Congressional Quarterly Press, 1981).

11. Peters, *The American Speakership*, 4.

12. Rohde and Shepsle, "Leaders and Followers," 118. Emphasis mine.

13. Fred I. Greenstein, *Personality and Politics* (Chicago: Markham, 1969), 42.

14. Ibid., 42–43.

15. Ibid., 45. Emphasis in original.

16. Ibid., 50.

17. Ibid., 50–51.

18. Ibid., 117.

19. Richard F. Fenno, Jr., *Home Style* (Boston: Little, Brown, 1978), 79, 91, 124–26.

20. Stephen Skowronek, "Presidential Leadership in Political Time," in *The Presidency and the Political System*, 2d ed., ed. Michael Nelson (Washington: Congressional Quarterly Press, 1988), 154.

21. Ibid., 155.

22. On characterizing the institutional development of the House in terms of periods of equilibrium and periods of instability or institutional messiness, see Kenneth A. Shepsle, "The Changing Textbook Congress," in *Can the Government Govern?*, ed. John E. Chubb and Paul E. Peterson (Washington: Brookings Institution, 1989); and Steven S. Smith, *Call to Order* (Washington: Brookings Institution, 1989), 250–52.

23. Two biographies of Reed have been written. Samuel W. McCall, *The Life of Thomas Brackett Reed* (Boston: Houghton Mifflin, 1914); William A. Robinson, *Thomas B. Reed: Parliamentarian* (New York: Dodd, Mead, 1930). Both are useful, but the Robinson volume offers a much more detailed portrait of Reed's congressional career.

24. Robinson, *Thomas B. Reed*, 197, 327, 331–33.

25. For a statement of Reed's views on territorial expansion, see Thomas B. Reed, "Empire Can Wait," *Illustrated American* (4 December 1897): 713–14.

26. Quoted in McCall, *Thomas Brackett Reed*, 82–83.

27. *Congressional Record*, Forty-sixth Congress, Second Session, 578–79.

28. *Congressional Record*, Forty-seventh Congress, First Session, 4306.

29. The Nationalists were a minor party that controlled nine seats in the Forty-seventh Congress. The final vote on Reed's motion was yeas 129, nays 22, not voting 142. De Alva Stanwood Alexander, *History and Procedure of the House of Representatives* (Boston: Houghton Mifflin, 1916), 204.

30. Thomas B. Reed, "Rules of the House of Representatives," *Century Magazine* 37 (March 1889): 794–95.

31. Thomas B. Reed, "Obstruction in the National House," *North American Review* 149 (October 1889): 425.

32. Ibid., 428.

33. On the politics of the dispersal of the jurisdiction of the Appropriations Committee during this period, see W. Thomas Wander, "Patterns of Change in the Congressional Budget Process, 1865–1974," *Congress and the Presidency* 9 (1982): 23–49; Charles Stewart III, *Budget Reform Politics* (Cambridge: Cambridge University Press, 1989).

34. Alexander, *History and Procedure of the House*, 62.

35. David W. Brady and Phillip Althoff, "Party Voting in the U.S. House of Representatives, 1890–1910: Elements of a Responsible Party System," *Journal of Politics* 36 (1974): 755–56.

36. David W. Brady, *Critical Elections and Congressional Policy Making* (Stanford, CA: Stanford University Press, 1988), 52.

37. Cooper and Brady, "Institutional Context and Leadership Style," 415.

38. Peter Swenson, "The Influence of Recruitment on the Structure of Power in the U.S. House, 1870–1940," *Legislative Studies Quarterly* 7 (1982): 21.

39. Ibid., 22.

40. M. P. Follett, *The Speaker of the House of Representatives* (New York: Longmans, 1896), 188.

41. See Nelson W. Polsby, "The Institutionalization of the U.S. House of Representatives," *American Political Science Review* 62 (1968): 144–68; Brady, *Critical Elections*, 79.

42. For more detailed treatments of Reed's ruling on the quorum issue, see Robinson, *Thomas B. Reed*, Chap. 10, and Follett, *Speaker of the House*, 184–94.

43. Quoted in Robinson, *Thomas B. Reed*, 47.

44. McCall, *Thomas Brackett Reed*, 167.

45. Lewiston *Evening Journal* (8 December 1902), quoted in Richard Stanley Offenberg, *The Political Career of Thomas Brackett Reed* (Ph.D. dissertation, New York University, 1963), 95–96.

46. Robinson, *Thomas B. Reed*, 220.

47. Some material in this section is drawn from Randall Strahan, *New Ways and Means: Reform and Change in a Congressional Committee* (Chapel Hill: University of North Carolina Press, 1990), Chap. 5. Unattributed quotations are from interviews conducted for the book.

48. On the Rostenkowski family and Dan Rostenkowski's background in the Chicago Democratic organization, see Leo M. Snowiss, "Congressional Recruitment and Representation," *American Political Science Review* 60 (1966): 628–31, 639; Steven V. Roberts, "A Most Important Man on Capitol Hill," *New York Times Magazine* (22 September 1985): 44–55; Edward Kantowicz, *Polish-Ameri-*

can Politics in Chicago, 1888–1940 (Chicago: University of Chicago Press, 1975), 210–11.

49. Snowiss, "Congressional Recruitment," 630.

50. Ibid., 629.

51. Rostenkowski himself once commented on Wilbur Mills's reputation for mastery of Ways and Means issues: "The observation about Wilbur Mills was that in the daytime he works the *New York Times* crossword puzzle and at night he goes to bed with the tax code. I don't do either one of those." Lawrence J. Haas, "Rostenkowski's Way," *National Journal* 21 (22 July 1989): 1858.

52. On Mills's leadership style on the prereform committee, see John F. Manley, *The Politics of Finance* (Boston: Little, Brown, 1970). On the 1970s House reforms and their effects on the Ways and Means Committee, see Smith and Deering, *Committees in Congress*; and articles by Catherine E. Rudder: "Committee Reform and the Revenue Process," in *Congress Reconsidered*, ed. Lawrence C. Dodd and Bruce I. Oppenheimer (New York: Praeger, 1977); "The Policy Impact of Reform on the Committee on Ways and Means," in *Legislative Reform*, ed. Leroy N. Rieselbach (Lexington, MA: Lexington Books, 1978); "Tax Policy: Structure and Choice," in *Making Economic Policy in Congress*, ed. Allen Schick (Washington: American Enterprise Institute, 1983); and "Fiscal Responsibility and the Revenue Committees," in *Congress Reconsidered*, 3d ed., ed. Bruce I. Oppenheimer and Lawrence C. Dodd (Washington: Congressional Quarterly Press, 1985).

53. Smith and Deering, *Committees in Congress*, 177.

54. Dale Tate, "Ways and Means: Behind Closed Doors," *Congressional Quarterly Weekly Report* (8 October 1983): 2067; Jacqueline Calmes, "Few Complaints are Voiced as Doors Close on Capitol Hill," *Congressional Quarterly Weekly Report* (23 May 1987): 1059–60.

55. On patterns in Ways and Means members' goals after the 1970s reforms, see Smith and Deering, *Committees in Congress*, 90; Strahan, *New Ways and Means*, 75–78.

56. See David W. Rohde, "Variations in Partisanship in the House of Representatives, 1953–88: Southern Democrats, Realignment and Agenda Change" (Paper presented at the Eighty-fourth Annual Meeting of the American Political Science Association, n.p., 1–4 September 1988).

57. See John W. Ellwood, "The Great Exception: The Congressional Budget Process in an Age of Decentralization," in *Congress Reconsidered*, 3d ed.; Barbara Sinclair, "Agenda Control and Policy Success: Ronald Reagan and the 97th House," *Legislative Studies Quarterly* 10 (1985): 291–314.

58. Roger H. Davidson, "Committees as Moving Targets," *Legislative Studies Quarterly* 11 (1986): 32.

59. Peters, *The American Speakership*, 16. Emphasis in the original.

DAVID W. ROHDE

7 | Agenda Change and Partisan Resurgence in the House of Representatives

Agenda Change and Variations in Partisanship

In the view of most students of Congress, the influence of political parties in the House over the last century has been in decline. The period from 1889 to 1911, which encompassed the speakerships of "Czar" Thomas B. Reed and "Boss" Joseph G. Cannon, was characterized by dominant majority party leadership, extensive interparty conflict, and strong intraparty cohesion. After the revolt against Speaker Cannon in 1910, power was decentralized through the committee system, the leaders of which were beyond practical party control. This weakening of centralizing influences was exacerbated by growing intraparty divisions, particularly between northern and southern Democrats. By the time of Sam Rayburn's speakership (1940–61), he could neither command the organizational units of the House nor depend on the support of his party's members on the floor.[1]

During the late 1960s and early 1970s, the weakened position of parties was made even worse, according to most analysts, by the increased electoral independence of members from their parties and by congressional reforms that further decentralized the legislative process by increasing the influence of subcommittees.[2] Yet despite these trends, there was strong evidence during the 1980s of a resurgence of partisanship in the House. Party leaders had new powers and greater influence over the legislative process. Party majorities opposed one another more often on the floor, and members of both parties voted with their partisan colleagues more often. The present analysis is part

231

of an ongoing effort to explore the causes of this partisan resurgence. Previous work has discussed the central role of electoral forces: that changes in the electorate have led to greater homogeneity within the two congressional parties and greater differences between them. I have also argued that the expanded powers of the Democratic leadership, granted in the House reforms of the 1970s, helped promote an increase in partisanship.[3] In this study I examine another factor in this process: the role of agenda change.

Definitions of the Agenda and Some Theoretical Considerations

A number of different meanings have been attached to the term "agenda" by legislative scholars. Some analysts mean the nature of the vote taken and the procedures for determining outcomes. This meaning is often employed by formal theorists to explore the impact of procedures on outcomes. Other meanings of the term deal more with the substance of proposals, focusing on the issues or problems being dealt with or on the specific policy alternatives being considered on a particular issue.[4] In the current analysis I will use the term agenda to include all of these facets: procedures for choice, issues, and policy alternatives. The distinctions among them, however, will be considered at various points.

To understand the role of agenda change in the resurgence of partisanship, we must recognize that a given pattern of congressional voting is a response to a specific agenda: a mix of issues, sets of alternatives, and particular rules. Voting patterns are the consequence not only of what outcomes members want, based on their individual goals and political circumstances, but also of the choices they are offered. If the character of the choices changes, then voting responses may exhibit as much variation as they would in light of a wholesale turnover in membership.[5]

It is also important to note that the House controls its own agenda. The selection of issues, the shaping of alternatives, and the choice of decision rules are all done by the members. Outside forces like constituencies or presidential requests do have a major impact, but their effects are channeled through the actions of the members. The most important institutional arrangement affecting the content of the agenda is the committee system. Committees play a large role in determining which issues the House will address, and they are the primary locus for the discussion and drafting of alternatives. One committee—Rules—determines some of the procedures for the consideration of most major issues.

Thus it would be fair to say that decisions on the House floor, where the increase in partisan voting has been manifested, are in large measure responses to committee decisions. Changes in the makeup of the membership, which would in turn translate into changes in the mix of members' goals and issue preferences on various committees (as well as on the floor), would affect the nature of the House's agenda. So, too, would alterations in the institutional arrangements that govern the relationship between committees and the membership. It is my contention that membership change led to increased preference homogeneity (especially among the Democrats) and this, combined with the committee-centered House reforms of the 1970s altered the character of the agenda. This, in turn, fostered increased partisanship in floor voting.

Committee Reforms, Membership Change, and the House Agenda

The proximate cause of the committee reforms adopted by the Democratic caucus was the conviction among liberal Democrats that procedures within committees and on the floor were biased against their interests.[6] Committee chairmen had substantial powers over the organization and operation of their committees, and because of the automatic application of the seniority rule they were not responsible to anyone else in the House for their decisions. Chairmen and other senior committee Democrats were, moreover, disproportionately likely to be southern and conservative. They were frequently able to join in coalition with committee Republicans to produce policy alternatives that were at variance with the preferences of House Democrats, or to block action on liberal bills. Finally, when these policy alternatives came to the floor, the powers of committee leaders, in conjunction with rules that barred recorded votes on amendments in the Committee of the Whole, made it very difficult for rank-and-file Democrats to change committee proposals.

Democratic reformers struck at this institutional structure in a variety of ways. First, the "Subcommittee Bill of Rights" and related reforms reduced the autocratic power of committee chairmen.

Subcommittee chairmanships and memberships, as well as their staff, budgets, and jurisdictions were made largely independent of the whims of chairmen. The subcommittees were not, however, made autonomous the way full committees had been. Rather, the reforms vested final control over these matters in each committee's Democratic caucus. These changes reduced the power disparities among committee members along seniority lines, producing a more democratic decision-making environment. The expectation was that this would lead to policy outcomes that were more representative of overall committee sentiments.

Second, the creation of Democratic committee caucuses, coupled with the secret-ballot votes in the Democratic caucus on committee chairmen at the beginning of every Congress, made committee leaders responsible to the sentiments of the majority of the majority party to a degree unheard of since the early years of the century. Committee chairmen could be removed by the Democratic caucus if their actions were judged to be unacceptable, and the same thing could be done to subcommittee chairmen by the committee caucuses. These arrangements were intended to make committees produce policies that reflected the preferences of House Democrats. They were, moreover, actually used a number of times against both committee and subcommittee chairmen, demonstrating that their existence was not a hollow threat.

Third, the reformers strengthened the position of party leaders by granting the Speaker the power to refer legislation to more than one committee, by transferring responsibility for Democratic committee assignments to the leadership-dominated Steering and Policy Committee, by expanding the leadership's ability to employ suspension of the rules, and most importantly, by placing the Rules Committee firmly under the control of the Speaker.[7] These changes enhanced the ability of the leadership to influence who was assigned to committees—especially the top committees with the greatest policy impacts—and to affect the fate of legislation that committees had reported. The aim was to reinforce the responsiveness of committees to Democratic preferences when a party consensus existed, and to protect the interests of the rank and file on the floor.

Fourth, the bias in favor of committee judgments was undermined by the adoption of recorded teller voting on amendments, followed by the implementation of the electronic voting system. These changes made it possible to put members on the record on amendments, thus making them responsible to their constituencies rather than just to committee leaders. Electronic voting also made it feasible to vote on a large number of amendments, and Smith[8] shows that amendment activity expanded greatly in the wake of these reforms. These changes were two-edged. It was expected that giving this capability to the members on the floor would induce committees to be responsive to rank-and-file sentiments when they drafted legislation. If, on the other hand, a committee was not responsive to those sentiments, then members could override the committee and enact their preferences through amendments.

Finally, these reforms were reinforced by changes in the Democratic membership. In the early 1970s, the reformers represented a majority of the majority party, but they did not speak for all Democrats, nor did they command a majority of the House on many issues. Throughout the 1970s and during Reagan's first two years in office, House Democrats were divided on many issues, usually along North–South lines. Gradually, however, changes occurred that made the constituencies of northern and southern Democrats, and the members selected from them, more similar to each other and more different from those of Republicans. On the one hand, the enfranchisement of black voters in the South by the Voting Rights Act and the increasing propensity of conservative white voters to shift their allegiance to the Republican party, made average policy preferences among Democrats in southern districts more liberal and made average Republican preferences more conservative. At the same time, a significant number of "New-Liberal" northern Democrats were elected, many from formerly Republican districts. These members tended to share concerns about balancing the budget, were less hostile to defense spending than other northerners, and were less inclined to favor new large-scale government programs to solve social problems.[9] As a result, there was greater common ground on which to build a Democratic party consensus on previously divisive issues. For those members who might still be inclined to oppose the party (either due to constituency pressure or their own preferences), the greater party homogeneity interacted with the increased ability of the party to bestow rewards and punishments to reduce the tendency to deviate.

Thus the reforms were intended to reduce the independence of committees and their leadership, making them more responsive to the preferences of House Democrats, and those preferences grew more homogeneous over time. Elsewhere I have labeled the situation the reformers created as "conditional party government." The qualifier distinguishes the current situation from the "party government" days of Speakers Reed and Cannon, when leaders commanded their parties across virtually the full range of issues with which the House dealt. In the modern House, Democrats do not have partisan interests in every issue,[10] nor are they united on all issues where they have such an interest.

Conditional party government, as reflected in the reform effort and the years following, has a narrower focus. Its thrust is that party responsibility will exist only when an issue is salient to the party and the membership is fairly united on it. Under these circumstances, chairmen and members on relevant committees are expected not to act as roadblocks to the passage of party-supported policies, and the leadership is expected to use the powers granted to it to advance the party cause. Party leaders or committee chairmen who violate these expectations risk retaliation by the caucus.

Based on this perspective, one can offer some anticipated effects of the institutional changes on the House agenda and in turn trace their consequences for partisan voting on the floor. First, we would expect in the postreform period to find that the policy alternatives produced by committees more often represented the preferences of House Democrats,[11] and that conflict over proposed changes in them on the floor would have become more partisan. Second, we would expect that the majority leadership would increasingly use its powers to shape the agenda to advance Democratic policy interests—to protect satisfactory committee products and to provide for potential changes in unsatisfactory ones. Finally, we would expect these trends to have interacted with the easing of the floor amendment process so that the final products of legislative action—the bills passed by the House—would have more often reflected the preferences of the Democratic membership. Moreover, as a consequence of the growing homogeneity of the Democratic party, these trends should have become more pronounced over time. We would also not anticipate that these effects would be equal across issue areas, but that matter will be dealt with below as these expectations are elaborated and evidence is presented.

Partisan Consequences of Agenda Change

Leadership Powers and Committee Products

While most of the attention here will be given to leadership influence over bills after they are reported from committees, the reforms also expanded leadership involvement with committees before this stage. The power of multiple referral "has allowed the leadership to capitalize on existing sources of leverage, and in so doing extend its role and influence."[12] It enhances the Speaker's power over scheduling, and it is used for most legislation important to the leadership.[13] Moreover, the Speaker sometimes becomes the arbiter of inter-committee differences, negotiating compromises among the participants.[14]

After bills are reported, the leadership has a number of tools at its disposal. One is suspension of the rules. Bills passed under suspension of the rules require two-thirds approval. Traditionally, this device was used to consider noncontroversial legislation. However, given the restrictions the procedure imposes (only forty minutes of debate and no amendments permitted), it is also a useful device for protecting a committee's product when there is substantial support for *some* action to be taken (since two-thirds approval is needed for passage) but there is partisan disagreement over which alternative should be chosen. The reforms increased the number of days each month this procedure could be employed by the leadership, and previous analysis has shown that after the reform period it was used for an increasing number of bills about which there was significant disagreement. On those relatively controversial bills, moreover, the voting became increasingly partisan.

It seems clear, however, that the most important device the leadership has available to affect the fate of committee policies is the control over special rules. Most bills of consequence require a special rule from the Rules Committee to set the terms of floor debate. Because the Speaker had been granted sole appointment power for committee Democrats, it had become responsive to the leadership. Special rules could be crafted to protect the content of committee decisions, but only at the discretion of Democratic leaders. The Rules Committee was also very important in resolving conflicts between different versions of multiply referred bills.[15] These capabilities increased the incentives for committees to take into account leadership (and thus party) preferences when drafting bills.

Figure 7.1. **Partisanship on Votes on Special Rules, 84th–100th Congresses (Consensual Votes Excluded)**

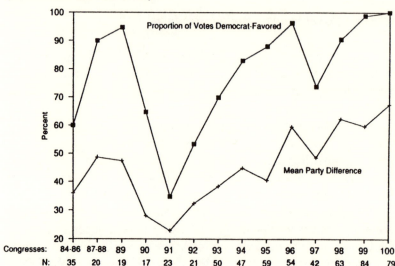

If the reforms did have the effect of inducing committee Democrats to produce policy alternatives that more often reflected Democratic party preferences, then we would expect that the leadership would use the ability to write special rules to protect the content of those bills. One way this would be reflected is that disagreement over the special rules themselves should have become more partisan and that the rules should have tended to be more often favorable to Democrats than to Republicans. Evidence regarding these points is contained in Figure 7.1, which displays data on partisanship in record votes on special rules from the 84th through the Hundredth Congresses (with "consensual" votes excluded).[16]

One line in the figure shows the proportion of rules votes on which the rule was "Democrat-favored." These are votes on which the proportion of Democrats voting in favor exceeds that proportion for the Republicans, indicating that the rule is more satisfactory to the Democrats. The other line shows the mean party difference (i.e., the absolute difference in the percentage of Democrats and Republicans voting "aye") on these votes, indicating the degree of interparty conflict. Both tell the same story. The proportion of votes on which the rule was Democrat-favored was in the middle range in the Eisenhower years, grew substantially after the successful fight in 1961 to expand the

Rules Committee, and then plummeted after the 1966 election and after the Nixon presidency gave a working majority in the House to the conservative coalition. The proportion began increasing again during the reform years and eventually peaked in the Hundredth Congress, when 100 percent of the rules were Democrat-favored. Similarly the mean party difference on these votes declined through the Ninety-first Congress, then steadily increased to the present. Thus the share of special rules that is more preferred by Democrats than Republicans has indeed increased, and votes in favor of those rules have become much more partisan. Leadership control of the Rules Committee has apparently led it to produce more rules favorable to Democratic positions, and the members of both parties see conflict about rules more in partisan terms.

Conflict over Alternatives: Committee Bills
and Floor Amendments

More direct evidence of changing reactions to the content of committee proposals can be had by examining data on floor amendments. If committee bills became more satisfactory to Democrats in the wake of reform, then Democrats should have become less likely to try to change them and Republicans should have become more likely to do so. Smith shows that the proportion of amendments sponsored by Democrats declined in the Ninety-third Congress (1973–74) and then remained steady after that. Smith's data, however, deal with all amendments, whether they involved conflicting views or not. In earlier analysis of the data used here, attention was confined to amendments decided by nonconsensual roll calls. That analysis showed that the proportion of amendments that were Democrat-favored declined from the Ninety-second Congress through the Carter years, rose again during Reagan's first term, and then declined to the pre-Reagan level (about 30 percent) during the Ninety-ninth and Hundredth Congresses.[17]

As we noted earlier, however, not all issues are equally likely to provoke partisan conflict. For the purposes of this analysis, we will deal only with broad issue categories, contrasting domestic issues with foreign and defense policy matters.[18] There is good reason to expect that partisan differences would be less pronounced in the two latter areas than on domestic matters, especially during the 1970s and before.

Parker and Parker's study of roll-call voting within House committees in the 1970s showed that Foreign Affairs and Armed Services were the only legislative committees with nonpartisan cleavage patterns. It also showed that pro- and anti-administration cleavages were important on both committees, and that both groups were bipartisan.[19]

Fenno had characterized the policy coalitions of the Foreign Affairs Committee as "executive-led," although the reforms appeared to undermine the committee's propensity to "rubber-stamp" presidential desires.[20] Much of the conflict within the committee revolved around the desirability of foreign economic aid, an issue to which many Republicans tended to react negatively. Thus we might expect the party of the president to be relevant to the amount of partisanship this issue provoked.

The Armed Services Committee has long been a bastion of support for the military and presidential desires to increase defense spending. There is also substantial evidence that Armed Services' membership is among the least representative of opinion in the House. For example, Ray, in a study of the committee in the 1970s, reported that it "has consistently drawn its new members from among those already the most supportive of the military industrial complex. . . ." Cox and McCubbins showed that it is committee Democrats that are specifically unrepresentative of opinion in their party.[21] Moreover, since the Vietnam War, defense policy is an issue that has divided House Democrats, particularly along sectional lines, although there is evidence that this cleavage declined significantly in the later years of the Reagan administration. The Democratic contingent on Armed Services remains quite sectionally unrepresentative of the party: in the 101st Congress, 52 percent of committee Democrats were southerners as compared to 33 percent of Democrats in the House. Therefore, we would expect that Democrats might continue to have disagreements with the content of defense bills, due to committee unrepresentativeness and the lack of a homogeneous party position, although this problem might have declined to some degree in the 1980s.

Figure 7.2 shows the proportion of amendments in each issue area that were Democrat-favored. The patterns are very consistent with our expectations. On domestic issues we see a steady decline from the Ninety-second Congress, when 43 percent of the amendments were more heavily supported by Democrats, to the Hundredth, when it was only 17 percent. Clearly, on domestic issues Democrats found

Figure 7.2. **Proportion of Amendments That Were Democrat-Favored, by Issue Area, 92d–100th Congresses (Consensual Votes Excluded)**

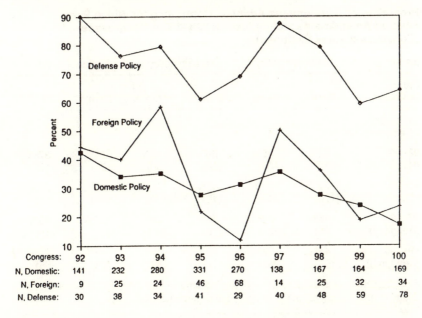

Congress:	92	93	94	95	96	97	98	99	100
N, Domestic:	141	232	280	331	270	138	167	164	169
N, Foreign:	9	25	24	46	68	14	25	32	34
N, Defense:	30	38	34	41	29	40	48	59	78

the committee-proposed agenda more and more satisfactory over time, while Republicans found it relatively less so and they tried more often to change it. On foreign policy issues, the Democrat-favored proportion of amendments was high in the Nixon-Ford years, dropped substantially under Carter (reflecting the great Republican dissatisfaction with his international approach), and rose again during Reagan's first Congress. This is consistent with the perspective that committee bills were responding to the preferences of the president, and the opposite party would have an incentive to try to change the proposals. Then from the Ninety-eighth through the Hundredth Congresses, as Democratic homogeneity increased, the Democrats' share of amendments trailed off to a level comparable to those on domestic issues.

On defense matters, Democrat-favored amendments accounted for an overwhelming share of the total at the beginning of the period. It declined during the Carter presidency, but then rebounded to earlier levels in Reagan's first term in reaction to committee approval of the president's proposed military expansion. In the Ninety-ninth and Hun-

Table 7.1

Proportion of Amendments Adopted, Controlling for Which Party Favored Amendments and for Issues: 92d–100th Congresses (Consensual Votes Excluded)

Issue:	Domestic policy		Foreign policy		Defense policy	
Party favoring:	Dem.	Rep.	Dem.	Rep.	Dem.	Rep.
Congresses (President)						
92–94 (Nixon-Ford)	42% (233)	35% (400)	36% (28)	43% (30)	15% (84)	37% (19)
95–96 (Carter)	38% (170)	40% (419)	47% (19)	40% (100)	13% (48)	54% (24)
97–98 (Reagan I)	48% (95)	33% (207)	56% (16)	36% (25)	27% (73)	40% (15)
99–100 (Reagan II)	44% (68)	22% (262)	50% (14)	30% (53)	41% (85)	27% (55)

Note: Cell entries are the percentage of amendments in that category that were adopted. (Number of amendments in the category are in parentheses.)

dredth Congresses, as the Democratic caucus deposed two successive Armed Services chairmen, Democrat-favored amendments dropped to a level equivalent to those in the Carter years. In this issue area, an unrepresentative committee and Democratic divisions produced policy alternatives that were unacceptable to many Democrats, leading them to seek a wide range of changes. More recently, caucus action against the committee's chairmen plus greater party agreement on defense has modified this tendency somewhat, but amendment-support patterns indicate that defense policies produced by committees are less satisfactory to House Democrats than other issues.[22]

Table 7.1 presents data on the proportion of these amendments that were adopted. (Because many Congress-party combinations had few cases on foreign and defense issues, Congresses were grouped.) On domestic issues, the adoption rate for Democratic amendments varied little, especially under Republican presidents. The Republican rate, on the other hand, dropped from 35 to 23 percent. On foreign-policy issues, adoption of Democrat-favored amendments increased under Carter and then stayed steady, while the Republican-favored rate was

Table 7.2

Mean Party Difference on Amendment Votes, Controlling for Which Party Favored Amendments and for Issues: 92d–100th Congresses (Consensual Votes Excluded)

Issue:	Domestic policy		Foreign policy		Defense policy	
Party favoring:	Dem.	Rep.	Dem.	Rep.	Dem.	Rep.
Congresses (President)						
92–94 (Nixon-Ford)	34% (233)	44% (400)	30% (28)	25% (30)	31% (84)	29% (19)
95–96 (Carter)	29% (170)	45% (419)	34% (19)	44% (100)	25% (48)	29% (24)
97–98 (Reagan I)	39% (95)	50% (207)	35% (16)	36% (25)	36% (73)	44% (15)
99–100 (Reagan II)	36% (68)	54% (262)	45% (14)	60% (53)	50% (85)	57% (55)

Note: Number of amendments in the category are in parentheses.

level until it fell during Reagan's second term. Finally on defense matters, the rate of passage for Democrats' amendments increased considerably over the Reagan years; for Republicans' amendments it increased under Carter, then declined substantially.

Space constraints do not permit exploration of the differing time sequences for these different amendment series, but they come to a common bottom line. By Reagan's second term, the likelihood of a Democrat-favored amendment being adopted was roughly similar across all three issues, as was the likelihood for Republican-favored proposals; however, the first probability was 50 to 100 percent higher than the second. As committee-produced policies came to reflect better the preferences of the majority party, the Democrat-controlled House became much more resistant to Republican changes than to Democratic ones.

This interpretation is reinforced by data on the mean party difference on amendment votes, shown in Table 7.2. On domestic issues, there is greater partisanship on Republican-favored amendments than on Democratic ones from the beginning of the series onward. On the former set, however, the mean party difference increases over time, while on Democratic-favored amendments there is no such trend. That is, over time the defense of committee bills against Republican efforts to change them grew more partisan, while the voting on Democrat-supported changes did not exhibit any notable change in partisanship. If committee bills were becoming more representative of Democratic views, then party members should have found it easier to cohere in defense of those bills than to join together in seeking changes.

The patterns are more complex on foreign and defense votes. On foreign policy, there is an increase in the mean party difference on both sets of amendments, but the increase is about two and one-half times greater on Republican-favored amendments than on Democratic ones. The number of cases in the Democrat-favored category is small throughout the series. A more detailed analysis will be necessary in the future to determine whether this trend is due to increased Democratic willingness to challenge the president, or just appears to be so due to variations in the content mix of these small subsets.

Finally, on defense policy the increase in partisanship was substantial on both sets of amendments, although even here it was somewhat larger on Republican-favored proposals. This appears partly to reflect the continuing unrepresentativeness of the Democrats on the Armed Services Committee, and partly the modification of the committee's product over time. Increasing Democratic homogeneity on defense made it easier for them to join together to defend the committee when it reflected the party's view, and easier to challenge the committee when it did not. On the latter point, the annual defense authorization bill was among the rare instances where the agenda powers of the majority leadership were used to facilitate challenges to the content of a committee's bill. Moreover, many of these challenges and the leadership's procedural maneuvers were supported by the Armed Services chairman, Les Aspin of Wisconsin.

So we see that regarding amendments, a larger share of them became Republican-favored over time (particularly on domestic issues), a smaller proportion of Republican amendments were successful, and partisan conflict increased substantially in voting on those amendments. Thus on this aspect of the agenda, the increase in partisanship appears to reflect both increased Democratic homogeneity and a shift in the character of committee products to represent better Democratic preferences.

Figure 7.3. **Percent of Bills and Joint Resolutions on Domestic Issues That Were Democrat-Favored on Initial Passage, 84th–100th Congresses (Consensual Votes Excluded)**

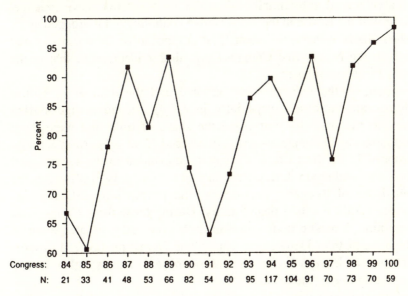

The Final Product: Bill Passage

Here the different aspects of our discussion come together. If committees have tended to produce proposals that better represent Democrats' views and if changed floor procedures have facilitated altering those proposals when they were not so representative, then we should find evidence that the end product of these deliberations—the bill as passed by the House—became more often satisfactory to the Democrats over time.

Figure 7.3 shows the proportion of bills and joint resolutions on domestic issues that were Democrat-favored on the vote on initial passage.[23] The variations seem to demonstrate the influence of the forces we have been discussing, as well as the impact of divided partisan control of the government and variations in Democratic strength. The proportion of bills that were Democrat-favored was low in the two earliest Eisenhower Congresses, increased with the infusion of a large number of Democrats after the 1958 election, and then increased again when the Democrats gained control of the presidency. This reflection of Democratic preferences was sustained through the "Great Society" Congress (the Eighty-ninth), but the proportion of Democrat-favored bills decreased substantially when the 1966 election gave practical control of the House to the conservative coalition, and it dropped again when Nixon became president. The proportion of Democrat-favored bills in the Ninety-first Congress was almost identical to that in the early Eisenhower years.

Then, as the reforms were adopted and the number of House Democrats increased (especially in 1974), the advantage shifted back to the majority party, and the share of bills that were more supported by Democrats steadily increased. That proportion actually dropped in the first Carter Congress, rebounded in the second, and then declined again during Reagan's first two years in office. In the remainder of Reagan's presidency, the proportion of Democrat-favored bills reached near totality. During these three Congresses, only nine domestic nonconsensual bills received a greater share of Republican than Democratic votes. The Democrat-favored proportion was as high or higher in each of these Congresses than in any preceding one in the series.

The comparatively small number of foreign- and defense-policy bills requires us to group Congresses for analysis, and these grouped data are presented in Table 7.3. On foreign policy, the Democrat-favored portion of bills rises and falls with control of the presidency, being higher when the Democratic party held the White House and lower when it did not. This pattern held until Reagan's second term, when every foreign-policy bill was Democrat-favored. Like the situation with amendments, the small numbers involved suggest that a more detailed analysis is desirable before reaching any firm conclusions. It does appear, however, that this change reflected a greater willingness on the part of Democrats, through the combination of committee and floor action, to challenge the president's judgments on foreign policy, since Reagan formally opposed passage of nine of the fifteen Democrat-favored bills voted on in the two Congresses.

Regarding defense issues, even with the small number of cases, the pattern is quite clear. Throughout and after the Vietnam War, the Democratic party's divisions over military policy gave control over outcomes to the conservative coalition. Thus unlike either of the other issue categories, Republican-favored outcomes were the rule

Table 7.3

Proportion of Democrat-Favored Bills and Joint Resolutions, and Mean Party Difference on Initial Passage: Foreign- and Defense-Policy Issues, by Administration, 84th–100th Congresses (Consensual Votes Excluded)

Congresses (President)	Percent Democrat-favored	N	Mean party difference	
			Dem. bills	Rep. bills
Foreign policy				
84–86 (Eisenhower)	81	(26)	12%	16%
87–90 (Kennedy-Johnson)	96	(44)	31%	8%
91–94 (Nixon-Ford)	77	(62)	15%	13%
95–96 (Carter)	88	(32)	28%	9%
97–98 (Reagan I)	70	(20)	29%	31%
99–100 (Reagan II)	100	(15)	43%	[N=0]
Defense policy				
84–86 (Eisenhower)	50	(2)	[N=1]	[N=1]
87–90 (Kennedy-Johnson)	90	(10)	28%	[N=1]
91–94 (Nixon-Ford)	16	(31)	10%	20%
95–96 (Carter)	30	(23)	26%	16%
97–98 (Reagan I)	31	(16)	53%	24%
99–100 (Reagan II)	55	(20)	56%	49%

throughout the administrations of Nixon, Ford, and Carter, and into Reagan's first term. During the last half of the Reagan years, however, the increased homogeneity of the Democrats permitted them to

Figure 7.4. **Mean Party Difference on Initial Passage of Bills and Joint Resolutions on Domestic Issues, Controlling for Which Party Favored Passage, 84–100th Congresses (Consensual Votes Excluded)**

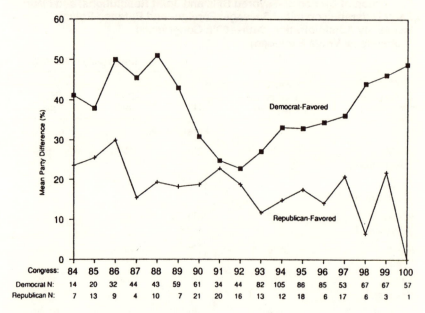

Congress:	84	85	86	87	88	89	90	91	92	93	94	95	96	97	98	99	100
Democrat N:	14	20	32	44	43	59	61	34	44	82	105	86	85	53	67	67	57
Republican N:	7	13	9	4	10	7	21	20	16	13	12	18	6	17	6	3	1

put together a party consensus broad enough to control a large share of the outcomes.

We can conclude this analysis with an examination of the data on partisan voting on the passage of these bills. Figure 7.4 shows the mean party difference on domestic issues, controlling for which party most favored the bill. Because virtually all bills that reach the stage of a vote on final passage are successful, a Republican-favored bill means—almost by definition—that the Democratic party is divided on the issue. These cases involve the conservative coalition in action: cohesive Republicans joined by varying number of Democrats (mostly southerners) to control the outcome. Such instances will mute partisanship, and so the data for Republican-favored bills show a relatively small mean party difference and little trend over time.[24] On Democrat-favored bills, however, we see a considerable decline in partisanship after the Eighty-ninth Congress, in the wake of Republican election victories in 1966 and 1968 and Democratic divisions over the "Great Society" agenda. The mean party difference began a slow and steady increase from the low point of the Ninety-second Congress through the

Ninety-seventh and then exhibited an equivalent increase over just the next six years.

For defense- and foreign-policy bills, the pattern on Republican-favored measures is fairly similar to that for domestic issues: relatively low partisanship and little change over time until the Reagan years.[25] On Democratic-favored policy bills, there was a modest variation before Reagan as the partisan control of administrations shifted, reflecting the Republicans' greater inclination to support the initiatives of presidents of their party. The pattern was different during the Reagan administration, as the Democrats' tendency to defer to the president on this issue declined and they more frequently created their own foreign-policy alternatives. As noted earlier, the president opposed nine of the fifteen bills in this category in his second term, while the comparable figure for the first term was only three of fourteen (and all three dealt with foreign trade).

Finally, partisan disagreement on Democrat-favored defense bills was modest under Democratic presidents, and virtually nonexistent under Nixon–Ford. Here too, however, things were different during the Reagan presidency, with larger mean party differences than on the corresponding bills in either of the other set of issues. The growth of party conflict was partly due, as with Republican-favored bills, to changes in the particular issues in the defense category.[26] But it was also a consequence of a shift in the responses to continuing agenda items, particularly the annual defense authorization bill.

The changing voting patterns on this matter are shown in Figure 7.5, which gives the percent of Republicans and northern Democrats voting in favor of passage of the bill each year from 1971 through 1988.[27] Throughout the years from the Nixon through the Carter administrations, Republican support was virtually unanimous, while between one-fifth and one-third of the northern Democrats voted against. During Reagan's first term, the president pressed for a substantial expansion of military spending. At first he got almost everything he wanted, but over the next few years (because of troubles in the economy and growing deficits) spending began to fall somewhat short of projections. Northern Democrats increasingly thought that defense spending was too high and opposed the bill in greater numbers, while growing numbers of conservative Republicans believed that the bills didn't give the president enough of what he requested and began voting against them too.

Figure 7.5. **Percentage of Republicans and Northern Democrats Supporting Initial Passage of the Defense Authorization Bill, 1971–1988**

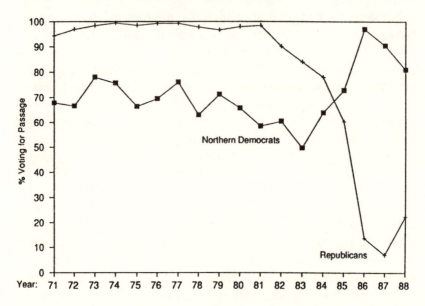

In 1984 the balance between approval and refusal of administration requests apparently became more tolerable to northerners, and the proportion of them voting for the bills began to increase. Then in 1985, after the Democratic caucus deposed Armed Services Chairman Melvin Price of Illinois and replaced him with Les Aspin, the combination of committee and floor action produced the first Democrat-favored defense bill since the Johnson administration, with increased northern Democratic support and greater Republican opposition. In the next three years more Democratic unity on specific defense items, coupled with the leadership's use of its agenda management powers, gave the Democrats victory on most contested questions. The Democrats' preferences were reflected in the bills, the Republicans' were not, and the mean party difference on those three votes was seventy-eight points.

To summarize these results regarding bill passage, while there have been variations across issues, the basic pattern has been the same. After the reform years, the combination of committee and floor action produced an increasing proportion of bills that were more satisfactory to Democrats than Republicans. On the decreasing number of

Republican-favored bills, the average party difference remained relatively low. On Democrat-favored bills, however, the better representation of the party's preferences produced greater and greater partisan disagreement. Thus like the pattern on amendments, increasing partisanship on votes on bill passage seems partly to reflect the greater preference homogeneity among Democrats, and also to be the consequence of a difference in the character of the agenda items that the combination of committee action and floor amendments put before the House.

Agendas and Partisanship: The Causes of Change

This chapter has sought to explore the role of agenda change in the resurgence of partisanship in the House. I have argued that voting patterns are responses to an agenda, that the House controls its legislative agenda, and that the character of votes changes in response to both shifts in the distribution of members' preferences and alterations in the institutional arrangements through which decisions are made.

Previous analysis has shown that regional and district-level electoral changes since the mid-1960s have produced congressional parties that were more internally homogeneous and more distinct from one another. Moreover, institutional reforms within the Democratic party have made those Democrats who hold power more responsible to the party membership. Those reforms (and others passed by the full House) have also created a more egalitarian distribution of power within committees and have made it easier to alter committee proposals on the floor. The intent of the reforms was to facilitate the passage of policy alternatives on important issues that reflected the preferences of House Democrats. To that end, the institutional structures that shaped the agenda—within committees and on the floor—were altered.

Therefore, in assessing the role of the agenda in increasing partisanship, this analysis has sought evidence that the reforms have contributed to systematic changes in the nature of the agenda and that those changes were linked to more partisan patterns of support. The evidence presented relates to three stages of decision making. We saw that the special rules that governed floor consideration of major bills became progressively more satisfactory to Democrats than to Republicans after the reforms, and that the average party difference on votes on contested rules increased sharply. This reflected the Democratic leadership's new control over the Rules Committee and greater inclination to use special rules to advantage proposals favored by House Democrats.

Regarding amendments, the evidence showed that an increasing proportion were Republican-favored, that Republican amendments became more difficult to pass, and that partisanship on Republican amendments rose significantly. Thus floor conflict over alternatives increasingly became a matter of a cohesive Democratic party defending committee proposals against Republican attempts to change them, reflecting greater Democratic satisfaction with committee decisions. There were, however, important variations across issues, especially with respect to defense.

Finally, with respect to initial House passage of bills, we saw that the combined effects of committee and floor action produced progressively higher proportions of Democrat-favored bills on domestic issues, given the variations in party resources (i.e., seats and presidential control) available to Democrats. Because of the special circumstances of defense and foreign policy, this effect was not apparent on those issues until the Reagan years. The increase in partisan voting on bill passage was due to increased Democratic cohesion in favor of, and declining Republican support for, Democrat-favored bills, and to the increased representation of those measures on the agenda.

Therefore, the conclusion warranted by the analysis is that greater preference homogeneity within the Democratic party interacted with the reforms of the 1970s to alter the House's agenda in ways that better reflected the wishes of House Democrats. At the same time, the Republican minority also became more cohesive and more conservative. The agenda changes in turn combined with the greater party homogeneity to produce more partisan conflict over alternatives and outcomes on the floor. Across a wide range of issues the frequent pattern became Democrats defending committee products against changes proposed by Republicans. No longer accurate was the picture of House decision making in which committees, controlled by senior conservatives, dominated outcomes which were then "rubber-stamped" on the floor. Also inaccurate (particularly on important issues) was the description that portrayed the House as generally characterized by atomistic subcommittee government, in which parties were of little consequence, and stalemate and inaction were the rule. Relatively cohesive parties and their leaders had become important elements in determining decision rules, in selecting issues for consideration, in shaping alternatives, and in deciding outcomes.

Conclusion

If we accept, at least as a working assumption, the accuracy of the theory discussed here, then we can consider the future prospects for congressional parties and partisanship in light of its components. I have argued that the driving force behind the resurgence of partisanship has been electoral change. As northern and southern Democratic constituencies became more similar, the preferences of their Democratic representatives did also. A second important influence was the institutional reforms that made committees more responsible and more responsive to the Democratic rank and file and that strengthened party leaders. Finally, the distribution of political resources between the parties (such as seats held or control of the presidency) also had an impact.

Regarding the Democrats' constituency base, the question is whether new issues will emerge or old issues will resurface to divide Democratic constituencies and undermine party homogeneity and cohesion. If the pressure of large deficits subsides or if a "peace dividend" ever really appears, then old disagreements about the magnitude of federal domestic spending will likely become more prominent. On the other hand, with the changes occurring in the Soviet Union and Eastern Europe, intraparty conflict over foreign and defense issues will probably decline even more. Thus it does not seem that there is much prospect in the near future for widespread constituency-based disagreements on issues among Democrats. Some issues will always come along to divide them, as the recent capital gains dispute illustrates. It does not seem likely, however, that divisions of the magnitude produced by civil rights, Vietnam, and the Great Society will be seen again soon.

Nor does it seem likely that the Democrats' reforms that were adopted in the 1970s will be reversed. They appear to be serving the interests of the majority quite well, and there is little apparent dissatisfaction. Democratic majorities in committee and in the full caucus should retain the ability to control and shape the agenda and to impose sanctions on committee or party leaders who impede the progress of Democrat-favored initiatives. Indeed, at the committee level, the trend toward better representation of party preferences may grow even stronger, as new loyalist chairmen come to power, especially on the major committees.

On the other hand, the transition in the speakership from Wright to Foley has muted partisan conflict to a degree because Speaker Foley is inclined toward a less aggressive use of the powers at the leadership's disposal to shape the agenda and to stimulate cohesiveness than his predecessor. Yet one should not overestimate the likely impact of this transition. The strategies and tactics of leaders are shaped in large measure by the preferences and attitudes of the members they represent, and strong pressures from his Democratic colleagues have led Foley toward a more aggressive approach in 1990, including greater use of restrictive rules to enhance the prospects for Democratic policy initiatives.

Finally, it does not seem likely that the change in occupants of the White House or a shift in the distribution of seats in the House between the parties will significantly alter the observed trends toward greater partisanship. To be sure the new leadership both in the House and the White House has mitigated the animosity that was apparent under Wright and Reagan, and Bush's own policy preferences are more moderate than those of his predecessor. However, the president and the Democratic majority speak for fundamentally different political coalitions, and they support significantly different priorities. And despite Bush's high approval ratings in public opinion polls, there has been no lack of conflict with the House and no strong record of success for the president. As one analysis indicated, "George Bush fared worse in Congress than any other first-year president elected in the postwar era."[28] The president's position won on only 50 percent of the eighty-six House roll calls where one was identified and on only 30 percent of the fifty-six votes on which a majority of Democrats opposed the president and a majority of Republicans supported him. It seems likely that interbranch relations in the Bush presidency will be characterized by greater civility, but not by a lack of partisan conflict.

While we may see an increase in the share of House seats held by Republicans over the next few election cycles, which may restore some of the "balance-of-power" role played by conservative Democrats in the early 1980s, it does not seem probable that the GOP will win control of the House. Yet even if that did occur, it does not appear likely that this would significantly alter the patterns of partisanship in the House. Again, the inter-party differences are electorate-based, and these will persist regardless of which party has majority status. Moreover, the House GOP members have apparently concluded for themselves that part of the Democrats' increased success in the legislative process is due to the reform provisions they adopted, and the Republicans have passed rules patterned on them. Republican caucuses were created on every committee, party and committee leaders were obligated to support party positions, and the Republican leaders were empowered to create task forces on particular bills and were given greater influence over committee assignments. Partisanship in the operation of the House of Representatives will remain strong as long as the conditions that produced it persist. This seems likely for the foreseeable future.

Notes

The major support for the project of which this paper is a part came from the National Science Foundation through grant SES 89–09884. During the project's initial stages, support was also received from the Dirksen Congressional Center and from Michigan State University's Research Initiation Grant program. I want to acknowledge the research assistance of James Meernik throughout the development of the project. More recent assistance was provided by Renée Smith. Roll-call data were supplied by the Interuniversity Consortium for Political and Social Research, which bears no responsibility for the analyses or interpretations presented here.

1. Useful discussions of the era of strong parties and of the revolt against Cannon can be found in Charles O. Jones, "Joseph G. Cannon and Howard W. Smith: An Essay on the Limits of Leadership in the House of Representatives," *Journal of Politics* 30 (August 1968): 617–46; and Joseph Cooper and David W. Brady, "Institutional Context and Leadership Style: The House from Cannon to Rayburn," *American Political Science Review* 75 (June 1981): 411–25. On the impact of electoral divisions and decreased leadership powers, see David Brady, Joseph Cooper, and Patricia A. Hurley, "The Decline of Party in the U.S. House of Representatives, 1887–1968," *Legislative Studies Quarterly* 4 (August 1979): 381–408. The situation in the Rayburn years is discussed by Cooper and Brady, "Institutional Context."

2. The growth of electoral independence is examined by Melissa P. Collie and David W. Brady, "The Decline of Partisan Voting Coalitions in the House of Representatives," in *Congress Reconsidered*, 3d ed., ed. Lawrence C. Dodd and Bruce I. Oppenheimer (Washington: Congressional Quarterly Press, 1985), 272–87. On the negative effects of the congressional reforms on parties, see Leroy N. Rieselbach, *Congressional Reform* (Washington: Congressional Quarterly Press, 1986).

3. On the effects of electoral forces, see David W. Rohde, "Variations in

Partisanship in the House of Representatives, 1953–1988: Southern Democrats, Realignment, and Agenda Change" (Paper presented at the Eighty-fourth Annual Meeting of the American Political Science Association, Washington, D.C., 1–4 September 1988). The impact of strengthened Democratic party leadership is examined in Rohde, *Parties and Leaders in the Postreform House* (Chicago: University of Chicago Press, 1991).

4. For example, John Kingdon, *Agendas, Alternatives, and Public Policies* (Boston: Little, Brown, 1984) defined the agenda as the list of problems being debated, and he distinguished it from alternatives. Other analysts used the term to include both issues and alternatives. See Barbara Sinclair, *Congressional Realignment, 1925–1978* (Austin: University of Texas Press, 1982); and Paul Light, *The President's Agenda* (Baltimore: Johns Hopkins University Press, 1983).

5. Thus changes in aggregate voting patterns could conceivably be the consequence of nothing more than a shift in the mix of issues or of types of votes. For example, if certain issues or votes (e.g., amendments) are more likely to produce partisan responses and if the proportion of all votes represented by those matters increases, then we would expect aggregate partisanship to increase. Previous analysis (Rohde, "Variations in Partisanship") indicates that the resurgence of partisanship is not simply the consequence of this type of shift in the mix of votes. Increased partisan voting is apparent across broad-issue and vote-type categories.

6. For evidence regarding this contention and a discussion of the specific reforms referred to below, see Norman J. Ornstein, "Causes and Consequences of Congressional Change," in *Congress in Change*, ed. Norman Ornstein (New York: Praeger, 1975), 88–114; Burton D. Sheppard, *Rethinking Congressional Reform* (Cambridge: Schenkman, 1985); and Rohde, *Parties and Leaders*, Chap. 2.

7. For discussions of these specific leadership-strengthening moves, see Melissa P. Collie and Joseph Cooper, "Multiple Referral and the 'New' Committee System in the House of Representatives," in *Congress Reconsidered*, 4th ed., ed. Lawrence C. Dodd and Bruce I. Oppenheimer (Washington: Congressional Quarterly Press, 1989), 245–72; Steven S. Smith and Bruce A. Ray, "The Impact of Congressional Reform: House Democratic Committee Assignments," *Congress and the Presidency* 10 (Autumn 1983): 219–40; Stanley Bach, "Suspension of the Rules, the Order of Business, and the Evolution of Legislative Procedure in the House of Representatives" (Paper presented at the Eighty-second Annual Meeting of the American Political Science Association, Washington, D.C., 28–31 August 1986); and Stanley Bach and Steven S. Smith, *Managing Uncertainty in the House of Representatives* (Washington: Brookings Institution, 1988).

8. Steven S. Smith, *Call to Order* (Washington: Brookings Institution, 1989), Chap. 2.

9. For evidence on Democratic divisions in the 1970s, see Barbara Sinclair, *Congressional Realignment*. Changes in southern districts are considered in Rohde, "Variations in Partisanship," and *Parties and Leaders*, Chap. 3. The latter also discusses the impact of the "New Liberals."

10. Thus we should not be surprised to find one committee with a jurisdiction that only rarely provokes partisan interest (e.g., Merchant Marine and Fisheries) operating with roughly the same degree of autonomy as in the past, while others that often deal with partisan matters are more greatly affected by the changes. See

Gary W. Cox and Mathew D. McCubbins, *Parties and Committees in the U.S. House of Representatives*; Steven S. Smith and Forrest Maltzman, "Declining Committee Power in the House of Representatives" (Paper presented at the Eighty-fifth Annual Meeting of the American Political Science Association, Atlanta, Georgia, 31 August–3 September 1989); and Rohde, *Parties and Leaders*, Chap. 3.

11. We would also expect that committees would rarely, if ever, prevent issues the party wants considered from getting on the agenda and to the floor. This effect seems to have taken hold almost immediately. At the end of 1975, Representative Philip Burton (D- CA) said, "For the first time in memory there was not a single instance when a committee chairman blocked a major bill." Quoted in James L. Sundquist, *The Decline and Resurgence of Congress* (Washington: Brookings Institution, 1981), 380.

12. Collie and Cooper, "Multiple Referral," 265. When a bill involves the jurisdiction of more than one committee, the Speaker may refer it to several committees sharing jurisdiction.

13. See Barbara Sinclair, "House Majority Party Leadership in the Late 1980s," in *Congress Reconsidered*, 4th ed., 313–15.

14. See Roger H. Davidson, "The New Centralization on Capitol Hill," *The Review of Politics* (1988): 358–59.

15. For discussion of these Rules Committee activities see Bach and Smith, *Managing Uncertainty*, 41–45. Committees could be protected by granting a "closed" rule (which prohibited amendments entirely), but during the 1970s the Rules Committee began employing the less extreme device of "restrictive" rules. This procedure would usually prohibit some amendments, but not all. It might also employ a number of other "innovations" to structure debate. See Bach and Smith, *Managing Uncertainty*, 74–86.

16. The Eighty-fourth Congress was chosen as the starting point for this project because it began the unbroken period of Democratic control of the House. Included are both votes on passage and votes on moving the previous question to bar potential changes in the rule. In both cases an "aye" vote supports the rule. There were relatively few votes in the early years of the series, so those Congresses were grouped. "Consensual" votes are votes with majorities of 90 percent or more.

17. The evidence cited can be found in Smith, *Call to Order*, 34, and Rohde, *Parties and Leaders*, Chap. 5. The discussion and evidence below will deal only with first-degree amendments. As Smith (*Call to Order*, 183–87) shows, second-degree amendments (i.e., amendments to amendments) can be used by committees to counter attempts to change their proposals, and thus may not indicate any dissatisfaction with the committee's product. In the amendment analysis, only Congresses from the Ninety-second on are considered since there were so few record votes on amendments before recorded-teller voting. The "Democrat-favored" measure seems better than controlling for the party of the sponsor, since amendment proponents frequently find it useful to seek a sponsor from the other party to present an image of bipartisanship.

18. Defense issues include defense organization and military security issues (like foreign military aid) but not things like military construction and veterans' benefits, which are classified as domestic issues. Foreign-policy issues include

nonmilitary foreign aid and foreign trade matters. A small set of votes that deal with internal House matters (e.g., election of the Speaker, legislative appropriations) are excluded from the analysis.

19. Glenn R. Parker and Suzanne L. Parker, *Factions in House Committees* (Knoxville: University of Tennessee Press, 1985), 249, 265–68.

20. Richard F. Fenno, *Congressmen in Committees* (Boston: Little, Brown, 1973), 27. On the effects of the reforms on Foreign Affairs, see Norman J. Ornstein and David W. Rohde, "Shifting Forces, Changing Rules, and Political Outcomes: The Impact of Congressional Change on Four House Committees," in *New Perspectives on the House of Representatives*, 3d ed., ed. Robert Peabody and Nelson Polsby (Chicago: Rand McNally, 1977), 253–61.

21. Bruce A. Ray, "The Responsiveness of U.S. Congressional Armed Services Committees to their Parent Bodies," *Legislative Studies Quarterly* 5 (November 1980): 515; Cox and McCubbins, *Parties and Committees*, Chap. 7. See also Parker and Parker, *Factions in House Committees*, 126–31.

22. The combined effects of the election of less conservative southerners and New Liberal northerners has meant that on some issues Democratic caucus sentiment is less liberal than in the 1970s, while on others (e.g., defense) it is more liberal. At the same time, Republican preferences have generally become more conservative. As committee bills have come to reflect Democratic preferences better, Republican amendments have sometimes sought to embarrass Democrats without real hope of passage, while in other cases they are real threats to the content of the policy supported by the committee. Restrictive rules have been used on various occasions to limit both types of strategies.

23. "Initial" passage excludes votes on conference reports or veto overrides. This limits consideration to the House's judgment on content before disagreements with the Senate have been bargained away. "Regular" passage excludes passage by suspension of the rules, the incidence of which we know varied greatly over time. "Bills and joint resolutions" exclude simple and concurrent resolutions, which don't involve presidential approval. Similarly we exclude those few joint resolutions that involve passage of constitutional amendments. With that one exception, bills and joint resolutions are equivalent.

24. It is true that there was a sharp decrease in the Ninety-eighth Congress, but this involved only six bills. No data are included for the Hundredth Congress because there was only one case.

25. The increase in partisanship at the end of the foreign-policy series reflects the small N (five cases), and the impact of a few bills on which Democratic support was comparatively low for Reagan initiatives. On defense, the big jump was due to a shift of the issues on the agenda. There were five bills on Contra aid and two on the MX missile in the second term (with a mean party difference of sixty points), while there were none dealing with either issue in the first term.

26. For example, three of the bills here also dealt with Contra aid.

27. Southern Democrats are not included because the annual variation of those voting "aye" was only between 94 and 100 percent.

28. Janet Hook, "Bush Inspired Frail Support for First-Year President," *Congressional Quarterly Weekly Report* (30 December 1989): 3540. The data cited in this paragraph on presidential position votes are taken from that issue and from earlier issues throughout the year.

BARBARA SINCLAIR

8 | The Evolution of Party Leadership in the Modern House

The 1980s saw the emergence of strong, policy-oriented majority party leadership in the House of Representatives. By the Hundredth Congress (1987–88), there had developed a majority party leadership that, compared to other post–World War II leaderships, is more involved in and more decisive in organizing the party and the chamber, setting the House agenda, and determining legislative outcomes.[1] Why, in what is generally characterized as a weak party era and in a legislature often characterized as fragmented, did strong leadership emerge?

The development of strong leadership is the result, I argue, of a significant change in the costs and benefits to Democratic members of such leadership and of the behavior on their part that makes such leadership possible. The 1970s reforms, combined with the constraints of the 1980s political environment, greatly increased the difficulty of enacting legislation, especially legislation Democrats find satisfactory. The decline in inter-committee reciprocity and the rise of floor amending activity, split control, and huge budget deficits made passing major legislation more difficult. The party leadership possesses critical resources that, if Democratic members acquiesce in their use, can significantly increase the probability of legislative success. Through control of the Rules Committee, the leadership can structure the floor choice situation so as to reduce uncertainty and advantage the committee majority's position. Through the expanded whip system, the leadership can collect information and mobilize votes and thereby provide important aid to a bill's proponents. To the extent that passing legislation is necessary to the advancement of their goals, the Democratic membership, Democratic committee contingents, and Democratic committee leaders all can at least potentially benefit from strong leadership.

259

Moreover, during this same period, the costs of strong leadership declined as the effective ideological heterogeneity of the Democratic membership declined and as the political environment made the free-lance, Lone Ranger sort of policy entrepreneurship prevalent in the 1970s much less feasible.

Substantiating this explanation of the changing role of the House majority party leadership in the post–World War II period is the essay's purpose. Doing so requires an explicit theoretical apparatus. By assumption, legislation is the currency of congressional life; members of Congress care about what is and is not placed on the discussion agenda, what is and is not brought up for decision, and what is and is not passed because the advancement of their goals of reelection, policy, and influence is affected thereby. In assuming members are concerned not only with what they can and must talk about and vote on but also with what passes, this research follows Fenno, not Mayhew, in assuming also that members have multiple goals.[2]

Majority party members of the House expect the party leadership as their elected agent to facilitate the advancement of their goals, especially though not exclusively, in those ways that require collective action. Specifically, they expect the leadership to facilitate the passage of legislation. Leaders attempt to meet their members' expectations because they value their leadership positions.

Leadership in legislatures can be conceptualized as having been instituted to ameliorate problems of collective action.[3] The passage of legislation requires coordination and coalition building, yet even though members do have an interest in seeing legislation passed, it may well not be in any member's individual interest to bear the costs of the necessary coordination and coalition building. Leaders are designated to perform these tasks and are, in effect, paid with influence. That is, leaders are given by their members certain resources to enable them to carry out the tasks with which they are charged. Of necessity, these are resources that enable the party leadership to involve itself in and affect the outcomes of the legislative process. Of course, the magnitude of the resources granted can vary enormously and, over the course of House history, has, in fact, done so.

The strength of the majority party leadership—its capacity for involving itself and being decisive in the legislative process—derives from the resources members have given the leadership and from the extent to which members are willing to let leaders exploit those resources. The former are relatively fixed at a given point in time by rules, though they do change over time as they did during the period under study here. The Speaker's right to nominate all Democratic members of the Rules Committee and the large leadership staffs are examples. The latter is potentially more variable. Members' willingness to vote for rules reported by the leadership-controlled Rules Committee or to listen to leadership advice on how to shape a passable bill may vary even though rules granting resources remain unchanged.

From the perspective of the individual majority party member, party leadership strength is a double-edged sword. The stronger the leadership, the more it can help in passing legislation the member wants or, of course, in obtaining other outcomes the member desires, such as keeping legislation off the floor or from enactment. But the stronger the leadership, the more it can help others pass legislation or obtain other outcomes that are detrimental to the member's goal advancement. A strong leadership may even be able to "coerce" the member, through the use of favors, to act in a way he would not otherwise act.

It follows then that the balance of benefits to costs to members should determine leadership strength. When benefits are perceived as significantly outweighing costs for a substantial majority, members should be more willing to grant their leadership additional resources and/or to allow their leaders to exploit fully the resources they already possess. Conversely, when costs are perceived as higher than benefits, party leadership strength should decrease.

Since the granting or taking away of resources usually involves changes in House or party rules and, consequently, is subject to collective action problems, one would not, of course, expect instantaneous adjustments. Institutional change may lag behind a change in costs and benefits. Party leadership strength, however, depends also upon the willingness of members to allow leaders to fully exploit the resources they possess and this can change quickly in response to alterations in costs and benefits.

Party Leadership during the Committee Government Era

"A modern Democratic Speaker," Congressman Dick Bolling wrote in the mid-1960s, "is something like a feudal king—he is first in the land; he receives elaborate homage and respect; but he is dependent on the powerful lords, usually committee chairmen, who are basically hostile to the objectives of the national Democratic party and the Speaker. . . . Rayburn was frequently at odds with the committee oligarchs, who rule their own committees with the assured arrogance of absolute monarchs."[4]

The period from approximately 1920 through 1970 can be characterized as an era of committee government in the House of Representatives.[5] Legislation was the product of a number of autonomous committees headed by powerful chairmen who derived their positions from their seniority on the committee. The chairman's great organizational and procedural powers over his committee and structural advantages, such as the lack of recorded votes on floor amendments, led to a system of reciprocity or mutual deference among committees that protected most legislation from serious challenge on the floor of the House.

Committee leaders and committee majorities saw little benefit in strong, active party leadership; leadership assistance was seldom a prerequisite to legislative success. Moreover, the Democratic party's ideological heterogeneity during much of this period made strong leadership potentially costly—to party subgroups and to the leadership itself. When members differ radically in the legislation they need for reelection or prefer as good public policy, leadership involvement on behalf of one group's legislative aims may be a direct threat to another's goals. Consequently, within this system, the role of the majority party leadership was restricted.

Committee assignments potentially provide the leadership with its most significant role in organizing the party and the chamber. During the committee government era, the seniority rule for choosing committee chairmen and the structure of the Committee on Committees limited the leadership's role. No mechanism for removing recalcitrant committee chairmen existed. The party leadership exerted considerable influence over the initial assignment of members to committees, but the Committee on Committees consisted of Ways and Means Democrats and did not officially include the party leadership.

Since Franklin Roosevelt's time, when the president and the congressional majority were of the same party, the president has set the majority party's and Congress's policy agenda. During the committee government era, when control of Congress and the White House was divided, the majority party's policy agenda consisted of whatever emerged from the autonomous committees. The House Democratic party lacked any mechanism for developing a party agenda or for imposing one upon powerful committee chairmen.

The party leadership's role in the policy process was largely restricted to facilitating passage at the floor stage of legislation written by autonomous committees.[6] Party leaders seldom if ever interceded in committee to shape legislation; the chairmen's power and norms of deference to committee worked against such involvement.

Even the leadership's role at the floor stage was somewhat restricted. Although the Speaker as presiding officer had considerable control over the flow of legislation to and on the floor, the independence of the Rules Committee during this period meant that the party leadership's control over the scheduling of legislation for floor consideration was only partial.[7] Inter-committee reciprocity meant that most committees could expect to pass most of their legislation on the floor without great difficulty; consequently committees and their chairmen did not often require help from the leadership. On the other hand, on those highly controversial issues that were fought out on the floor, the leadership often confronted a deep North–South split and had great difficulty in successfully building winning coalitions.

An examination of the Ninety-first, the last pre-reform congress, illustrates the restricted scope and rate of leadership activity during the committee government era and the conditions that fostered such a modest role.

To make rigorous comparisons with the Congresses to be discussed below possible, the congressional agenda needs to be specified. *Congressional Quarterly*'s list of major legislation, augmented by those measures on which key votes occurred (again according to *Congressional Quarterly*) is used to define the agenda. This produces a list of legislation considered major by very close contemporary observers.

Assessing leadership agenda setting activities requires classifying the items on the congressional agenda as to source. The president's core agenda is defined as those items mentioned in the State of the Union address or its equivalent and in special messages of some prominence. Routine administration requests for reauthorization of legislation without major change do not qualify the items for agenda status. Majority party leadership agenda setting, if it occurs, will become manifest in the Speaker's speech upon being elected to his office at the beginning of a Congress, the party's reply to the president's State of the Union address, the leadership's reply to special presidential addresses, or in major news conferences.

Of the fifty items on the Ninety-first Congress agenda, almost half (48 percent) were from the president's agenda. Draft reform, postal reform, welfare reform, and extension of the surtax were among the Nixon proposals to which Congress gave agenda space. In the Ninety-first Congress, agenda setting by the Democratic House leadership was minimal at best. "The Speaker's philosophy, according to his friends, is that the Democrats' role under the Nixon Presidency should be to keep the Kennedy and Johnson programs from being stripped by the Republicans."[8] In his speech upon being elected Speaker, McCormack proposed no agenda and, in fact, made no issue references. In response to the three-way 1968 presidential election contest, McCormack and Minority Leader Gerald Ford, on January 7, 1969, jointly endorsed electoral college reform. Only this could be remotely considered agenda setting.

If the leadership played little role in setting the congressional agenda, how active was it in other aspects of the legislative process within the House? Leadership involvement may take a variety of forms: the leadership may involve itself in the shaping of legislation, in the structuring through procedure of the floor choice situation, in vote mobilization, or in other aspects of legislative strategy. Again, in order to make comparisons over time possible, global measures based upon these modes of activity but not attempting to make fine distinctions among them are constructed. The first measure intended to distinguish some involvement from none is based upon answers to the following questions: (1) Was the bill a part of the leadership's agenda? (2) Did the Speaker or the majority leader advocate passage during floor debate? (3) Did *Congressional Quarterly*'s account report the leadership as being involved? If any one of the answers is "yes," the leadership is considered as having been involved. A second, more refined measure distinguishes major from minor involvement on the basis of the mode or modes of involvement reported by *Congressional Quarterly*. Four modes are distinguished: (a) the leadership uses its control over scheduling, the Rules Committee, or other procedure to advantage the legislation; (b) the leadership is involved in a floor vote mobilization effort; (c) the leadership is centrally involved in some other aspect of legislative strategy or (d) the leadership participates in shaping the content of the legislation by talking or negotiating with or among the committee(s) or with the Senate or with the president. Major leadership involvement is defined as engaging in (d), shaping legislation, or in any two of the other activities (e.g., 1, 2, a, b, c).

The House majority party leadership was involved in less than half (46 percent) of the items on the congressional agenda in the Ninety-first Congress; on only 28 percent of the items was leadership involvement major. In a number of cases, the leadership used its scheduling powers to advantage legislation. On draft reform legislation, the major battle was on the rule, with liberals trying to open up the closed rule to allow amendments aimed at broad-scale draft reform. The Democratic leadership, working with its Republican counterpart, suddenly postponed the vote because, as Republican whip Les Arends said, "We thought we'd be stronger in the morning."[9] Similarly, the leadership postponed consideration of the anti-poverty program reauthorization for ten days to give proponents time to mobilize against an amendment turning the program over to the states. Either the Speaker or the majority leader spoke on the floor in a number of instances. Both spoke against further cuts in foreign aid during consideration of the foreign aid authorization bill in 1969; Albert urged the House to override Nixon's veto of the Hill–Burton bill while both urged an override of the Department of Housing and Urban Development appropriations bill veto. In a limited number of cases, the leadership's role was major: it was involved in negotiating a compromise with Nixon on education funding in the Labor–Health, Education, and Welfare appropriations bill; McCormack led vote mobilization on the Voting Rights Act extension after the committee's initial floor defeat; Albert was deeply involved in negotiating the terms of the resolution that led to the unseating of Adam Clayton Powell. Yet, compared to later leaderships, the McCormack–Albert team's involvement was neither frequent nor broad in scope. With the exception of matters affecting the chamber itself, involvement tended to be restricted to the floor stage of the legislative process, it often seems to have been stimulated by trouble on the floor, and it seldom entailed any involvement in the substance of legislation.

If the party leadership's involvement was restricted, committees by and large did not need much help. The major and often controversial measures that make up the congressional agenda as here defined were subject to a mean of only 1.5 amendments decided by teller or roll call, and only 0.4 such amendments per bill were adopted. Because amendments can vary so much in importance, all amendments adopted were examined as were other votes (e.g., on recommittal, passage, conference report). A committee was judged to have clearly won on the floor if its measure passed without the acceptance of any amendments of consequence.[10] By this tough standard, the committee clearly won on the floor on 70 percent of the measures on the congressional agenda; it clearly lost on only 13 percent. A foreign trade bill illustrates the power of some committee chairmen to prevail on the floor. When the previous question on the closed rule for consideration of the bill failed, Ways and Means Chairman Wilbur Mills said his committee had instructed him to have the bill considered only under a closed rule and threatened to pull the bill off the floor if the vote was not reversed. Enough of those members who had hoped to amend the legislation but wanted a bill even more did change their votes, a closed rule was adopted, and the bill passed the House as written by the committee.

The chairman's power and the system of inter-committee reciprocity were not the only bases for committee success. Although control of Congress and the presidency was divided, committee majorities frequently agreed with the president and thus were spared a formidable opponent. On almost half (47 percent) of the classifiable agenda items, the president and the committee agreed; on only 40 percent were they directly at odds.

The frequency of agreement reflects to some extent the murky ideological thrust of the Nixon administration; for example, welfare reform, a core item on the president's agenda, elicited agreement from the committee of jurisdiction but was opposed by both liberals and conservatives on the floor. More important, however, was the ideological split within the Democratic party. Frequently, conservative Democrats combined with Republicans on the committee to report a bill satisfactory to the president, but much less so to the liberal wing of the Democratic party.

The Democratic membership's ideological heterogeneity in the late 1960s and early 1970s manifested itself in a startlingly high rate of disagreement between the reporting committee and liberals.[11] Of the items that reached the floor and on which there was some conflict, fully one-third provoked such a disagreement. The issues involved ranged from food stamp reform to pollution control to emergency home financing legislation to the depletion allowance to Vietnam-related matters. During the Ninety-first Congress, floor coalitions were seldom partisan; of the agenda items that reached the floor, only 13 percent evoked partisan alignments while 53 percent split northern and southern Democrats.

Reform and Its Impact on Party Leadership

If committee majorities and committee chairmen did not, by and large, need party leadership help to advance their legislative goals and consequently saw little benefit in strong leadership, and the ideological heterogeneity of the Democratic party made strong leadership potentially costly, why did the 1970s reforms include leadership-strengthening changes? Briefly put, the answer lies in the fact that liberal Democrats, a majority of the party membership but junior and underrepresented in positions of committee influence, were much less favorably situated than more senior and more conservative members to advance their goals. Both policy and participation goals were at issue. Using their strength in the Democratic caucus, the reformers—most of whom were northern liberals—made a series of changes intended to enhance the responsiveness of the House legislative process to the policy preferences of party majorities and to increase opportunities for rank-and-file participation in the legislative process.

To elaborate, the House Democratic party during most of the 1950s was fairly evenly divided between southerners, most of whom were conservative, and northerners, who were predominantly liberal but included moderates and a few conservatives. Elections in the late 1950s and the 1960s brought into the House a large number of liberal northern Democrats who found the committee government system ill-suited to advancing their goals. The powerful committee chairmen were largely conservative southerners; they, not the party leadership or the party as a whole, set the policy agenda and determined the substance of legislation. The chairmen thwarted the liberals' policy goals by blocking liberal legislation and frustrated their desire to participate meaningfully in the legislative process by the often autocratic way they ran their committees.[12]

Policy-related dissatisfactions were the initial motivating force behind the reform movement in the House. Liberals complained that the seniority system and the committee assignment process resulted in committee chairmen and the membership of the most important committees being unrepresentatively conservative. And no procedure or forum for holding chairmen or committee majorities responsible to the party majority existed.

In the 1950s the Rules Committee, controlled by a bipartisan conservative coalition, frequently had prevented liberal legislation from reaching the floor or had exacted substantive concessions as the price for allowing House consideration. The 1961 packing of the committee only partially solved the problem. During the Ninety-first Congress, for example, the committee refused a rule and thus killed a liberal-sponsored bill establishing a federal consumer agency.

Inter-committee reciprocity seemed to work better for conservative-dominated than for predominantly liberal committees. Certainly, in the Ninety-first Congress conservative committees were more successful on the floor than liberal ones. Of the six instances in which committees were "rolled" on the floor (that is, where the committee clearly lost) five involved the generally liberal committees of Education and Labor, Banking, and Judiciary.[13] In the sixth case, Ways and Means was defeated on the floor on the question of indexing social security payments; Mills nevertheless prevented the provision from becoming law in that Congress by refusing to go to conference. In one instance—extension of the Voting Rights Act—leadership involvement helped the committee pull out a floor victory after the conference committee had reversed the damage done during initial House floor consideration. In the other cases, however, the leadership was either not involved or not successful.

Especially in the aftermath of the loss of the overwhelming numbers they had commanded in the mid-1960s and the replacement of a skillful progressive ally with the often-hostile Nixon as president, liberals did need help in advancing their legislative goals. Some of the reforms had the effect of strengthening the party leadership because they weakened the leadership's principal internal competitor for influence, the committee chairmen. In some cases, the party leadership was strengthened to act as a counterweight to the committee chairmen, who were the primary target of the reforms. Some rules changes were, however, clearly and directly aimed at making the party leadership more capable of facilitating the advancement of the party majority's legislative goals.[14]

The requirement that committee chairmen and the chairmen of Appropriations subcommittees win majority approval in the Democratic caucus was intended to make them responsive to the party majority, which was now clearly a liberal majority. A provision for regular meetings of the Democratic caucus provided a forum in which rank-and-file members could inform Democratic committee contingents of their views and a few instances of the caucus instructing committees put committees on notice that they had better listen to strongly held caucus sentiments.

Policy and responsiveness motives also underlay the shifting of the committee assignment function from Ways and Means to the new Steering and Policy Committee, which the Speaker chairs and a number of whose members he appoints. Ways and Means Democrats were seen as too conservative and not accountable to the party. The Steering and Policy Committee was designed to be both representative and responsive, its membership a combination of members elected from regional groups, elected party leaders, and leadership appointees.

Granting the Speaker the right to nominate all Democratic members and the chairman of the Rules Committee subject only to ratification by the caucus was clearly intended to give the leadership true control over the scheduling of legislation for the floor. By making Rules Democrats dependent upon the Speaker for their position on the committee, reformers made the committee an arm of the leadership. At the same time they reserved for the caucus the power of confirming the Speaker's nominees and wrote into caucus rules a procedure by which the caucus could instruct the Rules Committee on the character of rules.

In addition to policy dissatisfactions, desires to increase rank-and-file members' opportunities for meaningful participation in the legislative process motivated the reform movement. A series of rules changes, some principally aimed at expanding participation opportunities, others also motivated by policy concerns, had the effect of increasing opportunities and incentives for participation in committee and on the floor. In an effort to spread positions of influence, members were limited to chairing no more than one subcommittee each. The subcommittee bill of rights removed from committee chairmen the power to appoint subcommittee chairmen and gave it to the Democratic caucus of the committee; it guaranteed subcommittees automatic referral of legislation and adequate budget and staff. The supply of resources available to Congress and its members (most importantly staff) was expanded and distributed much more broadly among members. The institution of the recorded teller vote in the Committee of the Whole changed the dynamics of the floor stage, increasing the incentives for offering amendments and often for opposing the committee's position. Sunshine reforms opened up most committee markups and conference committee meetings to the media and the public, encouraging members to use those forums for grandstanding as well as for policy entrepreneurship.

The policy and participation goals that motivated the 1970s reforms need not be irreconcilable over the long run, though both cannot be maximized simultaneously. In the early years, the goals did come into conflict and, despite the augmentation of leadership resources expressly for the purpose of furthering policy goals, participation goals won out.

In the 1974 elections, fought in the midst of a recession and in the aftermath of Watergate, Democrats made a net gain of forty-nine seats in the House. The class of 1974 provided the votes in the Democratic caucus to pass the final round of rules changes that collectively constitute the reforms and, using new procedures, to depose three committee chairmen. When three extremely senior members, all southerners and two of them conservatives, were voted out of committee chairmanships they had held for years, all committee chairmen were put on notice: responsiveness to the caucus was a prerequisite to retaining their position.

Strengthened by their big electoral gains and facing a president weakened by his unelected status and his unpopular pardon of Richard Nixon, House Democrats, especially liberals, believed the Ninety-fourth Congress offered them an unusually favorable opportunity for advancing their legislative goals. Under pressure from such members, Speaker Albert played an aggressive agenda-setting role. In late 1974, he appointed a task force to draft an economic recovery program. The president took this effort sufficiently seriously that, on January 13, the day the task force's report was released, Ford gave a televised speech on economic and energy policy to try to preempt the Democratic program. In Albert's speech upon being elected Speaker on January 14 and in his televised response to Ford's January 15 State of the Union address, he talked in some detail about the Democratic agenda of energy and economic stimulus programs.[15]

The Democratic leadership's agenda constituted 17 percent of the forty-eight measures on the Ninety-fourth Congress congressional agenda, while President Ford's agenda accounted for 23 percent. Clearly, Ford's political weakness precluded his dominating the agenda as Nixon had during the Ninety-first, and the House Democratic leadership took advantage of that weakness to play a prominent agenda-setting role.

The Democratic leadership was considerably more active on the congressional agenda in the Ninety-fourth Congress than its counterpart in the Ninety-first had been. The Albert-O'Neill team involved itself in 60 percent of the agenda items—up from 46 percent in the Ninety-first Congress; in 40 percent of the measures, leadership involvement was major, compared to 28 percent in the Ninety-first. In addition to the measures on its own agenda, which dealt mostly with energy and economic stimulus, the leadership was active on a wide variety of other issues ranging from tax legislation to a congressional pay raise, from budget resolutions to lobbying reforms to aid to New York City.

Thus in response to the expectations of a sizable majority of its members, the House Democratic leadership played an aggressive agenda-setting role and increased its rate of involvement in the legislative process. However, despite the increased resources that reforms had granted party leaders, their members' desire to participate more fully in the legislative process which had, in part, fueled the reform movement and the ideological heterogeneity of the party presented the leadership with problems it could not surmount in the Ninety-fourth Congress.

H.R. 6860, an energy bill, provides a good example of the problems. The Arab oil embargo of 1973–74 had put energy conservation at the top of everyone's agenda. Ford sent Congress a multi-part energy package in January 1975; its conservation strategy was based on higher energy prices. Leadership-appointed Democratic task forces in the House and Senate had been at work and unveiled a Democratic plan on February 27. Ways and Means Democrats then came up with their own plan but only with great difficulty. On a 19–16 vote, the committee reported out a bill that oil state conservatives and Republicans opposed and liberals considered not tough enough.

Ways and Means had traditionally brought its bills to the floor under a closed rule; during the Ninety-first Congress, for example, five of the measures on the congressional agenda were reported by Ways and Means and all—including welfare reform and foreign trade legislation—were protected from floor amendments by closed rules. Reformers, in a move aimed specifically at Ways and Means, established a procedure by which Rules could be instructed by caucus vote to allow amendments. On H.R. 6860, Ways and Means did not even ask for a closed rule; the rule it requested and was granted was basically an open one.

Originally having scheduled the bill for May floor action, the party leadership postponed consideration after a deluge of amendments indicated the level of opposition. When the bill was brought up in June, 21 noncommittee amendments were offered. Amendments came from both ends of the ideological spectrum and from the perspectives of a variety of interests. Six amendments passed, including the Stark amendment deleting the twenty-cent gas tax, which constituted the heart of the bill. Democrats were badly split on many of the amendments, but on the Stark killer amendment not even a majority of northern Democrats supported the committee. Although the bill subsequently passed the House, the amending process had emasculated the bill and it never became law. Thus on a core item of the Democratic leadership's agenda, the Democratic membership splintered. The reforms facilitated the public expression of and thereby perhaps amplified the party's ideological heterogeneity.

The reforms did make committees and their chairmen more responsive to the predominantly liberal Democratic caucus. The frequency of disagreement between the reporting committee and liberals fell from 33 percent in the Ninety-first Congress to 14 percent in the Ninety-fourth. And, by increasing chairmen's responsiveness, the reforms strengthened the leadership's hand. Waldman quotes a contemporary leadership staffer as saying, "The three chairmen being thrown out has affected the willingness of chairmen to cooperate with the leadership. In 1973 when we voted on them, they didn't get the message. They took the positive vote as continuing support for them. In 1975, when three were deposed, they got the message. That was important."[16] The conservative chairman of the Appropriations Committee, told that Speaker Albert intended to have Steering and Policy pass a resolution urging Appropriations to report funding for emergency jobs, replied, "Let's avoid that. . . I'll do it. I'll do whatever you want."[17] Chairman Mahon not only got the bill reported out of his committee but actively worked to pass it and to override Ford's veto.

The new relationships created by the reforms appear to have changed leadership behavior as well. In the Ninety-first Congress, when the leadership involved itself in measures which split the reporting committee and liberals, it took sides, supporting the committee and opposing the liberals. By and large, this was not an ideological response by the leadership; it also supported liberal committees against their conservative foes on the floor. Rather, the leadership appears to have interpreted its role as entailing support, tacit or active, for all committee-reported legislation whatever its ideological hue; given the lack of an active caucus to serve as a counterweight to committees as enunciators of party policy positions, that reading of member expectations was, from the perspective of leaders interested in keeping their leadership positions, the least risky one. In the Ninety-fourth Congress, with the caucus active and expecting responsiveness from its party as well as its committee leaders, the party leadership's role on measures that divided the reporting committee and liberals changed. Rather than automatically supporting the committee, the leaders tended to act as mediators or damage controllers. On other measures as well, the leadership was occasionally willing to take on a committee as it had not been in the Ninety-first. The party leadership, for example, refused to schedule a food-stamp reform bill, thereby protecting the many freshmen Democrats who did not want to vote on the legislation, especially not on the issue of food stamps for strikers. The leadership believed that, in the wake of the Hayes sex-payroll scandal, refurbishing the image of the party and the chamber required passing a meaningful reform package; doing so required pressuring the House Administration Committee, which lost power under the leadership plan.

While the new responsiveness of committee chairmen and committees to the caucus gave the leadership increased leverage, the legislative consequences of members' desires to participate more extensively made the leadership's task much more difficult and often overwhelmed the effect of the new leverage. Democrats were no longer willing to allow Ways and Means to bring its legislation to the floor under closed rules. In addition to the energy bill, two major tax bills were considered under rules allowing floor votes on some amendments. The leadership may have obtained control of the Rules Committee but it could not use that control to protect legislation on the floor with restrictive rules. It had every reason to expect its membership to refuse to acquiesce in such use of the leadership's new resources. In fact, the only item on the congressional agenda brought to the floor under a closed rule was the leadership-supported resolution to strip the House

Administration Committee of its control over members' perquisites.

Increased participation by rank-and-file members took a number of forms, the easiest to document and the most problematic for the party leadership being the increase in amending activity on the floor. As a result of the reforms, incentives for offering floor amendments increased and the costs of doing so decreased. As Smith shows, the number of floor amendments decided on a teller or recorded vote rose from 55 in 1955–56 to 107 in 1969–70; with the institution of the recorded teller, it jumped to 195 in 1971–72 and, with electronic voting, it jumped again to 351 in 1973–74.[18] During the Ninety-fourth Congress (1975–76), 372 such amendments were offered on the floor and during the Ninety-fifth, 439.

The major legislation on the congressional agenda as here defined shows the impact of this change in floor behavior. From the pre-reform Ninety-first Congress to the reformed Ninety-fourth, the mean number of amendments decided on a teller or recorded vote to items on the congressional agenda more than tripled from 1.5 to 5.3; the mean number of amendments per measure adopted increased more than fourfold from 0.4 to 1.8. The increase in floor amending activity made legislation more vulnerable to change on the floor. The success of committees in passing their legislation intact decreased. While during the Ninety-first Congress the committee of origin had clearly won on the floor on 70 percent of the measures that reached the floor, in the Ninety-fourth the committee won on 57 percent. Yet given the larger Democratic margin in the Ninety-fourth and the weakened president, Democratic committee contingents might reasonably have expected to increase their win rate.

The continuing deep North–South split within the Democratic party exacerbated the problems that increased floor participation created. Only 28 percent of the measures on the congressional agenda evoked partisan alignments on the House floor, while on 40 percent, northern and southern Democrats split.

As a result, despite its huge Democratic membership, the Ninety-fourth Congress was a legislative disappointment to Democrats. Committees were successful on balance in enacting legislation in their preferred form on less than half (48 percent) of the items on the congressional agenda compared to 57 percent in the Ninety-first.[19] The Democratic agenda proposed by the party leadership did not fare well. The leadership clearly prevailed on the floor on only half the items and won on balance on final disposition on half.

Even when Democrats were in substantial agreement, legislative success often proved elusive. On those measures pitting two-thirds or more of House Democrats against the president, the oversized Democratic membership produced a high rate of floor success; the Democrats' position clearly prevailed on 83 percent of such measures.[20] The Democrats' win rate on final disposition was, however, much lower; they won on balance on only 44 percent. Ford made extensive use of the veto and Democrats were seldom able to maintain sufficient cohesion to override.

Such meager legislative results from a Congress in which Democrats seemed so favorably situated led to intense criticism of the majority party leadership.[21] Speaker Albert was pilloried for not being sufficiently active and assertive. From the leaders' point of view, however, the problem was a lack of willingness to follow. As a senior staffer said, "People . . . want leadership for the other guys, the guys who don't agree with them. They want the leadership to get those who defect from the positions they desire, but they don't want to be told what to do."[22]

In the House and in the Democratic caucus, majorities can change rules that then bind all the members. Some of the participation-enhancing reforms, which benefited the minority Republicans as well as liberal Democrats, were made through the Legislative Reorganization Act, which required approval of the full House. The leadership-strengthening changes were made in the caucus, where liberal Democrats had a clear majority. But, while the party leadership may be given enhanced resources by majority vote, very substantially more than a majority of party members must be willing to exhibit restrained and cooperative behavior before the leadership is able to exploit its new resources. For example, passing a rule that enhances a controversial bill's probability of floor success will, in all likelihood, require the assent of a large proportion of the Democrats, as Republicans are likely to oppose it. When a party is ideologically split, as the House Democrats were in the 1970s, one faction or the other is unlikely to be willing to act in such a way as to make strong leadership possible. For southern Democrats, reelection needs and policy preferences frequently dictated behavior inimical to their liberal colleagues' policy goals. As a result of the reforms, such members in their capacity as committee leaders did have to be responsive to the sentiments of party majorities; but, in their capacity as ordinary members voting on the floor, they were under no such injunction.

In the Ninety-fourth Congress, the leadership's difficulties were by no means caused only by a conservative minority faction. Many of the northern Democrats who had supported party-strengthening changes nevertheless did not act in a way that allowed the leadership to exploit its new resources. Having multiplied opportunities and incentives for rank-and-file participation, the reforms exacerbated the collective action problem inherent in passing legislation. The new resources granted leaders were not, of course, sufficient to make it possible for leaders to coerce their members into behaving cooperatively; successful coalition building consequently required that members as individuals be willing to compromise and to exercise restraint. Success frequently depended upon a large proportion of northerners being willing to eschew exploiting readily available participation opportunities, since the leadership could not count on many southern votes. Many northern Democrats were unwilling to forego the immediate payoffs of free-lance policy entrepreneurship for the more distant and less certain payoff of policy results. The former could be obtained through individual activity, through the offering of floor amendments for example, while the latter required collective action and, given also the ideological split among Democrats and a hostile president, was less certain.

Leadership Adaption to the Postreform Environment

By the mid-1970s, the reforms had transformed the legislative process in the House. Increased participation by rank-and-file members at both the committee and the floor stage, the growing attractiveness of the free-lance entrepreneurial style, and large numbers of inexperienced subcommittee chairmen multiplied the number of significant actors and radically increased uncertainty.[23] Democratic committee contingents, Democratic committee leaders and the Democratic membership needed help passing their legislation and looked to the party leadership for that help. After his election, so did Democratic President Jimmy Carter. The problem the party leadership faced was providing that help without constricting the participation opportunities members prized and within the context of continuing ideological heterogeneity.

The leadership team of Speaker Tip O'Neill and Majority Leader Jim Wright, which began its service in 1977, developed over time a set of strategies for coping with the new House.[24] In addition to being heavily engaged in doing favors for individual members as all leaderships in the post-1910 period have been, the party leadership put great emphasis upon developing its service role. The leadership increasingly provided services—such as scheduling sensitive to members' needs and timely information—to the Democratic membership collectively. When resources are so broadly distributed that almost any member can cause trouble, the leaders have an immediate interest in maintaining rank-and-file satisfaction. A second strategy involved including as many members as possible in the coalition-building process. This strategy of inclusion entailed expanding and using formal leadership structures, such as the whip system, and bringing other Democrats into the coalition-building process on an ad hoc basis, through bill-specific task forces, for example. In the new House environment the core leadership was too small to undertake the task of successful coalition building alone; including other members provided needed assistance. The strategy of inclusion was also a way for leaders to satisfy members' expectations that they play a significant part in the legislative process but to do so in a manner beneficial to the party and the leadership.

Finally, the leadership greatly refined the quintessential legislative strategy of using its control over procedure to structure the choice situation members confront. By giving the Speaker control of the Rules Committee, the reforms greatly enhanced the leadership's tools for structuring the floor choice situation. In the mid-1970s, members' desires for maximum participation opportunities constrained the leadership's use of this resource. By the late 1970s, however, many Democrats were having second thoughts about the wide open amending process on the floor. The unrestricted amending process was resulting in frequent lengthy and late sessions; Republicans were becoming increasingly adept at drafting amendments that confronted Democrats with a no-win choice; and legislative compromises, carefully crafted in committee, were being picked apart on the floor. In August 1979, over forty Democrats signed a letter to the Speaker complaining about the length of floor sessions and calling for more frequent use of restrictive rules.[25] The Rules Committee, in response to a variety of new floor problems, had made increasing use of complex rules; now, in concert with the party leadership, it increasingly reported rules that restricted amending activity to some extent.[26] During the 1980s such rules were to become a key element of leadership strategy.

Party Leadership during a Period
of Partisan Adversity

During the Ninety-seventh Congress, the first of his presidency, Reagan was in a stronger position vis-à-vis House Democrats than Nixon had been in 1969. Reagan had won with a larger margin, Republicans had picked up more House seats and had won control of the Senate, and, having run an issue-based campaign, Reagan could claim a policy mandate.

Nevertheless, House Democrats did make some attempt to counter Reagan with their own agenda. Although O'Neill in his speech accepting election as Speaker simply pledged cooperation, in April he announced a Democratic economic program which had been drafted by a task force chaired by Dick Gephardt. During the first half of 1981, the political tides were running too strongly in Reagan's favor, and this agenda-setting attempt sank without a trace; it produced neither legislation nor good publicity. In 1982, however, House Democrats, helped by the developing recession, were a little more successful. A leadership-appointed task force chaired by Jim Wright drafted an economic program consisting mostly of various sorts of jobs programs which did become an important part of the congressional agenda. Of the forty-five measures that constituted the congressional agenda, 44 percent were from the president's agenda; 9 percent were Democratic leadership agenda items. Thus, while a politically potent president dominated the agenda-setting process in the Ninety-seventh Congress, the Democratic House leadership played a greater role than its counterpart had in the Ninety-first, even though conditions were less favorable for Democrats in 1981–82 than in 1969–70.

The president's political strength and the deep policy divisions between Reagan and House Democrats made the Ninety-seventh Congress a very difficult one for House Democrats and their leadership. The major measures on the congressional agenda were much more likely to pit a preponderance of House Democrats against the president in the Ninety-seventh than they had in the Ninety-first (45 percent versus 18 percent). Certainly, Reagan's agenda was a much greater threat to Democrats' legislative goals than Nixon's or Ford's had been; 45 percent of the items on his agenda pitted Reagan against two-thirds or more of House Democrats while only 8 percent of Nixon's and 27 percent of Ford's did. Just how potent a threat Reagan posed in the

Ninety-seventh Congress is suggested by the fact that on fully half the battles pitting the president against House Democrats, Reagan was on the offensive advocating policy change and thus threatening Democrats with an outcome worse than the status quo; Democrats were on the defensive attempting to defeat or alter Reagan-supported measures, a situation in which even winning meant only preserving the status quo. In contrast, during the Ninety-first Congress Nixon was on the offensive in 25 percent of such battles and in the Ninety-fourth Ford was never able to assume the offensive.

Clearly, under such dire circumstances, House Democrats needed help in furthering their goals through legislation. The majority party leadership did, in fact, increase its rate of activity; the leadership was involved in 67 percent of the measures on the congressional agenda; in 38 percent of the items, its involvement was major.

Nevertheless, the legislative success rate of Democratic committee contingents and of the Democratic membership was low in the Ninety-seventh Congress. Committee majorities won on balance on final disposition 48 percent of the measures on the congressional agenda in the Ninety-seventh Congress compared with 57 percent in the Ninety-first and 70 percent in the Hundredth. The Ninety-seventh winning proportion of 48 percent is not very different from the 49 percent in the Ninety-fourth; however, as discussed above, the stakes were considerably higher in the Ninety-seventh than in the Ninety-fourth. In fact, the committees' win rate when the committee and the president disagreed was much lower in the Ninety-seventh than in any of the other Congresses—22 percent versus between 47 percent and 65 percent. In the Ninety-seventh Congress, on measures pitting House Democrats against the president, Democrats won on final disposition only 28 percent of the measures. In the early 1980s, then, Democrats were having great difficulty not only in passing legislation that would advance their goals but even in blocking legislation inimical to their goals.

The series of bad losses—on the budget resolution, the reconciliation bill making major spending cuts, and the tax-cut bill, especially—that the House Democrats and their leadership sustained in 1981 led to intense criticism of the leadership as weak and ineffective. Yet, in fact, the O'Neill–Wright team continued to develop its leadership strategies and made increasingly aggressive use of its control over special rules to structure the choice situation on the floor.[27] In the Ninety-first and

Ninety-fourth Congresses about 20 percent of the measures on the congressional agenda were considered under a complex or closed rule; in the Ninety-seventh, 43 percent were. During that Congress, every item on the leadership's agenda was considered under a closed or a complex rule compared with half in the Ninety-fourth; 71 percent of the measures in which the leadership was involved in a major way were considered under such a rule in the Ninety-seventh compared with 32 percent in the Ninety-fourth.

House Democrats' losses were not the result of unusually low cohesion in the Ninety-seventh Congress. On seven crucial votes on Reagan's domestic program in 1981, a mean of 84.5 percent of Democrats voted together. Leadership mobilization efforts and, presumably, the drastic character of Reagan's proposals produced impressive Democratic cohesion. But, because of the reduced size of the Democratic membership and even more impressive Republican cohesion (95 percent), Democrats lost most of these votes. Since Republicans controlled the Senate, Democrats' policy preferences fared even less well in terms of final disposition than on the House floor; thus the very low win rates on final disposition.

By the early 1980s, the majority party leadership was centrally involved in the major legislative battles in a way the party leadership in the Ninety-first Congress had not been. During a president's first two years, his agenda usually is the focus of congressional attention and often of conflict and that was certainly the case in 1981–82. The O'Neill–Wright team was active on 75 percent of Reagan's agenda items, while the leadership in the Ninety-first had been active on only 42 percent of Nixon's. Furthermore, by the Ninety-seventh Congress, the party leadership was increasingly directing the coalition-building effort from early in the process, not just aiding a committee when it encountered trouble at the floor stage.[28]

Clearly, then, the 1970s reforms which made legislation more vulnerable to alteration on the floor and the 1980s political environment of conflict between a conservative confrontational president and House Democrats did make passing legislation Democrats favor much more difficult and thus increased the Democrats' need for help in advancing their goals through legislating. I have argued that the majority party leadership intensified its activity in response to this need.

The 1970s and 1980s, in addition, witnessed a change in the structure of legislation that contributed to majority party members' greater need for the sort of assistance that only the party leadership can provide. Increased jurisdictional conflicts among committees and the House's inability to realign jurisdictions created a need for an outside arbiter when committee leaders could not agree.[29] The multiple-referral rule, instituted in 1975, formalized the Speaker's role and gave him new powers to set reporting deadlines for legislation referred to more than one committee. In the Ninety-fourth Congress, about 6 percent of measures on the congressional agenda as here defined were multiply referred; this grew to 12 percent in the Ninety-seventh and 28 percent in the Hundredth. Over these three Congresses, the leadership was, on average, involved in 81 percent of multiply referred measures.

In the 1980s deep policy divisions between President Reagan and House Democrats resulted in much more frequent employment of omnibus measures. The major battles came to revolve around budget resolutions, reconciliation bills, and other omnibus measures centering on questions of basic priorities. During the Ninety-seventh Congress, Reagan had used these measures as vehicles for his agenda. After the 1982 elections, in which Democrats won back twenty-six House seats, stalemate became an ever-present threat. The inability of the president and House Democrats to agree on individual appropriations bills or of either to impose its preferences upon the other resulted in frequent use of continuing resolutions, which are omnibus appropriations bills. Since such continuing resolutions are must-pass legislation and thus difficult for a president to veto, they also provided Democrats with a vehicle for enacting into law provisions that Reagan would have vetoed had they been sent to him as freestanding legislation. Much the same is true of reconciliation bills: they too are major, multi-provision measures which are difficult for a president to veto and, they have been used to force upon Reagan legislation he would not otherwise have accepted. Reconciliation bills, however, became such a prominent part of the congressional agenda because they provided the vehicle through which the unpalatable decisions necessitated by the huge deficits could be bundled; a package in which all shared the pain was passable, if often with difficulty, while separate bills cutting popular programs and raising revenues might well not have been. Finally, in their effort to compete with the White House for media attention and public credit, House Democrats began to package legislation on issues such as trade and drugs into high-profile omnibus measures. As a result of all these processes, omnibus measures increased as a proportion of the congressional agenda from none in the Ninety-first Congress to 8 percent in the Ninety-fourth (all budget resolutions) to 20 percent in the first two Congresses of the 1980s.

Because of the number and magnitude of issues and sometimes also the number of committees involved in omnibus measures, putting together and passing such legislation often requires negotiation and coordination activities beyond the capacity of committee leaders. Furthermore, on such high-stakes, broadly encompassing measures, committee leaders lack the legitimacy to speak for the membership as a whole. Thus as omnibus measures became more prominent on the congressional agenda, the need for leadership involvement increased. In fact, the party leaders were active on every omnibus measure in the Congresses under study.

In the 1970s and early 1980s, then, the potential benefits of stronger leadership increased as institutional changes and changes in the political environment increased the Democratic membership's and Democratic committee contingents' need for help in advancing their goals through legislating.

Leadership activity did increase in the mid-1970s and early 1980s, as was shown earlier, but the full development of strong leadership, it was hypothesized, depended upon a decline in the costs of strong leadership. Specifically, the ideological heterogeneity of the Democratic party in the 1970s retarded the development of strong leadership, while the party's growing homogeneity in the 1980s made that development possible.

Voting was more partisan and House Democrats more cohesive on party votes in the late 1980s than at any time in the last four decades. In the Hundredth Congress, the typical Democrat voted with a majority of his party colleagues on 88 percent of those votes that divided Democrats and Republicans. This average party unity score is the highest for Democrats from 1925 to the present. For the period 1951 through 1970, the House Democrats' average party unity score was 77.6 percent; this fell to 73.8 percent for the period 1971–82. After the 1982 election, the scores began rising and averaged 85.3 percent for the period 1982–88. During these last three Congresses, the proportion of roll calls on which a majority of Democrats voted against a majority of Republicans also increased, averaging 55.4 percent compared with 37.2 percent during the 1971–82 period.

David Rohde has shown that in the past two decades the electoral constituencies of northern and southern Democrats became more similar.[30] The political climate of the 1980s may also have contributed to this high cohesion by placing some policy options that split Democrats completely beyond the realm of the politically feasible. What is important here, however, is its impact upon the structure of conflict and upon the costs of strong leadership. The ideological heterogeneity of the Democratic party in the early 1970s manifested itself in frequent disagreements between a committee majority and Democratic liberals. Of all the agenda items that reached the House floor and elicited some conflict in the Ninety-first Congress, fully 33 percent saw liberal Democrats in opposition to the committee majority's position. By the Hundredth Congress, only 5 percent did.

In the Ninety-first Congress, over half the measures on the congressional agenda divided northern from southern Democrats on the House floor. By the Hundredth Congress, 61 percent of floor coalitions were partisan and only 11 percent were characterized predominantly by a split between northern and southern Democrats.

The political climate of the 1980s, House members report, has constricted the opportunities for policy entrepreneurship.[31] Our data on agenda setting provide some evidence that this perception has, in fact, influenced member behavior. Certainly, the agenda-setting role of identifiable individuals or groups other than the president or the leadership was less in the 1980s than in the 1970s, declining from about 35 percent in the 70s to 16 percent in the Ninety-seventh Congress and 23 percent in the Hundredth. The impact of the big deficits can be seen in the character of the legislation successfully placed on the congressional agenda by identifiable individuals or groups in the Hundredth Congress. Although in all but two cases the agenda setter was in the liberal camp broadly defined, only one of the bills in question cost money. Only the legislation providing an apology and reparations to Japanese-Americans interned during World War II entailed a significant cost to the government. By implication, the deficit depressed entrepreneurial activity.

When the environment precludes free-lance entrepreneurship, when policy battles between Democratic committee contingents and significant groups within the party are rare rather than standard, when major legislation most frequently splits Democrats from Republicans rather than northern from southern Democrats, the potential costs of strong leadership to House Democrats have clearly decreased.

Party Leadership in the Late 1980s

In the Hundredth Congress, the longer-term trends in the costs and benefits of strong leadership in conjunction with short-term factors conducive to strong leadership culminated in the strongest, most policy-oriented and most successful majority-party leadership of the post–World War II era.

By the Hundredth Congress, the party leadership's role in organizing party and chamber had expanded greatly beyond the restricted role of committee government era Speakers or the self-restricted role of early postreform era Speakers.[32] Through his predominant influence in the committee assignment process, his sole authority to nominate Democratic members of Rules, his appointments to the Steering and Policy Committee, to the expanded whip system, and to select committees and his choice of the Democratic Congressional Campaign Committee chairman, the Speaker can affect the decisions these units make through the choice of personnel and can do favors for members that strengthen his hand in coalition-building efforts.

Under conditions of divided control, agenda setting is a critical component of policy leadership. When the Speaker publicly highlights and legislatively advantages selected initiatives, he increases those bills' probability of passing and the majority party's chances of getting credit for them. If the party membership is not too ideologically heterogeneous, an adept party leadership can put together an agenda that includes something really important to every member and nothing electorally devastating to any. For most members, such party leadership agenda setting is much more likely to advance both their policy and reelection goals than the alternatives: agenda setting by a president of the other party and the agenda as the unplanned resultant of the decisions of many committees acting independently. The prerequisites for such agenda setting are leadership resources for significantly advantaging legislation and a reasonable level of ideological homogeneity. The reforms of the 1970s gave the leadership the requisite resources; the necessary homogeneity developed during the 1980s. The magnitude of the policy differences between Reagan and congressional Democrats, as well as Reagan's skill at using the media to further his own agenda and to depict the Democratic party in a negative light, intensified Democrats' need for their leadership to counter the president by engaging in agenda setting.

The party leadership in the Hundredth Congress played a highly aggressive agenda-setting role. In December 1986, immediately after being chosen the Democrats' nominee for Speaker, Jim Wright outlined a policy agenda for the majority party and the House: Deficit reduction achieved in part through a tax increase, clean-water legislation, a highway bill, trade legislation, welfare reform, and a farm bill were included. In his acceptance speech after being elected Speaker on January 6, 1987, and in his televised reply to Reagan's State of the Union address on January 31, Wright further specified and publicized the agenda, adding aid to education, aid to the homeless, and insurance against catastrophic illness. Leadership agenda items accounted for 33 percent of the 1987–88 congressional agenda; the president's agenda accounted for only 23 percent.

Special political conditions facilitated the Speaker's aggressive agenda setting. President Reagan had been weakened by the Iran-Contra scandal, the loss of a Senate majority, and his lame-duck status. House Democrats believed that they finally had the opportunity to pass legislation stymied during six years of the Reagan administration—if they were disciplined enough to exploit the opportunity. The House Democrats wanted policy leadership.

The party leadership responded with an unprecedented rate and scope of activity. The leadership involved itself in 83 percent of the items on the congressional agenda and, in 60 percent of the measures, its involvement was major. Although special political circumstances in the Hundredth Congress highlighted the benefits of strong leadership and thus account for some of the increase in leadership agenda-setting and legislative involvement, the increase was clearly the continuation of a trend, not simply an anomaly.

The broad scope of leadership activity in the Hundredth also represented the continuation of trends underway since at least the late 1970s. Contemporary party leaders are more frequently involved in shaping the substance of legislation than their predecessors of the committee government era. The party leadership itself now sometimes directly negotiates over substance with other key actors, such as Senate leaders and the president. In September 1987, when the Gramm–Rudman budget balancing legislation was being rewritten; in November 1987, when a two-year budget agreement between Congress and the White House was being worked out; and in December 1987, when the continuing resolution to fund the entire government for most of

1988 was at issue, the key players for the House were not the committee chairmen but the party leadership. In negotiations with the Bush administration on a Contra-aid package and on the budget in 1989, party leaders again played central roles. In each of these cases, decisions highly consequential to the party and the membership as a whole were at stake; most involved broadly encompassing omnibus legislation and negotiations with cabinet-level administration officials. As the elected agent of the majority party, the leadership has a basis for speaking for and making agreements on behalf of the majority that other entities lack.

The leadership sometimes plays a direct role in within-House negotiations, particularly on multiply referred or omnibus measures, where an arbiter or coordinator outside the committee or committees of origin is most likely to be necessary. On matters of great interest and consequence to the membership as a whole, the leadership may set guidelines or parameters for a committee, as the Speaker did for the Budget Committee in 1987.[33] The leaders are always engaged in behind-the-scenes efforts to get members at loggerheads to compromise and to persuade committee leaders to be responsive to majority sentiment in the party.

The leadership's increased involvement in shepherding legislation to passage at the floor stage has been made possible by the expansion and ingenious use of the whip system and by the aggressive and creative use of special rules.

The expansion of the whip system that began in the early 1970s had, by the Hundredth Congress, resulted in an organization with eighty-one members, most of whom were appointed by the party leadership. On legislation of consequence, the party leadership will conduct a whip count to ascertain the level of support among Democrats. Usually shortly before the leadership intends to bring the legislation to the floor, the regional whips will be instructed to ask the members in their zones how they intend to vote. If the count indicates insufficient support, due either to opposition or to a large number of undecideds, a task force will be formed. All the whips and the Democratic members of the committee of origin who supported the bill will be invited to take part. The task force, working from the initial count, distributes names of all Democrats not listed as supporting the party position among its members. Their task is to talk to those Democrats, to ascertain their voting intention, and to persuade a number sufficient for victory to support the party position. During the Hundredth Congress, task forces functioned in about seventy instances, and about 60 percent of House Democrats served on one or more task forces.

Control over the Rules Committee and members' greater willingness to acquiesce in restrictive rules has allowed the leadership to make increasingly aggressive use of this key resource to structure the choice situation on the floor. During the Hundredth Congress, 76 percent of the measures on the congressional agenda were considered under a closed or a complex rule—up from 43 percent in the Ninety-seventh Congress. That 85 percent of leadership agenda items and 81 percent of the measures on which the leadership was active were considered under such rules indicates that the use of complex and often restrictive rules has become a normal component of leadership strategy.

If, as here posited, the active help of a strong leadership increases the probability of passing legislation in the form preferred, Democratic committee contingents and the Democratic membership should have been more legislatively successful in the late 1980s than in comparable earlier Congresses when the leadership was weaker and less active. In fact, committee success was considerably higher in the Hundredth Congress than in any of the earlier Congresses under study on those measures where the president opposed the committee. Committees won on the House floor on 73 percent of their measures in the Hundredth; the range for the earlier Congresses was 46 percent to 60 percent. On final disposition, committees won on balance on 65 percent of their measures, compared with between 22 percent and 52 percent in the earlier Congresses.

On those measures pitting House Democrats against the president, Democrats were more successful on the House floor—91 percent versus between 61 percent and 83 percent—and much more successful in terms of final disposition—78 percent versus between 28 percent and 44 percent—in the Hundredth Congress than in the other Congresses under study. The comparison between the Ninety-fourth and the Hundredth is especially instructive since in both cases House Democrats faced a weakened president. Yet despite Democrats' much bigger numbers in the Ninety-fourth Congress (291 versus 258), they were more legislatively successful in the Hundredth.

A brief look at the 101st Congress substantiates the claim that the strong leadership evident in the Hundredth was not an anomaly but the culmination of a trend. The 1988 elections brought in a new Republican president but little change in the makeup of Congress; 1989 saw Speaker Jim Wright forced to resign under an ethics cloud and the succession of Tom Foley, previously majority leader, to the speakership. One would not expect leadership agenda setting to be as aggressive during the first Congress of a new presidency as during a lame-duck president's last; furthermore, the Democrats' traumatic leadership upheaval also took its toll. Yet Wright, in 1989 in his speech upon being reelected Speaker and in his reply to Bush's first speech to a joint session of Congress, and Foley, in reply to Bush's 1990 State of the Union address, did lay out a set of priorities considerably more extensive than O'Neill had in the first Reagan Congress. The scope and rate of leadership involvement in the legislative process appears to have changed little. To be sure, Tom Foley's leadership style is different from Jim Wright's. Foley consults even more widely; he tends to give the contending sides somewhat longer to work out their differences before stepping in personally, and he delegates more broadly to others on the leadership team. Yet because most of the same institutional and political barriers to passing legislation Democrats favor still exist, the members still need leadership help and the new leadership team provides it. The team works out political and jurisdictional conflicts among Democrats, as Foley himself did on child care; coordinates complex multiply referred legislation, as caucus chairman Steny Hoyer did on the Americans with Disabilities Act; and negotiates with the White House, as Majority Leader Gephardt did on the budget in 1990. The leadership protects legislation with carefully crafted rules and, using the whip system, mobilizes votes. Democrats did not win as often in the 101st as in the Hundredth, but repeating that phenomenal win rate was never a realistic possibility. Under conditions of divided control, winning depends not only upon the congressional leadership's strength and adeptness but also upon the president's resources and skills. And a newly elected president, even one with as little of a mandate or demonstrated coattails as Bush, nevertheless commands greater resources than a lame-duck president.

The Future of Leadership

If, as argued here, party leadership strength depends upon its costs and benefits to majority party members, what are the prospects for the

future? The institutional changes that increased the benefits of strong
leadership are not likely to be reversed in the foreseeable future. A
return to the system of autonomous committees and inter-committee
reciprocity is inconceivable. Consequently majority party members
will continue to need the party leadership's brokering, coordinating,
procedural advantaging and mobilization services in order to pass legislation. The political circumstances that increased the benefits to
Democrats of strong leadership are potentially more variable. George
Bush is a less conservative and confrontational president than Ronald
Reagan was, but the budget deficit continues to produce sharp conflicts
over priorities between congressional Democrats and the president.
Thus, Democrats continue to need a strong leadership. Were the deficit
to somehow disappear or a Democratic president to be elected, the
balance of costs and benefits of strong leadership would certainly
change. Paradoxically, the disappearance of the budget deficit as a
constraint might increase the costs of strong leadership to Democrats.
To be sure, the decrease in ideological heterogeneity that reduced those
costs is in considerable part a function of long-term changes in the
supportive constituencies of southern Democrats and those changes are
not likely to be reversed. In addition, however, the political climate of
the 1980s, especially the big deficits, placed some policy options that
split Democrats completely outside the politically feasible range,
thereby decreasing apparent ideological heterogeneity. Were these
constraints to be lifted, the Democratic membership's effective ideological heterogeneity might again increase. Furthermore, while leaders
and members have developed ways of reconciling members' desires to
participate meaningfully in the legislative process with strong leadership, those solutions might not hold up in a political climate more
conducive to free-lance policy entrepreneurship. Without the constraints of a big deficit and of a conservative political climate which
make liberal policy entrepreneurship unlikely to succeed, the costs of
the restraint members need to exercise in order to make strong leadership possible rise. The impact of a Democratic president upon the costs
and benefits of strong leadership to members would depend very much
upon the political circumstances leading to his or her reelection. If the
president were elected with a broadly based issue mandate the result
would be to increase the benefits and decrease the costs of strong
leadership, for a time at least. However, to the extent the election of a
Democratic president altered the political climate so as to make party-

splitting options feasible or free-lance entrepreneurship more attractive, its impact upon leadership strength would be negative.

Strong majority party leadership in the House in the late twentieth century seems more fragile than the strong leadership of the nineteenth century because it is not based upon strong parties external to Congress. We can predict only that party leadership in the House will remain strong so long as majority party members as individuals gain more than they lose from strong leadership.

Notes

This research is based in part upon a fifteen-month period of participant observation in the office of the Speaker and upon interviews with members and staff. I would like to thank Jim Wright and his staff for giving me an unprecedented opportunity to see leadership in operation from the inside and all those people who took some of their precious time to talk with me. This research was supported in part by intramural grant funds from the Academic Senate, University of California, Riverside, and by a grant from the Dirksen Congressional Leadership Research Center.

1. John Berry, *The Ambition and the Power* (New York: Viking, 1989); Roger Davidson, "The New Centralization on Capital Hill," *The Review of Politics* 49 (1988): 345–63; Lawrence Dodd and Bruce Oppenheimer, "Consolidating Power in the House: The Rise of a New Oligarchy," in *Congress Reconsidered,* 4th ed., ed. Dodd and Oppenheimer (Washington: Congressional Quarterly Press, 1989); David Rohde, "Democratic Party Leadership, Agenda Control, and the Resurgence of Partisanship in the House" (Paper presented at the Eighty-fifth Annual Meeting of the American Political Science Association, Atlanta, Georgia, 31 August–3 September 1989); Kenneth Shepsle, "The Changing Textbook Congress," *Can the Government Govern?*, ed. John H. Chubb and Paul Peterson (Washington: Brookings Institution, 1989); Barbara Sinclair, "The Changing Role of Party and Party Leadership in the U.S. House" (Paper delivered at the Eighty-fifth Annual Meeting of the American Political Science Association, Atlanta, Georgia, 31 August–3 September 1989); Steve Smith and Forrest Maltzman, "Declining Committee Power in the House of Representatives" (Paper delivered at the Eighty-fifth Annual Meeting of the American Political Science Association, Atlanta, Georgia, 31 August–3 September 1989); Janet Hook, "Speaker Jim Wright Takes Charge in the House," *Congressional Quarterly Weekly Report* 45, no. 28 (11 July 1987): 1483–88; Richard E. Cohen, "Quick-Starting Speaker," *National Journal*, 30 May 1987, 1409–13.

2. Richard Fenno, *Congressmen in Committees* (Boston: Little, Brown, 1973) and *Home Style* (Boston: Little, Brown, 1978); David Mayhew, *Congress: The Electoral Connection* (New Haven: Yale University Press, 1974). See also Richard L. Hall, "Participation and Purpose in Committee Decision Making," *American Political Science Review* 81 (1987): 105–27.

3. David Rohde and Kenneth A. Shepsle, "Leaders and Followers in the

House of Representatives: Reflections on Woodrow Wilson's 'Congressional Government,' " *Congress and the Presidency* 14 (1987): 111–33; Mathew Mc-Cubbins and Terry Sullivan, eds., *Congress Structure and Policy* (Cambridge, Eng.: Cambridge University Press, 1987). See also Joseph Cooper and David W. Brady, "Institutional Context and Leadership Style: The House from Cannon to Rayburn," *American Political Science Review* 75 (1981): 411–25; and Charles O. Jones, "House Leadership in an Age of Reform," in *Understanding Congressional Leadership*, ed. Frank H. Mackaman (Washington: Congressional Quarterly Press, 1981), 117–34.

4. Richard Bolling, *House Out of Order* (New York: E. P. Dutton and Co., 1965), 70.

5. See Richard F. Fenno, "The Internal Distribution of Influence: The House," in *The Congress and America's Future*, ed. David B. Truman (Englewood Cliffs, NJ: Prentice-Hall, 1965).

6. Randall B. Ripley, *Party Leaders in the House of Representatives* (Washington: Brookings Institution, 1967).

7. Bruce I. Oppenheimer, "The Changing Relationship between House Leadership and the Committee on Rules," in *Understanding Congressional Leadership*.

8. *Congressional Quarterly Weekly Report* (9 January 1970): 85.

9. *Congressional Quarterly Almanac* 1969:350.

10. *Congressional Quarterly*'s judgment, the content of the amendment and the extent to which the committee fought the amendment were the bases of judgment. There were few borderline cases; which amendments are key is almost always clear because all relevant actors are agreed. Consequently, coding clear losses is also straightforward; they occur when key votes—on major substitutes, killer amendments, or, of course, recommittal, passage, etc.—are lost. Not all cases fall into the clear win or the clear loss category; a committee may defeat some but not all major amendments. Such cases were placed into intermediate categories which are, however, less reliable and are not reported here.

11. *Congressional Quarterly*'s account is relied upon. *Congressional Quarterly*'s reports of liberal opposition to a committee-reported bill are usually corroborated by roll-call evidence, but sometimes liberals were not able to force a recorded vote.

12. See Bolling, *House Out of Order*.

13. Only instances of floor action that required a majority vote are included. That is, failed veto override attempts are not counted.

14. On the reforms, see Lawrence C. Dodd and Bruce I. Oppenheimer, *Congress Reconsidered* (New York: Praeger, 1977).

15. *Congressional Quarterly Weekly Reports* (25 January 1975): 177–78; (1 March 1975): 426–37; (28 June 1975): 1332–33.

16. Sidney Waldman, "Majority Party Leadership in the Contemporary House: The 94th and 95th Congresses" (Unpub. manuscript, Haverford College, 1978), 12.

17. Ibid., 17.

18. Steven Smith, *Call to Order: Floor Politics in the House and Senate* (Washington: Brookings Institution, 1989).

19. On the basis of the *Congressional Quarterly* account, a judgment was made as to whether the committee and, where relevant, the president and House

Democrats as a group had on balance won or lost on final disposition. This judgment is often somewhat more subjective than the classification concerning winning and losing on the floor, where votes provide an important guide. Because most major legislation that is enacted involves some compromise after committee consideration—most frequently in conference—the classification of winning on balance is considerably less demanding than the classification of winning on the floor and just requires that the committee (or the president or House Democrats) achieved a favorable compromise. Where a measure involved a clear-cut conflict between two sides and the result appeared to be an even compromise, the measure is placed into a middle, no clear winner, category.

20. For a measure to be included in this category the president must have a clear publicly stated position, two-thirds or more of House Democrats must vote together on all important roll calls on the measure, and the president's position and that of House Democrats must be directly opposed.

21. See Waldman, "Majority Party Leadership," *Congressional Quarterly Weekly Report* (28 June 1975): 1332–33.

22. Waldman, "Majority Party Leadership," 3.

23. Barbara Sinclair, *Majority Leadership in the U.S. House* (Baltimore: Johns Hopkins University Press, 1983); Burdette Loomis, "The 'Me' Decade and the Changing Context of House Leadership," in *Understanding Leadership*.

24. Ibid. See also Lawrence C. Dodd, "The Expanded Roles of the House Democratic Whip System: The 93rd and 94th Congresses," *Congressional Studies* 7 (1979): 27–56.

25. Smith, *Call to Order*, 40–41.

26. Sinclair, *Majority Leadership*, 82; Oppenheimer, *Congress Reconsidered*; Stanley Bach, "Special Rules in the House of Representatives: Themes and Contemporary Variations," *Congressional Studies* 8 (1981): 37–57, and "The Structure of Choice in the House of Representatives: The Impact of Complex Special Rules," *Harvard Journal on Legislation* 18 (1981): 553–602.

27. See Sinclair, *Majority Leadership*, and Stanley Bach and Steven S. Smith, *Managing Uncertainty in the House of Representatives* (Washington: The Brookings Institution, 1988).

28. Sinclair, *Majority Leadership*.

29. Melissa P. Collie and Joseph Cooper, "Multiple Referral and the 'New' Committee System in the House of Representatives," in *Congress Reconsidered*, 4th ed.; Roger H. Davidson, Walter J. Oleszek, and Thomas Kephart, "One Bill, Many Committees: Multiple Referrals in the U.S. House of Representatives," *Legislative Studies Quarterly* 13 (1988): 3–28.

30. David Rohde, "Variations in Partisanship in the House of Representatives: Southern Democrats, Realignment and Agenda Change" (Paper presented at the Eighty-fourth Annual Meeting of the American Political Science Association, Washington, D.C., 1–4 September 1988).

31. David E. Price, "From Outsider to Insider," in *Congress Reconsidered*.

32. See Waldman, "Majority Party Leadership"; Sinclair, "House Majority Party Leadership in the Late 1980s," in *Congress Reconsidered*, 4th ed.

33. Dan Palazzolo, "The Speaker's Relationship with the House Budget Committee" (Paper presented at the Annual Meeting of the Midwest Political Science Association, Chicago, Illinois, 13–15 April 1989).

DONALD C. BAUMER

9 Senate Democratic Leadership in the 101st Congress

In 1989 Senate Democrats elected George Mitchell of Maine as their majority leader. In just his tenth year of service in the Senate, Mitchell became majority leader with less seniority than any person to hold that office since Lyndon Johnson in the 1950s; yet in the 101st Congress he established himself as perhaps the strongest party leader since Johnson. The Senate that George Mitchell leads is, however, dramatically different from the institution that Lyndon Johnson was able to dominate. In this chapter I examine Mitchell's leadership in the 101st Congress and offer an explanation of the factors that enabled him to succeed, and those that set limits upon him. Among the principal factors are the special character of the Senate, a small and elite institution; the peculiar political milieu of the postreform period, shaped by the attitudes of the new American politicians, many products of the House of Representatives; the circumstance of divided government that has placed upon congressional Democrats an obligation to develop party policy positions; and Senator Mitchell's personality and style, which helped him get elected and facilitated his leadership of the Senate. George Mitchell led the Senate by a combination of personal qualities that are peculiar to him and institutional innovations that are peculiar to modern legislative politics. This combination produced in the Senate a leadership system that was different in fundamental respects from that which emerged in the House of Representatives during the same period, and which also differed from that which had preceded it in the Senate. In order to establish the nature and extent of this change in Senate leadership, I begin by briefly reviewing Senate leadership, beginning with the tenure of Lyndon Johnson.

Senate Leadership, 1955–1988

The evolution of the Senate from the 1950s to the 1980s can be described rather succinctly: a tradition-laden institution run by a self-selected group of "Senate types" was transformed into a body in which self-promoting individualism and collective disorder became predominant characteristics. William S. White's "inner club" that supposedly controlled the Senate in the immediate postwar period and sponsored Lyndon Johnson's rise to power had disintegrated by the time Johnson left the Senate in 1960.[1] Johnson's legendary "one man rule" as majority leader was actually quite short-lived; it was evident mainly in the Eighty-fourth and Eighty-fifth Congresses (1955–58). During this period Johnson centralized power in the Senate through an extensive intelligence and communication system and through his own extraordinary effort, zeal, and personality.[2] By the Eighty-sixth Congress, however, Johnson was being vigorously challenged by young Senate liberals such as Philip Hart, Eugene McCarthy, Edmund Muskie, and William Proxmire. Interestingly, the Senate's tradition as an institution that allowed its members numerous prerogatives helped to make the demands of these liberal insurgents for a greater spreading of power within the chamber more appealing.

Upon Johnson's departure, his former Democratic colleagues in the Senate were clearly looking for a very different type of leader, and Mike Mansfield was definitely that. His low-keyed, hands-off approach to leadership and his laconic, deferential personality stood in marked contrast to those of his aggressive, domineering predecessor.[3] Mansfield shared power, responsibility, and information widely among his fellow senators. He was quoted in 1961 as saying "I'm not the leader, really. They don't do what I tell them. I do what they tell me."[4] In 1969 Randall Ripley concluded an article on power in the postwar Senate by commenting "The present Senate is not composed of a few omnipotent and happy senior senators and a great many impotent and unhappy junior senators. Most senators are content with their lot. A central reason for their contentment is that the opportunity to develop both institutional power and personal power is available to all."[5]

Thus by the 1970s independence, egalitarianism, and issue entrepreneurship were the central features of the "new" Senate.[6] The famous "Johnson Rule," whereby incoming senators were guaranteed their choice of one major committee assignment before any senator was given two, was a major step down the road toward egalitarianism.[7] Since then the number and prominence of subcommittees have increased, giving virtually every senator of the majority party (and most from the minority party) a policy power base. The steady expansion in staff capacity has helped senators with reelection, policy/issue promotion in areas outside their committees, and media relations, thus contributing to independence and entrepreneurship.[8] The increased visibility of senators and openness of the institution further have contributed to the self-promoting inclinations of senators. Casualties in the changeover to this new Senate style were the old norms of apprenticeship, specialization, reciprocity, and to some extent courtesy. The result, to borrow a phrase from Roger Davidson, has been the creation of a truly "untidy chamber."[9]

The internal changes occurring in the Senate (and the House) in the late 1960s and 1970s were being driven by outside, contextual forces. Members faced a rapidly changing political world that included an unpopular war, demands for social justice at home, increased interest group activity, declining party loyalty, candidate-centered elections, and a pervasive media role in politics. Reformers within Congress were determined to make the institution more responsive to this new political world. Most of the institutional changes they sought were directed at decentralizing power so that more members could claim credit for legislative accomplishments, achieve influence within the chamber more rapidly, and improve their prospects for reelection.[10] In general, the reforms worked against the possibility of strong central leadership. There was, however, some recognition that fragmentation and egalitarianism could be taken too far, that no one could achieve their goals if the chamber was immobilized.[11]

This recognition was most evident in the House, where the reforms of the early 1970s—that helped to bring about greater decentralization by giving more power to subcommittee chairman and the caucus, while taking power away from committee chairman—included changes that enhanced the power of the leadership, particularly the Speaker. For example, the committee assignment function was taken away from the Ways and Means Committee and given to the twenty-four member Steering and Policy Committee, which includes four members of the leadership, eight appointees of the Speaker, and is chaired by the Speaker.[12] The Speaker was also given more control over the referral of legislation to committees, including the use of multiple referrals, the creation of temporary committees, and the ability to set deadlines for committees to report legislation.[13] Another important change gave the Speaker sole power to appoint members of the Rules Committee, which greatly enhanced his control of legislative scheduling.[14] House Speaker Tip O'Neill gradually learned how to exploit these opportunities so as to increase his power and influence over the chamber.[15]

In the Senate the democratizing reforms of the late 1960s and 1970s did not include as many new grants of authority to the leadership. In part, this reflected the fact that Democratic floor leaders already had an impressive list of formal powers: they chaired the Conference, the Policy Committee, and the Steering Committee. After Johnson, however, these formal powers were used mostly to serve or accommodate members rather than to steer them. Mansfield, who served as majority leader from 1960–76, assumed a largely passive role in conferences, routinized Steering Committee decisions, and he worked for consensus in Policy Committee deliberations.[16] His successor, Robert Byrd (majority leader from 1976–80 and 1986–88, and minority leader between 1980 and 1986), took a personal interest in Steering Committee decisions in order to provide valuable favors for his colleagues, hosted few conferences, and reduced the Policy Committee to a staffing operation (it rarely, if ever met).[17] Senate leaders did gain a bit more control over floor activity through changes made in 1975 and 1979 in the rules for invoking cloture. The 1975 rule change reduced the majority needed to stop filibusters from two-thirds to three-fifths, and the 1979 reform restricted postcloture activity to one hundred hours.[18]

Senate Democrats got a taste for some of the disadvantages of institutional untidiness when they confronted Republican administrations under Richard Nixon and Gerald Ford between 1968 and 1975. Responding to the frustration of his colleagues about the course of foreign and domestic policy, Mansfield worked through the Democratic Policy Committee and the Conference to discuss and pass resolutions that outlined party positions (the most notable of these was a 1971 resolution calling for withdrawal from Vietnam). In both 1971 and 1973 Senate Democrats created broad-gauged agendas of party policy (foreign and domestic) in an effort to combat Nixon policies, but few of these resolutions were ever enacted by the full Senate. In the end, Mansfield held to his tradition of deference to committee chairmen and individual members, and he never attempted to enforce any sort of party discipline on behalf of the stated policy objectives.[19]

The Watergate experience gave Congress a renewed sense of the importance of its role as a check on the chief executive, which continued to make relations between the two branches somewhat conflictual even when the Democrats regained the White House.[20] Byrd's loyalty was very much divided between his colleagues and the president during the Carter administration. In an illustrative episode, he first parcelled out the president's 1977 national energy plan to various Senate committees against the wishes of the administration but then teamed up with Vice President Mondale to salvage natural gas legislation that was drowning in a postcloture filibuster by using strong-arm parliamentary tactics.[21] Byrd's greatest strength as a floor leader was his mastery of Senate floor procedures. He also accumulated a huge stockpile of credits from favors rendered, and he hoarded and selectively disseminated information, which gave him influence. He could be intensely partisan, but Byrd was never willing and/or able to use his influence to bring his colleagues together in support of a program of party-based policy objectives. Under his leadership individualism and entrepreneurship flourished.

The Democrats lost control of the Senate after the 1980 national elections, and they did not regain it until after the 1986 elections. Howard Baker, minority leader since 1977, assumed the role of majority leader, and for about one year he rode a crest of Republican optimism and unity to achieve many policy successes. The most notable of these was the Senate's quick and easy passage of critical Reagan budget and tax legislation in 1981, which put a great deal of pressure on the House to act in a similar fashion. Baker's skill as a negotiator enabled him to find compromises that maintained the peace between arch-conservatives, most of whom were newcomers; moderate Republicans, many of whom were committee chairmen; and the Reagan White House. He also continued a practice that Byrd had followed of meeting with committee chairmen on a weekly basis in order to maintain tight control over the scheduling of floor business (in consultation with the White House and the minority leader).[22] Overall, in 1981 Baker delivered to Reagan the kind of cohesive partisan support that had not been seen on Capitol Hill since the heyday of Lyndon Johnson's Great Society.[23]

During 1982–83 Baker encountered more difficulty. A recession during an election year, the widening gulf among Senate Republicans and between moderate senators and the White House, and his commitment to patience and kindness in dealing with his colleagues conspired to produce stalemate and disorder in the Senate. Baker's majorities were small (fifty-four in the Ninety-seventh Congress and fifty-five in the Ninety-eighth), and even a little disunity was crippling. Baker did have some notable successes, such as the passage of the Tax Equity and Fiscal Responsibility Act of 1982. But two years of trying to lead a group that refused to be led was enough for Baker, and he announced his intention to retire after the Ninety-eighth Congress. On an institutional front, Baker made a determined, but unsuccessful, effort to introduce television coverage of Senate floor debates. However, in 1986 the Senate did vote in television and for a further reduction (to thirty hours) in the time allowed for postcloture discussion.[24]

Senate Republicans chose Robert Dole as their majority leader in 1984. Dole was known to be a tough partisan fighter who would be an assertive leader while maintaining some independence from the White House. This was the combination many of his colleagues thought was needed after Baker's experience. Republicans lost two Senate seats in the 1984 election, despite Reagan's decisive victory, had twenty-two incumbents up for reelection in 1986, which put their slim majority (fifty-three) in great peril, and recognized that Reagan could not help them much in the future. They needed to establish their own record. Unity would be essential in the effort to establish a record, and Dole was recognized as someone who was more inclined toward aggressive persuasion than deference. It is noteworthy that the context of the Ninety-ninth Senate led Republicans, who vividly displayed the individualism associated with the new Senate during the Ninety-eighth Congress, to want strong leadership. Dole himself said: "Most senators want leadership—if they wanted someone to just call meetings, or someone who will always check with each and every senator, they wouldn't want me."[25]

Dole delivered pretty much as expected. He was very assertive in conferences, insisting that all or nearly all Republican senators commit themselves to a party position before entering legislative battles. Dole allowed many senators to be involved in shaping decisions, but the need for party unity was stressed as never before. Many key votes in 1985–86 were very close. The most memorable of these occurred in the spring of 1985, when Senator Pete Wilson of California was wheeled onto the Senate floor in his hospital bed to cast the forty-ninth (and tying) vote for a Dole budget resolution, and Vice President Bush was then able to decide the matter for Republicans.

Not surprisingly, strong Republican partisanship encouraged Democrats in the same direction, so that the normally restrained partisanship of the Senate evaporated, and partisan fangs were frequently exposed. Dole supported Reagan administration positions on several important matters, such as the confirmation of Daniel Manion for a federal judgeship and South African sanctions; but he also opposed the administration on matters like subsidized grain sales to the Soviet Union, which he hoped would help Senate Republicans establish an independent record.[26] Despite Dole's efforts, Republican unity sometimes broke down, but he was the forceful leader most of his colleagues seemed to want.

According to Barbara Sinclair, House leaders under Speaker Jim Wright gradually built upon the leadership potential that resulted from the reforms of the 1970s to achieve genuinely strong leadership in the Hundredth Congress.[27] Employing a three-pronged strategy that involved generous provision of services to members to aid in coalition building, the structuring of choices for the chamber in ways that served the policy ends of the leadership, and the expansion of leadership organizations and circles to include as many members as possible (strategy of inclusion), the Wright–Foley–Coelho team was able to establish an agenda (clean water, aid for the homeless, a trade bill, catastrophic health insurance, welfare reform, and tax increases) and move it through the chamber. Speaker Wright also became much more aggressive in his use of the media to convey Democratic messages to the public and, of course, benefited greatly from the weakened presidency of Ronald Reagan following the Iran-Contra scandal. Sinclair predicted a continuation of strong leadership in the House both because of the resources and skills possessed by contemporary leaders, and "even more important, [because] its membership wants such leadership."[28]

Senate Democrats were unable to achieve the same level of policy integration and cohesion as their House counterparts in the Hundredth Congress. Byrd continued to show little interest in policy leadership—he did not convene the Policy Committee to discuss issues or pass resolutions, nor did he try to establish a policy agenda as Wright did. Thus most policy matters were left to the discretion of committee chairmen. Byrd never attempted to consolidate power over budgetary decisions, which have dominated congressional politics since the early 1980s.[29] His service orientation fed the entrepreneurial appetites of some members, but there were increasing signs that this was no longer enough. A survey of twenty-six senators conducted in 1987 uncovered considerable support for, among other things, "stronger discipline among members, and more attention to the partisan and congressional agenda."[30] Byrd's inability to project a favorable media image also contributed to increasing dissatisfaction with his leadership and helped to stimulate interest, especially among newcomers, in "strong leadership."

The interest in stronger leadership was also a product of divided government, which members were beginning to recognize as a normal condition rather than an aberration. Conflict with the Reagan administration and declining public confidence in Congress were powerful forces that helped to make the *idea* of strong leadership popular on Capitol Hill.[31] In April 1988 Byrd announced his intention to resign as majority leader at the end of the Hundredth Congress, and a new era in Senate leadership loomed on the horizon. This chapter examines the activities of the new Democratic leadership during the 101st Congress in a preliminary attempt to explore the question of whether stronger, more policy-oriented leadership is likely or even possible in the Senate of the 1990s.[32]

A New Leader for Senate Democrats

Senate leadership elections are shrouded in secrecy.[33] Candidates, some of whom are unannounced, seek commitments of support from their colleagues in face-to-face meetings. Senators are often quite creative about offering reassurance while keeping their final options open. The Democratic leadership race in 1988 featured three candidates: George Mitchell of Maine, J. Bennett Johnston of Louisiana, and Daniel K. Inouye of Hawaii. All three acknowledged the need for "quality-of-life" reforms, but Mitchell was the most outspoken on this issue.[34] An October 1988 head count taken by freshman senators found Johnston ahead with fifteen supporters, Mitchell next with fourteen, and Inouye behind with eleven.[35] But, when the vote was finally taken in late November, Mitchell won with surprising ease.[36] Mitchell's effectiveness on television, proven during the Iran-Contra hearings when he clearly outshone Investigating Committee Chairman Inouye, his obvious intelligence and judicious style combined with a willingness to take positions (for example, he was a strong advocate of environmental protection and progressive income taxation), and Johnston's conservatism and lack of telegenic qualities conspired to raise this junior senator above his more experienced opponents into the leadership position.[37]

The context of the Senate Democratic leadership election was dominated by the election of George Bush to the presidency, giving the Republicans control of the executive branch for the fifth time in the last six elections. But Bush's victory stood in contrast to Reagan's 1980 election in several important respects. First, congressional Democrats did well in 1988, adding to their majorities in both the House and Senate.[38] Second, Bush's victory was not accompanied by a substantive policy mandate (except "no new taxes"); polls showed that voters had faith in the way Republican presidents managed the economy and provided for defense but sided with the Democrats on the need for expanded federal benefits in the areas of education, housing, the environment, and assistance to the elderly.[39] Third, congressional Democrats had gained some experience at governing during the Hundredth Congress. They had passed some important legislation (clean water, omnibus trade, welfare reform and catastrophic health legislation) with little or no help from the White House, and they had even overturned Reagan administration policies on the budget, South Africa, and Central America.

Thus Wright's strong leadership in the House and fresh leadership in the Senate raised interesting possibilities for congressional Democrats. Should they view themselves as a governing party or an opposition party? Should they try to work with the White House to pursue mutual policy objectives or use their control of Congress to emphasize for the public partisan differences with regard to policies and values? Could they do both?

Mitchell's principal objectives upon assuming the leadership were to pursue a strategy of inclusion, to implement quality-of-life reforms, and to work in good faith with the White House and Senate Republicans to clear legislative roadblocks on important matters. He quickly demonstrated his commitment to sharing the powers and responsibilities of leadership by breaking with tradition and making Inouye chairman of the Steering Committee. He also tapped three members of the class of 1986 to serve as leadership lieutenants—Tom Daschle of South Dakota as co-chairman of the Policy Committee, Wyche Fowler of Georgia as assistant floor leader, and John Breaux of Louisiana as head of the Democratic Senatorial Campaign Committee (DSCC). All three of these members had served on leadership committees in the House and were familiar with the coalition-building strategies that had been employed there under O'Neill and Wright. Mitchell's first substantive promise—to produce a Democratic legislative agenda by mid-March—was announced with inclusiveness as its theme. The new leader said, "We Senate Democrats should have our own agenda for action, . . . objectives that we should strive to attain. All senators should be able to participate in this process. And if you involve people in the decision-making process, you are more likely to get their support later."[40]

New Leadership Apparatus

On January 4, 1989, a seemingly important event occurred amidst little or no fanfare: the Senate Democratic Policy Committee (DPC) met for the first time in twelve years.[41] Senator Fritz Hollings of South Carolina, who was a member of Mike Mansfield's Policy Committee in 1971, expressed pleasure and excitement about the reactivation of the DPC. Mitchell outlined his plans for the year, emphasizing the importance of a legislative agenda, and Daschle described the steps that had already been taken toward development of one. Daschle had been meeting individually with committee chairmen since December, asking them to prepare prioritized lists ("must do," "could do," and "might do") of legislation within their jurisdictions that they would like to move to the floor during the 101st Congress. Since Mitchell's core support resided with the younger members (as chairman of the DSCC, he helped to recruit the class of 1986), the committee chairmen had to be approached with caution and care. Their cooperation was essential if the agenda creation process was to get off the ground.

By the end of January, Daschle had successfully completed the meetings with committee chairmen, and, along with other DPC members, he had also met with representatives of major interests—labor, the elderly, women's and civil rights groups, small business and real estate associations—to gather their input. By February, the committee had a draft of a *Legislative Agenda* for formal consideration, and on March 17 the *Legislative Agenda* of the Senate Democratic Conference was approved and released.

The basic issue of contention during DPC meetings in February

and early March was how specific the agenda should be in identifying legislation Senate Democrats intended to enact. Daschle and
Mitchell wanted to be fairly specific (initial drafts of the agenda
listed specific legislation they hoped to pass under issue headings
like defense, education, environment, housing, etc.), but many members were concerned that an agenda composed of specific items
might be used by the press and Republicans as a "scorecard," which
could be politically damaging to Democrats. This concern eventually
led Daschle to adopt a very broad thematic format for the agenda in
order to gain DPC approval, and it almost derailed the entire project
when all Democratic senators met to approve the DPC *Legislative
Agenda* on March 15, 16, and 17.[42]

During these meetings quibbling over wording and disagreement
about content (stemming largely from the scorecard concern) eventually led to the suggestion that the *Legislative Agenda* go out under
Mitchell's name rather than as a product of the Senate Democratic
Conference. Mitchell intervened strongly, telling his colleagues that he
expected them to approve an agenda by March 17. They did, but their
compliance was partially induced by the appearance of an Associated
Press wire story describing the agenda and conveying the impression
that its approval was a certainty. No one either claimed credit or accepted blame for the early release of the agenda; and it is, perhaps, an
appropriate irony that the *Legislative Agenda* never attracted much
attention in the major media markets. A story about it appeared on the
fourth page of the *Washington Post* and the twenty-eighth page of the
New York Times on Saturday, March 18; little or nothing was said
about it on television.

Senator Mitchell also successfully implemented the quality-of-life
schedule he promised his colleagues, but as with the agenda, not without some difficulty. The Mitchell Senate meets for three weeks and
then takes a week off, does not hold votes on Mondays or Fridays,
does not have votes after 7:00 P.M. on Tuesdays and Wednesdays,
takes four weeks off in August, and aspires to finish its legislative
sessions by October (in election years) or Thanksgiving (in 1989).
Like his predecessors, however, Mitchell's patience has been stretched
to the limit at times by his colleagues' absenteeism and competing
commitments, which prevent the chamber from moving ahead legislatively.[43] On June 9, 1990, he stated on the Senate floor, "It is intolera-
ble that the Senate cannot function if one of a few senators has

something else to do on one of the three days of the week of the three weeks of the month that the Senate is supposed to be in session and working."[44] His typical response to these problems was to threaten to alter the quality-of-life schedule—hold votes on Mondays and Fridays, have early morning roll calls, or shorten the August recess.

A traditional function of the DPC has been to help the majority leader with the scheduling of legislation for floor consideration. As all observers of the modern Senate attest, the scheduling function is extremely complicated, time-consuming and problematic, largely because any single senator can tie up floor debates for a long period of time if he/she so desires.[45] The majority leader, working with the minority leader, tries to accommodate the concerns of as many senators as possible, hoping to achieve unanimous consent agreements (specifying length of debate, restricting nongermane amendments, and setting a date and time for final vote) before moving important items to the floor.[46] Deals and agreements can be struck at almost any time, or impasses can persist indefinitely, making it very difficult to predict when or if legislation will get through the Senate.

The majority leader is expected to bring some order to the Senate's scheduling chaos. Mostly this is done by being an informational hub. The leader maintains constant lines of communication with committee chairmen and bill sponsors, members of task forces and negotiating teams searching for compromises on contentious issues, the minority leader and the administration, and interested outside parties. Managing the Senate's schedule also demands that the leader make a number of difficult substantive and procedural decisions—when to push committee chairman to produce expected legislation or agree to modifications in legislation, whether compromise proposals preserve vital partisan interests and thus merit the leader's endorsement, when to put bills on the floor (with or without a unanimous consent agreement) and when to take them off—and then communicate these decisions to his party colleagues. Often such decisions are made under rushed, last-minute conditions, and an ongoing complaint among senators is that they often have a difficult time keeping track of their own institution's schedule.

In an effort to respond to this problem and, more generally, to improve communication between the leadership and members, Mitchell and Daschle defined a new, more service-oriented mission for the DPC.[47] The first product of the reoriented DPC was an upgraded and expanded set of publications. Beginning in May of 1989, new DPC publications were issued that aimed to provide Democratic members with timely, in-depth, substantive and political information on bills, pending issues, the schedule, and the statements and views of the majority leader.[48] House publications, particularly those of the Democratic Study Group (DSG) provided part of the inspiration for these revised DPC publications. By 1990, the DPC had also set up an in-house television station that broadcasted scheduling information and other messages from the leadership whenever the Senate was in session (the Republicans had had one of these for several years).[49] If nothing else, the DPC can be credited with bringing some measure of twentieth-century technology into the Senate.

Although these new DPC services did not dramatically alleviate the difficulties and frustrations associated with Senate scheduling, they were recognized and appreciated in the offices of most Senate Democrats. It was not unusual for senators to use DPC reports on the floor, and many staff members came to rely upon them in the preparation of speeches and press statements. There were still complaints about the accuracy and timeliness of information (some of this was caused by the fact that the DPC services staff was not directly linked to the majority leader and his floor staff), but much more information about the plans and views of the leadership was available to Senate Democrats under Mitchell than had been the case under Byrd.

In addition to serving as a communication network, the DPC also became an important educational forum in the 101st Congress. It sponsored two major retreats—in Williamsburg in July 1989, and in Charlottesville in July 1990—where a series of expert panels analyzed and discussed with senators designated topics, including foreign policy, the budget, the economy, health care, the environment, and education. In 1990 the DPC held weekly luncheon meetings on Thursdays that became issue seminars in which committee or subcommittee chairmen or outsiders would brief members on selected topics. These issue seminars were open to all Democratic members and proved quite popular (fifteen to twenty-five members attended most of them). Policy Committee luncheons on Thursdays became a part of many senators' weekly routines.

Thus the DPC carved out an important niche for itself as a discussion forum and a service provider, but it did not serve as any sort of "executive committee" for the majority leader—he did not use it to help him develop or discuss legislative strategies.[50] In fact, Mitchell played a limited role in most DPC discussions. He adopted the DPC floor and foreign policy staff, and left the services and educational functions to Daschle. Formal discussions of legislative strategies, to the extent that they took place at all, occurred in the Democratic Conference.

Conference luncheons were held on Tuesdays, and the discussion typically focussed on immediate and pressing legislative matters. Members searched, with mixed success, for partisan strategies that could be maintained on the floor. Mitchell was active in these discussions but did not generally dominate them—he was neither as deferential as Mansfield or Baker nor as assertive as Dole. He offered his opinions, sometimes forcefully, reported on meetings with Senate Republicans or the White House, and waited for consensus to emerge. Another active participant was Senator Breaux, who regularly reported on electoral stirrings and developments. It is difficult to obtain much information about conference discussions (staff are excluded and members are pledged to confidentiality), but the word "frustrating" came up frequently in comments about them. By the end of the second session, Mitchell's control over the conference was said to have increased substantially.

Senate Democrats as a Governing Force

The introduction to the *Legislative Agenda* that Senate Democrats developed for the 101st Congress includes the following statements: "The Democratic Majority in the Senate is committed to two fundamental purposes—standing up for the principles in which we believe, and sitting down with a new administration to build the cooperation which we believe the nation needs"; and "Our job as Democrats and members of the Senate, is not to oppose the administration automatically, but to propose policies and pursue them cooperatively." Although some of his colleagues had, and continue to have, doubts about whether one can simultaneously stand up for Democratic principles and work cooperatively with a Republican administration, the leader's actions during the 101st Congress indicated that he believed such a balancing act was possible. Mitchell was determined to work with the Bush administration to pass policies that he and other Senate Democrats regarded as important priorities.

During the 101st Congress, in most areas of domestic policy and many aspects of foreign policy, Senator Mitchell and the Democratic congressional leadership generally acted in ways suggestive of a governing party. They tried to pass policies that served important Democratic interests (minimum wage, clean air, child care), and they rejected executive proposals they regarded as demagogic (flag-burning amendment) or excessively damaging to well-established interests (deep cuts in domestic programs). This approach had natural appeal—it was designed to enable members achieve their policy goals, please constituent groups, and ultimately to help Democratic incumbents get reelected and the party to maintain its majority. The inclination toward a governing party posture reflected the fact that congressional Democrats had many program and policy responsibilities, stemming from many years of directing or co-directing domestic policy, that could not be ignored. As mentioned above, they also had some experience at governing during the last few years of the Reagan administration.

But passing new policies in a era of divided government almost inevitably means making compromises with Republicans, especially the president. Democrats lacked the numbers (55 in the Senate, 259 in the House) and cohesiveness to force their preferences on a president with veto authority, which gave the leaders no choice but to negotiate with Republicans in most of the policy situations they faced. Therefore, the governing party approach really meant coalition government and placed a great deal of responsibility on congressional leaders to strike the right bargains. The process of negotiation invariably leads to significant concessions on matters of policy and principle, which can engender confusion and frustration among ideological partisans, group allies and citizens.[51] Thus an important potential disadvantage of the governing party approach is that it does not always help the party define itself to voters, and it can result in situations where the president is able to derive more benefit from the policy actions that are taken (because of his greater visibility) than the Democrats who initiated and pursued them.

Coalition government strategies had particular appeal for Senator Mitchell because the upper chamber has a long tradition of bipartisanship (strained somewhat in recent years), he did not have a governing majority (sixty votes are needed to control the Senate floor), and he was especially confident of his ability to get at least half a loaf in negotiations with other elected officials. It also played into the inclusion theme in that sharing the negotiating duties with committee chairmen and other policy leaders would allow many members to feel they played a part in the process and would put the leader in a position to share both credit and blame. Therefore, an emphasis on bipartisan approaches to policy making seemed to fit well with the realities of the 101st Senate.

In the end, Senate Democrats under Mitchell achieved a number of legislative successes and, despite its low profile, the *Legislative Agenda* provided a reasonably good blueprint of Senate activities in the 101st Congress. In contrast to the Hundredth Congress, the Senate acted first on many Democratic legislative initiatives. Some of the prominent specifics from the agenda on which the Senate successfully acted included: thrift-industry reforms, education initiatives, vocational-education reauthorization, rural development and the 1990 farm bill, a defense-authorization bill, new clean-air standards, a new minimum-wage law, child-care assistance, expanded funding for anti-drug programs, an overhaul of housing programs, parental- and medical-leave legislation, Hatch Act revisions, new congressional-ethics and campaign-finance reform, whistleblower protections, anti-discrimination provisions for the handicapped, new civil rights legislation, and new immigration reforms.

Of course, many of the bills the Senate passed never became law. Campaign finance reform and congressional ethics (limiting honoraria) and the education initiatives never worked their way out of the congressional process. President Bush vetoed parental- and medical-leave legislation, Hatch Act revisions, and the 1990 Civil Rights Act. He also vetoed the minimum wage bill preferred by Democrats but eventually accepted a scaled-down increase in the minimum wage. Indeed, all sixteen of the president's vetoes during the 101st Congress were sustained. Thus most of the legislative successes of the 101st Congress were not pure Democratic victories; final legislation was shaped in important ways by the preferences of Republicans and the Bush administration.[52] The bills that did become law bore the hallmarks of coalition government.

Aggregate analysis of Senate voting reveals a pattern of increasing partisanship during the 101st Congress, which is an indication that Mitchell's partisan instincts became somewhat sharper as he became more familiar with his new job. The party-unity index—the percentage of roll calls in which a majority of Democrats opposed a majority of Republicans—fell during the first session to its third lowest level in thirty-five years (going from 42 percent in 1988 to 35 percent in 1989), but rose in the second session to its highest level since 1981 (54 percent). Party loyalty among Democrats—the percentage of members who voted with their party on party unity votes—rose from 78 percent in 1988 and 1989 to 80 percent in 1990.[53]

Successful legislative leadership in the modern Senate requires the majority leader to devote a great deal of attention to, and exhibit a good deal of skill over Senate floor proceedings. The floor has become an important decision-making arena because most important bills are subject to a series of floor amendments (committee products rarely gain universal acceptance), and passing legislation normally involves many procedural and substantive votes.[54] Delaying tactics and obstructionism (quorum calls, procedural motions, introducing numerous amendments) are common as the contemporary breed of policy-active senators makes great use of the prerogatives granted them by the loose rules governing Senate floor proceedings. Thus the final content and ultimate fate of legislation is often determined on the floor, which makes the job of overseeing floor debate especially critical and onerous. It is, perhaps, the most demanding feature of the day-to-day life of Senate leaders.

As mentioned previously, one of Robert Byrd's main assets as a floor leader was his mastery of parliamentary procedures. With increasing numbers of amendments being proposed, with more filibusters being threatened and undertaken, and with cloture votes becoming routine occurrences, his skill in this area seemed well suited to the modern Senate. Dealing with Byrd over several years forced Senator Dole to develop his parliamentary repertoire, and by the Hundredth Congress, Senate debate had become something of a parliamentary chess game. Senator Mitchell exhibited little interest in the arcane aspects of Senate floor procedure. His approach to floor debate and procedure was straightforward—he announced his intentions and then tried to use ordinary and well-understood procedural channels to achieve his legislative goals. Dole and the Republicans seldom resorted to extraordinary procedural devices in their efforts to thwart the Democrats during the 101st Congress, and when they did, Byrd was still available to unravel their parliamentary knots. Thus in the Mitchell Senate duels between the leaders were much less likely to involve the use of complicated and obscure rules and procedures.

Mitchell's conduct and performance on the floor were widely

praised by Democrats. His first major test came in the debate over John Tower's confirmation as secretary of defense in March of 1989. This debate was prolonged and bitter, but Mitchell faced several challenges by Dole and other Republicans squarely, and he successfully managed the rejection of Tower on a close 47–53 vote. One of the most dramatic exchanges in this debate pitted Mitchell against New Hampshire Republican Warren Rudman. Rudman insisted that FBI evidence of Tower's alcohol abuse was inconclusive, saying "One thing I learned in 24 years of practicing law is how to read evidence . . ."; at which point Mitchell, a former judge, retorted, "I think I know how to do that just as well as you do."[55]

Since then Mitchell has shown many times that he can be intelligent, resourceful, and strong on the floor. Another memorable episode occurred on July 17, 1990, when Mitchell pressed for cloture to limit debate on and amendments to the Civil Rights Act of 1990. Dole exploded with anger when he realized that Mitchell had the votes he needed (fifty-four Democrats and eight Republicans supported the cloture petition), saying, "This senator's never voted against a civil rights bill. But he has never had one shoved down his throat before." Dole's extended tirade laced with accusations of abuse by the majority leader caused even Mitchell to get angry, and he responded by saying, "If there is one thing I have tried to do since I became majority leader, it is to establish a sense of fairness and comity in the Senate."[56] On the next day the Senate passed a very liberal civil rights bill.

Of course, rhetorical sparring with the opposition is only a part of the majority leader's floor responsibilities. Debate on most bills is managed by sponsors from the committees in which they were formulated (usually full or subcommittee chairmen), but the leader and his floor staff must keep tabs on these debates to ensure that they proceed as planned. Mitchell held formal meetings with Dole before recesses to set the floor schedule for the upcoming weeks, but most of his meetings with the minority leader were informal and ad hoc. Their offices are close together in the Capitol, and they frequently ran into each other on the way to the floor or could be seen huddling in the rear of the chamber to work out a deal. Similarly, the minority and majority floor staffs have continual communication, much of it informal.

At any given time, there were several Democratic negotiating teams at work trying to iron out differences with Republicans on important legislation, and developments in these negotiations constituted another important element in the leader's decisions about floor activities. Mitchell carefully monitored ongoing discussions and offered his views on contested issues, but he generally gave the leaders of negotiating teams (usually committee chairmen) a good deal of latitude to come up with acceptable agreements.

The best example of Majority Leader Mitchell using his leadership position to successfully establish a viable coalition with the administration in order to achieve a policy breakthrough was the passage of clean-air legislation in the early months of 1990. Mitchell made passage of a new clean-air bill his top legislative priority for the second session of the 101st Congress, and Bush announced a similar intention during his 1990 State of the Union Address. Of course, there were major differences to be resolved between the Senate Environment Committee's bill (S. 1630) and the president's proposal (S. 1490), both of which had been put forward in 1989. Environmentalists strongly supported S. 1630, and Mitchell brought it to the floor in late January. He quickly pulled it off the floor, however, when it was clear that he did not have the votes to stop a Republican filibuster. He and Dole then put together a group of negotiators, and head-to-head talks with the White House began.

Mitchell, as majority leader and the former chairman of the Environmental Protection Subcommittee, played a major role in these negotiations, which ran through most of February. On March 1 a compromise agreement was announced; Bush, Mitchell, and Dole took turns praising it. Although the agreement more or less split the difference between provisions of the earlier bills in the key areas of automobile emission limits, restrictions on toxic pollutants, and acid-rain regulations; environmentalists were visibly unhappy, while industry seemed relieved. Richard Ayres of the National Clean Air Coalition challenged Mitchell's strategy of direct negotiations with the administration by saying, "The back-room dealing has generated bad deals for the American people."[57] Despite this type of criticism from long-time political allies, the majority leader pushed ahead, vowing to fend off "deal-breaking" amendments on the floor so as to keep the negotiated package intact and avoid a presidential veto.

Mitchell eventually succeeded in this effort, but not without a good deal of drama, and a remarkable amount of collaboration with the White House and Dole. Peak drama occurred on March 29, when an amendment by Robert Byrd to compensate coal miners who might lose their jobs as a result of new acid-rain regulations finally made its way on to the floor. Dole said the amendment would bring about a veto, but Byrd, who holds more IOUs than anyone on Capitol Hill, went all out to pass his amendment. On the day of the vote, Byrd thought he had fifty votes, but he ended up with only forty-nine.[58] During the month-long clean air debate, Mitchell opened his office to administration officials, sharing information about pending amendments and head counts with them; he needed more than thirty Republican votes in order to stop the Byrd amendment. At the last minute, Mitchell and Republican Whip Alan Simpson (Wyoming) arranged a phone conversation between a wavering Joe Biden of Delaware and White House Chief of Staff John Sununu in order to convince Biden that the Byrd amendment would indeed trigger a veto.[59] This was truly coalition government at work.

The majority leader expended a good deal of political capital in order to achieve the clean air victory. He made repeated personal appeals to his colleagues for help in defeating a series of popular but "deal-breaking" amendments, and at every critical juncture he was able to obtain the help he needed. Democratic colleagues who supplied crucial votes, often going against their policy preferences or constituent interests, offered the same explanation: "I did it for the leader." His success with a bill of such magnitude and complexity (nearly 700 pages of scientific and regulatory language) also enhanced Mitchell's reputation as a floor engineer. However, the triumph was mainly a personal one for Mitchell; many liberal Democrats felt that there was little or no political payoff in the bill. As one staffer put it, "About all we could say about it to our environmental friends is that we supported every strengthening amendment."

Leader of the Opposition

It should come as no surprise that decisions made in a complicated and fluid environment such as that just described would be subject to a good deal of second guessing. The most common complaints about Mitchell's leadership among Democrats revolved around the same theme—that he was insufficiently partisan in many of his actions and decisions. Some thought he should use his control over the schedule to try to embarrass Republicans by forcing them to vote as often as possible on proposals highlighting their unpopular stands, such as opposition to abortions for victims of rape and incest. Others thought that sometimes the leader bent too far in a bipartisan direction in his quest to move legislation through the chamber. For example, many questioned why Mitchell continued to pursue negotiations on an omnibus anti-crime bill after nearly a week of debate and two failed cloture votes had taken place in early June of 1990. Eventually an agreement was reached and a bill was passed, but in the process Democrats were forced to vote for a ban on assault weapons (a very difficult vote for some westerners and midwesterners) and for death penalty provisions (a painful vote for many liberals) several times.[60]

These kinds of criticisms indicated a desire for greater use of opposition party tactics. Such tactics might include pushing through highly partisan legislation and inviting presidential vetoes in order to accentuate partisan differences, or even avoiding action on important matters and risking short-run damage to constituent groups and society at large in the hope of gaining political ammunition that could be used against the president in subsequent elections. In general, the Democratic leadership of the 101st Congress was willing to follow these kinds of strategies only when there were no entrenched Democratic interests at stake.[61]

Although the constitutional separation of powers makes the answer to the question of whether Democrats, who control Congress, or Republicans, who control the White House, should view themselves as the opposition party inherently ambiguous, on the airwaves the president normally reigns supreme and Congress often appears as an opposition force.[62] Still, many congressional Democrats would like nothing better than to see their leaders attempt to do something about the party's image problem by making greater use of the media to emphasize Democratic legislative accomplishments and Republican (presidential) shortcomings. They view with alarm the gradual narrowing of the gap between those who identify themselves as Democrats and Republicans and are especially concerned about the fact that among younger voters Democrats have no advantage at all over Republicans.[63] As noted earlier, an important reason for Mitchell's success in his run for the majority leader post was the widespread perception among Democratic senators that he would be an effective media voice.

During the 101st Congress Democratic senators exhibited a great deal of interest in communicating a better message to the American people. Early in 1989 Breaux, Daschle, and Fowler held periodic meetings to discuss "message" and other leadership strategies. They were aware that the Republicans had well-thought-out message strategies (coordinated by the White House) for every major legislative battle and felt it important for Democrats to do something to offset this advantage.

By the summer of 1989, enough interest in message strategies had surfaced in DPC meetings and Democratic Conferences to stimulate Mitchell to appoint an "Issues Task Force." This group managed to put together a few floor statements and suggestions for the leader about possible approaches to better communication with the public, but it never blossomed because the leader was uncomfortable with the whole idea of using the Senate as a vehicle for communicating a partisan message to the public.[64] Mitchell stated on several occasions that he did not want the DPC to be "political" (a somewhat odd statement to make about a party committee), and in response to criticism about his reluctance to be more aggressive in the message area he said: "I would make a serious mistake if I determined that my principal responsibility was to figure out how to elect a Democratic president."[65]

Senator Mitchell was, however, outspoken in his criticism of the Bush administration several times, on several different issues. In the late summer and early fall of 1989, the leader attacked the administration for its "ambivalence . . . about the dramatic transformations now under way in the Eastern bloc," and he quickly followed by publicly scolding the president "for his eagerness to amend the Constitution" after the Senate rejected a flag desecration amendment Bush supported.[66] He then called the president's position on abortion "wrong" and "terribly harsh on the poorest, most vulnerable women" after Bush vetoed an appropriations bill that would have allowed federal financing of abortions for victims of rape and incest; and in December of 1989 and January of 1990 he repeatedly blasted the president for his willingness to reestablish normal relations with the Chinese government, saying: "There are times when what America stands for is more important than economic or geopolitical considerations. This is one of those times."[67] In these instances, to the delight of many of his partisan colleagues, he acted in the classic manner of an opposition party leader.

However gratifying these rhetorical outbursts may have been for partisans, they did not appear to have much impact on the public or the administration. Mitchell's presentations were invariably thorough and articulate, but he may have been a bit too cerebral for the popular media; he did not always deliver the thirty-second sound bites they were looking for. Furthermore, Mitchell was not in a position to simply command media attention; he had to share it with committee chairmen and senators with presidential aspirations, some of whom had long and well-established relationships with the small (compared to the White House) Capitol Hill press corps.[68] Also, the press often had its own ideas about what was newsworthy, and in the 101st Congress this was usually scandals—from Jim Wright to the S&Ls.[69]

Although Mitchell did not make aggressive courtship of the media an important part of his leadership, he did receive considerable exposure. From December 1988 through October 1990, his number of mentions in the *National Newspaper Index* exceeded that of every senator and Speaker Foley.[70] He also was mentioned and/or appeared frequently on the evening news, though slightly less often than Dole.[71] Still, the leader's low-keyed approach to media coverage is considered a problem by many Democrats within the Senate. They would like to see Mitchell include more media advisers on his staff, and/or avail himself of the many experienced Democratic media consultants in Washington. One top aide to a Democratic senator said, "I talk to Bob Squire every day, but I'm not sure anyone in the leader's office even has his phone number."

Within the chamber Senator Mitchell did at times find himself in the position of an opposition leader. The most notable instance of this occurred in the fall of 1989 on the issue of capital gains taxation. In late September the House Democratic leadership lost an important vote (190–239) on a measure to reduce capital gains taxes, which was supported by the White House and brought together the conservative coalition in a classic manner.[72] In the Senate the first critical capital gains fight took place in the Finance Committee (Mitchell is a member) when a proposal by ranking Republican Bob Packwood of Oregon to amend the revenue package for the budget reconciliation bill to include a capital gains tax reduction failed on a 10–10 vote late in the evening of October 3. Mitchell then boldly announced his intention to prevent a Senate floor vote on capital gains during 1989.

Mitchell needed forty-one votes to uphold this pledge because under the so-called Byrd Rule extraneous amendments to reconciliation bills required sixty votes; therefore, Republicans would need sixty votes to attach capital gains provisions to the reconciliation bill when it went to the floor. Alternatively, the Republicans could try to bring a free-standing capital gains bill to the floor, but it could be filibustered and they would need sixty votes to invoke cloture.[73] President Bush took the rare step of visiting the Capitol on October 6 to meet with Republican leaders (and briefly with Mitchell), and afterward he reiterated his commitment to securing a capital gains tax cut in 1989.[74] For nearly a month the majority leader battled and negotiated with the White House over this issue and, in the end, he prevailed. By early November, the president had announced his willingness to drop capital gains provisions from the reconciliation bill that was being debated in conference in exchange for a "clean" debt-limit bill and an additional $14 billion in FY 1990 spending cuts.[75] Mitchell received generally high marks from his colleagues for this display of strong leadership even though many middle-of-the-road Democrats would have liked to have had a chance to vote for a capital gains tax reduction.

Center-Stage Politics

The 1989 battle of the budget ended with little fanfare. Throughout the fall the public's attention was captured by dramatic events in Eastern Europe. Before Thanksgiving, Congress managed to pass budget legislation that apparently met both the president's and Gramm-Rudman-Hollings (GRH) requirements, and the first session of the 101st Congress ended.[76] But a sluggish economy and relentless spending in entitlement programs resulted in a FY 1990 deficit of more than $150 billion (not including spending for the S&L bailout), rather than the $100 billion maximum called for under GRH. Thus with a structural deficit in the $200-billion range and a FY 1991 GRH target of $64 billion, there was no apparent way of avoiding serious engagement with the budget issue in the summer and fall of 1990. Democrats and Republicans, Congress and the White House, locked horns in a long-postponed center-stage political battle over the budget that tested the mettle of participants and starkly displayed the meaning of divided government for the public.

Although it is difficult for an outsider to assess with certainty the role played by the various participants in the budget battle of 1990, Senator Mitchell appeared to be both a dominant actor and major winner by the time the agreement was eventually reached. The budget summit began in May, but Mitchell assumed a relatively low-profile role in the talks during the late spring and early summer.[77] He gave Budget Committee Chairman James R. Sasser and Finance Committee Chairman Lloyd Bentsen the opportunity to negotiate with the Republicans on most substantive matters, and Senator Wyche Fowler was given the important political role of deciding what sort of agreement could be sold on the Senate floor.[78] House Majority Leader Richard A. Gephardt was the leading media spokesperson for congressional Democrats.

The most important development in this early period of the talks was President Bush's acknowledgment that "tax revenue increases" were necessary to balance the FY 1991 budget.[79] Mitchell's immediate reaction to the president's reversal of his famous "no new taxes" campaign pledge was subdued, but he made a major contribution to the talks a few weeks later when he said that he would not accept the president's proposal for a capital gains tax cut (as part of a revenue package) unless the top marginal tax rate was raised.[80]

Mitchell's pronouncement enraged House Republicans, who shortly afterward passed a resolution among themselves to not allow tax increases to be a means of deficit reduction for FY 1991. The budget talks bogged down, as partisan recriminations went back and forth, and Mitchell was often singled out as the target of angry Republicans.[81] Congress then recessed for most of August, and budget negotiations were postponed until September. Mitchell's strong stand on the issue of tax fairness helped to prolong the negotiations and was recognized at the time as a political risk. Among insiders, it was widely believed that House Democrats would have given the president most of what he wanted on capital gains without extracting much of a concession. Mitchell went out on a limb for a principle that would eventually become the central issue of the budget battle. This was a clear indication of the confidence he had in his own ability to prevail in negotiations, and a demonstration of strong leadership.

The budget talks resumed at Andrews Air Force Base in early September, but ten days of intense negotiations went nowhere as capital gains and tax fairness continued to divide participants. By mid-September the negotiations devolved to a smaller group (Mitchell, Dole, Foley, Gephardt, Michel, Sununu, Darman, and Brady) and the meetings moved to the Capitol. Meanwhile, the GRH clock was running out, and the size of the impending sequester was enormous—over $100 billion, which would mean cuts of more than 40 percent in the government accounts included in the sequester.[82] In the House both liberal Democrats and conservative Republicans showed increasing signs of restlessness about the inability of summiteers to find an agreement. At the last possible moment (September 30), the president and congressional leaders gathered in the Rose Garden to announce that a budget deal had been reached. There were few happy faces among the negotiators as the president described the plan, which featured increased taxes on gasoline, cigarettes, beer, plane tickets and other luxury items, tax incentives for small businesses, and cuts in Medicare.[83]

A government shutdown was avoided when Congress passed a continuing resolution on September 30 that included a suspension of the GRH deficit targets. (The president had agreed not to veto such a resolution if a budget deal producing $50 billion in FY 1991 deficit savings and $500 billion in deficit reduction over five years was in the works.) But on October 5 the House rejected the summit plan (179–254), which neither conservative Republicans nor liberal Democrats liked. The demise of the summit plan stemmed mainly from the administration's inability to convince House Minority Whip Gingrich and his followers to support it. At this point, chaos seemed imminent. The government began a shutdown on October 6 after Bush vetoed a continuing resolution, but within a few days new talks started, new resolutions were passed, and Bush agreed to keep the government running until the nineteenth.[84]

The failure of the summit package changed the nature of the budget battle. Unable to control his own troops, Bush's principal remaining bargaining tool was the veto, but many doubted that he would actually let the government shut down just before an election. House Democrats moved quickly, bringing forth an alternative proposal developed by Dan Rostenkowski's Ways and Means Committee that would have raised tax rates for top income brackets, provided tax relief for the working poor, imposed a 10 percent surtax on all income above $1 million, excluded 50 percent of capital gains from taxation up to a lifetime cap of $200,000, and placed additional taxes on alcohol, cigarettes, airline tickets, and luxury items. It did not, however, include additional gasoline taxes, tax incentives for small businesses, or cuts in Medicare.[85] This package focused everyone's attention on the question of whether the president would agree to higher tax rates on high income in exchange for a reduction in the capital gains tax rate.

Between October 9 and 11, the president changed his answer to this question three or four different times in an incredible display of indecision that gave the Democrats an advantage for the remainder of the budget battle. First, he said he would consider a trade-off of this sort, then he told Republican senators he would not, then he told Ways and Means leaders he would, and finally he said that he was taking no position on the matter; he would leave it to Congress to decide.[86]

Although Mitchell saw much he liked in the House plan, he cooperated with Dole in steering a budget reconciliation bill that closely resembled the summit package through the Senate knowing that tax rates would be on the table in conference. On October 19, House and Senate conferees sat down to resolve the differences in their reconciliation bills, and the president signed another continuing resolution to keep the government running. Meanwhile, the media gave increasing attention to the fairness issue, as the White House seemed especially intent on making sure the surtax on millionaires was removed from the package.

A 1991 budget agreement was finally approved on October 27. It featured higher tax rates (up to 31 percent) for the wealthy, tax cuts for the poor, a five-cents-per-gallon increase in gasoline taxes, other excise taxes (on beer, cigarettes, airline tickets, and luxuries), tax breaks for small businesses and energy producers, some cuts in Medicare, and a whole new budget process. Deficit savings were projected at $42.5 billion for FY 1991 and $496.5 billion over five years.[87] Although Congress cannot be said to have gained much in the eyes of voters from this extended fight with the president, the Democrats definitely came out ahead in substantive terms—the final deal was much closer to their preferences than what the administration initially proposed—and they appeared to have beaten the president politically as well. Among Washington insiders Bush's reputation was substantially diminished, while Mitchell's was enhanced; and on November 6 the voters gave the Democrats nine additional House seats and one more Senate seat.

Conclusion

The outcome of the budget battle solidified Mitchell's position as a formidable leader, and it made the 101st Congress a successful one for Senate Democrats. The Senate Democratic majority had reestablished itself as a force in national politics by setting legislative goals and achieving them. Their new leader had gained respect and loyalty, and the election produced an unexpected increment to their majority. Still, there was a good deal of ugliness associated with these successes; many voters and politicians reacted with anger and dismay at the spectacle of divided government at work. One doesn't have to share the gloomy outlook of James Sundquist, who has argued that voter confusion and meaningless elections are inevitable outgrowths of divided government because true national leadership is impossible in such a setting, to recognize that divided government has limited appeal.[88] But stronger legislative leadership of the Mitchell–Wright variety may help to offset some of the disadvantages of divided rule by giving voters a better sense of the congressional majority's positions.

In the end, Mitchell's greatest strengths were old-fashioned ones: perseverance and intelligence. He benefited from a political context that made effective leadership possible (congressional Democrats' long and frustrating experience with Republican presidents, Wright's success in the Hundredth Congress, the willingness of his colleagues to support a stronger leader) and from new leadership machinery (the agenda, DPC services, inclusion strategies); but the critical element was his own extraordinary ability.[89] He first demonstrated that he could handle Dole (on and off the floor), he then mixed patience with occasional assertiveness in convincing his colleagues to support certain policy positions, and finally he showed that he could go head-to-head with the administration and win. He entered the 102nd Congress as the strongest Senate Democratic majority leader since Lyndon Johnson.

This favorable assessment should not be construed as being unambiguous; Senator Mitchell displayed several potential weaknesses or points of vulnerability. Mitchell's pursuit of coalition government left him open to the charge of being insufficiently partisan, especially in his approach to scheduling and media relations. His deference to powerful committee chairmen led some to question the extent of his control over the policy priorities of Senate Democrats. And his propensity to perform most leadership tasks himself, with only a small, insulated inner circle of advisers to assist him, caused many to wonder what could have been accomplished with a more fully developed leadership operation.

The insufficient partisanship criticism is not altogether compelling. Senate Democrats simply do not share a full enough sense of partisan identity to encourage or support a leader who is more aggressively partisan—a long-standing problem with Democrats. The principles that liberals regard as fundamental (government regulation, income redistribution, racial and gender equality) are considered problematic by many other Democrats. It is instructive to remember that early in the 101st Congress, many Senate Democrats were afraid that an ambitious agenda would make them look bad because they were unsure of their ability to enact policies. In the end, Democrats would have benefited from having the agenda serve as a scorecard, but the price of legislative success under divided government is bipartisanship.

It also seems clear that Congress is not especially well suited to the task of serving as the institutional base from which to launch a campaign to change public perceptions about political parties and public policies. Too much of the important work that Congress does is undecipherable to the public, as was illustrated by a March 1990 poll conducted by a group called "Democrats for the 90s," which found that over 60 percent of voters were unable to volunteer a response to the question: "What issues do you think the Democrats in Congress are handling best?"[90] Democrats' success in using the fairness issue to their advantage in the budget battle was due in large part to the mistakes and poor judgment of the White House. Nevertheless, if Senator Mitchell expects Democratic senators to continue supporting him on issues that may hurt them at home, he should try to develop message strategies that give senators a sense that cohesive partisanship can help them with their constituents. This seems especially important with the 1992 election looming because Senate Democrats have a large number of seats (twenty) on the line.

Deference to committee chairmen seemed like a very rational course to follow for a first-term leader who had limited seniority himself. Given what we have seen so far, one would expect Mitchell to carefully build his base of knowledge, influence, and support so that he can deal with the chairmen from a position of strength in the future. It should also be noted that when the leader did assert himself (on capital gains, clean air, the civil rights bill, and the FY 1991 budget), he received the backing he needed. One of Mitchell's great strengths is his ability to use diplomacy to achieve his own goals, which should enable him to turn the presence of strong Democratic committee chairmen into an asset rather than a liability.

Unfortunately for Senator Mitchell, there are only so many hours in a day and only so much one person can accomplish. He needs to develop a much more extensive staffing operation to support and augment his leadership. The DPC was reinvigorated during the 101st Congress, but it remained underutilized. The committee itself could be used as a source of advice and assistance with legislative scheduling and strategy, which could help to prepare the way for conference discussions; and the staff could be much better integrated into the leader's activities. The DPC is also a logical vehicle for mounting a more ambitious Democratic message effort. Perhaps it is not surprising that someone of Mitchell's enormous personal ability would not be especially skilled at assembling a large and effective organizational apparatus. But in the years to come, as national politics becomes ever more complicated and pervasive, his ability to complement the personal with the organizational may prove crucial in determining whether he can expand the base of power he created in the 101st Congress to establish a lasting legacy of strong majority party leadership in the Senate.

Senator Mitchell's capacity to do so will be affected by the four factors mentioned in the beginning of this chapter. The Senate has changed in many ways, but it is still fundamentally a small and elite institution in which members function autonomously. Therefore, in order to cope with such a membership Senate leaders will have to continue to devise new leadership strategies, such as those Mitchell sought to develop in the 101st Congress. It is in no way surprising that the members upon whom he relied were transplants from the House of Representatives, where many new leadership techniques had been developed during the previous fifteen years. Yet new techniques alone, no matter how well organized and executed, will not enable a Senate majority leader to govern. In addition, Senator Mitchell and his successors will have to rely on their own ability to identify legislative priorities and engineer compromises. In this respect, the circumstances of divided government will present both opportunities and difficulties. While it is not easy to get Democrats to agree on policy, their incentive to agree is greatly increased by the necessity of establishing Democratic policy positions from which to govern or in opposition to those of a Republican administration. Still, the enduring realities of Senate individualism and autonomy make it unlikely that strong central leadership will be sustained over a long period of time.

Notes

1. For a description of "Senate types" and the "inner club," see William S. White, *The Citadel: The Story of the United States Senate* (New York: Harper & Row, 1956). Another classic work on the old Senate is Donald R. Matthews, *U.S. Senators and Their World* (Chapel Hill: University of North Carolina Press, 1960). For a statement on the change in the Senate before Lyndon Johnson stepped down as majority leader, see Nelson W. Polsby, "Goodbye to the Inner Club," *Congressional Behavior*, ed. Nelson W. Polsby (New York: Random House, 1971).

2. The "one man rule" quote came from Robert L. Peabody, "Senate Party Leadership: From the 1950s to the 1980s," in *Understanding Congressional Leadership*, ed. Frank H. Mackaman (Washington: Congressional Quarterly Press, 1981), 71.

3. For an excellent comparison of the leadership of Johnson and Mansfield, see John G. Stewart, "Two Strategies of Leadership," in *Congressional Behavior*, 61–92.

4. As quoted by Roger H. Davidson, "Senate Leaders: Janitors for An Untidy Chamber?" in *Congress Reconsidered*, 3d ed., ed. Lawrence C. Dodd and Bruce I. Oppenheimer (Washington: Congressional Quarterly Press, 1985), 231.

5. Randall B. Ripley, "Power in the Post-World War II Senate," *Journal of Politics*, 31, no. 2 (May 1969): 465–92; reprinted in *Studies of Congress*, ed. Glenn R. Parker (Washington: Congressional Quarterly Press, 1985), 317.

6. For accounts of the "new" Senate, see Michael Foley, *The New Senate* (New Haven: Yale University Press, 1980); Barbara Sinclair, *The Transformation of the Senate* (Baltimore: Johns Hopkins University Press, 1989); Norman J. Ornstein, Robert L. Peabody, and David W. Rohde, "The Senate Through the 1980s: Cycles of Change," in *Congress Reconsidered*, 3d ed.

7. On the "Johnson rule," see Ripley, "Power in the Post-World War II Senate," 308; Peabody, "Senate Party Leadership," 58.

8. On staff, see Harrison W. Fox, Jr., and Susan Webb Hammond, *Congressional Staff: The Invisible Force in American Lawmaking* (New York: Free Press, 1977); Michael J. Malbin, *Unelected Representatives: Congressional Staff and the Future of Representative Government* (New York: Basic Books, 1980); Norman J. Ornstein and David Rohde, "Resource Usage, Information, and Policymaking in the Senate," in *Senators: Offices, Ethics and Pressures*, a compilation of papers prepared for the Commission on the Operation of the Senate, 94th Congress, Second Session (Washington: U.S. Government Printing Office, 1977), 37–46. On staff and reelection, see Gary C. Jacobson, *The Politics of Congressional Elections*, 2d ed. (Boston: Little, Brown and Company, 1987). On policy-issue promotion and agenda-setting, see Sinclair, *The Transformation of the Senate*.

9. Davidson, "Senate Leaders."

10. On congressional reforms, see Roger H. Davidson and Walter J. Oleszek, *Congress against Itself* (Bloomington: Indiana University Press, 1977); Leroy Rieselbach, *Congressional Reform* (Washington: Congressional Quarterly Press, 1986).

11. See Charles O. Jones, "House Leadership in an Age of Reform," in *Understanding Congressional Leadership*, 117–34.

12. See Chap. 8 by Barbara Sinclair. See also "Majority Party Leadership Strategies for Coping with the New U.S. House," in *Understanding Congressional Leadership*, 187.

13. For details, see Melissa P. Collie and Joseph Cooper, "Multiple Referral and the 'New' Committee System in the House of Representatives," in *Congress Reconsidered*, 4th ed., ed. Lawrence C. Dodd and Bruce I. Oppenheimer (Washington: Congressional Quarterly Press, 1989), 245–72.

14. See Bruce I. Oppenheimer, "House Leadership and the Rules Committee," in *Understanding Congressional Leadership*, 207–25.

15. See Barbara Sinclair, *Majority Party Leadership in the U.S. House* (Baltimore: Johns Hopkins University Press, 1983).

16. Stewart, "Two Strategies of Leadership," 69–78.

17. Peabody, "Senate Party Leadership," 70–81.

18. The Senate's famous rule 22 for invoking cloture was first adopted in 1917. It specified that Senate floor debates could be stopped if a cloture petition, signed by sixteen senators, was filed and later endorsed by two-thirds of senators "present and voting." The 1975 change in rule 22 provided that cloture could be invoked if three-fifths of the entire Senate membership voted for it. Between 1975 and 1979 various procedural motions were not counted against the one hour that each senator had for postcloture discussion. Thus by introducing large numbers of amendments before cloture and then demanding a reading of the amendments, quorum calls, and roll-call votes on each of them, a senator or two could tie up the chamber for a very long time. The 1979 change in rule 22 reduced the effectiveness of this option by setting a hundred-hour limit on all postcloture discussion. For details, see Walter J. Oleszek, *Congressional Procedures and the Policy Process*, 3d ed. (Washington: Congressional Quarterly Press, 1989), 222–29.

The Senate also formalized procedures for multiple referrals in 1977, giving joint responsibility to both the majority and minority leaders for initiating such actions. In practice, the leaders have deferred to committee chairmen on the need for multiple referrals. For details, see Roger H. Davidson, "Multiple Referral of Legislation in the U.S. Senate," in *The Changing World of the U.S. Senate*, ed. John Hibbing (Berkeley, CA: The Institute of Governmental Studies, 1990), 139–56.

19. For a description of Mansfield's efforts during these years, see Donald A. Robinson, "If Senate Democrats Want Leadership: An Analysis of the History and Prospects of the Majority Policy Committee," in *Policymaking Role of the Leadership in the Senate*, papers compiled for the Commission on the Operation of the Senate, 94th Congress, Second Session (Washington: U.S. Government Printing Office, 1976), 40–57; Andrew J. Glass, "Mansfield Reform Sparks 'Quiet Revolution' in the Senate," *American Government and Public Policy*, ed. John F. Manley (New York: Macmillan, 1976).

20. See James L. Sundquist, *The Decline and Resurgence of Congress* (Washington: The Brookings Institution, 1981).

21. This episode is described by Oleszek, *Congressional Procedures*, 226–28.

22. On Byrd's use of committee chairmen in the scheduling function, see Peabody, "Senate Party Leadership," 70–81. For details on Baker's stint as Sen-

ate majority leader, see Norman Ornstein, Robert L. Peabody, and David W. Rohde, "Party Leadership and the Institutional Context: The Senate from Baker to Dole" (Paper delivered at the Eighty-second Annual Meeting of the American Political Science Association, Washington, D.C., 28–31 August 1986); Ornstein, Peabody, and Rohde, "Change in the Senate: Toward the 1990s," in *Congress Reconsidered*, 4th ed., 13–37.

23. Senate Republicans achieved a presidential support score of 84 percent in 1981, which was their highest score since 1955, and this equaled House Democratic support for Johnson in 1964. See Norman J. Ornstein et al., *Vital Statistics on Congress, 1984–85 Edition* (Washington: American Enterprise Institute, 1984), 180–81.

24. For an excellent account of the debate over television in the Senate, see Richard F. Fenno, Jr., "The Senate through the Looking Glass: The Debate over Television," *Legislative Studies Quarterly* 14 (August 1989). On the 1986 change in cloture, see Oleszek, *Congressional Procedures*, 228–29.

25. As quoted by Ornstein, Peabody, and Rohde, "Party Leadership," 34.

26. This account of Dole's leadership relies heavily on Ornstein, Peabody, and Rohde, "Party Leadership."

27. Barbara Sinclair, "House Majority Party Leadership in the Late 1980s," in *Congress Reconsidered*, 4th ed., 307–29.

28. Ibid., 328.

29. In the House the leadership had recognized the importance of budgetary politics and had moved to establish a large measure of control over it. See Lawrence C. Dodd and Bruce I. Oppenheimer, "Consolidating Power in the House," *Congress Reconsidered*, 4th ed., 39–64.

30. The survey was conducted by the Center for Responsive Politics, *Congressional Operation: Congress Speaks, A Survey of the Hundredth Congress* (Washington: Center for Responsive Politics, 1988), and is cited in Roger H. Davidson, "The Senate: If Everyone Leads, Who Follows?" in *Congress Reconsidered*, 4th ed., 294–95.

31. For an interesting discussion of the relationship between congressional leadership and change, conflict with presidents, and public confidence in governmental institutions, see Lawrence C. Dodd, "A Theory of Congressional Cycles: Solving the Puzzle of Change," in *Congress and Policy Change*, ed. Gerald C. Wright, Jr., et al. (New York: Agathon Press, 1986), 3–44.

32. This research began, in a preliminary way, during my stint as a Congressional Fellow in Senator Tom Daschle's office (December 1988 through August 1989). During that time, Senator Daschle and several of his aides were generous in sharing their thoughts and some specialized information (internal memoranda) about Senate leadership, especially the Democratic Policy Committee, with me. Beginning in September 1989 and continuing to the present, I have conducted over forty interviews, mainly with high-level Senate staffers (past and present), in an effort to study more systematically and comprehensively Senate Democratic leadership in the 101st Congress. Nearly everyone I interviewed insisted upon confidentiality, and many did not want to be identified, even in a footnote. Therefore, in order to protect everyone, I have deemed it best to list no one.

33. For a thorough discussion of congressional leadership elections, see Robert L. Peabody, *Leadership in Congress* (Boston: Little, Brown and Company, 1976).

34. So-called quality-of-life issues became increasingly important in the Senate during the 1980s. They had to do mainly with the number of late night sessions, time for members to visit constituents, and methods for streamlining floor procedures and disentangling floor debates. In 1985 a group of senators led by David Pryor (D-AR) and John Danforth (R-MO) called for a more predictable schedule, with fewer late night votes and more recesses, and rules changes to help prevent deadlocks, such as limitations on nongermane amendments and debate on motions to proceed. Senate wives even formed a Ladies of the Senate Quality-of-Life Committee. See Davidson, "The Senate," 289. In 1988 freshmen Democratic senators led by Thomas Daschle of South Dakota pushed similar reforms and were instrumental in Mitchell's successful bid for the leadership post. See Richard Cohen, "Campaigning in the Club," *National Journal Reports*, 9 March 1988, 948–51.

35. See Richard Cohen, "Senate Democrats' Tight Race," *National Journal Reports*, 15 October 1989, 2604–5. The pattern of support for each candidate was quite distinctive. Johnston had nearly all the southerners and a few other conservatives, Inouye had many of the more senior senators, while Mitchell had eastern and midwestern liberals.

36. To be elected majority leader a candidate needs a majority vote from his party colleagues, in this case twenty-eight votes. On the first round, Mitchell received twenty-seven votes, while Inouye and Johnston had fourteen each. At that point, both Inouye and Johnston withdrew and Mitchell was elected unanimously. See Richard Cohen, "Making His Mark," *National Journal Reports*, 20 May 1989, 1234–36.

37. On Mitchell's judicious style, see Cohen, "Making His Mark"; on his views about tax reform, see Jeffrey Birnbaum and Alan S. Murray, *Showdown at Gucci Gulch* (New York: Vintage Books, 1987), 212.

38. The Democrats picked up three seats in the House and one in the Senate. For an analysis of the 1988 congressional election results, see Gary C. Jacobson, "Congress: A Singular Continuity," in *The Election of 1988*, ed. Michael Nelson (Washington: Congressional Quarterly Press, 1989), 127–52.

39. Data on the public's view of which party is better able to keep the country prosperous can be found in *Public Opinion* 11, no. 2 (July/August 1988), 32. The Republicans had an advantage in this category during most of the 1980s, the exceptions being 1980 and 1982. Data on public support for government benefits can be found in Warren E. Miller, Principal Investigator, *The American National Election Study, 1988: Pre- and Post-Election Survey*, ed. First ICPSR (University of Michigan, Center for Political Studies, Summer 1989). Specific findings were as follows: the percentage of the public favoring increased federal spending for the environment was 63 percent, for child care 56 percent, for Social Security 58 percent, for public schools 64 percent, for the homeless 65 percent, and for the elderly 76 percent.

40. As quoted by Richard E. Cohen, "Setting the Senate Democrats' Agenda," *National Journal Reports* (25 February 1989).

41. Party policy committees in the Senate were created through a 1947 appropriations bill after the House refused to include provisions for policy committees in the Legislative Reorganization Act of 1946. The Senate's commitment to establishing policy committees stemmed from the work of the La Follette-

Monroney Committee (Joint Committee on the Organization of Congress). The original idea (as described in the La Follette–Monroney Report) was for the policy committees to express formally within Congress "the main policies of the majority and minority parties." They have seldom, if ever, fulfilled this aspiration. Instead, they have been creatures of party leaders; their purpose and character have been shaped by the preferences of leaders. For details and descriptions, see Joint Committee on the Organization of Congress, "Organization of the Congress," Report No. 1011, U.S. Senate, 79th Congress, Second Session, 4 March 1946; Hugh A. Bone, "An Introduction to the Senate Policy Committees," *The American Political Science Review* 50 (June 1956): 339–59; Ralph K. Huitt and Robert L. Peabody, *Congress: Two Decades of Analysis* (New York: Harper & Row, 1969), 152–56; Robinson, "If the Senate Democrats Want Leadership"; Peabody, "Senate Party Leadership: From the 1950s to the 1980s"; George Reedy, *The U.S. Senate* (New York: Crown Publishers, Inc., 1986).

42. "The Legislative Agenda of the Senate Democratic Conference for the 101st Congress" included six substantive headings: Restore the Nation's Fiscal Integrity, Strengthening America's Economy, Strengthening America's Security, Preserving Our Environment, Protecting America's Families, and Building a Stronger Democracy. Under each heading were lists of items that varied substantially in specificity. The agenda contained specific statutory goals, such as passing a new minimum wage law; vague legislative objectives, such as "a serious and sustained effort to achieve a reasonable and fair budget plan"; nonlegislative goals, such as bringing those responsible for fraud in the thrift industry to justice; oversight objectives, such as implementing "super 301 procedures" (of the 1988 Omnibus Trade Act); and new ideas, such as doing something about global warming.

43. For a discussion of this topic, see Davidson, "The Senate," 288–89. During the Hundredth Congress Byrd used to hold "bed check" votes to keep senators in Washington during sessions. Sometimes he even ordered the sergeant-at-arms to physically escort senators to the floor to vote in midnight sessions. It should also be noted that the every-fourth-week-off schedule began under Byrd in 1988, but it was accompanied by a full Monday-through-Friday work week. Howard Baker also tried to follow a schedule that confined late night sessions to Thursdays.

44. See "Senate Chief at Boiling Point Over Absentees," *New York Times*, 10 June 1990.

45. See, for example, discussions by Peabody in "Senate Party Leadership: From the 1950s to the 1980s," 74–78; Davidson, "The Senate," 287–97; Oleszek, *Congressional Procedures*, Chap. 7–8.

46. For details on unanimous consent agreements, see Steven S. Smith and Marcus Flathman, "Managing the Senate Floor: Complex Unanimous Consent Agreements Since the 1950s," in *The Changing World of the U.S. Senate*, 157–82.

47. Under Byrd the DPC staff served mainly as a negotiating team for the leader. They negotiated with committee chairmen and other members on substantive and procedural matters, and they reported directly to Byrd. He used this information to plan the schedule. They also issued publications and kept track of members' voting records, but the DPC's orientation was toward personalized

service to the leader rather than provision of service to all Democratic members.

48. The "Legislative Bulletins" the DPC had issued previously, which provided background information on bills reaching the floor, were revamped to include more thorough explorations of the issues associated with a bill, a list of likely amendments to it, pro and con summaries (highlighting the views of the administration) of the merits of legislation, relevant statements by the majority leader and other senators, polling information, and quotes from news outlets. In addition, new "Daily Reports," providing the latest information on the schedule and carrying messages from the leader, augmented the revamped "Weekly Legislative Updates" and "Issue Alerts" (new), conveying the leader's recent remarks and views on important issues, and complemented the "Special Reports" (ongoing) the DPC issued to provide background information on significant upcoming legislation.

49. The DPC tried to get its own computer system installed so that DPC information could be accessed by senators at several locations around the Capitol (the Senate has relied on a centralized computer system for many years), but this effort remained incomplete by the end of the 101st Congress.

50. Robinson quotes Mansfield as describing the Policy Committee as the "executive committee" of the conference in "If Senate Democrats Want Leadership," 46.

51. For an example of this frustration, see Fred Barnes, "Leaders to Follow," *The New Republic*, 14 May 1989, 18–22.

52. For a summary of legislative action during the 101st Congress, see Janet Hook, "101 Congress Leaves Behind Plenty of Laws, Criticism," *Congressional Quarterly Weekly Report* 48, no. 44 (3 November 1990): 3683–3709; on Bush vetoes, see Rhodes Cook, "Popularity, Savvy Use of Veto, Leave Bush with 12–0 Record," *Congressional Quarterly Weekly Reports* 48, no. 25 (23 June 1990): 1934–35.

53. See Ronald D. Elving, "House Partisanship Scores High; Senate Goes Other Direction," *Congressional Quarterly Weekly Reports* 47, no. 52 (30 December 1989): 3546–50; Jill Zuckerman, "Thirty-Year High in Partisanship Marked 1990 Senate Votes," *Congressional Quarterly Weekly Reports* 48, no. 51 (22 December 1990): 4188–91.

54. See Sinclair, *The Transformation of the Senate*, 111–38.

55. Pat Towell, "Senate Spurns Bush's Choice in a Partisan Tug of War," *Congressional Quarterly Weekly Reports* 47, no. 10, 11 (March 1989): 534.

56. Both quotes can be found in Joan Biskupic, "Partisan Rancor Marks Vote on Civil Rights Measure," *Congressional Quarterly Weekly Reports* 48, no. 29, 21 (July 1990): 2312–16.

57. George Hager, "Senate-White House Deal Breaks Clean-Air Logjam," *Congressional Quarterly Weekly Reports* 48, no. 9 (3 March 1990): 654.

58. Displaced worker assistance was included in the final clean air bill that cleared conference in October. For a description, see Alyson Pytte, "A Decade's Acrimony Lifted in the Glow of Clean Air," *Congressional Quarterly Weekly Reports* 48, no. 43 (27 October 1990): 3587–92.

59. Phil Kuntz and George Hager, "Showdown on Clean-Air Bill: Senate Says 'No' to Byrd," *Congressional Quarterly Weekly Reports* 48, no. 13 (31 March 1990): 983; and Janet Hook, "Big Win for Majority Leader Marks His Rite of

Passage," *Congressional Quarterly Weekly Reports* 48, no. 14 (7 April 1990): 1045.

60. For an account, see Joan Biskupic, "Senate Comes Down to Wire on Anticrime Measure," *Congressional Quarterly Weekly Reports* 48, no. 26 (30 June 1990): 2061–62.

61. In some cases it is difficult to distinguish between opposition and governing party approaches. For example, family- and medical-leave and civil rights legislation ultimately came to the same fate—a presidential veto—but I would argue that they were products of different processes. The course followed by family-leave legislation had the look of opposition party action because both houses passed a bill that Republicans generally opposed and the Democrats more or less challenged the president to veto it, which he did. The veto was sustained, but Democrats immediately announced that family leave would be an issue in the 1990 elections. Although working women are clearly viewed by Democrats as part of their core constituency, there were no existing federal family- and medical-leave programs or benefits and, therefore, no entrenched interests built up around them. With regard to the civil rights bill, there were extensive efforts to find language on which civil rights groups and the White House could agree, but to no avail. This legislation followed the process of coalition government that worked in many other cases, but failure to find a compromise left civil rights Democrats with no choice in the end but confrontation.

62. See, for example, Samuel Kernell, *Going Public* (Washington: Congressional Quarterly Press, 1986); Doris Graber, *Mass Media and American Politics*, 3d. ed. (Washington: Congressional Quarterly Press, 1988).

63. In 1978 the pattern of partisan identification among the American electorate was: Republican, 21 percent; Democrat, 39 percent; and Independent, 38 percent. By 1988 it had changed to: Republican, 28 percent; Democrat, 35 percent; and Independent, 31 percent. For voters under thirty, partisan identification in 1988 was essentially the same at 27 percent. See William H. Flannigan and Nancy H. Zingale, *Political Behavior of the American Electorate*, 6th ed. (Boston: Allyn and Bacon, Inc., 1987); Warren E. Miller, *American National Election Study*.

64. The task force consisted of Sasser as chairman, Daschle, Breaux, Fowler, John Kerry of Massachusetts, Howard Metzenbaum of Ohio, and Paul Sarbanes of Maryland.

65. Quoted from Janet Hook, "Mitchell Learns Inside Game; Is Cautious as Party Voice," *Congressional Quarterly Weekly Reports* 47, no. 36 (9 September 1989): 2296.

66. Thomas L. Friedman, "Senate Leader Asserts U.S. Fails To Encourage Change in East Bloc," *New York Times*, 19 September 1989, A1, A14; Robin Toner, "Democrats Take Offensive on Abortion and Flag," *New York Times*, 23 October 1989, A16.

67. Robin Toner, "Beset by Critics Hungry for Dynamic Leader, Dogged Mitchell Lashes Back," *New York Times*, 17 October 1989, A18; John Felton, "Bush Bid To Fix Beijing Ties Strains Those with Hill," *Congressional Quarterly Weekly Reports* 47, no. 50 (16 December 1989): 3435.

68. See Stephen Hess, *The Ultimate Insiders* (Washington: The Brookings Institution, 1986); Sinclair, *The Transformation of the Senate*, Chap. 10.

69. In July of 1990, for example, Minnesota Senator David Durenberger's denunciation by the Senate for unethical financial dealings, which seemed to have very little lasting significance, received much more coverage than the passage of new, and potentially very significant, civil rights legislation.

70. *The National Newspaper Index* covers the *Los Angeles Times*, *New York Times*, *Washington Post*, *Christian Science Monitor*, and *Wall Street Journal*. My count had Mitchell with 188 entries, Speaker Foley with 168, Georgia Democrat Sam Nunn (Chairman of the Armed Services Committee) with 165, Dole with 143, North Carolina Republican Jesse Helms with 121, House Majority Leader Richard Gephardt with 98, and Ted Kennedy with 89.

71. Using figures compiled from the *Television News Index and Abstract* prepared by Vanderbilt University's Television News Archives, I had Mitchell appearing or being mentioned 187 times from January 1989 through October 1990. Figures for the others were as follows: Dole 227, Foley 161, Nunn 150, Kennedy 86, Gephardt 79, and Helms 52.

72. See Janet Hook, "Rout of Democratic Leaders Reflects Fractured Party," *Congressional Quarterly Weekly Reports* 47, no. 39 (30 September 1989): 2930.

73. See Ronald D. Elving, "Senate Deficit-Reduction Drive Runs Into Capital Gains Bog," *Congressional Quarterly Weekly Reports* 47, no. 40 (7 October 1989): 2616–19.

74. See Jackie Calmes and John R. Cranford, "Bush, Democrats Square Off on Bill to Cut Deficit," *Congressional Quarterly Weekly Reports* 47, no. 40 (7 October 1989): 2610–15.

75. In recent years "must-pass" legislation such as debt-limit and reconciliation bills have become magnets for all sorts of legislative proposals that have difficulty working their way through the process separately. This practice has been criticized by many legislators and executive officials. Thus the possibility of establishing a precedent for "clean" debt-limit and reconciliation bills had appeal in Congress as well as in the White House. See Jackie Calmes, "Riders Line Up for Free Trip on Must-Pass Debt Bill," *Congressional Quarterly Weekly Reports* 47, no. 42 (21 October 1989): 2767–69. On the president's decision to drop capital gains in 1989, see Jackie Calmes, "Bush Drops Gains Tax Drive, Shifts Focus to Deficit," *Congressional Quarterly Weekly Reports* 47, no. 44 (4 November 1989): 2927–30.

76. The final FY 1990 reconciliation package contained $14.7 billion in "hard" savings, but $4.6 billion of this came from continuing the sequester that Bush had been forced to order (under Gramm-Rudman-Hollings) on October 16. The rest of the savings came in the form of small cuts in domestic programs and from new revenues realized by closing tax loopholes and imposing new taxes on airline tickets and polluting chemicals. See Jackie Calmes, "Bush, Congress Reach Deal on Deficit Reduction Bill," *Congressional Quarterly Weekly Reports* 47, no. 47 (25 November 1989): 3221–23.

77. Congressional members of the FY 1991 Budget Summit included House Republicans Bob Michel of Illinois (minority leader), Newt Gingrich of Georgia (minority whip), Bill Archer of Texas (ranking member, Ways and Means), Bill Frenzel of Minnesota (senior member, Budget and Ways and Means), and Silvio Conte of Massachusetts (ranking member, Appropriations); House Democrats Tom Foley of Washington (Speaker), Richard Gephardt of Missouri (majority

leader), Bill Gray of Pennsylvania (majority whip), Dan Rostenkowski of Illinois (chairman, Ways and Means), Leon Panetta of California (chairman, Budget), and Jamie Whitten of Mississippi (chairman, Appropriations); Senate Republicans Pete Domenici (ranking member, Budget), Phil Gramm of Texas, Bob Packwood of Oregon (ranking member, Finance), and Mark Hatfield of Oregon (ranking member, Appropriations); and Senate Democrats Mitchell, Fowler, Byrd (chairman, Appropriations), Lloyd Bentsen of Texas (chairman, Finance), and Jim Sasser of Tennessee (chairman, Budget). The White House was represented by the president (very occasionally), Chief of Staff John Sununu, OMB Director Richard Darman, and Treasury Secretary Nicholas Brady.

78. Fowler's role is described by Susan F. Rasky, "Budget Position a Plum for First-Term Senator," *New York Times*, 29 June 1990, A12.

79. See Andrew Rosenthal, "3 Little Words: How Bush Dropped His Tax Pledge," *New York Times*, 29 June 1990, A1, A12. After the president's reversal was announced, a Gallup survey found that 54 percent of the public disapproved of it, but even higher percentages disapproved of his handling of the deficit (64 percent) and the S&L crisis (58 percent). His overall approval rating was 63 percent, its lowest level in a year. See Michael Oreskes, "Support for Bush Declines in Poll," *New York Times*, 11 July 1990, A10. Previous polls had shown that the public never believed that Bush would keep his promise not to raise taxes. See, for example, R.W. Apple, Jr., "Poll Finds Broad Support for Bush but Skepticism about Drugs and Taxes," *New York Times*, 26 September 1989.

80. Mitchell stated at this time that he would prefer a top tax rate of 35 percent, but that it ought to be at least 33 percent. See Ronald D. Elving, "Tax-Rate Bubble May Burst Under Budget Pressures," *Congressional Quarterly Weekly Reports* 48, no. 29 (21 July 1990): 2281–83.

81. See Susan Rasky, "The Target of Choice for the G.O.P.: Mitchell," *New York Times*, 3 August 1990, A17.

82. See George Hager, "Huge Automatic Cuts Loom As Summit Talks Stall," *Congressional Quarterly Weekly Reports* 48, no. 38 (22 September 1990): 2995–99.

83. See articles by David E. Rosenbaum and Susan F. Rasky, *New York Times*, 1 October 1990, A1, B8.

84. See George Hager and Pamela Fessler, "Negotiators Walk Fine Line To Satisfy Both Chambers," *Congressional Quarterly Weekly Reports* 48, no. 42 (20 October 1990): 3476–84.

85. For a comparison of the summit agreement, the House alternative, and the budget bill passed by the Senate, see Hager and Fessler, "Negotiators Walk Fine Line To Satisfy Both Chambers."

86. For an account, see articles by R.W. Apple and David E. Rosenbaum in the *New York Times*, 11 October 1990, A1, D22.

87. For a description of the final FY 1991 budget package, see George Hager, "One Outcome of Budget Package: Higher Deficits on the Way," *Congressional Quarterly Weekly Reports* 48, no. 44 (3 November 1990): 3710–13.

88. See James L. Sundquist, "Needed: A Political Theory for the New Era of Coalition Government in the United States," *Political Science Quarterly* 103, no. 4 (Winter 1988–89): 613–35.

89. Personalized leadership is, of course, not unusual for the Senate. See Patterson, "Party Leadership in the U.S. Senate," in *The Changing World of the U.S. Senate*, 89–91.

90. Robin Toner, "New Poll Indicates Confusion among Voters on Democrats," *New York Times*, 16 March 1990.

Contributors

Donald C. Baumer is associate professor of government at Smith College. His research interests are in American politics and public policy. He is co-author (with Carl E. Van Horn) of *The Politics of Unemployment* and *Politics and Public Policy*.

James E. Campbell is associate professor of political science at Louisiana State University. He has published numerous articles on elections, voting behavior, partisan alignment, and public opinion.

David T. Canon is assistant professor of political science at Duke University. He is author of a forthcoming book titled *Actors, Athletes, and Astronauts: Political Amateurism in the United States Congress*.

Allen D. Hertzke, coeditor of this volume, teaches political science at the University of Oklahoma, where he is assistant director of the Carl Albert Congressional Research and Studies Center. He is author of *Representing God in Washington*, a study of congressional lobbying by religious groups, along with a number of book chapters and articles.

L. Sandy Maisel is professor of government at Colby College. A specialist on political parties, nominations, and elections, he is author of *From Obscurity to Oblivion: Running in the Congressional Primary* and *Parties and Elections in America: The Electoral Process*.

Ronald M. Peters, Jr. is the director and curator of the Carl Albert Congressional Research and Studies Center at the University of Oklahoma. He is the author of *The Massachusetts Constitution of 1780: A Social Contract* and *The American Speakership: The Office in Histori-*

cal Perspective. He has also published articles on constitutional government and political theory.

David W. Rohde is professor of political science at Michigan State University, where he specializes in Congress and congressional elections. The author of numerous articles on Congress and other aspects of American politics, he is (with Paul Abramson and John Aldrich) the author of Congressional Quarterly's series of books interpreting congressional elections.

Barbara Sinclair is professor of political science at the University of California at Riverside. Her major research interests have been in congressional voting and leadership. She is the editor of *The Women's Movement: Political, Socio-Economic, and Psychological Issues*, and the author of *Congressional Realignment, 1925–1978*, *Majority Leadership in the U.S. House*, and *The Transformation of the U.S. Senate*.

Charles Stewart III is associate professor of political science at the Massachusetts Institute of Technology. Specializing in the application of formal modeling to an historical interpretation of politics, he is the author of *Budget Reform Politics: The Design of the Appropriations Process in the House, 1865–1921*.

Randall Strahan is assistant professor of political science at Emory University, where he specializes in the Congress and American politics. He is the author of *New Ways and Means: Reform and Change in a Congressional Committee*.

Carol M. Swain is assistant professor of political science at Princeton University. Her recently completed dissertation focuses on the politics of black representation in U.S. congressional districts.

Index